Perspectives in Neural Computing

Springer
London
Berlin
Heidelberg
New York
Barcelona
Budapest
Hong Kong
Milan
Paris
Santa Clara
Singapore
Tokyo

Also in this series:

J.G. Taylor
The Promise of Neural Networks
3-540-19773-7

Maria Marinaro and Roberto Tagliaferri (Eds)
Neural Nets - WIRN VIETRI-96
3-540-76099-7

Adrian Shepherd
Second-Order Methods for Neural Networks: Fast and Reliable Training Methods for Multi-Layer Perceptrons
3-540-76100-4

Jason Kingdon
Intelligent Systems and Financial Forecasting
3-540-76098-9

Dimitris C. Dracopoulos
Evolutionary Learning Algorithms for Neural Adaptive Control
3-540-76161-6

M. Kárný, K. Warwick and V. Kůrková (Eds)
Dealing with Complexity: A Neural Networks Approach
3-540-76160-8

John A. Bullinaria, David W. Glasspool and George Houghton (Eds)
4th Neural Computation and Psychology Workshop, London, 9-11 April 1997: Connectionist Representations
3-540-76208-6

Maria Marinaro and Roberto Tagliaferri (Eds)

Neural Nets WIRN VIETRI-97

Proceedings of the 9th Italian Workshop on Neural Nets, Vietri sul Mare, Salerno, Italy, 22-24 May 1997

Società Italiana Reti Neuroniche (SIREN)
•
International Institute for Advanced Scientific Studies "E.R. Caianiello" (IIASS)
•
IEEE NNC
•
Department of Computer Science and Applications, University of Salerno
•
Department of Information Science, University of Milan
•
Department of Physics "E.R. Caianiello", University of Salerno
•
Elsag Bailey (Genova)
•
IRSIP-CNR (Naples)
•
Instituto Italiano per gli Studi Filosofici (Naples)
•
Provincia di Salerno

Springer

Professor Maria Marinaro
Dipartimento di Fisica Teorica e S.M.S.A.,
Università di Salerno, 84081 Baronissi (SA), Italy
and
IIASS "E.R. Caianiello", Via G. Pellegrino 19, 84019 Vietri sul Mare, (SA), Italy

Dr Roberto Tagliaferri
Dipartimento di Informatica ed Applicazioni "R.M. Capocelli"
Università di Salerno, 84081 Baronissi (SA), Italy
and
IIASS "E.R. Caianiello", Via G. Pellegrino 19, 84019 Vietri sul Mare, (SA), Italy

Series Editor
J.G. Taylor, BA, BSc, MA, PhD, FInstP
Centre for Neural Networks,
Department of Mathematics, King's College,
Strand, London WC2R 2LS, UK

ISBN-13:987-1-4471-1522-9

British Library Cataloguing in Publication Data
A catalogue record for this book is available from the British Library

Library of Congress Cataloging-in-Publication Data
Italian Workshop on Neural Nets (9th : 1997 : Vietri sul Mare, Italy)
Neural nets, WIRN Vietri-97 : proceedings of the 9th Italian Workshop on Neural Nets, Vietri sul Mare, Salerno, 22-24 May 1997 / Maria Marinaro and Roberto Tagliaferri, eds.
p. cm. -- (Perspectives in neural computing)
Includes bibliographical references.
ISBN-13:987-1-4471-1522-9 e-ISBN-13:987-1-4471-1520-5
DOI: 10.1007/987-1-4471-1520-5
1. Neural networks (Computer science I. Marinaro, M.
II. Tagliaferri, Roberto. III. Title. IV. Series.
QA76.87.I58917 1997 97-26379
006.3'2--dc21 CIP

Softcover repint of the hardcover 1st edition 1998

Typesetting: Camera ready by contributors

34/3830-543210 Printed on acid-free paper

Preface

This volume contains the Proceedings of the 9th Italian Workshop on Neural Nets WIRN VIETRI-97, organised by the International Institute for Advanced Scientific Studies "Eduardo R. Caianiello" (IIASS), the Società Italiana Reti Neuroniche (SIREN) and the IEEE NNC Italian RIG.

As in the previous editions some invited and reviewed talks on updated subjects are presented in addition to the original contributions selected by the Refereeing Committee. Also included is Professor C.M. Bishop's Invited paper on:

- Latent Variables, Topographic Mappings and Data Visualization;

and two review talks that deal with updated topics:

- Fuzzy Neural Networks for Pattern Recognition;
- A Unifying View of Gradient Calculations and Learning for Locally Recurrent Neural Networks;

For publication the original contributions have been assembled into 4 sections: Applications, Architectures and Algorithms, Mathematical Models, Pattern Recognition and Robotics.

The Editors thank the invited speaker and all the participants for having contributed to the success of the Workshop by submitting high quality manuscripts, and also express gratitude to the Refereeing Committee for the high quality of the selection process.

Maria Marinaro
Roberto Tagliaferri

Organizing - Scientific Committee:

B. Apolloni *(Univ. Milano)*, A. Bertoni *(Univ. Milano)*, D.D. Caviglia *(Univ. Genova)*, P. Campadelli *(Univ. Milano)*, A. Colla *(ELSAG BAILEY - Genova)*, M. Frixione *(IIASS)*, C. Furlanello *(IRST - Trento)*, A. Esposito *(IIASS)*, G.M. Guazzo *(IIASS)*, M. Gori *(Univ. Firenze)*, F. Lauria *(Univ. Napoli)*, M. Marinaro *(Univ. Salerno - IIASS)*, F. Masulli *(Univ. Genova)*, P. Morasso *(Univ. Genova)*, G. Orlandi (Univ. Roma), T. Parisini (Univ. Trieste), E. Pasero *(Politecnico Torino)*, A. Petrosino *(INFM Salerno)*, M. Protasi *(Univ. Roma II)*, S. Rampone (IIASS), R. Serra (CRA Montecatini - Ravenna), F. Sorbello *(Univ. Palermo)*, R. Stefanelli *(Politecnico Milano)*, R. Tagliaferri *(Univ. Salerno)*, R. Vaccaro *(CNR Napoli)*.

Referees:

Alippi C., Apolloni B., Bertoni A., Burattini E., Burrascano P., Campadelli, P., Cantoni V., Caprile B., Caviglia D., Chella A., Colla A.M., d'Acierno A., Di Claudio E.D., Esposito A., Frattale Mascioli F.M., Frisone F., Frixione M., Furlanello C., Gori M., Lauria F., Marinaro M., Masulli F., Morasso P., Orlandi G., Plamieri F., Parisi R., Parisini, T., Pasero E., Petrosino A., Pirrone R., Rampone S., Serra R., Sorbello F., Sperduti A., Stefanelli R., Tagliaferri R.

The sponsorship and support of:

- Società Italiana Reti Neuroniche (SIREN)
- International Institute for Advanced Scientific Studies "E.R. Caianiello" (IIASS)
- IEEE NNC
- Department of Computer Science and Applications, University of Salerno
- Department of Information Science, University of Milan
- Department of Physics "E.R. Caianiello", University of Salerno
- Elsag Bailey (Genova)
- IRSIP-CNR (Naples)
- Instituto Italiano per gli Studi Filosofici (Naples)
- Provincia di Salerno

Are gratefully acknowledged

Contents

SECTION 1

INVITED PAPER

Latent Variables, Topographic Mappings and Data Visualization

Christopher M. Bishop
Neural Computing Research Group
Dept. of Computer Science and Applied Mathematics
Aston University, Birmingham, B4 7ET, U.K.

Abstract

Most pattern recognition tasks, such as regression, classification and novelty detection, can be viewed in terms of probability density estimation. A powerful approach to probabilistic modelling is to represent the observed variables in terms of a number of hidden, or latent, variables. One well-known example of a hidden variable model is the mixture distribution in which the hidden variable is the discrete component label. In the case of continuous latent variables we obtain models such as factor analysis. In this paper we provide an overview of latent variable models, and we show how a particular form of linear latent variable model can be used to provide a *probabilistic* formulation of the well-known technique of principal components analysis (PCA). By extending this technique to mixtures, and hierarchical mixtures, of probabilistic PCA models we are led to a powerful interactive algorithm for data visualization. We also show how the probabilistic PCA approach can be generalized to non-linear latent variable models leading to the Generative Topographic Mapping algorithm (GTM). Finally, we show how GTM can itself be extended to model temporal data.

1 Density Modelling

One of the central problems in pattern recognition and machine learning is that of density estimation, in other words the construction of a model of a probability distribution given a finite sample drawn from that distribution. Throughout this paper we will consider the problem of modelling the distribution of a set of continuous variables $t_1, \ldots, t_d$ which we will collectively denote by the vector $\mathbf{t}$.

A standard approach to the problem of density estimation involves parametric models in which a specific form for the density is proposed which contains a number of adaptive parameters. Values for these parameters are then determined from an observed data set $D = \{\mathbf{t}_1, \ldots, \mathbf{t}_N\}$ consisting of N data vectors. The most widely used parametric model is the normal, or Gaussian, distribution given by

$$p(\mathbf{t}|\boldsymbol{\mu}, \boldsymbol{\Sigma}) = (2\pi)^{-d/2}|\boldsymbol{\Sigma}|^{-1/2} \exp\left\{-\frac{1}{2}(\mathbf{t} - \boldsymbol{\mu})\boldsymbol{\Sigma}^{-1}(\mathbf{t} - \boldsymbol{\mu})^{\mathrm{T}}\right\} \tag{1}$$

where $\boldsymbol{\mu}$ is the mean, $\boldsymbol{\Sigma}$ is the covariance matrix, and $|\boldsymbol{\Sigma}|$ denotes the determinant of $\boldsymbol{\Sigma}$. A standard approach to the determination of these parameters is that of maximum likelihood which involves consideration of the log probability of the observed data set given the parameters, i.e.

$$\mathcal{L}(\boldsymbol{\mu}, \boldsymbol{\Sigma}) = \ln p(D|\boldsymbol{\mu}, \boldsymbol{\Sigma}) = \sum_{n=1}^{N} \ln p(\mathbf{t}_n|\boldsymbol{\mu}, \boldsymbol{\Sigma}) \tag{2}$$

in which it is assumed that the data vectors $\mathbf{t}_n$ are drawn independently from the distribution. When viewed as a function of $\boldsymbol{\mu}$ and $\boldsymbol{\Sigma}$, the quantity $p(D|\boldsymbol{\mu}, \boldsymbol{\Sigma})$ is called the *likelihood* function. Maximization of the likelihood (or equivalently the log likelihood) with respect to $\boldsymbol{\mu}$ and $\boldsymbol{\Sigma}$ leads to the set of parameter values which are most likely to have given rise to the observed data set. For the normal distribution (1) the log likelihood (2) can be maximized analytically, leading to the intuitive result (Anderson, 1958) that the maximum likelihood solutions $\widehat{\boldsymbol{\mu}}$ and $\widehat{\boldsymbol{\Sigma}}$ are given by

$$\widehat{\boldsymbol{\mu}} = \frac{1}{N}\sum_{n=1}^{N} \mathbf{t}_n \tag{3}$$

$$\widehat{\boldsymbol{\Sigma}} = \frac{1}{N}\sum_{n=1}^{N} (\mathbf{t}_n - \widehat{\boldsymbol{\mu}})(\mathbf{t}_n - \widehat{\boldsymbol{\mu}})^{\mathrm{T}} \tag{4}$$

corresponding to the sample mean and sample covariance respectively.

As an alternative to maximum likelihood, we can define priors over $\boldsymbol{\mu}$ and $\boldsymbol{\Sigma}$ use Bayes' theorem, together with the observed data, to determine the posterior distribution. An introduction to Bayesian inference with the normal distribution is given in (Bishop, 1995).

While the simple normal distribution (1) is widely used, it suffers from some significant limitations. In particular, it can often prove to be too flexible in that the number of independent parameters in the model can be excessive. This problem is addressed through the introduction of latent variables in Section 1.1. At the same time the normal distribution can also be insufficiently flexible since it can only represent uni-modal distributions. A more general family of distributions can be obtained by considering mixtures of Gaussians as discussed in Section 1.2. We consider each of these approaches in turn.

1.1 Latent Variables

Consider the number of free parameters in the normal distribution (1). Since $\boldsymbol{\Sigma}$ is symmetric, it contains $d(d+1)/2$ independent parameters. There are a further d independent parameters in $\boldsymbol{\mu}$, making $d(d+3)/2$ parameters in total. For large d this number grows like d^2, and excessively large numbers of data points may be required to ensure that the maximum likelihood solution for $\boldsymbol{\Sigma}$ is not ill-conditioned. One way to reduce the number of free parameters in the model is to consider a diagonal covariance matrix, which has just d free parameters. This, however, corresponds to a very strong assumption, namely that the components of $\mathbf{t}$ are statistically independent, and the model is therefore unable to capture the correlations between different components.

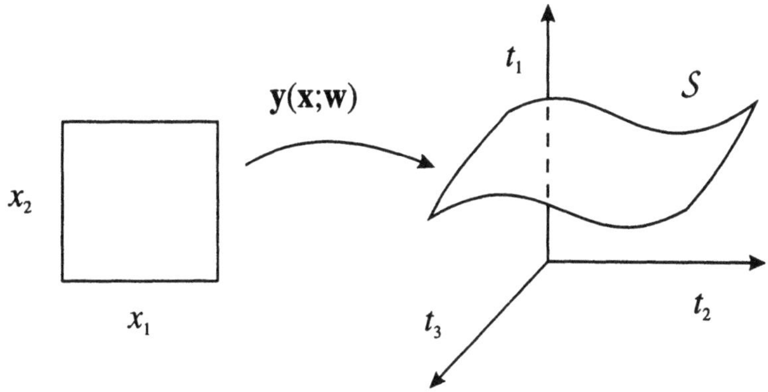

Figure 1: The non-linear function $\mathbf{y}(\mathbf{x};\mathbf{w})$ defines a manifold $\mathcal{S}$ embedded in data space given by the image of the latent space under the mapping $\mathbf{x} \rightarrow \mathbf{y}$.

We now show how the number of degrees of freedom within the model can be controlled, while still allowing correlations to be captured, by introducing *latent* (or 'hidden') variables. The goal of a latent variable model is to express the distribution $p(\mathbf{t})$ of the variables $t_1, \ldots, t_d$ in terms of a smaller number of latent variables $\mathbf{x} = (x_1, \ldots, x_q)$ where $q < d$. This is achieved by first decomposing the joint distribution $p(\mathbf{t}, \mathbf{x})$ into the product of the marginal distribution $p(\mathbf{x})$ of the latent variables and the conditional distribution $p(\mathbf{t}|\mathbf{x})$ of the data variables given the latent variables. We next assume that the conditional distribution factorises over the data variables, so that the joint distribution becomes

$$p(\mathbf{t}, \mathbf{x}) = p(\mathbf{x})p(\mathbf{t}|\mathbf{x}) = p(\mathbf{x}) \prod_{i=1}^{d} p(t_i|\mathbf{x}). \tag{5}$$

We then express the conditional distribution $p(\mathbf{t}|\mathbf{x})$ in terms of a mapping from latent variables to data variables, so that

$$\mathbf{t} = \mathbf{y}(\mathbf{x}; \mathbf{w}) + \mathbf{u} \tag{6}$$

where $\mathbf{y}(\mathbf{x}; \mathbf{w})$ is a function of the latent variable $\mathbf{x}$ with parameters $\mathbf{w}$, and $\mathbf{u}$ is an $\mathbf{x}$-independent noise process. If the components of $\mathbf{u}$ are uncorrelated, the conditional distribution for $\mathbf{t}$ will factorize as in (5). Geometrically the function $\mathbf{y}(\mathbf{x}; \mathbf{w})$ defines a manifold in data space given by the image of the latent space, as shown in Figure 1.

The definition of the latent variable model is completed by specifying the distribution $p(\mathbf{u})$, the mapping $\mathbf{y}(\mathbf{x}; \mathbf{w})$, and the marginal distribution $p(\mathbf{x})$. As we shall see later, it is often convenient to regards $p(\mathbf{x})$ as a *prior* distribution over the latent variables.

The desired model for the distribution $p(\mathbf{t})$ of the data is obtained by marginalizing over the latent variables

$$p(\mathbf{t}) = \int p(\mathbf{t}|\mathbf{x})p(\mathbf{x})\,d\mathbf{x}. \tag{7}$$

This integration will, in general, be analytically intractable except for specific forms of the distributions $p(\mathbf{t}|\mathbf{x})$ and $p(\mathbf{x})$.

One of the simplest latent variable models is called *factor analysis* (Bartholomew, 1987; Basilevsky, 1994) and is based on a linear mapping $\mathbf{y}(\mathbf{x};\mathbf{w})$ so that

$$\mathbf{t} = \mathbf{W}\mathbf{x} + \boldsymbol{\mu} + \mathbf{u}, \tag{8}$$

in which $\mathbf{W}$ and $\boldsymbol{\mu}$ are parameters, and the distribution $p(\mathbf{x})$ is chosen to be a zero-mean unit covariance Gaussian distribution $\mathcal{N}(\mathbf{0},\mathbf{I})$. The noise model for $\mathbf{u}$ is also a zero mean Gaussian with a covariance matrix $\boldsymbol{\Psi}$ which is diagonal, while the parameter $\boldsymbol{\mu}$ in (8) allows the conditional distribution to have a non-zero mean. Using (7) it is easily shown that the distribution $p(\mathbf{t})$ is also Gaussian, with mean $\boldsymbol{\mu}$ and a covariance matrix given by $\boldsymbol{\Psi} + \mathbf{W}\mathbf{W}^{\mathrm{T}}$.

The parameters of the model, comprising $\mathbf{W}$, $\boldsymbol{\Psi}$ and $\boldsymbol{\mu}$, can again be determined by maximum likelihood. There is, however, no longer a closed-form analytic solution, and so their values must be determined by iterative procedures. For q latent variables, there are $q \times d$ degrees of freedom in $\mathbf{W}$ together with d in $\boldsymbol{\Psi}$ and d in $\boldsymbol{\mu}$. The number of free parameters in this model therefore only grows linearly with d, and yet the model can still capture the dominant correlations between the data variables. We consider the nature of such models in more detail in Section 2.

1.2 Mixture Distributions

The density models we have considered so far are clearly very limited in terms of the variety of probability distributions which they can model since they can only represent distributions which are uni-modal. However, they can form the basis of a very general framework for density modelling, obtained by considering probabilistic *mixtures* of simpler parametric distributions. This leads to density models of the form

$$p(\mathbf{t}) = \sum_{i=1}^{M} \pi_i p(\mathbf{t}|i) \tag{9}$$

in which the $p(\mathbf{t}|i)$ represent the individual components of the mixture and might consist, for example, of normal distributions of the form (1) each with its own independent mean $\boldsymbol{\mu}_i$ and covariance matrix $\boldsymbol{\Sigma}_i$. The parameters π_i in (9) are called *mixing coefficients* and satisfy the requirements $0 \le \pi_i \le 1$ and $\sum_i \pi_i = 1$ so that $p(\mathbf{t})$ will be non-negative and will integrate to unity (assuming the individual component densities also have these properties).

The mixing coefficients can be interpreted as *prior* probabilities for the values of the label i. For a given data point $\mathbf{t}_n$ we can then use Bayes' theorem to evaluate the corresponding posterior probabilities, given by

$$p(i|\mathbf{t}_n) = \frac{\pi_i p(\mathbf{t}_n|i)}{\sum_j \pi_j p(\mathbf{t}_n|j)}. \tag{10}$$

The value of $p(i|\mathbf{t}_n)$ can be regarded as the *responsibility* which component i takes for 'explaining' data point $\mathbf{t}_n$.

The log likelihood for the mixture distribution takes the form

$$\mathcal{L}(\pi_i, \boldsymbol{\mu}_i, \boldsymbol{\Sigma}_i) = \sum_{n=1}^{N} \ln \left\{ \sum_{i=1}^{M} \pi_i p(\mathbf{t}|i) \right\}. \tag{11}$$

Maximization of this log likelihood is more complex than for a single component due to the presence of the sum inside the logarithm. An elegant and powerful technique for performing this optimization called the expectation-maximization (EM) algorithm (Dempster *et al.*, 1977). An introductory account of EM in the context of mixture distributions is given in (Bishop, 1995). The EM algorithm is based on the observation that, if we were given a set of indicator variables z_{ni} specifying which component i was responsible for generating each data point $\mathbf{t}_n$, then the log likelihood would take the form

$$\mathcal{L}_{\mathrm{C}}(\pi_i, \boldsymbol{\mu}_i, \boldsymbol{\Sigma}_i) = \sum_{n=1}^{N} \sum_{i=1}^{M} z_{ni} \ln \{\pi_i p(\mathbf{t}|i)\} \tag{12}$$

and its optimization would be straightforward. The $\{z_{ni}\}$ are regarded as 'missing data', and the data set $\{\mathbf{t}_n\}$ is said to be 'incomplete'. Combining $\{\mathbf{t}_n\}$ and $\{z_{ni}\}$ we obtain the corresponding 'complete' data set, with a log likelihood given by (12). Of course, the values of $\{z_{ni}\}$ are unknown, but their posterior distribution can be computed using Bayes' theorem, and the expectation of this distribution is just the set of responsibilities given by (10). The EM algorithm is based on the maximization of the expected complete-data log likelihood given from (12) by

$$\mathcal{L}_{\mathrm{C}}(\pi_i, \boldsymbol{\mu}_i, \boldsymbol{\Sigma}_i) = \sum_{n=1}^{N} \sum_{i=1}^{M} R_{ni} \ln \{\pi_i p(\mathbf{t}|i)\}. \tag{13}$$

It alternates between the E-step, in which the R_{ni} are evaluated using (10), and the M-step in which (13) is maximized with respect to the model parameters to give a revised set of parameter values. At each cycle of the EM algorithm the true log likelihood is guaranteed to increase unless it is already at a local maximum (Dempster *et al.*, 1977).

The EM algorithm can also be applied to the problem of maximizing the likelihood for a single latent variable model of the kind discussed in Section 1.1. We note that the log likelihood for such a model takes the form

$$\mathcal{L}(\mathbf{W}, \boldsymbol{\mu}, \boldsymbol{\Psi}) = \sum_{n=1}^{N} \ln p(\mathbf{t}_n) = \sum_{n=1}^{N} \ln \left\{ \int p(\mathbf{t}_n|\mathbf{x}_n) p(\mathbf{x}_n)\, d\mathbf{x}_n \right\}. \tag{14}$$

Again, this is difficult to treat because of the integral inside the logarithm. In this case the values of $\mathbf{x}_n$ are regarded as the missing data. Given the prior distribution $p(\mathbf{x})$ we can consider the corresponding posterior distribution obtained through Bayes' theorem

$$p(\mathbf{x}_n|\mathbf{t}_n) = \frac{p(\mathbf{t}_n|\mathbf{x}_n)p(\mathbf{x}_n)}{p(\mathbf{t}_n)} \tag{15}$$

and the sufficient statistics for this distribution are evaluated in the E-step. The M-step involves maximization of the expected complete-data log likelihood and is generally much simpler than the direct maximization of the true log likelihood. For simple models such as the factor analysis model discussed in Section 1.1 this maximization can be performed analytically. An iterative EM (expectation-maximization) algorithm for maximising the likelihood function for standard factor analysis was derived by Rubin and Thayer (Rubin and Thayer, 1982).

We can combine the technique of mixture modelling with that of latent variables, and consider a mixture of latent variable models. Again, the EM algorithm provides a natural framework for determination of the model parameters, and allows both the values of the component label i and of the latent variable $\mathbf{x}$ to be treated together as missing data.

In the subsequent sections of this paper we shall see how the concepts of latent variables and mixture distributions can be used in a fruitful partnership to obtain a range of powerful algorithms for density modelling, pattern classification and data visualization.

2 Probabilistic Principal Component Analysis

Principal component analysis is a well-established technique for dimensionality reduction, and a chapter on the subject may be found in practically every text on multivariate analysis. Examples of its many applications include data compression, image processing, data visualization, exploratory data analysis, and pattern recognition.

The most common derivation of PCA is in terms of a standardised linear projection which maximises the variance in the projected space (Hotelling, 1933). For a set of observed d-dimensional data vectors $\{\mathbf{t}_n\}$, $n \in \{1 \dots N\}$, the q *principal axes* $\mathbf{v}_j$, $j \in \{1, \dots, q\}$, are those orthonormal axes onto which the retained variance under projection is maximal. It can be shown that the vectors $\mathbf{v}_j$ are given by the q dominant eigenvectors (i.e. those with the largest associated eigenvalues λ_j) of the sample covariance matrix

$$\mathbf{S} = \frac{1}{N}\sum_{n=1}^{N}(\mathbf{t}_n - \widehat{\boldsymbol{\mu}})(\mathbf{t}_n - \widehat{\boldsymbol{\mu}})^{\mathrm{T}} \tag{16}$$

such that $\mathbf{S}\mathbf{v}_j = \lambda_j\mathbf{v}_j$. Here $\widehat{\boldsymbol{\mu}}$ is the sample mean, given by (3). The q principal components of the observed vector $\mathbf{t}_n$ are given by the vector $\mathbf{u}_n = \mathbf{V}^{\mathrm{T}}(\mathbf{t}_n - \widehat{\boldsymbol{\mu}})$, where $\mathbf{V}^{\mathrm{T}} = (\mathbf{v}_1, \ldots, \mathbf{v}_q)^{\mathrm{T}}$, in which the variables u_j are decorellated such that the covariance matrix for $\mathbf{u}$ is diagonal with elements $\{\lambda_j\}$.

A complementary property of PCA, and that most closely related to the original discussions of Pearson (Pearson, 1901), is that, of all orthogonal linear projections $\mathbf{x}_n = \mathbf{V}^{\mathrm{T}}(\mathbf{t}_n - \widehat{\boldsymbol{\mu}})$, the principal component projection minimises the squared reconstruction error $\sum_n \|\mathbf{t}_n - \hat{\mathbf{t}}_n\|^2$, where the optimal linear reconstruction of $\mathbf{t}_n$ is given by $\hat{\mathbf{t}}_n = \mathbf{V}\mathbf{x}_n + \widehat{\boldsymbol{\mu}}$.

One limiting disadvantage of both these definitions of PCA is the absence of a probability density model and associated likelihood measure. Deriving PCA from the perspective of density estimation would offer a number of important advantages, including the following:

- The corresponding likelihood measure would permit comparison with other density–estimation techniques and would facilitate statistical testing.
- Bayesian inference methods could be applied (e.g. for model comparison) by combining the likelihood with a prior.
- If PCA were used to model the class–conditional densities in a classification problem, the posterior probabilities of class membership could be computed.
- The value of the probability density function would give a measure of the novelty of a new data point.
- The single PCA model could be extended to a mixture of such models.

The key result of this section is to show that principal component analysis may indeed be obtained from a probability model (Tipping and Bishop, 1997b). In particular we show that the maximum-likelihood estimator of $\mathbf{W}$ in (8) for a specific form of latent variable models is given by the matrix of (scaled and rotated) principal axes of the data.

2.1 Relationship to Latent Variables

Links between principal component analysis and latent variable models have already been noted by a number of authors. For instance Anderson (Anderson, 1963) observed that principal components emerge when the data is assumed to comprise a systematic component, plus an independent error term for each variable having common variance σ^2. Empirically, the similarity between the columns of $\mathbf{W}$ and the principal axes has often been observed in situations in which the elements of $\boldsymbol{\Psi}$ are approximately equal (Rao, 1955). Basilevsky (Basilevsky, 1994) further notes that when the model $\mathbf{W}\mathbf{W}^{\mathrm{T}} + \sigma^2\mathbf{I}$ is exact, and therefore equal to $\mathbf{S}$, the factor loadings are identifiable and can be determined analytically through eigen-decomposition of $\mathbf{S}$, without resort to iteration.

As well as assuming that the model is exact, such observations do not consider the maximum-likelihood context. By considering a particular case of the factor analysis model in which the noise covariance is isotropic so that

$\Psi = \sigma^2\mathbf{I}$, we now show that even when the covariance model is approximate, the maximum-likelihood estimator $\mathbf{W}_{\text{ML}}$ is that matrix whose columns are the scaled and rotated principal eigenvectors of the sample covariance matrix $\mathbf{S}$ (Tipping and Bishop, 1997b). An important consequence of this derivation is that PCA may be expressed in terms of a probability density model, which we shall refer to as probabilistic principal component analysis (PPCA).

2.2 The Probability Model

For the isotropic noise model $\mathbf{u} \sim N(\mathbf{0}, \sigma^2\mathbf{I})$, equations (6) and (8) implie a probability distribution over $\mathbf{t}$-space for a given $\mathbf{x}$ given by

$$p(\mathbf{t}|\mathbf{x}) = (2\pi\sigma^2)^{-d/2} \exp\left\{-\frac{1}{2\sigma^2}\|\mathbf{t} - \mathbf{W}\mathbf{x} - \boldsymbol{\mu}\|^2\right\}. \tag{17}$$

In the case of an isotropic Gaussian prior over the latent variables defined by

$$p(\mathbf{x}) = (2\pi)^{-q/2} \exp\left\{-\frac{1}{2}\mathbf{x}^{\mathrm{T}}\mathbf{x}\right\}, \tag{18}$$

we then obtain the marginal distribution of $\mathbf{t}$ in the form

$$p(\mathbf{t}) = \int p(\mathbf{t}|\mathbf{x})p(\mathbf{x})d\mathbf{x} \tag{19}$$

$$= (2\pi)^{-d/2}|\mathbf{C}|^{-1/2} \exp\left\{-\frac{1}{2}(\mathbf{t} - \boldsymbol{\mu})^{\mathrm{T}}\mathbf{C}^{-1}(\mathbf{t} - \boldsymbol{\mu})\right\}, \tag{20}$$

where the model covariance is

$$\mathbf{C} = \sigma^2\mathbf{I} + \mathbf{W}\mathbf{W}^{\mathrm{T}}. \tag{21}$$

Using Bayes' rule, the *posterior* distribution of the latent variables $\mathbf{x}$ given the observed $\mathbf{t}$ is given by

$$p(\mathbf{x}|\mathbf{t}) = (2\pi)^{-q/2}|\sigma^2\mathbf{M}|^{-1/2} \times \exp\left[-\frac{1}{2}\{\mathbf{x} - \langle\mathbf{x}\rangle\}^{\mathrm{T}}(\sigma^2\mathbf{M})^{-1}\{\mathbf{x} - \langle\mathbf{x}\rangle\}\right], \tag{22}$$

where the posterior covariance matrix is given by

$$\sigma^2\mathbf{M} = \sigma^2(\sigma^2\mathbf{I} + \mathbf{W}^{\mathrm{T}}\mathbf{W})^{-1} \tag{23}$$

and the mean of the distribution is given by

$$\langle\mathbf{x}\rangle = \mathbf{M}^{-1}\mathbf{W}^{\mathrm{T}}(\mathbf{t} - \boldsymbol{\mu}). \tag{24}$$

Note that $\mathbf{M}$ is $q \times q$ while $\mathbf{C}$ is $d \times d$.

The log-likelihood for the observed data under this model is:

$$\mathcal{L} = \sum_{n=1}^{N} \ln\{p(\mathbf{t}_n)\}$$

$$= -\frac{Nd}{2}\ln(2\pi) - \frac{N}{2}\ln|\mathbf{C}| - \frac{N}{2}\mathrm{Tr}\left\{\mathbf{C}^{-1}\mathbf{S}\right\}, \tag{25}$$

where the sample covariance matrix $\mathbf{S}$ of the observed $\{\mathbf{t}_n\}$ is given by (16).

In principle, we could determine the parameters for this model by maximising the log-likelihood $\mathcal{L}$ using the EM algorithm of Rubin and Thayer (Rubin and Thayer, 1982). However, we now show that, for the case of an isotropic noise covariance of the form we are considering, there is an exact analytical solution for the model parameters.

2.3 Properties of the Maximum-Likelihood Solution

Our key result is that the log-likelihood (25) is maximised when the columns of $\mathbf{W}$ span the principal subspace of the data. To show this we consider the derivative of (25) with respect to $\mathbf{W}$:

$$\frac{\partial \mathcal{L}}{\partial \mathbf{W}} = N(\mathbf{C}^{-1}\mathbf{S}\mathbf{C}^{-1}\mathbf{W} - \mathbf{C}^{-1}\mathbf{W}), \tag{26}$$

which may be obtained from standard matrix differentiation results (see (Krzanows and Marriott, 1994), pp 133). In (Tipping and Bishop, 1997b) it is shown that, with $\mathbf{C}$ given by (21), the only non-zero stationary points of (26) occur for:

$$\mathbf{W} = \mathbf{U}_q(\mathbf{\Lambda}_q - \sigma^2\mathbf{I})^{1/2}\mathbf{R}, \tag{27}$$

where the q column vectors in $\mathbf{U}_q$ are eigenvectors of $\mathbf{S}$, with corresponding eigenvalues in the diagonal matrix $\mathbf{\Lambda}_q$, and $\mathbf{R}$ is an arbitrary $q \times q$ orthogonal rotation matrix. Furthermore, it is also shown that the stationary point corresponding to the *global maximum* of the likelihood occurs when $\mathbf{U}_q$ comprises the *principal* eigenvectors of $\mathbf{S}$ (i.e. the eigenvectors corresponding to the q largest eigenvalues) and that all other combinations of eigenvectors represent saddle-points of the likelihood surface. Thus, from (27), the columns of the maximum-likelihood estimator $\mathbf{W}_{\mathrm{ML}}$ contain the principal eigenvectors of $\mathbf{S}$, with scalings determined by the corresponding eigenvalue and the parameter σ^2, and with arbitrary rotation.

It may also be shown that for $\mathbf{W} = \mathbf{W}_{\mathrm{ML}}$, the maximum-likelihood estimator for σ^2 is given by

$$\sigma^2_{\mathrm{ML}} = \frac{1}{d-q}\sum_{j=q+1}^{d} \lambda_j, \tag{28}$$

which has a clear interpretation as the variance 'lost' in the projection, averaged over the lost dimensions. Note that the columns of $\mathbf{W}_{\mathrm{ML}}$ are not orthogonal since

$$\mathbf{W}_{\mathrm{ML}}^{\mathrm{T}}\mathbf{W}_{\mathrm{ML}} = \mathbf{R}^{\mathrm{T}}(\mathbf{\Lambda}_q - \sigma^2\mathbf{I})\mathbf{R}, \tag{29}$$

which is not diagonal for $\mathbf{R} \neq \mathbf{I}$. In common with factor analysis, there exists a family of solutions related by rotations of the latent variable coordinates. This is also true of many iterative algorithms for determining principal components. However, unlike factor analysis, we can determine $\mathbf{R}$ by noting from (29) that the rows of $\mathbf{R}$ correspond to the eigenvectors of $\mathbf{W}_{\mathrm{ML}}^{\mathrm{T}}\mathbf{W}_{\mathrm{ML}}$. That the rotational ambiguity may be resolved is a consequence of the scaling of the eigenvectors by $(\mathbf{\Lambda}_q - \sigma^2\mathbf{I})$.

In summary, we can obtain a probabilistic principal components model by finding the q principal eigenvectors and eigenvalues of the sample covariance matrix. The density model is then given by a Gaussian distribution with mean $\boldsymbol{\mu}$ given by the sample mean, and a covariance matrix $\mathbf{W}\mathbf{W}^{\mathrm{T}} + \sigma^2\mathbf{I}$ in which $\mathbf{W}$ is given by (27) and σ^2 is given by (28).

3 Mixtures of Probabilistic PCA

We now extend the latent variable model of Section 2 by considering a mixture of probabilistic principal component analysers (Tipping and Bishop, 1997a). It is straightforward to obtain an EM algorithm to determine the parameters π_i, $\boldsymbol{\mu}_i$, $\mathbf{W}_i$ and σ_i^2. The E-step of the EM algorithm involves the use of the current parameter estimates to evaluate the responsibilities of the mixture components i for the data points $\mathbf{t}_n$, given from Bayes' theorem by

$$R_{ni} = \frac{p(\mathbf{t}_n|i)\pi_i}{p(\mathbf{t}_n)}. \tag{30}$$

In the M-step, the mixing coefficients and component means are re-estimated using

$$\widetilde{\pi}_i = \frac{1}{N}\sum_{n}^{N} R_{ni} \tag{31}$$

$$\widetilde{\boldsymbol{\mu}}_i = \frac{\sum_n^N R_{ni}\mathbf{t}_n}{\sum_n^N R_{ni}}, \tag{32}$$

while the parameters $\mathbf{W}_i$ and σ_i^2 are obtained by first evaluating the weighted covariance matrices given by

$$\mathbf{S}_i = \frac{\sum_{n=1}^N R_{ni}(\mathbf{t}_n - \widetilde{\boldsymbol{\mu}})(\mathbf{t}_n - \widetilde{\boldsymbol{\mu}})^{\mathrm{T}}}{\sum_{n=1}^N R_{ni}} \tag{33}$$

and then applying (27) and (28).

3.1 Example Application: Hand-written Digit Classification

One potential application for high-dimensional density models is handwritten digit recognition. Examples of gray-scale pixel images of a given digit will generally lie on a lower-dimensional smooth continuous manifold, the geometry of which is determined by properties of the digit such as rotation, scaling and thickness of stroke. One approach to the classification of such digits (although not necessarily the best) is to build a model of each digit separately, and classify unseen digits according to the model to which they are most 'similar'.

Hinton *et al.* (Hinton *et al.*, 1997) gave an excellent discussion of the handwritten digit problem, and applied a 'mixture' of conventional PCA models, using soft reconstruction-based clustering, to the classification of scaled and smoothed 8-by-8 gray-scale images taken from the CEDAR U.S. postal service database (Hull, 1994). The models were constructed using an 11,000-digit subset of the '*br*' data set (which was further split into training and validation sets), and the '*bs*' test set was classified according to which model best reconstructed each digit. We repeated the experiment with the same data using the probabilistic PCA mixture approach utilising the same choice of parameter values ($M = 10$ and $q = 10$). The same method of classification was used, and the best model on the validation set misclassified 4.64% of the digits in the test set. Hinton *et al.* (Hinton *et al.*, 1997) reported an error of 4.91%, and we would expect the improvement to be a result partly of the localised clustering of the PPCA model, but also the use of individually-estimated values of σ_i^2 for each component, rather than a single, arbitrarily-chosen, global value.

One of the advantages of the PPCA methodology is that the definition of the density model permits the posterior probabilities of class membership to be computed for each digit and utilised for subsequent classification. After optimizing the parameters M and q for each model to obtain the best performance on the validation set, the model misclassified 4.61% of the test set. An advantage of the use of posterior probabilities is that it is possible to reject (using an optimal criterion) a proportion of the test samples about which the classifier is most 'unsure', and thus improve the classification performance. Using this approach to reject 5% of the test examples resulted in a misclassification rate of 2.50%.

4 Hierarchical Mixtures for Data Visualization

An interesting application for the PPCA model, and mixtures of PPCA models, is to the problem of data visualization. By considering a further extension to a hierarchical mixture model, we are led to a powerful interactive algorithm for visualization which retains a probabilistic framework and which can provide considerable insight into the structure of data in spaces of high dimensionality.

4.1 Visualization using Probabilistic PCA

Consider first the use of a single PPCA model for data visualization. In standard principal component analysis, the data points are visualized by orthogonal projection onto the principal components plane (spanned by the two leading eigenvectors). For our probabilistic PCA model this projection is modified slightly. From (22) and (24) it may be seen that the *posterior mean* projection of $\mathbf{t}_n$ is given by $\langle \mathbf{x}_n \rangle = \mathbf{M}^{-1}\mathbf{W}^{\mathrm{T}}(\mathbf{t}_n - \widehat{\boldsymbol{\mu}})$. When $\sigma^2 \to 0$, $\mathbf{M}^{-1} \to (\mathbf{W}^{\mathrm{T}}\mathbf{W})^{-1}$ and $\mathbf{W}\mathbf{M}^{-1}\mathbf{W}^{\mathrm{T}}$ then becomes an orthogonal projection, and so PCA is recovered (although the density model then becomes singular, and thus undefined). For $\sigma^2 > 0$, the projection onto the manifold becomes skewed towards the origin as a result of the prior over $\mathbf{x}$. Because of this, $\mathbf{W}\langle \mathbf{x}_n \rangle$ is *not* an orthogonal projection of $\mathbf{t}_n$. We note, however, that information is not lost because of this skewing, since each data point may still be optimally reconstructed from the latent variable by taking the skewing into account. With $\mathbf{W} = \mathbf{W}_{\mathrm{ML}}$ the required reconstruction is given by

$$\hat{\mathbf{t}}_n = \mathbf{W}_{\mathrm{ML}}\{\mathbf{W}_{\mathrm{ML}}^{\mathrm{T}}\mathbf{W}_{\mathrm{ML}}\}^{-1}\mathbf{M}\langle\mathbf{x}_n\rangle, \tag{34}$$

and is derived in (Tipping and Bishop, 1997b). Thus the latent variables convey the necessary information to reconstruct the original data vector optimally, even in the case of $\sigma^2 > 0$.

The data set can therefore be visualized by mapping each data point onto the corresponding posterior mean $\langle\mathbf{x}_n\rangle$ in the two-dimensional latent space. Note that this type of visualization plot satisfies a topographic property in that points in data space which are sufficiently close will map to points in latent space which are also close.

We illustrate the visualization properties of this model using a toy data set consisting of 450 data points generated from a mixture of three Gaussians in three-dimensional space. Each Gaussian is relatively flat (has small variance) in one dimension, and two of these clusters lie 'on top' of each other, while the third is well separated from the first two. The structure of this data set has been chosen order to demonstrate the benefits of the interactive hierarchical approach developed in Section 4.3. A two-dimensional latent variable model is trained on this data set, and the result of plotting the posterior means of the data points is shown in Figure 2.

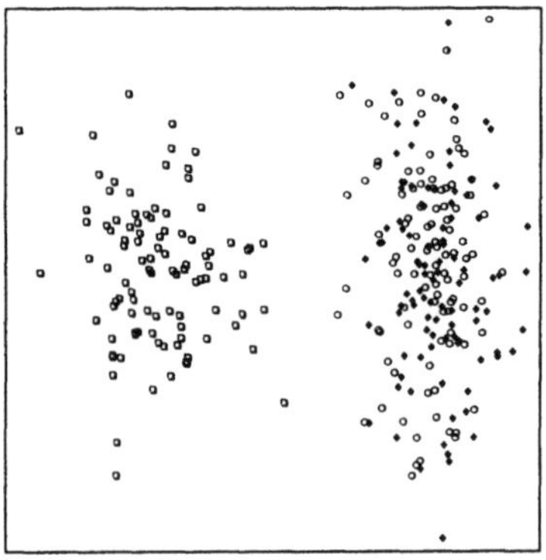

Figure 2: Plot of the posterior means of the data points from the toy data set, obtained from the probabilistic PCA model, indicating the presence of (at least) two distinct clusters.

4.2 Mixture Models for Data Visualization

Next we consider the application of a simple mixture of PPCA models to data visualization. Once a mixture of probabilistic PCA models has been fitted to the data set, the procedure for visualizing the data points involves plotting each data point $\mathbf{t}_n$ on each of the two-dimensional latent spaces at the corresponding posterior mean position $\langle \mathbf{x}_{ni} \rangle$ given by

$$\langle \mathbf{x}_{ni} \rangle = (\mathbf{W}_i^{\mathrm{T}} \mathbf{W}_i + \sigma_i^2 \mathbf{I})^{-1} \mathbf{W}_i^{\mathrm{T}} (\mathbf{t}_n - \boldsymbol{\mu}_i). \tag{35}$$

As a further refinement, the density of 'ink' for each data point $\mathbf{t}_n$ is weighted by the corresponding responsibility R_{ni} of model i for that data point, so that the total density of 'ink' is distributed by a partition of unity across the plots. Thus, each data point is plotted on every component model projection, while if a particular model takes nearly all of the posterior probability for a particular data point, then that data point will effectively be visible only on the corresponding latent space plot.

We shall regard the single PPCA plot introduced in Section 4.1 as the top level in a hierarchical visualization model, in which the mixture model forms the second level. Extensions to further levels of the hierarchy will be developed in Section 4.3.

The model can be extended to provide an interactive data exploration tool as follows. On the basis of the single top-level plot the user decides on an appropriate number of models to fit at the second level, and selects points $\mathbf{x}^{(i)}$ on the plot, corresponding, for example, to the centres of apparent clusters. The resulting points $\mathbf{y}^{(i)}$ in data space, obtained from $\mathbf{y}^{(i)} = \mathbf{W}\mathbf{x}^{(i)} + \boldsymbol{\mu}$, are then used to initialize the means $\boldsymbol{\mu}_i$ of the respective sub-models. To initialize the matrices $\mathbf{W}_i$ we first assign the data points to their nearest mean vector $\boldsymbol{\mu}_i$ and then compute the corresponding sample covariance matrices. This is a hard clustering analogous to K-means and represents an approximation to the posterior probabilities R_{ni} in which the largest posterior probability is replaced by 1 and the remainder by 0. For each of these clusters we then find the eigenvalues and eigenvectors of the sample covariance matrix and hence determine the probabilistic PCA density model.

The visualization process can be enhanced further by providing information at the top level on the location and orientation of the latent spaces corresponding to the second level. This can be achieved by considering the orthogonal projection of the latent plane in data space onto the corresponding plane of the parent model, as illustrated in Figure 3.

Consider the application of this procedure to the toy data set introduced in Section 4.1. At the top level we observed two apparent clusters, and so we might select a mixture of two models for the second level, with centres initialised somewhere near the centres of the two clusters seen at the top level. This leads to the two-level visualization plot shown in Figure 4.

4.3 Hierarchical Mixture Models

We now extend the mixture representation of Section 1.2 to give a hierarchical mixture model. Our formulation will be quite general and can be applied to hierarchical mixtures of any parametric density. So far we have considered a two-level system consisting of a single latent variable model at the top level

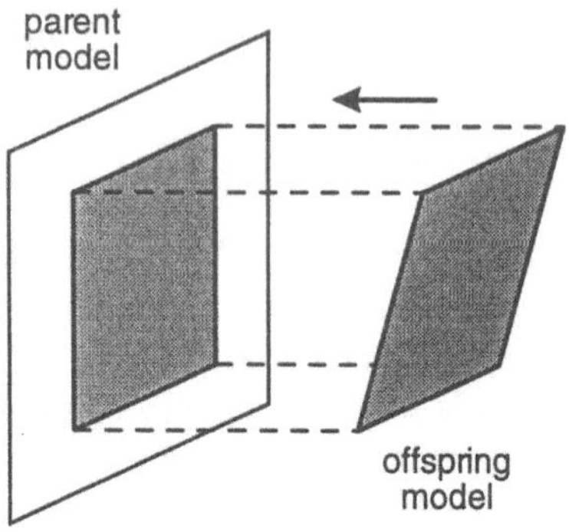

Figure 3: Illustration of the projection of one of the latent planes onto its parent plane.

and a mixture of M_0 such models at the second level. We can now extend the hierarchy to a third level by associating a group $\mathcal{G}_i$ of latent variable models with each model i in the second level. The corresponding probability density can be written in the form

$$p(\mathbf{t}) = \sum_{i=1}^{M_0} \pi_i \sum_{j \in \mathcal{G}_i} \pi_{j|i} p(\mathbf{t}|i,j) \tag{36}$$

where $p(\mathbf{t}|i,j)$ again represent independent latent variable models, and $\pi_{j|i}$ correspond to sets of mixing coefficients, one set for each i, which satisfy $0 \leq \pi_{j|i} \leq 1$ and $\sum_j \pi_{j|i} = 1$. Thus each level of the hierarchy corresponds to a generative model, with lower levels giving more refined and detailed representations. This model is illustrated in Figure 5.

The determination of the parameters of the models at the third level can again be viewed as a missing data problem in which the missing information corresponds to labels specifying which model generated each data point. When no information about the labels is provided the log likelihood for the model (36) would take the form

$$\mathcal{L} = \sum_{n=1}^{N} \ln \left\{ \sum_{i=1}^{M_0} \pi_i \sum_{j \in \mathcal{G}_i} \pi_{j|i} p(\mathbf{t}|i,j) \right\} \tag{37}$$

and the model would collapse to a simple mixture model. If, however, we were given a set of indicator variables z_{ni} specifying which model i at the second level generated each data point $\mathbf{t}_n$ then the log likelihood would become

$$\mathcal{L} = \sum_{n=1}^{N} \sum_{i=1}^{M_0} z_{ni} \ln \left\{ \pi_i \sum_{j \in \mathcal{G}_i} \pi_{j|i} p(\mathbf{t}|i,j) \right\}. \tag{38}$$

In fact we only have partial, probabilistic, information in the form of the posterior responsibilities R_{ni} for each model i having generated the data points $\mathbf{t}_n$,

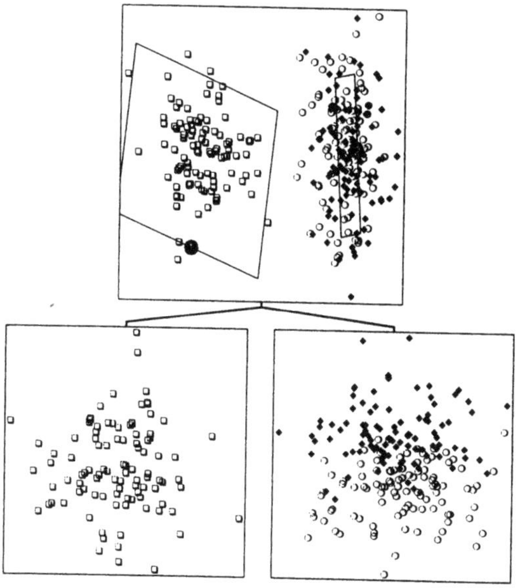

Figure 4: The result of applying the two-level visualization algorithm to the toy data set. At the second level a mixture of two latent variable models has been fitted and the data plotted on each latent space using the approach described in the text. In addition, the two latent planes have been visualized by projection back onto the top-level model. The left-hand plane at the second level is almost perpendicular to the top-level plane (as can be seen by its projection) giving further insight into why the two clusters which appear well separated on the left-hand second-level model appear to be overlapping at the top level.

obtained from the second level of the hierarchy. The corresponding log likelihood is obtained by taking the expectation of (38) with respect to the posterior distribution of the z_{ni} to give

$$\mathcal{L} = \sum_{n=1}^{N} \sum_{i=1}^{M_0} R_{ni} \ln \left\{ \pi_i \sum_{j \in \mathcal{G}_i} \pi_{j|i} p(\mathbf{t}|i,j) \right\} \tag{39}$$

in which the R_{ni} are constants. In the particular case in which the R_{ni} are all 0 or 1, corresponding to complete certainty about which model in the second level is responsible for each data point, the log likelihood (39) reduces to the form (38).

Maximization of (39) can again be performed using the EM algorithm, as discussed in (Tipping and Bishop, 1996). This has the same form as the EM algorithm for a simple mixture, discussed in Section 1.2, except that in the E-step, the posterior probability that model (i, j) generated data point $\mathbf{t}_n$ is given by

$$R_{ni,j} = R_{ni} R_{nj|i} \tag{40}$$

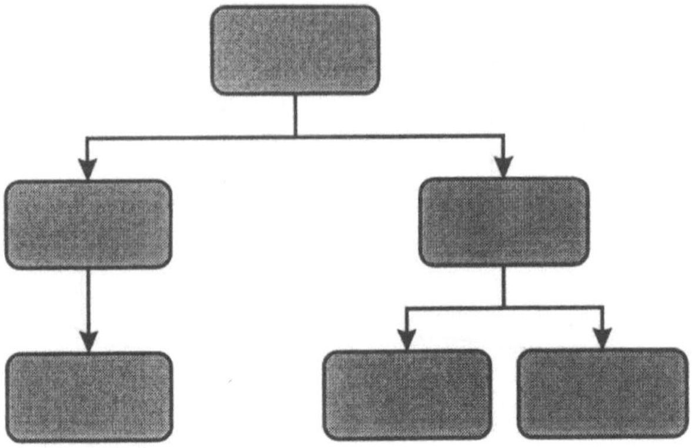

Figure 5: An example structure for the hierarchical mixture model.

in which

$$R_{nj|i} = \frac{\pi_{j|i} p(\mathbf{t}_n|i,j)}{\sum_{j'} \pi_{j'|i} p(\mathbf{t}_n|i,j')}. \tag{41}$$

This result automatically satisfies the relation

$$\sum_{j \in \mathcal{G}_i} R_{ni,j} = R_{ni} \tag{42}$$

so that the responsibility of each model at the second level for a given data point n is shared by a partition of unity between the corresponding group of offspring models at the third level. It is straightforward to extend this hierarchical approach to any desired number of levels.

The result of applying this approach to the toy data set is shown in Figure 6.

4.4 Example: Oil Flow Data

We now illustrate the application of the hierarchical visualization algorithm by considering an example data set arising from a non-invasive monitoring system used to determine the quantity of oil in a multi-phase pipeline containing a mixture of oil, water and gas (Bishop and James, 1993). The diagnostic data is collected from a set of three horizontal and three vertical beam-lines along which gamma rays at two different energies are passed. By measuring the degree of attenuation of the gammas, the fractional path length through oil and water (and hence gas) can readily be determined, giving 12 diagnostic measurements in total. In practice the aim is to solve the inverse problem of determining the fraction of oil in the pipe. The complexity of the problem arises from the possibility of the multi-phase mixture adopting one of a number of different geometrical configurations. Our goal is to visualize the structure of the data in the original 12-dimensional space. A data set consisting of 1000

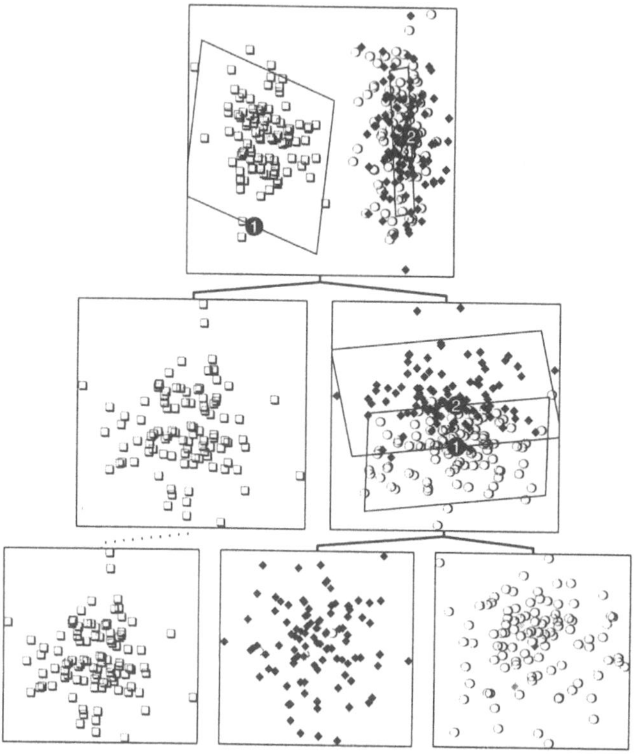

Figure 6: Plot of the complete three-level hierarchy for the toy data set. At the third level the three clusters have been almost perfectly separated. The structure of this particular hierarchical model is as shown in Figure 5.

points is obtained synthetically by simulating the physical processes in the pipe, including the presence of noise determined by photon statistics. Locally, the data is expected to have an intrinsic dimensionality of 2 corresponding to the two degrees of freedom given by the fraction of oil and the fraction of water (the fraction of gas being redundant). However, the presence of different configurations, as well as the geometrical interaction between phase boundaries and the beam paths, leads to numerous distinct clusters. It would appear that a hierarchical approach of the kind discussed here should be capable of discovering this structure. Results from fitting the oil flow data using a 3-level hierarchical model are shown in Figure 7.

In the case of the toy data, the optimal choice of clusters and sub-clusters is relatively unambiguous and a single application of the algorithm is sufficient to reveal all of the interesting structure within the data. For more complex data sets, it is appropriate to adopt an exploratory perspective and investigate alternative hierarchies, through the selection of differing numbers of clusters and their respective locations. The example shown in Figure 7 has clearly been

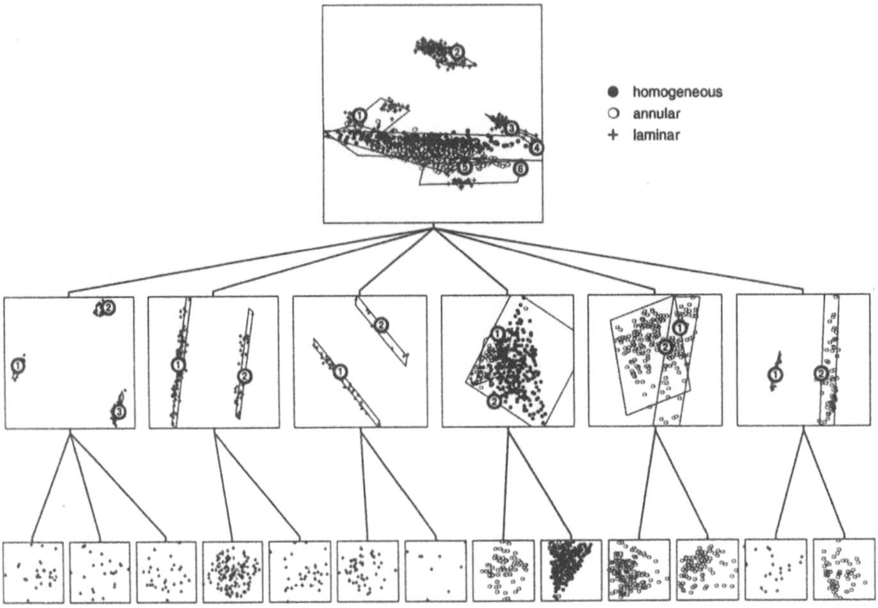

Figure 7: Results of fitting the oil data. The symbols denote different multi-phase flow configurations corresponding to homogeneous (•), annular (∘) and laminar (+). Note how the apparently single cluster, number 2, in the top level plot is revealed to be two quite distinct clusters at the second level.

highly successful. Note how the apparently single cluster, number 2, in the top level plot is revealed to be two quite distinct clusters at the second level. Also, data points from the 'homogeneous' configuration have been isolated and can be seen to lie on a two-dimensional triangular structure in the third level. Inspection of the corresponding value of σ^2 confirms that this cluster is confined to a nearly planar sub-space, as expected from the physics of the diagnostic data for the homogeneous configurations.

5 Non-linear Models: The Generative Topographic Mapping

The latent variable models we have considered so far are based on a mapping from latent variables to data variables of the form (6) in which the function $\mathbf{y}(\mathbf{x}; \mathbf{w})$ is linear in $\mathbf{x}$. Thus the manifold $\mathcal{S}$ in data space, shown in Figure 1 is hyper-planar. Data living on a manifold which is not hyper-planar (for example the hand-written digits data considered in Section 3.1) can then be approximated using a mixture of linear latent variable models. An alternative approach, however, would be to consider a latent variable model which is *non-linear*.

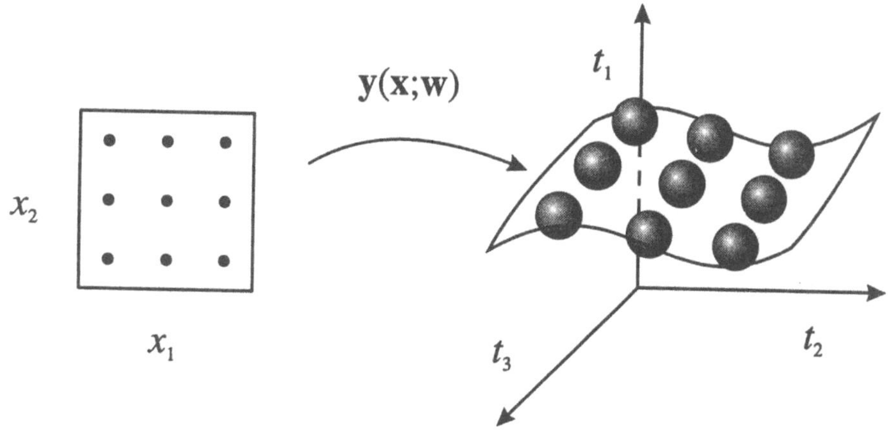

Figure 8: In order to formulate a tractable non-linear latent variable model, we consider a prior distribution $p(\mathbf{x})$ consisting of a superposition of delta functions, located at the nodes of a regular grid in latent space. Each node $\mathbf{x}_i$ is mapped to a corresponding point $\mathbf{y}(\mathbf{x}_i;\mathbf{w})$ in data space, and forms the centre of a corresponding Gaussian distribution.

The difficulty with using a non-linear mapping function $\mathbf{y}(\mathbf{x};\mathbf{w})$ in (6) is that in general the integration over $\mathbf{x}$ in (7) will become analytically intractable. However, by making careful model choices a tractable, non-linear model, called the *Generative Topographic Mapping* or GTM, can be derived (Bishop *et al.*, 1997). In particular, the prior distribution $p(\mathbf{x})$ over latent space is given by a sum of delta functions centred on the nodes of a regular grid in latent space

$$p(\mathbf{x}) = \frac{1}{K}\sum_{i=1}^{K}\delta(\mathbf{x}-\mathbf{x}_i) \tag{43}$$

in which case the integral in (7) can again be performed analytically. The conditional distribution $p(\mathbf{t}|\mathbf{x})$ is chosen to be an isotropic Gaussian with variance σ^2. Each point $\mathbf{x}_i$ is then mapped to a corresponding point $\mathbf{y}(\mathbf{x}_i;\mathbf{w})$ in data space, which forms the centre of a Gaussian density function, as illustrated in Figure 8. From (7) and (43) we see that the distribution function in data space then takes the form

$$p(\mathbf{t}|\mathbf{W},\sigma^2) = \frac{1}{K}\sum_{i=1}^{K}p(\mathbf{t}|\mathbf{x}_i,\mathbf{W},\sigma^2) \tag{44}$$

which corresponds to a *constrained* Gaussian mixture model (Hinton *et al.*, 1992) since the centres of the Gaussians, given by $\mathbf{y}(\mathbf{x}_i;\mathbf{w})$, cannot move independently but are related through the function $\mathbf{y}(\mathbf{x};\mathbf{w})$. Note that, provided the mapping function $\mathbf{y}(\mathbf{x};\mathbf{w})$ is smooth and continuous, the projected points $\mathbf{y}(\mathbf{x}_i;\mathbf{w})$ will necessarily have a *topographic* ordering in the sense that any two points $\mathbf{x}_A$ and $\mathbf{x}_B$ which are close in latent space will map to points $\mathbf{y}(\mathbf{x}_A;\mathbf{w})$ and $\mathbf{y}(\mathbf{x}_B;\mathbf{w})$ which are close in data space.

5.1 An EM Algorithm for GTM

Since GTM is a form of mixture model it is natural to seek an EM algorithm for maximizing the corresponding log likelihood. By choosing a particular form for the mapping $\mathbf{y}(\mathbf{x}; \mathbf{w})$ we can obtain an EM algorithm in which the M-step has a simple form. In particular we shall choose $\mathbf{y}(\mathbf{x}; \mathbf{w})$ to be given by a generalized linear regression model of the form

$$\mathbf{y}(\mathbf{x}; \mathbf{w}) = \mathbf{W}\boldsymbol{\phi}(\mathbf{x}) \tag{45}$$

where the elements of $\boldsymbol{\phi}(\mathbf{x})$ consist of M fixed basis functions $\phi_j(\mathbf{x})$, and $\mathbf{W}$ is a $d \times M$ matrix. Generalized linear regression models possess the same universal approximation capabilities as multi-layer adaptive networks, provided the basis functions $\phi_j(\mathbf{x})$ are chosen appropriately. The usual limitation of such models, however, is that the number of basis functions must typically grow exponentially with the dimensionality q of the input space (Bishop, 1995). In the present context this is not a significant problem since the dimensionality is governed by the number of latent variable variables which will typically be small. In fact for data visualization applications we generally use $q = 2$.

In the E-step of the EM algorithm we evaluate the posterior probabilities for each of the latent points i for every data point $\mathbf{t}_n$ using

$$R_{in} = p(\mathbf{x}_i | \mathbf{t}_n, \mathbf{W}, \sigma^2) \tag{46}$$

$$= \frac{p(\mathbf{t}_n | \mathbf{x}_i, \mathbf{W}, \sigma^2)}{\sum_{i'=1}^{K} p(\mathbf{t}_n | \mathbf{x}_{i'}, \mathbf{W}, \sigma^2)}. \tag{47}$$

Then in the M-step we obtain a revised value for $\mathbf{W}$ by solving a set of coupled *linear* equations of the form

$$\boldsymbol{\Phi}^{\mathrm{T}}\mathbf{G}\boldsymbol{\Phi}\mathbf{W}^{\mathrm{T}} = \boldsymbol{\Phi}^{\mathrm{T}}\mathbf{R}\mathbf{T} \tag{48}$$

where $\boldsymbol{\Phi}$ is a $K \times M$ matrix with elements $\Phi_{ij} = \phi_j(\mathbf{x}_i)$, $\mathbf{T}$ is a $N \times d$ matrix with elements t_{nk}, $\mathbf{R}$ is a $K \times N$ matrix with elements R_{in}, and $\mathbf{G}$ is a $K \times K$ diagonal matrix with elements

$$G_{ii} = \sum_{n=1}^{N} R_{in}(\mathbf{W}, \sigma^2). \tag{49}$$

We can now solve (48) for $\mathbf{W}$ using standard matrix inversion techniques, based on singular value decomposition to allow for possible ill-conditioning. Note that the matrix $\boldsymbol{\Phi}$ is constant throughout the algorithm, and so need only be evaluated once at the start. Also in the M-step we update σ^2 using the following re-estimation formula

$$\sigma^2 = \frac{1}{Nd} \sum_{n=1}^{N} \sum_{i=1}^{K} R_{in}(\mathbf{W}, \sigma^2) \left\| \mathbf{W}\boldsymbol{\phi}(\mathbf{x}_i) - \mathbf{t}_n \right\|^2. \tag{50}$$

When using GTM for data visualization we can again plot each data point at the point on latent space corresponding to the mean of the posterior distribution, given by

$$\langle \mathbf{x}|\mathbf{t}_n, \mathbf{W}, \sigma^2\rangle = \int \mathbf{x}p(\mathbf{x}|\mathbf{t}_n, \mathbf{W}, \sigma^2)\, d\mathbf{x} \tag{51}$$

$$= \sum_{i=1}^{K} R_{in}\mathbf{x}_i. \tag{52}$$

It should be borne in mind, however, that as a consequence of the non-linear mapping from latent space to data space the posterior distribution can be multi-modal in which case the posterior mean can give a very misleading summary of the true distribution. An alternative approach is therefore to evaluate the mode of the distribution, given by

$$i^{\max} = \arg\max_{\{i\}} R_{in}. \tag{53}$$

In practice it is often convenient to plot both the mean and the mode for each data point, as significant differences between them can be indicative of a multi-modal distribution.

One of the motivations for the development of the GTM algorithm was to provide a principled alternative to the widely used 'self-organizing map' (SOM) algorithm (Kohonen, 1982) in which a set of unlabelled data vectors $\mathbf{t}_n$ ($n = 1, \ldots, N$) in a D-dimensional data space is summarized in terms of a set of reference vectors having a spatial organization corresponding to a (generally) two-dimensional sheet. These reference vectors are analogous to the projections of the latent points into data space given by $\mathbf{y}(\mathbf{x}_i; \mathbf{w})$. While this algorithm has achieved many successes in practical applications, it also suffers from some significant deficiencies, many of which are highlighted in (Kohonen, 1995). They include: the absence of a cost function, the lack of any guarantee of topographic ordering, the absence of any general proofs of convergence, and the fact that the model does not define a probability density. These problems are all absent in GTM. The computational complexity of the GTM and SOM algorithms is similar, since the dominant cost in both cases is the evaluation of the Euclidean distanced between each data point and each reference point in data space, and is the same for both algorithms.

Clearly, we can easily formulate a density model consisting of a mixture of GTM models, and obtain the corresponding EM algorithm, in a principled manner. The development of an analogous algorithm for the SOM would necessarily be somewhat ad-hoc.

5.2 Geometry of the Manifold

An additional advantage of the GTM algorithm (compared with the SOM) is that the non-linear manifold in data space is defined explicitly in terms of the analytic function $\mathbf{y}(\mathbf{x}; \mathbf{w})$. This allows a whole variety of geometrical properties of the manifold to be evaluated (Bishop *et al.*, 1996). For example, local magnification factors can be expressed in terms of derivatives of the basis functions appearing in (45). Magnification factors specify the extent to which the area of a small patch of the latent space of a topographic mapping is magnified on projection to the data space, and are of considerable interest in both neuro-biological and data analysis contexts. Previous attempts to consider magnification factors for the SOM were been hindered because the manifold is only defined at discrete points (given by the reference vectors).

We can determine the properties of the manifold, including magnification factors, using techniques of differential geometry as follows (Bishop *et al.*, 1996). Consider a standard set of Cartesian coordinates x^i in the latent space. Since each point P in latent space is mapped by a continuous function to a corresponding point P' in data space, the mapping defines a set of curvilinear coordinates ξ^i in the manifold in which each point P' is labelled with the coordinate values $\xi^i = x^i$ of P, as illustrated in Figure 9. Throughout this paper we shall

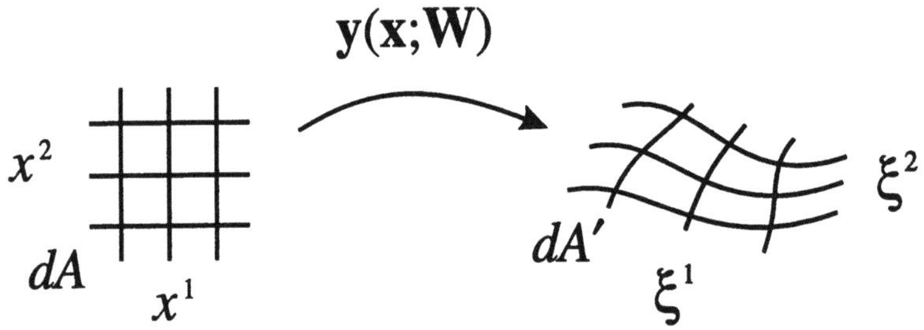

Figure 9: This diagram shows the mapping of the Cartesian coordinate system x^i in latent space onto a curvilinear coordinate system ξ^i in the q-dimensional manifold $\mathcal{S}$.

use the standard notation of differential geometry in which raised indices denote contravariant components and lowered indices denote covariant components, with an implicit summation over pairs of repeated covariant-contravariant indices.

We first discuss the metric properties of the manifold $\mathcal{S}$. Consider a local transformation, at some point P' in $\mathcal{S}$, to a set of rectangular Cartesian coordinates $\zeta^i = \zeta^i(\boldsymbol{\xi})$. Then the squared length element in these coordinates is given by

$$ds^2 = \delta_{\mu\nu} d\zeta^\mu d\zeta^\nu = \delta_{\mu\nu} \frac{\partial \zeta^\mu}{\partial \xi^i} \frac{\partial \zeta^\nu}{\partial \xi^j} d\xi^i d\xi^j = g_{ij} d\xi^i d\xi^j \tag{54}$$

where g_{ij} is the metric tensor, which is therefore given by

$$g_{ij} = \delta_{\mu\nu} \frac{\partial \zeta^\mu}{\partial \xi^i} \frac{\partial \zeta^\nu}{\partial \xi^j}. \tag{55}$$

We now seek an expression for g in terms of the non-linear mapping $\mathbf{y}(\mathbf{x})$. Consider again the squared length element ds^2 lying within the manifold $\mathcal{S}$.

Since $\mathcal{S}$ is embedded within the Euclidean data space, this also corresponds to the squared length element of the form

$$ds^2 = \delta_{kl} dy^k dy^l = \delta_{kl} \frac{\partial y^k}{\partial x^i} \frac{\partial y^l}{\partial x^j} dx^i dx^j = g_{ij} dx^i dx^j \tag{56}$$

and so we have

$$g_{ij} = \delta_{kl} \frac{\partial y^k}{\partial x^i} \frac{\partial y^l}{\partial x^j}. \tag{57}$$

Using (45) the metric tensor can be expressed in terms of the derivatives of the basis functions $\phi_j(\mathbf{x})$ in the form

$$\mathbf{g} = \mathbf{\Omega}^{\mathrm{T}} \mathbf{W}^{\mathrm{T}} \mathbf{W} \mathbf{\Omega} \tag{58}$$

where $\mathbf{\Omega}$ has elements $\Omega_{ji} = \partial \phi_j / \partial x^i$. It should be emphasised that, having obtained the metric tensor as a function of the latent space coordinates, many other geometrical properties are easily evaluated, such as the local curvatures of the manifold.

Our goal is to find an expression for the area dA' of the region of $\mathcal{S}$ corresponding to an infinitesimal rectangle in latent space with area $dA = \prod_i dx^i$. The area element in the manifold $\mathcal{S}$ can be related to the corresponding area element in the latent space by the Jacobian of the transformation $\xi \rightarrow \zeta$

$$dA' = \prod_\mu d\zeta^\mu = J \prod_i d\xi^i = J \prod_i dx^i = J dA \tag{59}$$

where the Jacobian J is given by

$$J = \det \left(\frac{\partial \zeta^\mu}{\partial \xi^i} \right) = \det \left(\frac{\partial \zeta^\mu}{\partial x^i} \right). \tag{60}$$

We now introduce the determinant g of the metric tensor which we can write in the form

$$g = \det(g_{ij}) = \det \left(\delta_{\mu\nu} \frac{\partial \zeta^\mu}{\partial x^i} \frac{\partial \zeta^\nu}{\partial x^j} \right) = \det \left(\frac{\partial \zeta^\mu}{\partial x^i} \right) \det \left(\frac{\partial \zeta^\nu}{\partial x^j} \right) = J^2 \tag{61}$$

and so, using (59), we obtain an expression for the volume element in curvilinear coordinates in the form

$$\frac{dA'}{dA} = J = \det{}^{1/2} \mathbf{g}. \tag{62}$$

Although the magnification factor represents the extent to which areas are magnified on projection to the data space, it gives no information about which directions in latent space correspond to the stretching. We can recover this information by considering the decomposition of the metric tensor in terms of its eigenvectors and eigenvalues. This information can be conveniently displayed by selecting a regular grid in latent space (which could correspond to the reference vector grid, but could also be much finer) and plotting at each grid point an ellipse with principal axes oriented according to the eigenvectors, with principal radii given by the square roots of the eigenvalues. The standard area magnification factor is given from (62) by the square root of the product of the eigenvalues, and so corresponds to the area of the ellipse.

As an illustration of the GTM algorithm and the evaluation of magnification factors we consider a data set of measurements taken from the genus *Leptograpsus* of rock crabs. Measurements were taken from two species classified by their colour (orange or blue) with the aim of discovering morphological differences which would allow preserved specimens (which have lost their colour) to be distinguished. The data set contains 50 examples of each sex from each species, and the measurements correspond to length of frontal lip, rear width, length along mid-line, maximum width of carapace, and body length. Since all of the variables correspond to length measurements, the dominant feature of the crabs data is an overall scaling of the data vector in relation to the size of the crab. To remove this effect each data vector $\mathbf{t}_n = (t_{1n}, \ldots, t_{dn})^{\mathrm{T}}$ is normalized to unit mean, so that

$$\widetilde{t}_{kn} = t_{kn} \Bigg/ \sum_{k'=1}^{d} t_{k'n}. \tag{63}$$

The latent space visualization of the crabs data is shown in Figure 10 together with the local magnification factor. It can be seen that the two species

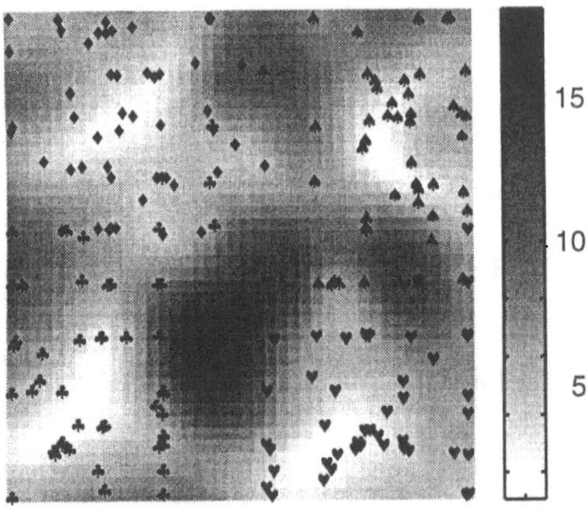

Figure 10: Plot of the latent-space distribution of the crabs data, in which ♣ denotes blue males, ♢ denotes blue females, ♡ denotes orange males, and ♠ denotes orange females. The grey-scale background shows the corresponding magnification factor as a function of the latent space coordinates.

form distinct clusters, with the manifold undergoing a relatively large stretching in the region between them. Within each cluster there is a partial separation of males from females.

The corresponding plot of the local eigenvector decomposition of the metric is given in Figure 11, and shows both the direction and magnitude of the stretching.

Figure 11: Plots of the local stretching of the latent space, corresponding to the example in Figure 10, using the ellipse representation discussed in the text.

6 Temporal Models: GTM Through Time

In all of the models we have considered so far, it has been assumed that the data vectors are independent and identically distributed. One common situation in which this assumption is generally violated in where the data vectors are successive samples in a time series, with neighbouring vectors having typically a high correlation. As our final example of the use of latent variables, we consider an extension of the GTM algorithm to deal with temporal data (Bishop *et al.*, 1997). The key observation is that the hidden states of the GTM model are discrete, as a result of the choice of latent distribution $p(\mathbf{x})$, which allows the machinery of hidden Markov models to be combined with GTM to give a non-linear temporal latent variable model. The structure of the model is illustrated in Figure 12.

The hidden states of the model at each time step n are labelled by the index i_n corresponding to the latent points $\{\mathbf{x}_{i_n}\}$. We introduce a set of transition probabilities $p(i_{n+1}|i_n)$ corresponding to the probability of making a transition to state i_{n+1} given that the current state is i_n. The emission density for the hidden Markov model is then given by the GTM density model (44). It should be noted that both the transition probabilities $p(i_{n+1}|i_n)$ and the parameters $\mathbf{W}$ and σ^2 governing the GTM model are common to all time steps, so that the number of adaptive parameters in the model is independent of the length of the time series. We also introduce separate prior probabilities π_{i_1} on each of the latent points at the first time step of the algorithm.

If we allow a fully connected matrix of independent transition probabilities connecting every state at time n to every state at time $n+1$, then the number

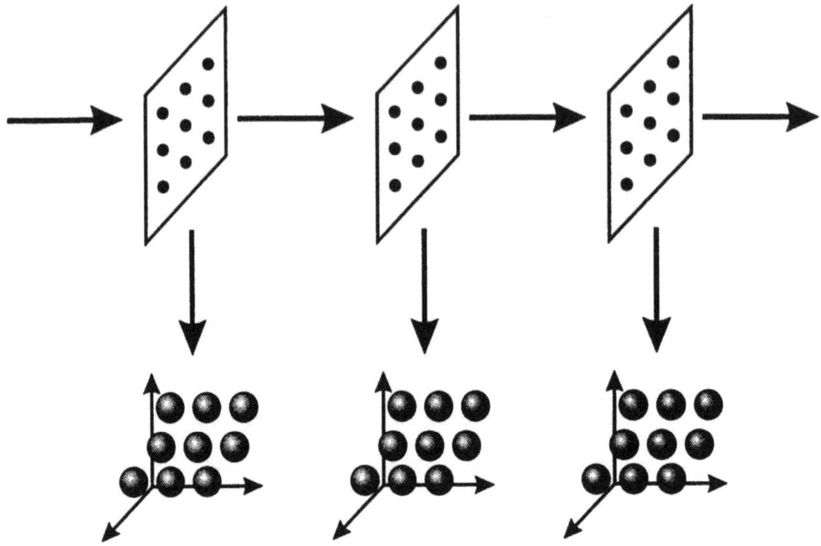

Figure 12: The temporal version of GTM consists of a hidden Markov model in which the hidden states are given by the latent points of the GTM model, and the emission probabilities are governed by the GTM mixture distribution. Note that the parameters of the GTM model, as well as the transition probabilities between states, are tied to common values across all time steps.

of independent parameters would be prohibitively large. For example, if we have 100 hidden states in the GTM model corresponding to a 10×10 grid of latent points (a relatively small model) then we would have 10^4 independent transition probability parameters to be determined (slightly less in fact due to the constraint that probabilities must sum to one). This would require an excessive amount of training data.

Also it fails to capture any prior knowledge which we might possess about the nature of the transitions between different time steps. In many applications we would like different regions of the latent space to correspond to different 'regimes' of the time series. We might then expect smooth changes in latent space within a regime and relatively rare jumps to other regimes, as in the helicopter data example discussed below. An approximate way to capture this prior knowledge is to allow groups of transitions to be governed by a common parameter. We denote the kth group from state i_n by $\mathcal{G}_{i_n k}$ and we introduce indicator variables $C_{ki_n i_{n+1}}$ which equal 1 if state i_{n+1} is in group $\mathcal{G}_{i_n k}$ and 0 otherwise. The transition probability from state i_n to a state in group k will be denoted $\eta_{i_n k}$, and will satisfy $\sum_k \eta_{i_n k} N_{i_n k} = 1$ where $N_{i_n k}$ denotes the number of states in group $\mathcal{G}_{i_n k}$. The transition probability from state i_n to state i_{n+1} is then given by

$$p(i_{n+1}|i_n) = \sum_k \eta_{i_n k} C_{ki_n i_{n+1}}. \tag{64}$$

Again we can obtain an EM algorithm for maximizing the likelihood for the temporal GTM model. In the context of hidden Markov models, the EM algorithm is often called the Baum-Welch algorithm, and is reviewed in (Rabiner, 1989). The E-step involves the evaluation of the posterior probabilities of the hidden states at each time step, and can be accomplished efficiently using a technique called the *forward-backward* algorithm since it involves two counter-directional propagations along the Markov chain. The M-step equations again take the form given in Section 5.1.

As an illustration of the temporal GTM algorithm we consider a data set obtained from a series of helicopter test flights. The motivation behind this application is to determine the accumulated stress on the helicopter airframe. Different flight modes, and transitions between flight modes, cause different levels of stress, and at present maintenance intervals are determined using an *assumed* usage spectrum. The ultimate goal in this application would be to segment each flight into its distinct regimes, together with the transitions between those regimes, and hence evaluate the overall integrated stress with greater accuracy.

The data used in this simulation was gathered from the flight recorder over four test flights, and consists of 9 variables (sampled every two seconds) measuring quantities such as acceleration, rate of change of heading, speed, altitude and engine torque. A sample of the data is shown in Figure 13.

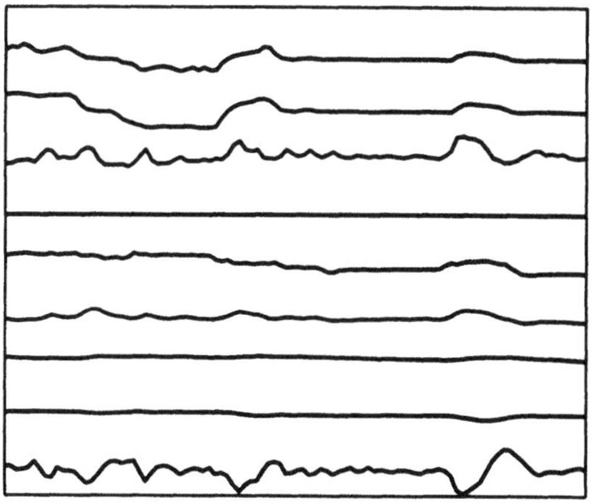

Figure 13: Sample of the helicopter data showing the evolution of 9 different dynamical quantities such as acceleration, speed, and engine torque as a function of time.

We consider a GTM model having a 15×15 grid of states in latent space. For each latent state i_n, the transition probabilities to states at the next time step are collected into 10 separate groups, in which 9 of the groups correspond to those states i_{n+1} which are within a distance of ± 1 units in latent space from state i_n, while the 10th group consists of all remaining stages i_{n+1}. We expect that, in the trained model, different regions of the latent space will correspond to different flight regimes. The first group of transition probabilities then allows evolution of the data vector within a given flight regime to be modelled, while transitions to distant flight regimes can be represented by the second group. Note that this does not capture all of the likely behaviour of the time series. For instance, if transitions between two particular regimes are much more frequent than between some other pair of regimes, this cannot be represented in the model just described.

Figure 14 shows the posterior probability distribution in latent space for a trained temporal GTM model, in which the posterior probabilities for a given temporal sequence have been evaluated using the forward-backward algorithm as described earlier.

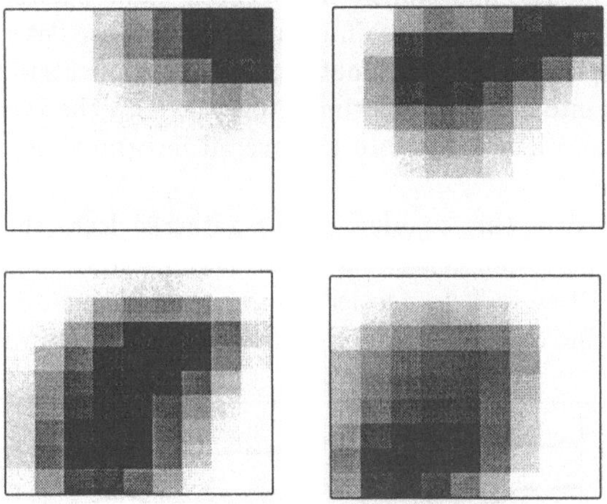

Figure 14: Plots of the posterior probability distribution in latent space at 4 time steps, corresponding to a transition from one flight regime to another.

7 Discussion

In this paper we have surveyed a number of hidden variable models for representing the distributions of continuous variables. We considered examples involving discrete, continuous and mixed hidden variables, together with linear and non-linear models for the distribution of observed variables conditioned on the hidden variables.

These models can conveniently be expressed in terms of probabilistic graphical structures, which provides insight into the corresponding inference and learning algorithms. For example, we saw that two key operations are the inference of the posterior distribution of the hidden variables given the observed variables (corresponding to the E-step of the EM algorithm) and the evaluation of the likelihood function which involves summing or integrating over all possible configurations of the hidden variables. For the models considered in this paper, the integration over continuous hidden variables was possible because of simple (linear and Gaussian) choices for the model structure. In the case of discrete hidden variables we considered models in which only one of the hidden states can be active at any one time, giving rise to the standard mixture distribution.

The graphical viewpoint, however, also helps to motivate the development of new classes of probabilistic model. For instance, more general representations for discrete hidden states could also be considered. However, for many models this leads to intractable algorithms since the number of *configurations* of hidden states may grow exponentially, rather than linearly, with the number of hidden variables. The development of controlled approximations to deal with such models is currently the focus of extensive research within the graphical modelling and neural computing communities.

Acknowledgements

The author would like to thank the following for their contributions to the work reported in this paper: Geoffrey Hinton, Iain Strachan, Markus Svensén, Michael Tipping and Christopher Williams.

References

Anderson, T. W. (1958). *An Introduction to Multivariate Statistical Analysis.* New York: John Wiley.

Anderson, T. W. (1963). Asymptotic theory for principal component analysis. *Annals of Mathematical Statistics* **34**, 122–148.

Bartholomew, D. J. (1987). *Latent Variable Models and Factor Analysis.* London: Charles Griffin & Co. Ltd.

Basilevsky, A. (1994). *Statistical Factor Analysis and Related Methods.* New York: Wiley.

Bishop, C. M. (1995). *Neural Networks for Pattern Recognition.* Oxford University Press.

Bishop, C. M., G. E. Hinton, and I. G. D. Strachan (1997). GTM through time. Accepted for publication in Proceedings IEE Fifth International Conference on Artificial Neural Networks, Cambridge, U.K.

Bishop, C. M. and G. D. James (1993). Analysis of multiphase flows using dual-energy gamma densitometry and neural networks. *Nuclear Instruments and Methods in Physics Research* **A327**, 580–593.

Bishop, C. M., M. Svensén, and C. K. I. Williams (1996). Magnification factors for the GTM algorithm. To appear in Proceedings Fifth IEE International Conference on Artificial Neural Networks.

Bishop, C. M., M. Svensén, and C. K. I. Williams (1997). GTM: the generative topographic mapping. Accepted for publication in Neural Computation. Available as NCRG/96/015 from `http://www.ncrg.aston.ac.uk/`.

Dempster, A. P., N. M. Laird, and D. B. Rubin (1977). Maximum likelihood from incomplete data via the EM algorithm. *Journal of the Royal Statistical Society, B* **39** (1), 1–38.

Hinton, G. E., P. Dayan, and M. Revow (1997). Modeling the manifolds of images of handwritten digits. *IEEE Transactions on Neural Networks* **8** (1), 65–74.

Hinton, G. E., C. K. I. Williams, and M. D. Revow (1992). Adaptive elastic models for hand-printed character recognition. In J. E. Moody, S. J. Hanson, and R. P. Lippmann (Eds.), *Advances in Neural Information Processing Systems*, Volume 4, pp. 512–519. Morgan Kauffmann.

Hotelling, H. (1933). Analysis of a complex of statistical variables into principal components. *Journal of Educational Psychology* **24**, 417–441.

Hull, J. J. (1994). A database for handwritten text recognition research. *IEEE Transactions on Pattern Analysis and Machine Intelligence* **16**, 550–554.

Kohonen, T. (1982). Self-organized formation of topologically correct feature maps. *Biological Cybernetics* **43**, 59–69.

Kohonen, T. (1995). *Self-Organizing Maps.* Berlin: Springer-Verlag.

Krzanowski, W. J. and F. H. C. Marriott (1994). *Multivariate Analysis Part I: Distributions, Ordination and Inference.* London: Edward Arnold.

Pearson, K. (1901). On lines and planes of closest fit to systems of points in space. *The London, Edinburgh and Dublin Philosophical Magazine and Journal of Science, Sixth Series* **2**, 559–572.

Rabiner, L. R. (1989). A tutorial on hidden Markov models and selected applications in speech recognition. *Proceedings of the IEEE* **77** (2), 257–285.

Rao, C. R. (1955). Estimation and tests of significance in factor analysis. *Psychometrika* **20**, 93–111.

Rubin, D. B. and D. T. Thayer (1982). EM algorithms for ML factor analysis. *Psychometrika* **47** (1), 69–76.

Tipping, M. E. and C. M. Bishop (1996). Hierarchical latent variable models for data visualization. Technical Report NCRG/96/028, Neural Computing Research Group, Aston University, Birmingham, UK. Submitted to IEEE PAMI.

Tipping, M. E. and C. M. Bishop (1997a). Mixtures of principal component analysers. Technical Report NCRG/97/003, Neural Computing Research Group, Aston University, Birmingham, UK. Submitted to Neural Computation.

Tipping, M. E. and C. M. Bishop (1997b). Probabilistic principal component analysis. Technical report, Neural Computing Research Group, Aston University, Birmingham, UK. Submitted to Journal of the Royal Statistical Society.

SECTION 2

<u>REVIEW PAPERS</u>

Fuzzy Neural Networks for Pattern Recognition *

Andrea Baraldi
IMGA-CNR
Via Gobetti 101, 43100 Bologna, Italy
Ph.: +39-59-362388; Fax: +39-59-374506.
e-mail: andrea@aliseo.imga.bo.cnr.it

Palma Blonda
IESI-CNR
Via Amendola 163, 70126 Bari, Italy
Ph.: +39-80-5481612; fax +39-80-5484311
e-mail: blonda@iesi.ba.cnr.it

Alfredo Petrosino
INFM-University of Salerno
Via S. Allende, Baronissi (Salerno), Italy
Ph.: +39-89-761167; fax +39-81-761189
e-mail: alfredo@irsip.na.cnr.it

Abstract

The objective of this paper is to discuss a state-of-the-art of methodology and algorithms for integrating fuzzy sets and neural networks in a unique framework for dealing with pattern recognition problems, in particular classification procedures. Methods of pattern recognition are studied in two main streams, namely supervised and unsupervised learning. We propose our own definition of fuzzy neural integrated networks. This criterion is proposed as a unifying framework for comparison of algorithms. In the first part of the this paper, classification methods based on rule sets or numerical data are reviewed, together with specific methods for handling classification in image processing. In the second part of this paper, several fuzzy neural clustering models are reviewed and compared. These models are: i) Self-Organizing Map (SOM); ii) Fuzzy Learning Vector Quantization (FLVQ); iii) Carpenter-Grossberg-Rosen Fuzzy Adaptive Resonance Theory (CGR Fuzzy ART); iv) Growing Neural Gas (GNG); and v) Fully self-Organizing Simplified Adaptive Resonance Theory (FOSART).

*The introduction and Part I of this work have been authored by A. Petrosino, whereas Part II has been authored by A. Baraldi and P. Blonda.

Introduction

A lot of scientific effort has been dedicated to pattern recognition problems, especially classification procedures. These include linear classifiers, knowledge-based classification paradigms, as e.g. heuristic classification stemming from artificial intelligence fields, fuzzy logic based systems and neural networks. This underlines that a field of pattern recognition strongly follows recent achievements of different areas of science or engineering incorporating them for formation of more efficient and reliable classification algorithms. In particular, from the very beginning of the development of fuzzy sets it has been obvious that they have a strong impact on techniques of pattern recognition, both from the methodological viewpoint, i.e. it leads to treatment of fuzzy sets as a well-suited theory within which one can establish a plausible tool for modeling cognitive processes of the human being, and from the innovation viewpoint in the sense of the development of a lot of novel algorithms which, with suitable modifications, are useful for designing classification procedures. On the other side, neural networks offer today valuable tools for classification both in the sense of non parametric statistical pattern recognition and in their connotation of knowledge acquisition abilities from a family of training patterns and their distribution along the connections of the structure within their learning. The general tendency of merging fuzzy sets and neural networks has appeared quite early in the development of fuzzy sets [1]. Bearing in mind an evident overlap in the architectures characteristic for fuzzy sets and neural networks, these two complementary technologies can produce an efficient synergy for the design of "intelligent" classification procedures. So doing, the merits and demerits of each method against featuring elements of information processing in intelligent systems must be considered and analyzed. Table 1 reports such a comparison. From the table, it arises that neural networks enjoy four major advantages over many classical pattern recognition techniques: *adaptivity*, i.e. the ability to adjust when given new information; *speed* via massive parallelism; *fault tolerance* to missing, confusing and/or noisy data; *optimality* as regards error rates in classification systems. On the contrary, they suffer from low capability to clearly formulate knowledge extracted from data and treatment of imprecise and/or incomplete knowledge. Several researchers have considered the possibility of integrating the advantages of neural networks with those not less known of fuzzy sets, giving rising to *fuzzy neural integrated networks*.

Since the variety of approaches found nowadays is quite impressive, the interested reader may refer to [2,3] as being two representative sources with this regards. Here we will look at the synergy of fuzzy sets and neural networks from a broader perpective of methodology and methods in classification procedures. The paper is subdivided in two parts, relating algorithms for supervised and unsupervised recognition tasks. The first part covers methods for classification with the presence of supervision, together with a broader view of methodologies of integration fuzzy sets and neural networks in the same framework. Afterwards, methods of fuzzy neural clustering (classification with partial or any supervision) are studied in detail in the second part of the paper. We also

	FIS	ANN
Mathematical model	SG	SG
Learning ability	B	G
Knowledge representation	G	B
Expert knowledge	G	B
Nonlinearity	G	G
Optimization ability	B	SG
Fault tolerance	G	G
Uncertainty tolerance	G	G
Real-time operation	G	SG

Table 1: Comparison of Fuzzy Inference Systems (FIS) and Artificial Neural Networks (ANN). The terms for grading are good (G), slightly good (SG), slightly bad (SB) and bad (B).

provide an extensive and updated bibliography covering publications dealing with fuzzy neural synergism in pattern recognition.

PART I: FUZZY NEURAL NETWORKS FOR CLASSIFICATION

1 Fuzzy Pattern Recognition

To better understand the role of fuzziness in the design of pattern recognition systems, let us consider a decision-theoretic approach to pattern classification. When conventional probabilistic and deterministic classifiers are concerned, the features characterizing the input vectors are quantitative, i.e. numerical in nature. Features having imprecise or incomplete specification are usually either ignored or discarded from the design and test sets. The concept of *fuzzy set theory* [4,5] can be introduced into the pattern recognition process to cope with impreciseness arising from various sources. For example, instrumental error or noise corruption in the experiment may lead to partially reliable information available on a feature measurement. Again, in some cases the expense incurred in extracting a very precise value of a feature may be high or it may be difficult to decide on the most relevant features to be extracted. In these cases it may become convenient to use linguistic variables and hedges (small, medium, high, very, more and less, etc.) in order to describe the feature information. Again, uncertainty in classification may arise from the overlapping nature of classes; realistically speaking, the feature vector characterizing a specific pattern can and should allowed to have degrees of membership in more than one class. Similarly, another problem arises in pattern recognition when it is necessary to estimate the exact shape based upon the boundary that contains some or all of the sample points. Since the boundary should contain obscured portions not represented in the sampled points, each point is characterized by a multivalued or fuzzy degrees of belonging to certain classes.

Examples of how the uncertainty should be described depends on the context considered:

(a) involving the feature space

IF an object is ***elongated*** AND ***small*** AND it moves ***fast*** THEN it is in class ω_i

(b) involving the classification stage

IF an object is black AND cubic THEN it ***possibly*** is in class ω_i

(c) a combination of both

IF an object is ***elongated*** AND ***small*** AND it moves ***fast*** THEN it ***possibly*** is in class ω_i

where ***elongated***, ***small***, ***fast*** and ***possibly*** are linguistic variables.
Formally speaking, the design of a fuzzy pattern recognition system may be described as follows:

Problem formulation

Let X denote the pattern from the environment observed via the data acquisition process. The pattern is described in linguistic terms than in numerical fashion, i.e. the ith feature of X, X_i, is represented as a fuzzy set with membership function $\mu_{X_i} \in [0,1]$. We further assume that there exists finite number of classes $W = \{\omega_1, \omega_2, \ldots, \omega_c\}$. The goal is to find a fuzzy set Ω with membership function μ_Ω such that the value $\mu_{\Omega(\omega_i)}$, $i = 1, \ldots, c$, denotes the grade of membership of the pattern X to the ith class.

If there is a rule base consisting of a collection of fuzzy IF-THEN rules describing the classification process, e.g.

$$\mathcal{R}_j : \text{IF } x_1 \text{ is } A_1^j \text{ AND} \ldots \text{AND } x_n \text{ is } A_n^j \text{ THEN } (x_1, \ldots, x_n) \textbf{\textit{ possibly}} \text{ is in } \omega_l$$

the better way to classify an unknown pattern is to infer its belonging class on the basis of the rule base and the description of the pattern in linguistic terms or more generally characterized by numerical information. The aim of a *fuzzy inference system* (FIS) is to use these fuzzy IF-THEN rules to determine a mapping from fuzzy sets in the input universe of discourse $U \subset \mathcal{R}^n$ to fuzzy sets in the output discourse $V \subset \mathcal{R}$ based on fuzzy logic principles. As above mentioned, if the pattern is described in numerical fashion, a fuzzifier to the input and a defuzzifier to the output of the fuzzy logic system are added. The fuzzifier maps crisp (valued in $\{0,1\}$) points in U to fuzzy sets in U, and the defuzzifier maps fuzzy sets in V to crisp points in V. The relevance of using fuzzifier and defuzzifier should be looked for also in the capability of fuzzy logic system to integrate the processing both of numerical and linguistic information.

Generally and formally speaking in the framework of classification procedures, a fuzzy logic system with fuzzifier and defuzzifier is a multi-input-single-output (MISO) fuzzy inference system which computes the function $f : \mathcal{R}^n \rightarrow \mathcal{R}$, described by the following collection of single-output systems

Fact : x_1 is A'_1 AND $\cdots$ AND x_n is A'_n

Rule 1 : IF x_1 is A_1^1 AND $\cdots$ AND x_n is A_n^1 THEN y is B^1 ELSE

Rule m : IF x_1 is A_1^m AND $\cdots$ AND x_n is A_n^m THEN y is B^m ELSE

Conclusion : y is B'
where $(x_1, x_2, \ldots, x_n)^T \in U$ and $y \in V$.

In the setting of the MISO fuzzy inference system the fuzzifier, inference and defuzzifier get the following meanings:

Fuzzification:

The input x_i maps to the fuzzy set A'_i, $i = 1, \ldots, n$.

Inference:

Each fuzzy rule defines a fuzzy set $(A_1^j \text{ AND} \cdots \text{AND } A_n^j) \rightarrow B^j$ in the product space $U \times V$, i.e.

$$\mu_{\mathcal{R}^j}(x_1, \ldots, x_n, y) = \mu_{A_1{}^j}(x_1) \cdots \mu_{A_n{}^j}(x_n) \cdot \mu_{B^j}(y)$$

The conclusion B' can be deduced as

$$B' = (A'_1 \text{ AND} \cdots \text{AND } A'_n) \bullet R$$

where $\bullet$ denotes the max product compositional rule of inference and R is the fuzzy set union of rules, i.e.

$$\mu_{B'}(y) = \sum_{j=1}^{m} (\prod_{i=1}^{n} \mu_{A_i^j}(x_i)) \mu_{B^j}(y)$$

Defuzzification:

The output y^* is a representative point of B', i.e. if the center of area (COA) method is adopted

$$y^* = \frac{\int_V \mu_{B'}(y) y dy}{\int_V \mu_{B'}(y) dy}$$

The main theoretical result which characterizes the MISO fuzzy inference system is

Result

For any given real continuous function f on a compact set $U \subset \mathcal{R}^n$ and arbitrary $\epsilon > 0$ there exists a FIS with COA defuzzifier, product inference rule and single fuzzifier, i.e.

$$f(\mathbf{x}) = \frac{\sum_{j=1}^{m} y^i \left(\prod_{i=1}^{n} \mu_{A_i^j}(x_i)\right)}{\sum_{j=1}^{m} \left(\prod_{i=1}^{n} \mu_{A_i^j}(x_i)\right)}$$

where $y^i = \arg\sup_{y \in V}(\mu_{B^j}(y))$, such that

$$\sup_{\mathbf{x} \in U} |f(\mathbf{x}) - g(\mathbf{x})| < \epsilon$$

When only a training set $(\mathbf{x}^p, \mathbf{d}^p)$ is available (only numerical information), such that the classification of $\mathbf{x}$ is known as one of c classes with $d_i^p \neq 0$, one should require to describe the classification process in terms of fuzzy IF-THEN rules

$$\mathcal{R}_i : \text{IF } x_1^p \text{ is } A_{i_1}^K, \text{ AND} \cdots \text{AND } x_n^p \text{ is } A_{i_n}^K, \text{ THEN } \mathbf{x}^p \text{ is in } \omega_i \text{ with } CF^K$$

where $A_{i_j}^k$ is a fuzzy number modelled as fuzzy set (usually triangular), K is the number of fuzzy intervals in each axis, ω_i one of the c classes and $CF^K \in (0, 1]$ the grade of certainty of the fuzzy IF-THEN rule which models the linguistic term ***possibly*** as pointed before in this section.

Typical algorithms for extracting IF-THEN rules from numerical training data are based on: *a*) product space clustering; *b*) ellipsoidal covariance learning; *c*) direct matching. In the following a product space clustering algorithm is briefly sketched:

1. Determine a K^2 fuzzy partition of feature space.

2. Find class ω_y such that

$$\omega_y = \arg\max\{\beta_{\omega_t} | t = 1, \ldots, c\}$$

$$\beta_{\omega_t} = \sum_{\mathbf{x}^p \in \omega_t} \mu_{i_1}^K(x_1^p) \cdots \mu_{i_n}^K(x_n^p)$$

3. Determine the certainty factor CF^K as

$$CF^K = \frac{|\beta_{\omega_y} - \beta|}{\sum_{t=1}^{c} \beta_{\omega_t}} \qquad \beta = \frac{\sum_{\omega_t \neq \omega_y} \beta_{\omega_t}}{c - 1}$$

4. Assign $\mathbf{x}$ to ω_y such that

$$\omega_t = \arg\max\{\mu_{i_1}^K(x_1^p) \cdots \mu_{i_n}^K(x_n^p) | i_1, \ldots, i_n = 1, \ldots, K; K = 2, \ldots, L\}$$

2 Fuzzy Neural Integrated Systems

2.1 Objectives

Broadly speaking, we may characterize the neuro-fuzzy models according to the aim of using fuzzy technology in neural networks and/or neural technology in fuzzy systems. These objectives can be classified in three main classes:

- Provide fuzzy systems with automatic tuning abilities through neural learning in terms of tuning membership functions and fuzzy rules (*Neural Fuzzy Systems*).
- Augment the representation and interpretation abilities of ANN in terms of learning the mapping between input-output fuzzy sets (*Fuzzy Neural Networks*).
- Create hybrid systems where fuzzy logic techniques and neural networks are utilized separately to establish two decoupled subsystems which perform their own tasks involving different functions in the combined system (*Fuzzy Neural Hybrid Systems*).

While the first two systems are *supportive* combinations, the third exhibits *collaborative* combination and depends on the specific application task involved. In the sequel we limit ourselves to the first two models.

3 Neural Fuzzy Systems

3.1 Definition

A Neural Fuzzy System (NFS) is a connectionist model for the tuning and inference of fuzzy rules. The models distinguish for

- types of fuzzy rules
- types of inference
- static or dynamic.

According to this class of neuro-fuzzy models, fuzzy numbers are used to represent linguistic data. Conventionally, fuzzy numbers are defined by membership functions, such as bell shaped functions, triangular functions, trapezoidal functions, etc. For these forms, we only need a few simple parameters (e.g. the center and the width) to define them, but they can only display same normal situations. There are two kinds of way to process fuzzy numbers in Neural Fuzzy Systems: one is based on the sampling of the membership functions associated to each linguistic term, the other one uses a parametrized membership function whose characteristic parameters are learned from available data.

3.2 NFS based on sampled fuzzy sets

There are two different competitive approaches to sample fuzzy numbers: a) a discretized version of membership function for a fuzzy number in a universe of discourse with a discrete space; b) α-level sets of fuzzy numbers[1].
According to the first approach, if $[\alpha_1, \alpha_2]$ contains the support of all the A_i, plus the support of all the A' and $[\beta_1, \beta_2]$ contains the support of all the B_i, plus the support of all the B', a fuzzy set can be represented by a finite number of its membership values, i.e.

$$x_j = \alpha_1 + (j-1)(\alpha_2 - \alpha_1)/(N-1)$$

$$y_j = \beta_1 + (j-1)(\beta_2 - \beta_1)/(M-1)$$

where $1 \leq i \leq M$ and $1 \leq j \leq N$. A discrete version of the continuous training set consists of couples

$$(A_1^j, \ldots, A_n^j, \mu_{\Omega(\omega_l)})$$

An usual multilayer perceptron trained with the backpropagation algorithm is used to learn the associations between antecedents and consequents of the fuzzy IF-THEN rules. This approach, introduced in [6], suffers of the evident demerit to not explicitily give the position of the fuzzy number in the universe of discourse and its fuzziness. Again, the number of elements in an universe of discourse used to represent the membership function should be sufficiently great, leading to large memory capacity and processing time.
The second approach, introduced in [7], i.e. the α-level representation of membership function has gained more attention and interest. While the left and right limits of one of the α-level sets directly give the position of the fuzzy numbers, and the width is directly related to the fuzziness, this kind of representation provides fast inference computations requiring less memory capacity also for fuzzy numbers with a large number of elements in the universe of discourse. Also, the operations over α-level sets involve two-valued logic and the Zadeh extension principle, such as the addition and multiplication of fuzzy numbers can performed efficiently using α-level sets. Models of Neural Fuzzy Systems which follow this approach can be found in [8,9,10]. The operations in models [8,9] are performed by using internal arithmetic operations for α-level sets and fuzzy numbers are propagated through neural networks. The time of computations and the required memory capacities are $2p$ times of those of traditional neural networks, when p represents the number of α-level sets. In [10] a five-layered feedforward network, realizing a fuzzy inference system, is proposed, where inputs, outputs and weights can be fuzzy numbers of any shape. Based on interval arithmetics, a generalization of the normal back-propagation algorithm is prooposed to deal with fuzzy numbers in α-level representation. Since

[1] We recall that an α-level set of a fuzzy set X, X_α, is defined by

$$X_\alpha = \{x | \mu_X(x) \geq \alpha\}$$

where $0 \leq \alpha \leq 1$, $x \in X$.

except the input and output layers, numerical data are propagated through the neural fuzzy system, the operations are not time-consuming and the required memory capacity is small.
The above mentioned models are not able to learn fuzzy rules (*structure learning*), but at its best the form of membership functions can be learned (second approach). While in the models reported in [8,9] the input/output behaviour of fuzzy rules is approximated by a neural network without clear semantics, in that one reported in [10] the fuzzy rules are used to construct the network which has clear semantics (i.e. its structure is interpretable).

3.3 NFS based on parametrized fuzzy sets

The models belonging to this class of Neural Fuzzy Systems are characterized by a multilayer feedforward network with neurons which compute parametrized membership functions (Gaussians, trapezoidal, triangular or superposition of sigmoids) and operations as **T**-norm or **T**-conorm (or **S**-norm)[2]. The training is done by a backpropagaton-like error correction learning. Differently from the models cited in the previous section, the models belonging to this NFS class are able to perform structure learning and/or parameter learning.
In the following a brief review of the models FBFNN[11], ANFIS[14] and PossNN[16] is reported.

3.3.1 Fuzzy Basis Functions Neural Network (FBFNN)

The Fuzzy Basis Functions Neural Network (FBFNN)[11] bases its operations on the consideration that a fuzzy inference systems with product inference, singleton fuzzifier, centroid of area (COA) defuzzifier and Gaussian membership functions is an universal approximator. The network structure is three-layered (without input layer). The neurons at the input layer behave as fuzzy singleton fuzzifiers, while the neurons at the first layer compute the Gaussian membership functions (corresponding to the classical linguistic variables *small*, *medium*, *high*, etc), i.e.

$$\mu_{A_i^j} = a_i^j exp\left[-\frac{1}{2}\left(\frac{x_i - \bar{x}_i^j}{\sigma_i^j}\right)^2\right]$$

The neurons at the second layer combine the membership functions according to the product inference operations, while the output layer lineraly combines the neuron values of the previous layer. The fucntion computed by the network can be described in the form

$$f(\mathbf{x}) = \sum_{j=1}^{M} p_j(\mathbf{x})\theta_j \qquad p_j(\mathbf{x}) = \frac{\prod_{i=1}^{n} \mu_{A_i^j}(x_i)}{\sum_{j=1}^{M} \prod_{i=1}^{n} \mu_{A_i^j}(x_i)} \qquad 1 \leq j \leq M$$

[2] A **T** - norm (**S** - norm) is defined as a function $[0,1] \times [0,1] \rightarrow [0,1]$ which is commutative, monotone and associative. It also satisfies the boundary conditions : $x\mathbf{T}0 = 0, x\mathbf{T}1 = x$ e $x\mathbf{S}0 = 0$, $x\mathbf{S}1 = 1$.

where p_j are said *Fuzzy Basis Functions* (*FBF*).

Since $f(\mathbf{x})$ is linear in the parameter, some efficient linear parameter estimation methods can be used to train or design the FBFNN. Among others, tone should use the Backpropagation algorithm for the whole networkr or self-organization algorithms for lower layers for tuning the membership functions and a Least Mean Square algorithm for the output linear layer. A kind of hybrid structure-parameter learning method can be used to determine the proper number of significant FBFs automatically. The Gram-Schmidt orthogonal least squares (OLS) learning method is able to find the number of significant FBFs and their associated θ^j for the FBFNN.

The FBFNN permits one to build a non-parametric classifier able to approximate the Bayes discriminant function, being capable of membership function tuning and structure learning. At a glance, FBF networks seem to be nonlinear combinations of RBF or HyperBF [17] depending on the value of variances σ_i [12]. The main merit of this model should be found, however, in its capablity of exploiting linguistic knowledge available (structure identification problem) and information contained in data set (parameter estimation problem), by simply seeing the $f(\mathbf{x})$ as sum of $f_s(\mathbf{x})$ and $f_d(\mathbf{x})$, where the first has the parameters settled based upon the rule-base at disposal, while the second one tunes according to the data. The number of fuzzy rules of the FBFNN in classification problems with 1-out-C coding has been shown experimentally to be $o(c)$ [13].

3.3.2 Adaptive-Network-Based Fuzzy Inference System (ANFIS)

In [14] an adaptive-network-based fuzzy classifier is proposed. Given the general Takagi and Sugeno rule [15]

$$\mathcal{R}_j : \text{ IF } x_1 \text{ is } A_1^j \text{ AND } \ldots \text{ AND } x_n \text{ is } A_n^j$$
$$\text{THEN } y = f_j = a_0^j + a_1^j x_1 + a_2^j x_2 + \ldots + a_n^j x_n$$

the network is structured according to the involved operations. Specifically, the network is four-layered (without input) and each layer is characterized as follows:

Layer 1 Each neuron corresponds to a linguistic variable and computes the membership degree of input u to the specific linguistic label.

$$A_i(u) = exp\left[-\frac{1}{2}\left(\frac{u - a_{i1}}{b_{i1}}\right)^2\right]$$

where $\{a_{i1}, a_{i2}, b_{i1}, b_{i2}\}$ is the parameter set and are initially setted in such a way that the membership values satisfy, along each axis, the properties of ϵ-completeness, normality and convexity.

Layer 2 Each node computes the **T**- norm of the net input coming from the nodes of layer 1 labelled in the same way *rule nodes*.

Layer 3 Each node linearly combines the rule node activations.

Layer 4 Each node applies a sigmoidal function.

The training procedure applied only to weights between layer 0 (input layer) and layer 1, from layer 2 and layer 3 is based on an usual backpropagaton-like error correction learning made upon the error function computed at the output layer between the actual output and the target classification classes.
ANFIS is not able of structure learning, but only parameter learning (i.e. it cannot learn fuzzy rules but only fuzzy sets). The number of adjustable weights is $O((c+n)m)$, while the remaining network structure unchanges along the learning.

3.3.3 Possibilistic Neural Network (PossNN)

The neural network proposed in [16], named here PossNN, bases its operations on the possibility theory and is capable of structure learning. The development of a complete knowledge base in terms of fuzzy IF-THEN rules can be viewed as consisting of three main steps: a first *self-organizational* phase, which results in the determination of a preliminary set of rules that can be used to obtain the network structure; a second phase, named the calibration or tuning phase, consisting in the process of tuning the rules more preciously by supervised learning the parameters involved in their formulation; the third phase consists of the monitoring of the network performance and further tuning.

Let us suppose to have q *observations* $(A_i, B_i, E_i) \in X \times Y \times Z$, X, Y and Z being fuzzy sets corresponding to linguistic variables U, V e W. Given the network inputs $a_i, i = 1, \ldots, n$, $(n = card(X))$, the neurons y_i compute the possibilistic values, F and G being fuzzy sets

$$a_i = F(x_i) \qquad w_i = G(x_i)$$

$$net = \sum_i F(x_i)G(x_i) \qquad y_i = poss[F|G] = f(net)$$

The network structure consists of two layers ($n_X + n_Y + n_Z$ input and $v < q$ output) with weights a_{ij} (between x_j and output i), b_{ij} (between y_j and output i) and e_{ij} (between z_j and output i). Each output node computes three similarity measures

$$y_i^a = S((A(x_1), a_{i1}), \ldots, (A(x_n), a_{in}))$$
$$y_i^b = S((A(x_1), b_{i1}), \ldots, (A(x_n), b_{in}))$$
$$y_i^e = S((A(x_1), e_{i1}), \ldots, (A(x_n), e_{in}))$$

where $S((\alpha_1, \beta_1), \ldots, (\alpha_n, \beta_n)) = 1 - \frac{1}{n}\sum_{j=1}^{n} |\alpha_j - \beta_j|$, such that the real output value is

$$y_i = min\{y_i^a, y_i^b, y_i^e\}$$

As pointed out before the learning starts with a selforganization phase by SOFM. A rule production phase follows, i.e. let (A, B, C) be the centroid of each cluster, a rule is produced

$$\text{IF } V \textit{ is } A \text{ AND } U \textit{ is } B \text{ THEN } W \textit{ is } E$$

Lastly, tuning through error correction algorithms is applied to the network when the couple (A_i, B_i) is fed as input and the expected output is E_i.

3.4 Other models

In the sequel some other models are listed. We do not give details of these models, refeering the reader to the appropriate references.

- (Lin & Lin, 1995)[33] FALCON (Fuzzy Adaptive Learning Control Network).
- (Takagi & Hayashi, 1991)[34] NN-Driven Fuzzy Reasoning based on rules

$$\mathcal{R}_j : \text{IF } x_1 \text{ is } A_1^j \text{ AND } \ldots \text{ AND } x_n \text{ is } A_n^j \text{THEN } y = NN_s(x_1, \ldots, x_n)$$

- (Nauck and Kruse, 1995)[35] NEFCLASS for the data classification
- (Halgamuge and Glesner, 1994)[36] FuNe I
- (Pedrycz, 1992)[37] n-c-m layered network for modelling of rules

$$y_j = (v_{1j} \text{ AND } z_1) \text{ OR } \ldots \text{OR } (v_{cj} \text{ AND } z_c)$$

- (R. Yasdi, 1995)[38] neural modelling of rough set based rules.
- (H.M. Berenji, 1992)[39] GARIC (Generalized Approximate Reasoning based Intelligent Control).

4 Fuzzy Neural Networks

4.1 Definition

A Fuzzy Neural Network (FNN) is a neural network with crisp signals and weights and crisp transfer function.

- input and weights can be combined by a **T**-norm, **T**-conorm, or some other continuous operations
- net input can be aggregated with a **T**-norm, **T**-conorm or any other continuous function
- the output function can be any continuous function from input to output

4.2 Fuzzy neurons

In this section we will introduce and review basic properties of neurons developed with the aid of fuzzy arithmetic and logic operations. We will consider a collection of inputs x_i, $i-1,\ldots,n$, arranged in a vector form as $\mathbf{x} \in [0,1]^n$. the connections of the neurons will be denoted by w_{ij}. The first class of neurons realizes aggregation of the input signals by arithmetic operations, while the second one bases network operations by logic aggregation of fuzzy signals.

1. fuzzy arithmetic operations

   The neuron is described as

   $$y_j = f[(+)_{i=0}^{n} w_{ij}(\cdot)x_i]$$

   where $(+)$ and $(\cdot)$ are the usual fuzzy operations of addition and multiplication.

2. fuzzy logic operations

   $$y_j = f[\mathbf{S}_{i=0}^{n}[w_{ij}\mathbf{T}x_i]] \in [0,1]$$

   where $\mathbf{S}$ is the generalized OR operator e $\mathbf{T}$ the generalized AND.

One should stress that both the operations used in the construction of the neurons are strictly monotonic; as a result, they capture only excitatory characteristics of the neuron. To handle its inhibitory features and sustain the unit interval as a suitable range of coding of its input signals and the connections, the construct must be expanded by augmenting the existing inputs by their complements, $\bar{\mathbf{x}} = \mathbf{1} - \mathbf{x}$.
This is the case of the Fuzzy Neural Logic Networks [18]. According to the model, the weights are fuzzy relations between input and output. The weights are adjusted according to the formula

$$\mathbf{w}(t+1) = \mathbf{S}[\mathbf{w}(t), \Delta\mathbf{w}(t)] \qquad \Delta\mathbf{w}(t) = \mathbf{T}[\mathbf{z}, e(t)]$$

where $\mathbf{z}$ is a $(2n+2)$-dimensional vector $[\mathbf{x}, \mathbf{N}[\mathbf{x}]]$ $(\mathbf{N}[x] = 1 - x)$.

4.3 Other models

4.3.1 *(Krishnapuram, Lee, 1992)*

The model proposed in [19] becomes an $n - nc - c$ layered network when classification tasks are dealt with and c classes are considered. The peculiaruty of this kind of network is that the output neurons operate as fuzzy aggregators, in particular as

Generalized mean:

$$y = \left(\sum_{i=1}^{n} w_i x_i{}^p\right)^{1/p}$$

γ-model:

$$y = \left(\pi_{i=1}^{n} x_i^{\delta_i}\right)^{1-\gamma} \left(1 - \pi_{i=1}^{n}(1 - x_i^{\delta_i})\right)$$

where $\sum_{i=1}^{n} \delta_i = n \quad 0 \leq \gamma \leq 1,\ \gamma = \frac{a^2}{a^2+b^2}$ and $\delta_i = \frac{n d_i^2}{\sum_{k=1}^{n} d_k}$

The learning is again based on the Backpropagation algorithm applied to w_i in the generalized mean or to a, b, d_j in the γ-model.

4.3.2 *Fuzzy MultiLayer Perceptron (MLP) (Pal & Mitra, 1992)*

The model is a multi layer perceptron characterized by

- extension of the n-dimensional input to a $3n$-dimensional one

$$\mathbf{x} = [\mu_{low}(x_1), \mu_{medium}(x_1), \mu_{high}(x_1), \mu_{low}(x_2), \ldots, \mu_{high}(x_n)]$$

- the target output defined as

$$d_j = \mu_j(\mathbf{x}_i) \in [0,1] \quad \mu_j(\mathbf{x}_i) = \frac{1}{1 + (z_{ij}/F_d)^{F_e}}$$

  where $z_{ij} = \left(\sum_{k=1}^{n} [\frac{x_{ik} - m_{jk}}{v_{jk}}]^2\right)^{1/2}$ and $1/v_{jk}$ accounts for the releavance of the class variance, *i.e.* features with great variance are less specific of the corresponding class.

The model has been shown that in the case of non linearly separable patterns the target value changes to be crisp, i.e.

$$d_j \in \{0, 1\}$$

Consequently, its performance less discost from those of the usual MLP trained with the backpropagation algorithm.

4.4 Incremental Fuzzy Networks

The concept underlying this kind of networks is to create fuzzy subsets of the pattern space in the hidden layer and then aggregate the subsets to from a final decision in the output layer. In particular, these fuzzy neural networks create classes by aggregating several smaller fuzzy sets into a single fuzzy set class. Each fuzzy set is an n-dimensional box defined by a min point and a max point with a corresponding membership function. The so-called *hyperbox* fuzzy sets are aggregated to form a single fuzzy set class and this enables to create non-linearly separable classes. Learning in this network is performed by determining proper min-max points, i.e. by properly placing and adjusting hyperboxes in the pattern space. From the practical point of view, learning is a process of expansion, overlapping test and contraction. The Fuzzy ARTMAP network [51], the FALCON-ART [33] and the Fuzzy Min-Max Classifier [21] all utilize hyperbox fuzzy sets as the fundamental computing element, and they differ only for the rule of weights adjustment. In Fuzzy Min-Max Classifier (P. K. Simpson, 1992) it looks as

$$\mathbf{v}_{ji}^{(new)} = \min(v_{ji}^{old}, x_{ki}) \qquad \mathbf{w}_{ji}^{(new)} = \min(w_{ji}^{old}, x_{ki})$$

while in Fuzzy ARTMAP (G. Carpenter *et al.*, 1992) the learning process is quite more complex, i.e.

$$\mathbf{w}_J^{(new)} = \beta(\mathbf{I} \wedge \mathbf{w}_J^{(old)}) + (1-\beta)\mathbf{w}_J^{(old)}$$

where

$$J = \arg\max_j \left\{ \frac{|\mathbf{I} \wedge \mathbf{w}_j|}{\alpha + |\mathbf{w}_j|} | \mathbf{I} = (\mathbf{x}, \mathbf{x}^c), \frac{|\mathbf{I} \wedge \mathbf{w}_J|}{|\mathbf{I}|} \geq \rho \right\}$$

In Part II some considerations on the parameter values and capabilities of Fuzzy ARTMAP can be found.

Notes

- While in Fuzzy Min-Max Classifier each class corresponds to a category, in Fuzzy ARTMAP the same output can be associated to many categories.
- For purposes of control and function appoximation, any overlapping between hyperboxes are allowed.

5 IRIS Data Classification

In this section the comparisons of some of the above reviewed neuro-fuzzy algorithms on the *Iris* data are reported. *Iris* data are widely treated as the reference data set for pattern recognition [22]. It contains three categories of the species *Iris*, including *Iris setosa*, *Iris versicolor* and *Iris virginica*. These data are fifty four-dimensional patterns for each class. This data set has been preprocessed by using the product space clustering algorithm for extracting a first and large set of fuzzy IF-THEN rules. To the initial number of thirty IF-THEN rules, we apply the ANFIS model, while the models FBFNN, FMMC and Fuzzy ARTMAP have been applied to the original numerical data. The results for NEFCLASS and FuNe have been adapted from [35] and [36] respectively. In Table 2, the learning results of these models in terms of number of rules generated (for ANFIS, FBFNN, NEFCLASS and FuNe) and number of mistakes made over all the training patters are reported. These results were achieved by generating different network structures and picking up that one with the best classification performance related to the number of rules.

6 Fuzzy neural networks for image processing

Several models of fuzzy neural networks have been designed and employed to solve classical problems in pattern recognition when applied to image processing (see for instance [23,24]). They usually are based on the assumption that

	nr. rules	nr. mistakes
ANFIS	15	9
FBFNN	7	8
NEFCLASS	7	7
FuNe	7	6
FMLP	-	14
FARTMAP	-	13
FMMC	-	12

Table 2: IRIS data classification results

the images used in the processing framework are of similar nature and a set (although restricted) of images is available to the system for training purposes. Since this is not realistic in real-life situations, a self trained system independently from the images under exam is demanded. Here, we outline two models which try to attack these limitations: the model proposed by Ghosh *et al.*, 1993 [27,28] for object extraction purposes and that one proposed by Caianiello & Petrosino, 1994 for segmentation purposes. Both the models are based on the fact that the network output is described as a fuzzy set and a fuzziness measure [25,26] is used as a measure of error in the system (i.e. instability of the output network). The error measures adopted are the folowing:

- Fuzziness index

$$\gamma_p(A) = \frac{2}{n^{1/p}} \left[\sum_{i=1}^{n} \{min(\mu_A(x_i), 1 - \mu_A(x_i))\}^p \right]^{1/p}$$

- Fuzzy entropy

$$H(A) = \frac{1}{n \ln 2} \sum_{i=1}^{n} \{-\mu_A(x_i) \ln \mu_A(x_i) - (1 - \mu_A(x_i)) \ln(1 - \mu_A(x_i))\}$$

$$K_p = \sum_{\mathbf{x}} \left[\sum_{j} \left(\frac{y_j(\mathbf{x}) - \bar{y}_j(\mathbf{x})}{y_j(\mathbf{x}) - \underline{y}_j(\mathbf{x})} \right)^p \right]^{1/p}$$

where $\bar{y}_j = 1$ if $y_j \geq 0.5$, 0 otherwise, and $\underline{y}_j = 1 - \bar{y}_j$. The sets $\{\bar{y}_1, \ldots, \bar{y}_n\}$ and $\{\underline{y}_1, \ldots, \underline{y}_n\}$ represent respectively the nearest and furtherst crisp sets of the fuzzy set $\{y_1, \ldots, y_n\}$.

The error-correction algorithm is the basis of the learning phase, while the feature extraction mechanism is the featuring element of the models. In the following some details of the selected methods will be reported.

6.1 Object extraction network

The system reported in [27,28] is two layered (without input layer) and each layer of dimension $N \times M$ is characterized by the following considerations

- each neuron in a layer is connected to the corresponding of the previous layer and its neighbours.
- each output neuron is connected to the corresponding input.

Given this network structure, each node computes a sigmoidal funtion of the signals fed to it. The system is proved to be able to extract objects in noisy environments (up to standard deviations equal to the gray level range of the image under exam). The system is on the contrary characterized for an $N \times M$ image by $18NM$ adjustable weights when each neuron is connected to nine neurons in the previous layer (this is the case of the experiments reported in [27]).

6.2 Segmentation network

To attack the limitation induced in the Ghosh system as regards the number of adjustable weights and computational time, a system based on the minimization of fuzziness captured by rough fuzzy sets is proposed in [29,30]. The network is structured with an input layer, an output layer and two parallel hidden layers (whose neurons are labelled in the sequel as a^1_{ij} and a^2_{ij}), each of dimension $N \times M$. The operations are as follows

- each hidden neuron computes

$$a^1_{ij} = \mathbf{T}[x_{kl} | k \in \{i, \ldots, i+3\}, l \in \{i, \ldots, i+3\}]$$

$$a^2_{ij} = \mathbf{S}[a_{kl} | k \in \{i, \ldots, i+3\}, l \in \{i, \ldots, i+3\}]$$

- each output neuron computes the soft-max function

$$I_{ij} = \sum_l \left(a^l_{ij} - w^l_{ij}\right)^2 \qquad y_j = \frac{exp\{-I_j/\sigma^2\}}{\sum_k exp\{-I_j/\sigma^2\}}$$

The system is characterized by $O(2NM)$ adjustabel weights, leading to a not time consuming algorithm. The model is proved to efficiently behave in the context of region based segmentation of images [30] and edge detection also in presence of Gaussian noise with $\sigma = 12\%$ of the image dynamic range.

7 Introduction to Part II

The goal of this part of the paper is to review and compare functional features of clustering NNs that are termed or can be considered fuzzy. To our best knowledge, few examples of such comparative studies can be found in the literature (e.g., [40]). To make our comparison straightforward, we propose to treat these models within a unifying framework: by focusing our attention on fuzzification of unsupervised NN learning schemes, we propose our own definition of ***fuzzy clustering neural network***. Then we identify NN models that satisfy, in our opinion, this criterion.

The proposed unifying framework has been considered "interesting" and "quite reasonable" by some researchers [41]. However, other authors believe that, since "fuzziness can be incorporated at various levels to generate a fuzzy neural network, i.e., it can be at the input, output, learning or neural levels" [42], then our "claim of calling certain networks to be fuzzy/nonfuzzy seems improper and not acceptable" [41]. In both cases, comments pertaining to the proposed terminology "fuzzy clustering neural network" do not affect the core of this work, centered on the analysis of self-organization strategies adopted by clustering NNs.

The following study is organized in two parts. In the first part, the concepts of neuro-fuzziness, on-line and off-line learning, topologically correct mapping, and econet are discussed. In the second part, the basic functional features of several clustering NN algorithms are discussed. These models are: i) on-line learning, static-sizing, static-linking Self-Organizing Map (SOM) [43], [44]; ii) off-line learning, static-sizing, no-linking Fuzzy Learning Vector Quantization, FLVQ [45] (which was first called Fuzzy Kohonen Clustering Network, FKCN [46]); iii) on-line learning, dynamic-sizing, no-linking Carpenter-Grossberg-Rosen Fuzzy Adaptive Resonance Theory (CGR Fuzzy ART) [50], [51]; (Fuzzy SART) [54]; iv) on-line learning, dynamic-sizing, dynamic-linking Growing Neural Gas (GNG) [55], [56]; and v) on-line learning, dynamic-sizing, dynamic-linking Fully self-Organizing Simplified Adaptive Resonance Theory (FOSART) [57], [58]. We will conclude that of these models only SOM, GNG and FOSART develop an effective fuzzy clustering mechanism. This may sound paradoxical because only FOSART employ tools directly derived from fuzzy set theory (in detail, fuzzy set membership values).

7.1 On fuzzy clustering neural networks

A clustering NN model performs unsupervised detection of statistical regularities in a random sequence of input patterns.

Our attention is focused on fuzzification of clustering NN learning schemes. In the definition presented in [47], it is stated that an artificial NN model performs *fuzzy clustering* when it allows a pattern to belong to multiple categories to different degrees depending on the neurons' ability to recognize the input pattern. This approach is well known in the traditional field of coding techniques for data compression. Since the traditional c-means clustering algorithms feature a cost function (discretization error) characterized by many local minima, data compression techniques modify c-means algorithms by replacing their *Winner-Takes-All* strategy (WTA) with a soft-max adaptation rule [48]. A WTA learning strategy is purely competitive and allows no contextual adaptation. It is sensitive to initialization of templates, i.e., different initializations may lead to very different minimization results. In fact, WTA adaptations may not be able to get the system out of a poor local minimum when this lies in the proximity of the status where the system was started [56]. Unlike WTA learning, a *soft competitive learning* scheme is defined as a learning strategy that not only adjusts the winning cluster but also affects all cluster centers depending on their proximity to the input pattern. In general, soft competitive learning decreases the dependency on initialization and reduces the presence of dead units [56]. We observe that:

1. The fuzzy clustering definition provided in [47] is equivalent to the definition of soft-max adaptation rule traditionally employed in the field of data compression [48], i.e., a clustering NN is defined *fuzzy clustering neural network* iff it adopt a soft-max (non-crisp) adaptation rule.
2. As a corollary of point 1. above, a fuzzy clustering NN does not necessarily exploit mathematical tools provided by fuzzy set theory such as fuzzy set membership function and fuzzy set operations. For example, SOM pursues soft-max learning by means of biologically plausible update rules that employ no mathematical tool derived from fuzzy set theory.

It is to be noted that fuzzy membership functions are traditionally applied to clustering NNs in the intuitive belief that "vectors quantizers based on both winner and non-winner information about the relationship of an input pattern to the prototypes will be better representatives of the overall structure of the input data than those based on local information alone" [45]. Thus, several NN models, such as the Fuzzy c−means (FCM) and the Fuzzy Learning Vector Quantization (FLVQ) algorithms, combine local and global information in the computation of a fuzzy membership function [45], [46]. From a functional standpoint, exploitation of a fuzzy membership function in connectionist models is equivalent to introducing a contextual effect mechanism employing feed-sideways (intra-layer) connections.

8 On-line versus off-line NN models

Batch-mode updating is formally derived as a cost function minimization scheme exploiting gradient descent [59], while on-line weight updating is based on heuristics (e.g., SOM [43]). As a brief review of batch update and on-line update techniques, refer to [56]. Analitically, the difference between exact batch-mode and heuristic on-line updating is arbitrarily reduced by the adoption of "small" learning rates [61]. In general, "heuristic on-line weight updating departs to some extent from exact batch-mode" [59]. Although on-line learning is considered an extremely desirable property of any clustering neural model [47], especially in real-time applications, it typically results in systems that become order-dependent during training (in line with biological complex systems [60]). In some cases "the input data set may be so huge that batch methods become impractical. In other cases the input data comes as a continuous stream of unlimited length which makes completely impossible to apply batch methods" [56]. Moreover, on-line updating is consistent with neuron-based adaptation of local parameters. For example, it is known that when SOM processes two separate input categories characterized by different semantics and ranges, these input patterns are mapped into spatially segregated (but not topologically disjointed) areas of the output lattice. We would expect that adaptive parameters of neurons belonging to the two spatially segregated areas reflect the differences between probability density functions of the two training categories. Surprisingly, exploitation of *local* (neuron-based, connection-based) rather than *global* (network-based) variables has never been stressed in the development of on-line clustering NNs such as SOM [43], although it has been employed in Kohonen-based networks [55], [56]. For example, GNG, Fuzzy SART [54] FOSART employ local time and learning rate variables. In GNG a connection-based time variable is equal to the number of times one synapse is selected at adaptation steps. In Fuzzy SART and FOSART a neuron-based time variable is equal to the non-decreasing sum of the learning rate coefficients computed for that neuron at adaptation steps. The basic idea is that on-line adaptation of local parameters in competitive learning is expected to enhance the development of structured nets consisting of specialized subsystems (modules), in line with self-organizing neurological systems which are highly structured.

Exact non-sequential NNs, such as FCM and FLVQ [45], [46], do not depend on the order of the presentation sequence. In general, these algorithms employ global rather than local time and learning rate variables, i.e., time and plasticity values are the same for every neuron in the net. This is justified by considering that when fuzzy clustering mechanisms are employed, all the neurons acquire the same input pattern simultaneously. However, one may consider that fuzzy membership allows a pattern to belong to multiple categories to different degrees. Thus, in batch NNs the plasticity of every neuron is considered as being the same even though learning "histories" of neurons may differ significantly. This is clear if, for example, a local learning "history" is considered as the sum of the neuron learning rates at adaptation steps.

These considerations lead some authors to state that "the problem of learning in connectionist models is entering a second era in neural network research, where learning is no longer formulated simply as function optimization" [59]. With special regard to real-time applications, non-sequential NNs should be less effective than on-line NNs in self-organizing their architectures into specialized subsystems to decompose complex tasks into subproblems (in line with a classical engineering paradigm [60]).

9 Topologically correct mapping

The presentation of the Competitive Hebbian adaptation Rule (CHR) [62], introducing competition among synaptic links, represented a fundamental breakthrough in the evolution of Fully Self-Organizing artificial Neural Network models (FSONN). In this paper, a synaptic link is defined as a lateral connection between two neurons belonging to the same neural layer, and FSONN models are defined as those NN architectures capable of: i) dynamically generating/removing neurons; and ii) dynamically generating/removing synaptic links.

CHR generates synaptic links as follows. For a given pattern X_k, $k \in \{1, n\}$, where n is the total number of input patterns, let us consider: a) winner neuron $w1$ as the one featuring the shortest inter-pattern distance $d(X_k, T_{w1}) \leq d(X_k, T_i)$, $\forall i \in \{1, c\}$, where c is the total number of neurons, T_{w1} is the template pattern of neuron $w1$, and $d(X_k, T_i)$ is the Euclidean inter-pattern distance; and b) the second best neuron $w2$ as the one featuring activation value $d(X_k, T_{w2}) \leq d(X_k, T_i)$, $\forall i \in \{1, c\}$, $i \neq w1$. The exploitation of the Euclidean inter-pattern distance in competitive learning shapes neuron receptive fields as Voronoi polyedra [62]. According to CHR, if connection between $w1$ and $w2$ does not exist, it is generated.

It has been proved that CHR forms Perfect Topology Preserving Maps (PTPMs) [62]. To define a PTPM, let us consider an input manifold $X \subseteq R^D$ and a graph (network) G, consisting of vertices (neural units) i, $i = 1, ..., M$, such that a pointer $w_i \in X$ (also termed category template or prototype), belonging to the pointer set $S = \{w_1, ..., w_M\}$, is related ("attached") to vertex i. Given S, mapping ϕ_S from X onto the vertices of G is defined as

$$\phi_S : X \rightarrow G, \quad x \in X \rightarrow i^*(x) \in G, \tag{1}$$

where x is a feature vector (input pattern) and the vertex $i^*(x)$, also termed winner neuron, is determined by

$$\| w_{i^*(x)} - x \| \quad \leq \quad \| w_{i(x)} - x \|, \quad \forall i \in G, \tag{2}$$

where $\| \cdot \|$ is the *Euclidean* inter-vector distance. According to (1) and (2), a feature vector x is mapped to the vertex $i^*(x)$, the pointer $w_{i^*(x)}$ of which is closest to x. This is equivalent to stating that x is mapped to the vertex $i^*(x)$ whose Voronoi polyhedron $V_{i*(x)}$ encloses x. The Voronoi polyhedron of a neuron i is the receptive field of the neuron centered on w_i, and it is identified as $V_i \subseteq R^D$. The masked Voronoi polyhedron of neuron i is defined as $V_i^{(X)} = V_i \cap X \subseteq X$ [62].

Inverse mapping ϕ_S^{-1} from G onto X is defined as

$$\phi_S^{-1} : G \rightarrow X, \quad i \in G \rightarrow w_i \in X. \tag{3}$$

Two pointers w_i, w_j are termed adjacent on the feature manifold X if their masked Voronoi polyhedra are adjacent, i.e., if $V_i^{(X)} \cap V_j^{(X)} \neq 0$. Two vertices i, j in G are termed adjacent if they are connected by a synaptic link. Mapping ϕ_S from X to G is defined as neighborhood (adjacency) preserving if any pair of pointers w_i, w_j that are adjacent on X are assigned to vertices i, j that are adjacent in G. Mapping ϕ_S^{-1} from G to X is defined as neighborhood preserving if any pair of vertices i, j that are adjacent in G are assigned to locations w_i, w_j that are adjacent on X.

Thus, a PTPM is defined as a mapping ϕ_S from X to G such that ϕ_S, as well as inverse mapping ϕ_S^{-1} from G to X, are neighborhood (adjacency) preserving [62].

10 Artificial cognitive systems and ecological nets

To perform cognitive tasks, biological neural systems exploit: i) dishomogeneous nets, where several types of neurons are combined; ii) structured architectures, consisting of hierarchies of subnets; and iii) feed-back mechanisms, where feed-back information is provided by the external environment to the natural system in response to the system's actions [63]. It is *the presence of this feed-back interaction with the environment that characterizes all natural systems featuring cognitive capabilities* [60]. Some artificial neural systems feature none of the biological system properties listed above. For example, SOM [43] and the Hopfield network [64] are homogeneous systems; they feature no structured architecture and no *supervision* or *reinforcement* by or *feedback* from an external environment (also termed *supervisor*). In *reinforcement learning*, the neural system is allowed to react to each training case. It is then told whether its reaction was effective or not [65]. To increase their biological plausibility, artificial neural models should employ differentiated structures provided with dishomogeneous layers, specialized subnets, hierarchies of maps, etc. In parallel, the study of artificial neural nets as stand-alone systems should evolve to become the science of *ecological nets* (econets), where neural systems as well as their external environments are modeled [63]. Unlike Kohonen's networks, an ART system employs a structured architecture to self-adjust the network dimension to problem specific conditions. In particular, the ART *orienting subsystem* models the responses of the external environment to the learning activities of the *attentional subsystem* [50], [51], [52], [53]. Thus, an ART system belongs to the class of ecological nets.

11 SOM

Starting from the on-line Kohonen's Vector Quantization model (VQ, this achronym is used in this paper in line with [43]), which employs a WTA learning strategy, SOM develops a soft competitive learning technique largely based on heuristics derived from neurophysiological studies [43], [44].

11.1 Input parameters

• SOM employs an output array of neurons whose size c is fixed on an *a priori* basis (i.e., when no prior knowledge about the structure of the input manifold to be clustered is available to the user).
• The dimension of the output lattice (1-D to 3-D) must be set by the user. Implicitly this choice fixes the number of adjacent vertices, which is equivalent to fixing the number of synaptic links emanating from each neuron of the output lattice (see Section 4). For example, each neuron belonging to a 1-D lattice features two adjacent vertices, neurons belonging to a 2-D lattice feature eight adjacent vertices each, etc. This property of SOM is termed ***static-linking***. The peculiar feature of SOM is that it deals with the topological relationship of node adjacency in graph G without dealing with synptic links explicitly, as shown in equation (4) (see Subsection 6.2).
• It assumes that the initial position of clusters is known in advance. These initial positions can be randomly assigned or may be driven from sample vectors extracted from the input data set. This latter solution is likely to reduce dead units formation [56].
• It employs two user-defined monotone decreasing functions of time to compute: i) the learning rate $\alpha_{w1}(t)$ of winner neuron $w1$ (*cooling schedule*); and ii) the size $\sigma(t)$ of the resonance domain centered on the winner neuron. These two decreasing functions are further combined to compute the lateral excitatory signal generated by the winner and featuring the shape of a "bell curve" (see equation (4)). Time t is equal to the number of processing epochs (i.e., the number of times the input data set is presented to the system before convergence is reached). As a brief review of different monotonically non-increasing learning rates, refer to [56].
• It requires a convergence threshold (e.g., the maximum number of epochs t_{max}).

11.2 Description of the algorithm

• Geometrical (distance) relationships in the input (measurement) space are employed to enforce competitive learning mechanisms, i.e., for an input pattern X_k, $k \in \{1,n\}$, where n is the total number of patterns, winner neuron $w1$ is detected as the processing unit featuring the shortest inter-pattern distance $d(X_k,T_{w1}) \leq d(X_k,T_i)$, $\forall i \in \{1,c\}$, where T_{w1} is the template pattern of neuron $w1$, and $d(X_k,T_i)$ is the Euclidean or Hamming inter-pattern distance. The exploitation of the Euclidean inter-pattern distance in competitive learning shapes neuron receptive fields as Voronoi polyedra (see Section 4).
• Topological relationships among neurons belonging to an output lattice (graph, see Section 4) are employed to detect neighboring (contextual, soft-max) effects. In deeper detail, neurons belonging to the update neighborhood centered on winner neuron $w1$ are affected by a lateral excitatory signal, generated by the

winner, which is shaped as a "bell curve" (bubble strategy), such that [43]:

$$\alpha_i(t) = \alpha_{w1}(t) \cdot e^{-(\|r_i - r_{w1}\|^2/\sigma(t)^2)} \tag{4}$$

where $\alpha_i(t)$ is the learning rate of neuron i at time t, r_i and r_{w1} denote the spatial coordinates of the two output neurons i and $w1$ in the external lattice, and $\alpha_{w1}(t)$ and $\sigma(t)$ are the two user-defined monotone decreasing functions of time describing the amplitude and standard deviation of the Gaussian function respectively. Analysis of (4) reveals that: i) when $\sigma(t) = 0$, then nodes of SOM lose their contextual sensitivity, the SOM soft learning strategy becomes equivalent to a WTA strategy and SOM becomes equivalent to a c-means clustering procedure [48]; and ii) when $\alpha_{w1}(t) = 0$, then SOM reaches convergence.

• SOM employs the Kohonen weight adaptation rule to position optimally cluster prototypes that belong to the resonance domain (update neighborhood) centered on the winner neuron, such that:

$$T_i = T_i + \alpha_i(t) \cdot (X_k - T_i), \tag{5}$$

where $\alpha_i(t)$ is computed by means of (4) if $i \neq w1$, otherwise if $i = w1$ then $\alpha_{w1}(t)$ is computed according to the user-defined monotone decreasing function of time (see Subsection 6.1).

11.3 Architectural features

The main features of SOM are summarized: 1) on-line learning; 2) soft competitive learning (i.e., SOM satisfies the definition of fuzzy clustering NN adopted herein); 3) static-sizing; 4) static-linking, i.e., this model does not employ synaptic links explicitly to make neighboring neurons mutually coupled, see Subsection 6.1; 5) neuron receptive field information is represented as a single point identifying the receptive field center (cluster prototype); 6) the size of the neuron receptive field is not bounded by any user defined parameter; 7) network-based variables to be updated: time, learning rate; 8) neuron-based variables to be updated: receptive field center; 9) connection-based variables to be updated: none; 10) learning rate monotonically decreases with time (this is termed first Kohonen's learning constraint); 11) the size of the update neighborhood monotonically decreases with time (this is termed second Kohonen's learning constraint); 12) it does not minimize any known objective function, i.e., termination is not based on optimizing any model of the process or its data [46]; 13) no mathematical tool provided by fuzzy set theory is employed; 14) SOM does not model the responses of the external environment to its learning activities (i.e., it does not satisfy the econet definition adopted herein); 15) it does not develop independent subsystems (disjointed subnets); rather, input patterns are mapped into spatially segregated areas of the output lattice which are not topologically disjointed; and 16) it does not perform perfect topology preserving mapping, see Subsection 6.4.

11.4 Limitations

• SOM is order dependent (due to on-line learning), i.e., the final weight vectors are affected by the order of the input sequence and by the initial conditions [46].
• It should not be employed in topology preserving mapping when the dimension of the input space is larger than three. In fact, SOM tries to form a neighborhood preserving inverse mapping ϕ_S^{-1} from the lattice G to the input manifold X, but not necessarily a neighborhood preserving mapping ϕ_S from X to G [62]. To obtain a topologically correct map by running the SOM algorithm, the topological (adjacency) structure of the preset graph G has to match the topological structure of the unknown manifold X [62].

11.5 Advantages

• SOM can be employed as a vector requantization system.
• For some authors, "SOM was not intended for pattern classification. Rather, SOM attempts to find topological structures in the input data and display it in one or two dimensions" [66]. "SOM simply attempts to achieve a consistent spatial mapping of the training vectors to (usually) two dimensions" [41]. More precisely, it can be stated that SOM can be employed in topology preserving mapping iff the dimension of the input space is not larger than the dimension of the output lattice [62].

12 FLVQ

FLVQ [45] (which was first called FKCN [46]) has quickly gained popularity as a fairly successful batch clustering algorithm.

FLVQ design aims to improve performance and usability of on-line Kohonen's VQ and SOM algorithms by combining the on-line Kohonen weight adaptation rule with the fuzzy set membership function proposed by the batch FCM algorithm [45], [46]. This allows FLVQ to compute the learning rate and the "size" of the update neighborhood directly from the data. Thus, FLVQ employs a smaller set of user defined parameters than SOM.

Recent advances in the field have presented a broad family of batch FLVQ algorithms formally defined as a class of cost function minimization schemes. Hereafter, this class of batch vector quantizers will be referred to as the Extended FLVQ Family (EFLVQ-F) [67], [68], [69]. FLVQ updating can be seen as a special case of EFLVQ-F learning schemes for a restricted range of the weighting exponent. FLVQ is also related to several on-line fuzzy clustering algorithms such as the sequential Generalized LVQ (GLVQ) [70] and GLVQ Family algorithms (GLVQ-F) [71], and the class of on-line Fuzzy Algorithms for Learning Vector Quantization (FALVQ, whose proposed instances are termed FALVQ 1, FALVQ 2 and FALVQ 3) [66], [69]. Table 3 summarizes functional comparisons between these learning vector quantization algorithms. For a detailed analysis of these models, refer to [72].

		Batch updates	Sequential updates
Crisp learning		-	VQ
Soft learning	Membership function where m is constant	FCM, EFLVQ-F[1]	GLVQ-F[2]
	Membership function where $m = m_t$ is a function of time	FLVQ	-
	Other membership functions with no weighting exponent	-	GLVQ, FALVQ
	Width of the learning rate distrib. is constant	FCM, EFLVQ-F[1]	GLVQ[3], GLVQ-F[2]
	Width of the learning rate distrib. decreases with time	FLVQ	FALVQ
Cooling schedule (learning rate decreases with time)		EFLVQ-F[4]	VQ, FALVQ, GLVQ, GLVQ-F[5]
No cooling schedule		FCM, FLVQ	-

[1] see [67], p. 252 ($m = 2$).
[2] see [71], p. 1068 ($m = 2$).
[3] extended to the entire net.
[4] see [67], p. 251.
[5] see [69], p. 33.

Table 3:

12.1 Input parameters

• FLVQ requires the user to define number c of natural groups to be detected.
• It requires the initial and final weighting exponent m_0 and m_f, controlling the "amount of fuzziness" of the algorithm. In [45], the heuristic constraint $7 > m_0 > m_f > 1.1$ is recommended.
• Parameter t_{max} is defined as the maximum number of epochs.
• A convergence error ϵ is employed in the termination strategy.

12.2 Description of the algorithm

• Descending FLVQ employs a weighting exponent $m = m_t$ monotonically decreasing with time. The decreasing expression of m_t is [1]:

$$m_t = m_0 - (t \cdot \Delta m) \qquad \text{where } \Delta m = (m_0 - m_f)/t_{max} \tag{6}$$

• Unlike SOM, FLVQ employs metrical neighbors in the input space (analogously to GLVQ, GLVQ-F and FALVQ) rather than topological neighbors belonging to an output lattice. In particular, FLVQ computes a membership function providing the degree of compatibility of an input pattern with the vague concept represented by a cluster center. To compute this inter-pattern similarity measure, FLVQ combines winner and non-winner information as fol-

12.3 Architectural features

The main features of FLVQ are summarized: 1) off-line learning; 2) soft competitive learning afflicted by asymptotic misbehaviors (i.e., FLVQ does not fully satisfy the definition of fuzzy clustering NN adopted herein); 3) static-sizing; 4) no-linking (i.e., this model does not employ synaptic links to make neighboring neurons mutually coupled); 5) neuron receptive field information is represented as a single point identifying the receptive field center (cluster prototype); 6) the size of the neuron receptive field is not bounded by any user defined parameter; 7) network-based variables to be updated: time, learning rate; 8) neuron-based variables to be updated: receptive field center; 9) connection-based variables to be updated: none; 10) learning rate does not necessarily decrease with time monotonically, see Subsection 7.4 (i.e., it may not satisfy first Kohonen's learning constraint); 11) the size of the update neighborhood does not necessarily decrease with time monotonically, see Subsection 7.2 (i.e., it may not satisfy second Kohonen's learning constraint); 12) it does not minimize any known objective function, i.e., termination is not based on optimizing any model of the process or its data [46]; 13) it employs fuzzy set memberships provided by fuzzy set theory; 14) FLVQ does not model the responses of the external environment to its learning activities (i.e., it does not satisfy the econet definition adopted herein); 15) it does not develop independent subsystems (disjointed subnets); and 16) it does not perform perfect topology preserving mapping.

12.4 Limitations

• If trivial **Case A** is avoided, decreasing FLVQ causes learning strategy transitions from soft-max learning (**Case C**) to an adaptation strategy similar to WTA (**Case B**). As observed in [45], this update mechanism is roughly opposite to that of other NN models, like SOM. In SOM, all c learning rates (winner as well as non-winners) decrease towards 0 as t increases; vice versa, in FLVQ, (12) and (13) show that learning rate $\alpha_{i,k,t}$ may increase up to $1/n_i$ for the winner neuron when t increases (starting at $t = 0$ from a value which may be equal to $1/n$, see **Case A**), while the other $(c - 1)$ rates tend towards zero or $1/n$ (see **Case B**). Intuitively, this learning policy is not desirable because it does not provide prototypes with large initial plasticity values required to pursue fast (rough) initial learning.
• FLVQ features instability when its traditional termination criterion is employed, such that if $\sum_{i=1}^{c} ||T_{i,t} - T_{i,t-1}||^2 \leq \epsilon$, then FLVQ is terminated. Experimental tests reveal that clustering results improve when convergence is reached at m_f values close to 1, while ϵ is ignored [72].
• It can't be employed in topology preserving mapping.

12.5 Advantages

• FLVQ can be employed as a vector requantization system.
• FLVQ is order independent, i.e., the final weight vectors are not affected by the order of the input sequence and by the initial conditions when its traditional

lows:

$$u_{i,k,t} = \frac{\left(\frac{1}{\|X_k - T_i\|^2}\right)^{\frac{1}{(m_t-1)}}}{\sum_{j=1}^{c}\left(\frac{1}{\|X_k - T_j\|^2}\right)^{\frac{1}{(m_t-1)}}}, \qquad i = 1, 2, ..., c, \ k = 1, 2, ..., n, \qquad (7)$$

where c is the total number of categories, n is the total number of input patterns, X_k, $k \in \{1, n\}$, is an input pattern, and T_j, $j \in \{1, c\}$, is a cluster template. Equation (7) is a membership function because it satisfies the three conditions required to state that c fuzzy subsets are a fuzzy c-partition of X. These conditions are [79]: i) $u_{i,k}$ belongs to [0,1], $\forall i$, $\forall k$; ii) $\sum_{i=1}^{c} u_{i,k} = 1$, $\forall k$; and iii) $0 < \sum_{k=1}^{n} u_{i,k} < n$, $\forall i$. It is worth noting that equation (7) can be considered a ***soft-max output activation function***, where the outputs are constrained to sum to one, so they are interpretable as posterior probability estimates [74]. On the other hand, when condition ii) above is relaxed, Possibilistic Neural Network clustering models (PNN) are developed [73].

• The FLVQ learning rule is:

$$T_{i,t} = \quad T_{i,t-1} + \eta_{i,t} \cdot \sum_{k=1}^{n} w_{i,k,t}(X_k - T_{i,t-1})$$

$$= T_{i,t-1} + \sum_{k=1}^{n} \alpha_{i,k,t}(X_k - T_{i,t-1}) = \sum_{k=1}^{n} \alpha_{i,k,t} \cdot X_k, \quad i = 1, 2, ..., c, \qquad (8)$$

where

$$w_{i,k,t} = (u_{i,k,t})^{m_t}, \qquad (9)$$

$$\eta_{i,t} = \frac{1}{\sum_{k=1}^{n} w_{i,k,t}}, \qquad (10)$$

$$\alpha_{i,k,t} = \eta_{i,t} \cdot w_{i,k,t}. \qquad (11)$$

Equation (8) asserts that when $m_t = m$ is fixed, then FLVQ is equivalent to FCM [45]. By decreasing its weighting exponent m_t, descending FLVQ reduces the width of the learning rate distribution by means of model transitions. Although this property satisfies Kohonen's biologically driven learning constraint requiring the size of the update neighborhood to decrease monotonically (see Section 6), the initial learning phase of FLVQ may be affected by trivial (non-adaptive) vector quantization due to improper initialization of parameter m_t. This is demonstrated by the following analysis of FLVQ asymptotic behaviors.

Case A: $\lim_{m_t \to \infty}$. It is easy to verify that

$$\lim_{m_t \to \infty} T_{i,t} = T_{i,t-1} + \frac{1}{n}\sum_{k=1}^{n}(X_k - T_{i,t-1}) = \frac{1}{n}\sum_{k=1}^{n} X_k, \qquad i = 1, 2, ..., c. \quad (12)$$

Equation (12) shows that when $m_t \to \infty$, all FLVQ cluster centers collapse into the same point, i.e., all input patterns are mapped into the same prototype which is the center of gravity of the input data set. FLVQ shares with FCM this

asymptotic behavior leading to trivial vector quantization [72]. Unfortunately, once prototype collapse has occurred, FLVQ cannot recover its standard vector quantization capability by forcing model transitions from **Case A** to learning schemes **C** and **B** (see below) since equations (8) to (11) have no ability to move collapsed prototypes away from each other. This asymptotic behavior is acknowledged in [1], where it is recommended to keep m_t away from infinity to prevent numerical instability of FLVQ. Our analysis suggests that rather than numerical instability, limiting condition $m_t \rightarrow \infty$ causes prototype collapse in both FLVQ and FCM.
Case B: $\lim_{m_t \rightarrow 1}$. It can be demonstrated that $\lim_{m_t \rightarrow 1} w_{i,k,t} = 1$ if neuron i is the winner unit for pattern X_k, otherwise $w_{i,k,t}$ tends to zero. As a consequence,

$$\lim_{m_t \rightarrow 1} \{\alpha_{i,k,t}\} = \begin{cases} 1/n_i, \text{ if neuron } i \text{ is the winner unit for } X_k, \\ \quad \text{such that } 1 \leq n_i \leq n; \\ 0, \text{ if neuron } i \text{ is not the winner unit for } X_k, \\ \quad \text{and if } n_i \geq 1; \\ 1/n, \text{ if neuron } i \text{ is not the winner unit for } X_k, \\ \quad \text{and if } n_i = 0; \end{cases} \tag{13}$$

where n_i is the total number of times neuron i has been considered the best-matching unit during the last epoch. Equation (13) shows that this asymptotic behavior is similar but not equivalent to a WTA learning strategy pursuing strict excitation of the winner. In particular, condition $n_i = 0$ is equivalent to state that neuron i is a dead unit, i.e., (13) forces all dead units to collapse in the center of gravity of the input data set.
Case C: $m_t \in (1, \infty)$. When m_t is kept away from 1 (**Case B**) and infinity (**Case A**), the update neighborhood includes all c nodes characterized by unequal excitation. In line with SOM, the learning rate decreases with the distance from the winner node.
These theoretical conclusions about transitions of the FLVQ learning strategy as a function of decreasing m_t are consistent with those regarding FCM, EFLVQ-F and GLVQ-F [67], [68], [69], and [71], all these systems employing (7) as their membership function (see Table 3). This analysis is also consistent with the heuristic choice $7 > m_0 > m_f > 1.1$ recommended in [45].
• In [45], it is clarified that FLVQ, like SOM, does not optmize any known objective function, and that it is expected to reach termination when the FCM objective function is approximately minimized [46]. In [67], [68], [69], EFLVQ-F learning schemes are formally derived to minimize a given functional when m is constant. It is also shown that FLVQ updating can be seen as a special case of EFLVQ-F learning schemes for a restricted range of the weighting exponent. This does not mean, however, that FLVQ minimizes the EFLVQ-F functional since the hypothesis $m = constant$ does not hold true for FLVQ. We conclude that despite recent advances in the field, the objective function minimized by FLVQ is still unknown, as it is unknown the one minimized by SOM [72]. In line with Section 3, we believe that the absence of a known cost function may no longer be perceived as a structural drawback affecting either SOM or FLVQ.

termination criterion is removed.
• With respect to SOM, FLVQ requires a smaller set of input parameters.

13 CGR Fuzzy ART

In recent years, several ART models have been presented: ART 1 [52], ART 2 [53], and CGR Fuzzy ART [50]. ART 1 categorizes binary patterns with variance to their training sequences. This experimental evidence led to the development of the Improved ART 1 system (IART 1) [75]. ART 2, developed to detect regularities in analog data sequences, employs a computationally expensive architecture affected by difficulty in parameter selection. The CGR Fuzzy ART system, that can process binary as well as analog patterns while featuring none of the ART 2 drawbacks, was developed starting from a "fuzzification" of the choice function and match function employed in the ART 1 model. This means, however, that ART 1-based structural problems may also affect the CGR Fuzzy ART system design.

The structured organization of ART systems is made up of two subsystems. The ART *attentional subsystem* is a completely generic and homogeneous network performing learning by examples. It employs a neuron activation function providing a normalized degree of similarity between the input pattern and one template vector. It is worth noting that the activation function is "unidirectional", i.e., this inter-pattern similarity measure does not satisfy the commutative law. Then, the attentional subsystem selects the winner neuron as the best matching unit. The ART *orienting subsystem* models the responses of the external environment to the learning activities of the attentional subsystem. In particular, this subsystem employs a "unidirectional" *match function* to perform a *vigilance test*. This match function does not satisfy the commutative law either, and is complementary to the activation function. The vigilance test checks whether the degree of match between the input pattern and the winner template is above a user-defined normalized *vigilance threshold*. If the vigilance test is satisfied (i.e., *resonance* occurs), then the winner template is updated, otherwise a *mismatch reset condition* is managed as follows. The orienting subsystem inhibits the winner neuron and submits the second winner neuron to the vigilance test. This *search process* is repeated until either the vigilance test is passed or no more neurons are available for testing. In this second case, a new neuron is created such that its template (receptive field center) is equal to the input pattern. Coarser grouping of input patterns is obtained when the vigilance parameter is lowered.

13.1 Input parameters

• CGR Fuzzy ART employs parameter $\alpha \in [0.001, 1)$ to break ties in inter-pattern similarity measures (see (14)).
• It requires vigilance threshold $\rho \in [0, 1]$ to control neuron proliferation (see (15)). Parameters ρ and α are interrelated as illustrated in [76] (when ρ decreases, α must also decrease). A typical α value is 0.001 [51].

• Learning rate β is set within range $(0,1)$ (see (16)). We refer to β as the learning rate for *committed neurons* (i.e., for neurons that have been already initialized at generation time) [50].
• It requires a convergence threshold (e.g., the maximum number of epochs t_{max}).

13.2 Description of the algorithm

• CGR Fuzzy ART features bottom-up connections only, such that its attentional subsystem is flat, feed-forward and homogeneous, sharing these architectural properties with Kohonen networks. This conclusion is consistent with the following statement [50]: the CGR Fuzzy ART "weight vectors subsume both the bottom-up and top-down weight vectors of ART 1". Furthermore, this conclusion yields a major consequence concerning the meaning of the term "resonance" traditionally applied to ART-based systems. This term can no longer indicate "the basic feature of all ART systems, notably, pattern-matching between bottom-up input and top-down learned prototype vectors" [50], just as the term "resonance" has never been referred to pattern matching performed by a feed-forward Kohonen network. The term "resonance" means rather that CGR Fuzzy ART inherits what we believe is the basic feature of all ART systems, notably, the ART structured architecture consisting of a completely generic flat and homogeneous attentional network whose growing structure is controlled by an orienting subsystem which models the feed-back interaction of the attentional subsystem with the external environment. This understanding of the term "resonance" applied to ART-based systems is consistent with the following statement found in [51]: in the CGR Fuzzy ART model, "resonance occurs if the vigilance criterion is satisfied", i.e., feed-back phenomena are managed by the orienting subsystem exclusively.
• In the attentional subsystem, for a given pattern X_k, $k \in \{1,n\}$, where n is the total number of input patterns, winner unit $w1$ is detected as the neuron that satisfies the condition $\mu_{w1}(T_{w1}, X_k) = \max\{\mu_j(T_j, X_k), j = 1, ..., c\}$, where activation value $\mu_j(T_j, X_k)$ is computed as:

$$\mu_j(T_j, X_k) = \frac{\sum_{i=1}^{D} \min\{T_{j,i}, X_{k,i}\}}{\alpha + \sum_{i=1}^{D} T_{j,i}}, \qquad j = 1, ..., c, k = 1, ..., n, \tag{14}$$

where c is the total number of neurons, D is the input space dimension, and parameter α breaks ties in favor of the longer of the two vectors. Equation (14) measures to what normalized degree X_k matches T_j but it does not assess the reverse situation, i.e., to what degree T_j matches X_k. In other words, this activation function does not satisfy the commutative law, i.e., $\mu_j(T_j, X_k) \neq \mu_j(X_k, T_j)$.
• In the orienting subsystem, CGR Fuzzy ART employs a vigilance test defined as follows:

$$MF_1(T_{w1}, X_k) = \frac{\sum_{i=1}^{D} \min\{T_{w1,i}, X_{k,i}\}}{\sum_{i=1}^{D} X_{k,i}} \geq \rho. \tag{15}$$

The left side of the vigilance test is a match function that measures to what normalized degree T_{w1} matches X_k while it does not assess the reverse situation, i.e., $MF_1(T_{w1}, X_k)$ does not satisfies the commutative law. If the vigilance test is satisfied, then the attentional subsystem is activated to sequentially adjust the winner template according to (16). Otherwise, the mismatch reset condition and search process are activated (see above).

• CGR Fuzzy ART employs a WTA strategy. The weight transformation law applied to the winner template is [50]:

$$T_{w1} = (1 - \beta) \cdot T_{w1} + \beta \cdot (X_k - T_{w1}) \tag{16}$$

• When no existing neuron satisfies the vigilance test and a new processing unit $w1$ is allocated by the orienting subsystem, then (16) is substituted by $T_{w1} = X_k$ to initialize the uncommited neuron.

• Unlike Kohonen's clustering neural networks, CGR Fuzzy ART employs no cooling schedule, because the learning rate for commited neurons is constant in time.

• CGR Fuzzy ART substitutes the operators employed in the ART 1-based activation function and match function with fuzzy-like operations (intersection and cardinality, see (14) and (15)). To be correctly interpreted as fuzzy operations, these operations would have to be applied to fuzzy set membership values, rather than to the parameters (pattern and template vectors) of the fuzzy set membership function [47]. Since CGR Fuzzy ART employs no fuzzy membership function, then it cannot employ fuzzy operations derived from fuzzy logic either. Moreover, CGR Fuzzy ART adopts a WTA adaptation strategy, thus, it cannot be termed fuzzy according to Section 2.

13.3 Architectural features

The main features of CGR Fuzzy ART are summarized: 1) on-line learning; 2) hard competitive learning (i.e., CGR Fuzzy ART does not satisfy the definition of fuzzy clustering NN adopted herein); 3) dynamic-sizing (dynamic neuron generation: yes; dynamic neuron removal: no); 4) no-linking (i.e., this model does not employ synaptic links to make neighboring neurons mutually coupled); 5) neuron receptive field information is represented as a single point identifying the receptive field center (cluster prototype); 6) the size of the neuron receptive field is upper bounded by a user defined parameter; 7) network-based variables to be updated: time; 8) neuron-based variables to be updated: receptive field center; 9) connection-based variables to be updated: none; 10) learning rate is constant with time (i.e., it does not satisfy first Kohonen's learning constraint); 11) the size of the update neighborhood is not computed (i.e., it does not satisfy second Kohonen's learning constraint); 12) it does not minimize any known objective function, i.e., termination is not based on optimizing any model of the process or its data [46]; 13) no mathematical tool provided by fuzzy set theory is employed; 14) CGR Fuzzy ART models the responses of the external environment to its learning activities (i.e., it satisfies the econet definition adopted herein); 15) it does not develop independent subsystems (disjointed subnets); and 16) it does not perform perfect topology preserving mapping.

13.4 Limitations

• Experiments reveal that ART 1-based models are affected by pattern mismatching sensitive to the order of presentation of the input sequence [54], [75]. This is due to the fact that two non-commutative inter-pattern measures are analyzed in sequence to detect output values of the activation and match functions, respectively. In the first stage, winner neuron $w1$ is detected while ignoring the degree to which T_{w1} matches X_k. In the second stage, vigilance decisions are taken while ignoring the degree to which X_k matches T_{w1}.
• CGR Fuzzy ART is time consuming. Because two "unidirectional" similarity measures are analyzed in sequence, then ART 1-based models must schedule a search process. Sorting required by this search process increases computation time as $c \log c$ in a serial implementation [48]. For example, Fuzzy SART, by employing an activation function which satisfies the commutative law, no longer requires any search process [54]).
• It requires input data preprocessing (e.g., normalization or complement coding) to prevent category proliferation [50].
• Because it is uncapable of removing neurons, it may fit the noise, not just the signal, leading to overfitting.
• It can't be employed in topology preserving mapping.

13.5 Advantages

• Feed-back interaction between attentional and orienting subsystems allows CGR Fuzzy ART to self-adjust its size depending on the complexity of the clustering task.
• CGR Fuzzy ART can be employed as a vector requantization system.
• Distinct sample vectors are employed to initialize reference vectors. This choice reduces the risk of dead units formation and may reduce computation time with respect to random initialization.

14 GNG

GNG combines the growth mechanism inherited from the earlier proposed Growing Cell Structures [80] with the topology geration rule CHR [62]. GNG is capable of generating/removing synaptic links and neurons, i.e, GNG belongs to the class of FSONN models (see Section 4). In particular, starting with very few units (generally, two), one new unit is inserted every λ adaptation steps near the unit featuring the largest local error measure. In [82], it is anticipated that the future development of GNG will employ, besides the neuron insertion criterion described above, the following rule for neuron removal: every λ adaptation steps, the unit featuring lowest utility for error reduction is removed.

This utility measure is defined as the increase in overall distorsion error occurring if the unit of interest were removed from the set of templates (codebook). The utility $U(T_{w1})$ of codebook vector T_{w1}, $w1 \in \{1, c\}$, where c is the total number of neurons, is defined as follows [83]:

$$U(T_{w1}) = \sum_{X_k \in M_{w1}} d(X_k, T_{w2}) - d(X_k, T_{w1}) \tag{17}$$

where $k \in \{1, n\}$, such that n is the total number of input patterns, and $d(X_k, T_{w1})$ is the Euclidean distance. In (17), T_{w2} is the second best matching template for vector X_k, where $w2 \neq w1$, and M_{w1} is the subset of input patterns featuring template T_{w1} as the closest reference vector, i.e., $M_{w1} = \{X_k, k \in \{1, n\}$: neuron $w1$ satisfies the condition $d(X_k, T_{w1}) \leq d(X_k, T_j), \forall j \in \{1, c\}\}$.

14.1 Input parameters

• GNG employs two user-defined learning rates: $\epsilon_{w1} \in (0, 1)$ is applied to the winner neuron, while $\epsilon_n \in (0, 1)$, such that $\epsilon_n < \epsilon_{w1}$, is applied to neurons belonging to the update neighborhood. Typical values are: $\epsilon_{w1} = 0.05$, $\epsilon_n = 0.0006$ [56].
• Parameter $\lambda \in \mathcal{N}^+$ controls neuron generation at adaptation steps (see above).
• Parameters α and β are used to decrease the error variables, so that more recent signals are weighted stronger than previous ones [80]. Typical values are: $\alpha = 0.5$, $\beta = 0.0005$ [56].
• Parameter $a_{max} \in \mathcal{N}^+$ is the maximum age of a synaptic link. A typical value is: $a_{max} = 88$ [56].
• GNG employs a convergence parameter, such as the maximum number of neurons c_{max} [56].

14.2 Description of the algorithm

• In line with SOM, GNG employs geometrical (distance) relationships in the input (measurement) space to enforce competitive learning mechanisms. Let us consider: a) winner neuron $w1$ as the one featuring the shortest inter-pattern distance $d(X_k, T_{w1}) \leq d(X_k, T_i)$, $\forall i \in \{1, c\}$, where c is the total number of neurons, T_{w1} is the template pattern of neuron $w1$, and $d(X_k, T_i)$ is the the Euclidean distance; and b) the second best neuron $w2$ as the one featuring activation value $d(X_k, T_{w2}) \leq d(X_k, T_i)$, $\forall i \in \{1, c\}$, $i \neq w1$. The exploitation of the Euclidean inter-pattern distance in competitive learning shapes neuron receptive fields as Voronoi polyedra (see Section 4).
• As soos as neuron $w1$ is detected, the local error variable of winner neuron $w1$ is updated; for example, for requantization tasks, the increase of accumulated error E_{w1} is defined as

$$E_{w1} = E_{w1} + \| T_{w1} - X_k \|^2, \tag{18}$$

otherwise, for probability density function estimation,

$$E_{w1} = E_{w1} + 1. \tag{19}$$

• In line with SOM, topological relationships among neurons belonging to an output neuron lattice are employed to detect neighboring (contextual, soft-max) effects. In particular, GNG applies an update equation to the winner neuron $w1$ and to its (topologically) adjacent neighbors, i.e., the resonance neighborhood consists of all neurons adjacent to the winner (such that synaptic links $Lnk_{w1,i}$, $i \in \{1, c\}$, $i \neq w1$ do exist). Therefore, due to dynamic generation/removal of neurons and synaptic links, the resonance domain changes with time to include neurons that are topologically adjacent to winner $w1$. Nonetheless, this behavior does not strictly satisfy the Kohonen constraint requiring the size of the update neighborhood to decrease with time monotonically.
• Templates belonging to the update neighborhood are adapted according to the Kohonen weight adaptation rule. The update equation is

$$T_i = T_i + \epsilon_i \cdot (X_k - T_i), \tag{20}$$

where $\epsilon_i = \epsilon_{w1}$, which is user-defined (see Subsection 9.1), if $i = w1$, and $\epsilon_i = \epsilon_n$ if vertice i is adjacent to the winner (see above).
• With regard to generation of neurons, GNG employs the following strategy: one new units is inserted every λ adaptation steps near the unit featuring the largest local error measure, identified as unit q. In particular, the receptive field center of the new unit is located half way between the templates of units q and f, where f identifies the neuron featuring the maximum accumulated error among the neighbors of q (i.e., synaptic link $Lnk_{q,f}$ does exist). The local error of the new unit is set to $(E_q + E_f)/2$; then E_q and E_f are decreased by a fraction α.
• With regard to generation of synaptic links, GNG employs the following strategy. As soos as neurons $w1$ and $w2$ are detected, CHR is applied to $w1$ and $w2$ so that if connection $Lnk_{w1,w2}$ does not exist, it is generated (see Section 4). In either case, the age of the connection between $w1$ and $w2$ is reset to zero (the connection is "refreshed").
• With regard to removal of superfluous synaptic links and neurons, GNG employs the following strategy. After that CHR is applied to the neuron pair $w1$ and $w2$, and that connection $Lnk_{w1,w2}$ is refreshed, the age of all edges emanating from $w1$ is increased by one. Among these connections, edges whose age is larger than a_{max} are removed. If this results in units having no emanating edge, those units are removed.
• At the end of the current epoch: i) the error variables of all units are decreased by a fraction β; and ii) the convergence test is checked (e.g., it may involve parameter c_{max} or the mean accumulated error).

14.3 Architectural features

The main features of GNG are summarized: 1) on-line learning; 2) soft competitive learning (i.e., GNG satisfies the definition of fuzzy clustering NN adopted herein); 3) dynamic-sizing (dynamic neuron generation: yes; dynamic neuron removal: yes); 4) dynamic-linking (dynamic synaptic link generation: yes; dynamic synaptic link removal: yes); 5) neuron receptive field information is represented as a single point identifying the receptive field center (cluster prototype); 6) the size of the neuron receptive field is not bounded by any user defined parameter; 7) network-based variables to be updated: total number of neurons; 8) neuron-based variables to be updated: receptive field center, accumulated error; 9) connection-based variables to be updated: time; 10) learning rate is constant with time (i.e., it does not satisfy first Kohonen's learning constraint); 11) the size of the update neighborhood is constant with time (i.e., it does not satisfy second Kohonen's learning constraint); 12) it does not minimize any known objective function, i.e., termination is not based on optimizing any model of the process or its data [46]; 13) no mathematical tool provided by fuzzy set theory is employed; 14) GNG does not model the responses of the external environment to its learning activities (i.e., it does not satisfy the econet definition adopted herein); 15) it develops independent subsystems (disjointed subnets); and 16) it performs perfect topology preserving mapping.

14.4 Limitations

• It is not very easy to use, since it requires seven user-defined parameters whose meaning is not always straightforward.
• Sample vectors are not employed to initialize reference vectors. In particular, new neurons can be initialized outside the input manifold, and this increases computation time before convergence is reached.
• Its neurons feature no "cooling schedule" (in detail, the learning rate of these neurons is kept constant and equal to a value bigger than zero rather than decrease with time according to Kohonen's convergence constraints [43]); thus, GNG lacks in stability, i.e., the processing of a new data set deletes the structured submaps detected by the system during the previous processing stage (as shown by simulations on the www [56]). As a brief review of different monotonically non-increasing learning rates, refer to [56].
• The size of the update neighborhood does not decrease with time, as required by Kohonen's constraints.

14.5 Advantages

• GNG can be employed in: a) vector quantization, b) density function estimation, and c) structure detection in input data to be mapped topologically correctly onto submaps of an output lattice pursuing dimensionality reduction.
• Due to its insertion strategy, based on accumulated errors, it is robust against noise, i.e., it avoids overfitting.
• In the provided tests involving the 2-D two-spirals data set (194 patterns, 2 classes), an hybrid system (supervised + unsupervised) exploiting GNG as its first layer performs better than other NN models found in the literature [80]. The excellent adaptivity of GNG can be directly tested by simulations on the

www [56]. As a brief review of different monotonically non-increasing learning rates, refer to [56].
• GNG is computationally efficient because its computation time increases linearly as (c+ No. of links).

15 FOSART

FOSART combines properties of SOM, GNG, FCM, and Fuzzy SART algorithms. Its neurons employ a Radial Basis activation Function (RBF) yielding the normalized activation of the units. FOSART applies an ART-based vigilance test to control neuron proliferation [50], [54], and employs a new version of CHR, termed Pairwise Hyperspherical CHR (PHCHR), to generate synaptic links [62]. FOSART inherits from Fuzzy SART [54] the fuzzy membership function, which is derived from that developed in FCM [45], and the learning scheme (for both the winner neuron and the resonance neurons), which is consistent with Kohonen's biologically driven learning constraints [43]. In line with GNG, FOSART is able to dynamically generate and remove synaptic links as well as neurons. Thus, besides GNG also FOSART belongs to the class of FSONN models (see Section 4). FOSART aims to overcome GNG deficiencies listed in Subsection 9.4.

15.1 Input parameters

• Parameter $Ntrts \in [0,1]$ is an *a priori* estimate of the normalized amount of nutrients available to neurons for proliferation. This parameter is functionally equivalent to the normalized severity threshold ρ traditionally employed in ART-based models [10].
• Parameter $\tau \in (0,+\infty)$ is an *a priori* estimate of the time available to the system to perform the cognitive task. It is worth noting that parameters $Ntrts$ and τ, both characterizing the FOSART model, are provided with an intuitive and "plausible" physical meaning.
• Parameter $\epsilon \in (0,+\infty)$ is a convergence threshold employed in the convergence test.

15.2 Description of the algorithm

• FOSART belongs to the class of Gaussian RBF networks employing equal widths [74]. It is important to observe that when Gaussian RBFs with equal widths are employed in competitive learning, then neuron receptive fields are shaped as Voronoi polyedra, like when the Euclidean distance is adopted to compute inter-pattern dissimilarity [82].
• In line with SOM, FOSART employs geometrical (distance) relationships in the input (measurement) space to enforce competitive learning mechanisms. Let us consider: a) winner neuron $w1$ as the one featuring activation value Rbf_{w1} such that $Rbf_{w1} \geq Rbf_i, \forall i \in \{1,c\}$, where c is the total number of neurons; and b) the second best neuron $w2$ as the one featuring activation value

$Rbf_{w2} \geq Rbf_i, \forall i \in \{1,c\}, i \neq w1$. For a given input pattern X_k, $k \in \{1,n\}$, where n is the total number of patterns, the neuron transfer function RBF_i, $\forall i \in \{1,c\}$, is

$$Rbf_i(X_k) = exp\left[-\frac{1}{2} \cdot \sum_{d=1}^{D} \frac{(X_{k,d} - T_{i,d})^2}{\sigma_{i,d}^2}\right] \tag{21}$$

In equation (21), D is the input space dimension, T_i is the center of the Gaussian receptive field, and σ_i is the standard deviation of the Gaussian. Equation (21) provides FOSART with a normalized inter-pattern match degree to be employed in the ART-based vigilance test. It is important to stress that, in FOSART, no adaptation of $\sigma_{i,d}$, $d = 1, ..., D$, ever occurs. In detail,

$$\sigma_{i,d} = \sigma_i = \sigma = (1/Ntrts), \qquad d = 1, ..., D. \tag{22}$$

Equation (22) considers σ_i as being inversely related to user-defined parameter $Ntrts$; intuitively, this relationship means that when the number of neurons employed to map any given manifold X onto lattice G increases (this number being proportional to the available quantity of nutrients), then the size of the node receptive fields over X decreases.

• In line with SOM, topological relationships among neurons belonging to an output neuron lattice are employed to detect neighboring (contextual, soft-max) effects. In particular, FOSART (as well as GNG) applies an update equation to the winner neuron $w1$ and to its (topologically) adjacent neighbors, i.e., the resonance neighborhood consists of all neurons adjacent to the winner (such that synaptic links $Lnk_{w1,i}$, $i \in \{1,c\}$, $i \neq w1$ do exist). Therefore, due to dynamic generation/removal of neurons and synaptic links, the resonance domain changes with time to include neurons that are topologically adjacent to a winner $w1$. Nonetheless, this behavior does not strictly satisfy the Kohonen constraint requiring the size of the update neighborhood to decrease with time monotonically.

• To combine winner and non-winner information describing the position of the input pattern in the input space, FOSART computes a fuzzy membership function $U_i(X_k)$, $\forall k \in \{1,n\}$, $\forall i \in \{1,c\}$. The FOSART membership function is computed as:

$$U_i(X_k) = \frac{\frac{1}{1-Rbf_i}}{\sum_{l=1}^{c} \frac{1}{1-Rbf_l}}. \tag{23}$$

Equation (23) is a fuzzy membership function since it satisfies the three conditions required to state that c fuzzy subsets are a fuzzy c-partition of the input data set (see Subsection 7.2).

• The learning rate of the winner neuron $w1$ is computed as

$$\alpha_{w1} = U_{w1} \cdot (U_{w1})^{Time_{w1}/\tau}, \tag{24}$$

where U_{w1} is computed with (23), and $Time_{w1}$ is the age of the winner neuron. Coefficient α_{w1} is such that: i) it belongs to $(0, U_{w1}]$, where $U_{w1} \leq 1$; ii) it is a monotone decreasing function of $Time_{w1}$, in agreement with the Kohonen "cooling schedule"; and iii) it is a monotone increasing function of U_{w1}, i.e., α_{w1} decreases with distance from the input pattern. User-defined parameter τ has a clear physical meaning. When $Time_{w1} \geq (3 \cdot \tau)$, then $\alpha_{w1} \approx 0$, $\forall U_{w1} \in (0,1)$, i.e., neuron $w1$ reaches convergence. Thus, τ is an *a priori* estimate of the time available to the system to perform the cognitive task. It is important to stress that the age of the winner neuron $Time_{w1}$ is a real value, belonging to $[0, +\infty)$, equal to the non-decreasing sum of the learning rate coefficients computed for that neuron at adaptation steps (i.e., at each adaptation step neuron stability increases at the expense of neuron plasticity):

$$Time_{w1} = Time_{w1} + \alpha_{w1}. \tag{25}$$

• The learning rate of a resonance neuron i (such that synaptic link $Lnk_{w1,i}$ does exist) is computed as

$$\alpha_i = U_i \cdot (U_i)^{(Time_{w1}+Time_i)/\tau}. \tag{26}$$

In line with (25), $Time_i = Time_i + \alpha_i$. Learning rate α_i features the following properties: i) α_i belongs to $(0, U_i]$, where $U_i < U_{w1} \leq 1$, i.e., $\alpha_i < \alpha_{w1}$; ii) α_i is a monotone decreasing function of $Time_i$, in agreement with the Kohonen "cooling schedule"; and iii) α_i is a monotone increasing function of U_i, i.e., α_i decreases with distance from the input pattern. These properties feature overall consistency with the Kohonen bubble strategy identified by (4).
• The local error variable of winner neuron $w1$ is updated in line with GNG, see (18) and (19).
• Centers of Gaussians are updated according to the Kohonen weight adaptation rule. For winner node $w1$ the update equation is

$$T_{w1} = T_{w1} + \alpha_{w1} \cdot (X_k - T_{w1}), \tag{27}$$

where α_{w1} is computed according to (24). For neurons i adjacent to the winner, the update equation is

$$T_i = T_i + \alpha_i \cdot (X_k - T_i) \tag{28}$$

where α_i is computed according to (26).
• With regard to generation of neurons, FOSART employs the following ART-based vigilance test. Given $w1$ as the winner neuron categorizing pattern X_k, if $Rbf_{w1} < Ntrts$, then a new neuron is allocated to categorize X_k, such that, given c as the current number of neurons, then $c = c + 1$, $T_c = X_k$, and $\sigma_c = \sigma$ (in line with (22)). At this point, the conditional synaptic link generation rule PHCHR is applied to the neuron pair $w1$ and c (see below).
• With regard to removal of superfluous neurons, FOSART employs the following strategy. At the end of each epoch, neurons that, before reaching convergence, were never considered as winners in the course of the last epoch are removed. This mechanism: i) avoids overfitting, i.e., FOSART can be used with noisy data; and ii) avoids dead unit formation. It is interesting to observe that this criterion is consistent with Fritzke's definition of neuron utility. In particular, FOSART criterion for neuron removal can be described as follows:

when at the end of the current epoch, one neuron has not reached convergence and features Fritzke's utility computed by means of (17) equal to zero, then this neuron is removed.

• With regard to generation of synaptic links, FOSART employs the following strategy. Let us consider a generic FSONN model employing CHR. Whatever input pattern may be processed by FSONN, traditional CHR always generates one synaptic link to connect the winner node and the second winner node unless this link already exists. Unlike CHR, PHCHR generates a synaptic link to connect the winner node and the second winner node iff the length of this (potential) synaptic link (computed between centers of Gaussians in input space) is "fairly similar" to every length of synaptic links already irradiating from the two nodes. This means, for example, that an isolated neuron is unable to link to another neuron already belonging to a close-knit map of neurons. This also implies that for any given data set, PHCHR detects a number of submaps greater than or equal to CHR.

• With regard to removal of superfluous synaptic links, FOSART employs the following strategy. At the end of each iteration, synaptic links that were never considered as lying between the best and second best neuron in the course of the last epoch are removed.

• At the end of the last epoch Epc, the following convergence test is applied. For all neurons $i \in \{1, c\}$, if $(T_i(Epc) - T_i(Epc-1))$ is above ϵ, then convergence is not reached.

15.3 Architectural features

The main features of FOSART are summarized: 1) on-line learning; 2) soft competitive learning (i.e., FOSART satisfies the definition of fuzzy clustering NN adopted herein); 3) dynamic-sizing (dynamic neuron generation: yes; dynamic neuron removal: yes); 4) dynamic-linking (dynamic synaptic link generation: yes; dynamic synaptic link removal: yes); 5) neuron receptive field information (cluster prototype) is represented as: i) a single point identifying the receptive field center; and ii) a user-defined parameter σ defining a covariance matrix in the radial case; 6) the size of the neuron receptive field is upper bounded by a user defined parameter; 7) network-based variables to be updated: none; 8) neuron-based variables to be updated: receptive field center, accumulated error, time, learning rate, convergence; 9) connection-based variables to be updated: time; 10) learning rate monotonically decreases with time (i.e., it satisfies first Kohonen's learning constraint); 11) the size of the update neighborhood is constant with time (i.e., it does not satisfy second Kohonen's learning constraint); 12) it does not minimize any known objective function, i.e., termination is not based on optimizing any model of the process or its data [46]; 13) it employs fuzzy set memberships provided by fuzzy set theory; 14) FOSART models the responses of the external environment to its learning activities (i.e., it satisfies the econet definition adopted herein); 15) it develops independent subsystems (disjointed subnets); and 16) it performs perfect topology preserving mapping.

15.4 Limitations

• FOSART employs one up to three parameters which are defined by the application developer rather than by the user. In [57], these parameters are considered as significant prior structures [77], i.e., an important property of the model that must be "hard-wired or built-in, perhaps to be tuned later by experience, but not learned in any statistical meaningful way" [77].
• In several tests regarding satellite image clustering that are in progress, FOSART features Mean Square Error values larger than those obtained with SOM [78].
• The size of the update neighborhood does not decrease with time, as required by Kohonen's constraints.

15.5 Advantages

• Feed-back interaction between attentional and orienting subsystems allows FOSART to self-adjust its size depending on the complexity of the clustering task.
• Distinct sample vectors are employed to initialize reference vectors. This choice reduces the risk of dead units formation and may reduce computation time with respect to random initialization.
• FOSART can be employed in: a) vector quantization, b) density function estimation, and c) structure detection in input data to be mapped topologically correctly onto submaps of an output lattice pursuing dimensionality reduction.
• Due to its neuron removal strategy, it is robust against noise, i.e., it avoids overfitting. In the provided tests, the system is stable with respect to small changes in input parameters and in the order of the presentation sequence [57], [58].
• In the provided tests involving the 2-D Simpson data set (24 patterns) [47], the 2-D two-spirals data set (194 patterns, 2 classes) [80], a 3-D digitized human face (9743 patterns) [49], and the 4-D IRIS data set (150 patterns, 3 classes), FOSART performances are competitive with or better than those of other NN models found in the literature (VQ, Fuzzy Min-Max, FCM, FLVQ, FALVQ, GLVQ-F, ING). For example, typical error rates for unsupervised categorization of the IRIS data set are 10-16 mistakes [45]. In this case FOSART, scoring 11 mismatches, performs better than: i) the Fuzzy Min-Max neural network model, where the smallest number of misclassified patterns is 18 when the number of clusters is 3 [47]; ii) the off-line Fuzzy c-means algorithm affected by 15 misclassifications [81]; iii) the on-line Kohonen VQ algorithm affected by 17 misclassifications [81]; iv) the class of on-line FALVQ algorithms, affected by 16 misclassifications [66]; and v) the on-line GLVQ-F algorithms, affected by 16 misclassifications [71].
• FOSART is computationally efficient because its computation time increases linearly as (c+ No. of links).

Architectural features	CLUSTERING NNs				
	SOM	FLVQ	CGR F-ART	GNG	FOSART
on-line	Y	N	Y	Y	Y
learning strategy	SC	SC[1]	HC	SC	SC
neuron gener./remov.	N/N	N/N	Y/N	Y/Y	Y/Y
link gener./remov.	N/N	N/N	N/N	Y/Y	Y/Y
neuron receptive field informations	rfc	rfc	rfc	rfc	rfc, variance
neuron constrast or similarity measure	Eucl.dist.	Eucl.dist.	peculiar[2]	Eucl.dist.	Gaussian basis funct.
size of the neuron receptive field	NB	NB	UB	NB	UB
network-based (global) variables	time, lear.rate	time	time, lear.rate	no.neurons, lear.rate	none
neuron-based variables	rfc	rfc, lear.rate	rfc	rfc, accum.error	rfc, accum.error, time, lear.rate, converg.
connection-based variables	none	none	none	time	time
learning rate	MTD	TD	TC	TC	MTD
size of the update neighborhood	MTD	TD	NCP	TC	TC
objective function minimization	N	N	N	N	N
tools from fuzzy logic	none	mbf	none	none	mbf
econet	N	N	Y	N	Y
topologic.disjonted subnets	N[3]	N	N	Y	Y
PTPM	N[4]	N	N	Y	Y

Legenda
N = No, Y = Yes,
SC = Soft Competitive, HC = Hard Competitive,
NB = Not-Bounded, UB = Upper-Bounded,
rfc = receptive field center, mbf = membership function,
MTD = Monotonically Time Decreasing, TD = Time Decreasing,
TC=Time Constant, NCP = Not-Computed,
PTPM = Perfect Topology Preserving Mapping
[1]: FLVQ's learning strategy may be affected by asymptotic misbehaviors.
[2]: It does not satisfy the commutative property.
[3]: SOM maps different input patterns into spatially segregated areas of the output lattice.
[4]: SOM performs PTPM iff the dimension of the input space is not larger than the dimension of the output lattice.

Table 4:

16 Concluding remarks

Comparison of clustering NN models, syntesized in Table 4, shows that SOM, GNG and FOSART develop a soft-max adaptation strategy, i.e., these models satisfy the definition of fuzzy clustering neural network adopted herein. Paradoxically, among these architectures only FOSART exploits mathematical tools provided by fuzzy set theory (such as fuzzy set membership values). CGR Fuzzy ART employs a WTA strategy and no mathematical tool derived from fuzzy set theory. FLVQ is affected by asymptotic misbehaviors. Since GNG and FOSART inherits several features from SOM, the importance of SOM is outstanding. Several conclusions stem from our critical review. 1) The fuzziness of SOM shows that a network exploiting local rules derived from neurophysiological evidence can verify the definition of fuzzy clustering neural network proposed in this work, although no tool derived from fuzzy set theory is explicitly adopted. 2) An effective soft-max cooperative/competitive strategy makes neighboring PEs mutually coupled, i.e., they gain sensitivity to contextual effects; in architectural terms, mutually coupled PEs feature vertical (inter-layer) as well as horizontal (intra-layer) connections, which can be found in every biological cognitive system. 3) Within the framework of the multi-disciplinary science of artificial complex systems [60], mathematical tools derived from fuzzy set theory may be adopted to model contextual sensitivity effects due to cooperative/competitive local mechanisms. These mechanisms may be identified in advance by neurophysiological studies of biological neural systems (see point 1. above).

References

[1] J. M. Keller and D. J. Hunt. Incorporating fuzzy membership functions into the perceptron algorithm. *IEEE Trans. Pattern Analysis Machine Intelligence*, 7 (6), 693-699, 1985.

[2] C.-T. Lin and C. S. G. Lee. *Neural Fuzzy Systems*, Prentice Hall PTR, 1996.

[3] J.-S. R. Jang, C.-T. Sun and E. Mizutani, *Neuro-fuzzy and Soft Computing*, Prentice Hall PTR, 1997.

[4] L. A. Zadeh. Fuzzy sets. *Information Control*, 8, 338-353, 1965.

[5] L. A. Zadeh. Outline of a new approach to the analysis of compe systems and decision processes. *IEEE Trans. System Man and Cybernetics*, 1, 28-44, 1973.

[6] M. Umano, M. Mizumoto and K. Tanaka. FTDS systems: a fuzzy set manipulation system. *Information Science*, 14, 115-159, 1978.

[7] K. Uehara and M. Fujise. Fuzzy inference based on families of α-level sets. *IEEE Trans. on Fuzzy Ssytems*, 1 (2), 111-124, 1993.

[8] H. Ishibuchi and H. Tanaka. Fuzzy regression analysis using neural networks. *Fuzzy sets and systems*, 50, 257-265, 1992.

[9] H. Ishibuchi, R. Fujioka and H. Tanaka. Neural networks that learn from fuzzy if-then rules. *IEEE Trans. on Fuzzy Systems*, 1 (2), 85-97, 1993.

[10] C.-T. Lin and Y.-C. Lu. A neural fuzzy system with fuzzy supervised learning. *IEEE Trans. on System Man and Cybernetics*, 26 (5), 744-763, 1996.

[11] L. X. Wang and J. M. Mendel. Fuzzy basis functions, universal approximation and orthogonal least-squares learning. *IEEE Trans. on Neural Networks*, 3 (5), 807-814, 1992.

[12] H. M. Kim and J. M. Mendel. Fuzzy basis functions: comparisons with other basis functions. *IEEE Trans. on Fuzzy Systems*, 3 (2), 158-168, 1995.

[13] F. Casalino, F. Masulli and A. Sperduti. Rule specialization in networks of fuzzy basis functions. *Internat. Journal of Intelligent Automation and Soft Computing*, in press, 1997.

[14] J.-S. R. Jang. ANFIS: Adaptive-network-based fuzzy inference systems. *IEEE Trans. on System Man and Cybernetics*, 23 (3), 665-685, 1993.

[15] T. Takagi and M. Sugeno. Fuzzy identification of systems and its applications to modeling and control. *IEEE Trans. System Man and Cybernetics*, 15 (1), 116-132, 1985.

[16] R. R. Yager. Modeling and formulating fuzzy knowledge bases using neural networks. *Neural Networks*, 7 (8), 1273-1283, 1994.

[17] T. Poggio and F. Girosi. Networks for approaximation and learning. *IEEE Proceedings*, 78 (9), 1481-1497, 1990.

[18] M. M. Gupta. Fuzzy logic and neural networks, *Proc. of Tenth Intern. Conf. on Multicriterion Decision Making*, Taipei, 281-294, 1992.

[19] R. Krishnapuram and L. F. Lee. Fuzzy-set-based hierarchical networks for information fusion in computer vision. *Neural Networks*, 5, 335-350, 1992.

[20] S. K. Pal and S. Mitra. Multilayer perceptron, fuzzy sets and classification. *IEEE Trans. on Neural Networks*, 3 (5), 683-697, 1992.

[21] P. K. Simpson. Fuzzy min-max neural networks - Part I: Classification. *IEEE Trans. on Neural Networks*, 3 (5), 776-786, 1992.

[22] R. O. Duda and P. E. Hart. *Pattern Classification and Scene Analysis*, New York, John Wiley, 1973.

[23] W. E. Blanz and S. L. Gish. A connectionist classifier architecture applied to image segmentation. *Proc. 10th Intern. Conf. Pattern Recognition*, 272-277, Atlantic City, NJ.

[24] B. S. Manjunath, T. Simchony and R. Chelappa. Stochastic and deterministic networks for texture segmentation. *IEEE Trans. Acoustic Speech and Signal Processing*, 38 (6), 1039-1049, 1990.

[25] A. De Luca and S. Termini. A definition of nonprobabilistic entropy in the setting of fuzzy set theory. *Information Control*, 20, 301-312, 1972.

[26] A. Kandel. *Fuzzy Mathematical Techniques with Applications*, New-York, 1975.

[27] A. Ghosh, N. R. Pal and S. K. Pal. Self-organization for object extraction using a multilayer neural network and fuzziness measures. *IEEE Trans. on Fuzzy Systems*, 1 (2), 54-68, 1993.

[28] A. Ghosh. Use of fuzziness measures in layered networks for object extraction: a generalization. *Fuzzy sets and systems*, 72, 331-348, 1995.

[29] E. R. Caianiello and A. Petrosino. Neural networks, fuzziness and image processing. in Machine and Human Perception: Analogies and Divergencies, (V. Cantoni Ed.), 355-370, Plenum Press, New York, 1994.

[30] A. Petrosino. Rough fuzzy sets and unsupervised neural learning: applications in computer vision. in *New Trends in Fuzzy Logic*, (A. Bonarini *et al.* Ed.), 166-176, 1996.

[31] C.-T. Lin and C. S. G. Lee. Neural-network-based fuzzy logic control and description system. *IEEE Trans. on Computers*, 40 (12), 1320-1336, 1991.

[32] C.-T. Lin. A neural fuzzy control system with structure and parameter learning. *Fuzzy sets and systems*, 70, 183-212, 1995.

[33] C.J. Lin and C.-T. Lin. An ART-based fuzzy adaptive learning control network. *Proc. IEEE Intern. Conf. Fuzzy Systems*, 1, 1-6, Orlando, FL, 1994.

[34] H. Takagi and I. Hayashi. NN-driven fuzzy reasoning. *International Journal of Approximate Reasoning*, 5 (3), 191-212, 1991.

[35] D. Nauck and R. Kruse. NEFCLASS- A neuro-fuzzy approach for the classification of data. in *Proc. of 1995 ACM Symposium on Applied Computing*, (K. M. George *et al.* Ed.s), ACM Press, 1995.

[36] S. K. Halgamuge and M. Glesner. Neural networks in designing fuzzy systems for real world applications. *Fuzzy sets and systems*, 65, 1-12, 1994.

[37] W. Pedrycz. Fuzzy neural networks with reference neurons as pattern classifiers. *IEEE Trans. on Neural Networks*, 3 (5), 770-775.

[38] R. Yasdi. Combining rough sets learning and neural learning method to deal with uncertain and imprecise information. *Neurocomputing*, 7, 61-84, 1995.

[39] H. R. Berenji. A reinforment learning-based architecture for fuzzy logic control. *International Journal of Approximate Reasoning*, 6, 267-292, 1992.

[40] A. Baraldi and F. Parmiggiani. Fuzzy clustering: critical analysis of the contextual mechanisms employed by three neural network models. *SPIE Proc. on Applications of Fuzzy Logic Thecnology III* (B. Bosacchi, J. Bezdek Eds.), SPIE Vol. 2761, 261-270, 1996.

[41] Anonymous referee, *IEEE Trans. on Neural Networks*, 1997.

[42] S. Mitra and S. K. Pal. Self-organizing neural network as a fuzzy classifier. *IEEE Trans. on Systems, Man, and Cybernetics*, 24 (3), 385-399, 1994.

[43] T. Kohonen. The self-organizing map. *Proceedings of the IEEE* 78 (9), 1464-1480, 1990.

[44] T. Kohonen. *Self-organization and Associative Memory*, 2nd Edition, Spriger Verlag, Berlin, 1988.

[45] J. C. Bezdek and N. R. Pal. Two soft relative of learning vector quantization. *Neural Networks*, 8 (5), 729-743, 1995.

[46] E. C. Tsao, J. C. Bezdek and N. R. Pal. Fuzzy Kohonen clustering network. *Pattern Recognition*, 27 (5), 757-764, 1994.

[47] P. K. Simpson. Fuzzy Min-Max neural network-Part 2: Clustering. *IEEE Trans. on Fuzzy Systems*, 1 (1), 32-45, 1993.

[48] T. M. Martinetz, S. G. Berkovich and K. J. Schulten. Neural-gas network for vector quantization and its application to time-series prediction. *IEEE Trans. on Neural Networks* 4 (4), 558-569, 1993.

[49] M. Fontana, N. A., Borghese, and S. Ferrari, Image reconstruction using improved Neural-Gas. *Proc. Italian Workshop on Neural Networks '95* (M. Marinaro and R. Tagliaferri Eds.), Singapore, World Scientific, 260-265, 1995.

[50] G. Carpenter, S. Grossberg and D.B. Rosen. Fuzzy ART: fast stable learning and categorization of analog patterns by an adaptive resonance system. *Neural Networks*, 4, 759-771, 1991.

[51] G. Carpenter, S. Grossberg, N. Maukuzon, J. Reynolds and D. B. Rosen. Fuzzy ARTMAP: A neural network architecture for incremental supervised learning of analog multidimensional maps. *IEEE Trans. on Neural Networks*, 3 (5), 698-713, 1992.

[52] G. A. Carpenter and S. Grossberg. A massively parallel architecture for a self-organizing neural pattern recognition machine. *Computer Vision, Graphics, and Image Processing*, 37, 54-115, 1987.

[53] G. A. Carpenter and S. Grossberg. ART2: Self-organization of stable category recognition codes for analog input patterns. *Applied Optics*, 26 (23), 4919-4930, 1987.

[54] A. Baraldi and F. Parmiggiani. Fuzzy combination of the Kohonen and ART neural network models to detect statistical regularities in a random sequence of multi-valued input patterns. *Proc. Int. Conf. on Neural Networks '97*, Houston, TX, June 1997, in press.

[55] B. Fritzke. A growing neural gas network learns topologies. *Advances in Neural Information Processing Systems 7* (G. Tesauro, D. S. Touretzky, and T. K. Leen Eds.), Cambridge, MA: MIT Press, 625-632, 1995.

[56] B. Fritzke. Some competitive learning methods. Draft document, *http : //www. neuroinformatik.ruhr – uni – bochum.de/ini/VDM/ research/gsn/DemoGNG*, 1997.

[57] A. Baraldi and F. Parmiggiani. A fuzzy neural network model capable of generating/removing neurons and synaptic links dynamically. *Proc. of the II Italian Workshop on Fuzzy Logic* (A. Petrosino, Ed.), World Scientific, Singapore, 1997, in press.

[58] A. Baraldi and F. Parmiggiani. Novel neural network model combining radial basis function, competitive Hebbian learning rule, and fuzzy simplified adaptive resonance theory. *SPIE Proc. on Applications of Fuzzy Logic Technology IV*, San Diego, CA, July 1997, in press.

[59] M. Bianchini and M. Gori. Optimal learning in artificial neural networks: a review of theoretical results. *Neurocomputing*, 13 (2-4), 313-346, 1996.

[60] R. Serra and G. Zanarini. *Complex systems and cognitive processes.* Springer-Verlag, Berlin, 1990.

[61] D. E. Rumelhart, G. E. Hinton and R. J. Williams, Learning internal representations by error propagation, *Parallel Distributed Processing* (D. E. Rumelhart and J. L. McClelland, Eds.), 1, 318-362, MIT Press, Cambridge, MA, 1986.

[62] T. M. Martinetz and K. J. Schulten. Topology representing networks. *Neural Networks*, 7 (3), 507-522, 1994.

[63] D. Parisi. La scienza cognitiva tra intelligenza artificiale e vita artificiale. *Neuroscienze e Scienze dell'Artificiale: dal Neurone all'Intelligenza* (E. Biondi *et al.*, Eds.), Patron, Bologna, Italy, 321-341, 1991 (in Italian).

[64] J. J. Hopfield. Neural networks and physical systems with emergent collective computational abilities. *Proc. National Academy of Sciences*, 74, 2554-2558, 1982.

[65] T. Masters. *Signal and Image Processing With Neural Networks. A c++ Sourcebook.* Wiley, New York, 1994.

[66] N. B. Karayannis and P. Pai. Fuzzy algorithms for learning vector quantization. *IEEE Trans. on Neural Networks*, 7 (5), 1196-1211, 1996.

[67] N. B. Karayannis, and M. Ravuri. An integrated approach to fuzzy learning vector quantization and fuzzy c-means clustering. *Intelligent Engineering Systems Through Artificial Neural Networks* (C. H. Dagli *et al.* Eds.), 5, ASME Press, New York, NY, 247-252, 1995.

[68] N. B. Karayannis, J. C. Bezdek. An integrated approach to fuzzy learning vector quantization and fuzzy c-means clustering. *IEEE Trans. on Fuzzy Systems*, under review.

[69] N. B. Karayannis. Learning vector quantization: A review. *Int. Journal of Smart Engineering System Design*, in press, 1997.

[70] J. C. Bezdek, and N. R. Pal. Generalized clustering networks and Kohonen's self-organizing scheme. *IEEE Trans. on Neural Networks*, 4 (4), 549-557, 1993.

[71] N. B. Karayannis, J. C. Bezdek, N. R. Pal, R. J. Hathaway and P. Pai. Repair to GLVQ: A new family of competitive learning schemes. *IEEE Trans. on Neural Networks*, 7 (5), 1062-1071, 1996.

[72] A. Baraldi, P. Blonda, F. Parmiggiani, G. Pasquariello and G. Satalino. How is descending FLVQ sensitive to values of its weighting exponent?. *IEEE Trans. on Neural Networks*, submitted.

[73] K. Raghu and J. M. Keller. A possibilistic approach to clustering. *IEEE Trans. on Fuzzy Systems*, 1 (2), 98-110, 1993.

[74] ftp://ftp.sas.com/pub/neural/FAQ.

[75] F. Y. Shih, J. Moh and F. Chang. A new ART-based neural architecture for pattern classification and image enhancement without prior knowledge. *Pattern Recognition*, 25 (5), 533-542, 1992.

[76] J. Huang, M. Georgiopoulos and G. L. Heileman. Fuzzy ART properties. *Neural Networks*, 8 (2), 203-213, 1995.

[77] S. Geman, E. Bienenstock and R. Dourstat. Neural networks and the bias/variance dilemma. *Neural Computation*, 4 (1), 1-58, 1992.

[78] P. Blonda, G. Satalino, A. Baraldi and A. Bognani, "Neuro-fuzzy analysis of remote sensed antarctic data," *Proc. of the II Italian Workshop on Fuzzy Logic* (A. Petrosino, Ed.), World Scientific, Singapore, 1997, in press.

[79] Y. Pao. *Adaptive pattern recognition and neural networks.* Addison-Wesley, Reading, MA, 1989.

[80] B. Fritzke. Growing cell structures - A self-organizing network for unsupervised and supervised learning. *Neural Networks*, 7 (9), 1441-1460, 1994.

[81] S. Kim and and S. Mitra. Integrated Adaptive Fuzzy Clustering (IAFC) algorithm. *Proc. of the Second IEEE International Conference on Fuzzy Systems*, 2, 1264-1268, 1993.

[82] B. Fritzke. Personal communication, 1997.

[83] B. Fritzke. The LBG-U method for vector quantization - An improvement over LBG inspired from neural networks. *Neural Processing Letters*, 5 (1), 1997, in press.

A Unifying View of Gradient Calculations and Learning for Locally Recurrent Neural Networks

Paolo Campolucci, Aurelio Uncini, Francesco Piazza+*

Dipartimento di Elettronica ed Automatica, Università di Ancona,
via Brecce Bianche, 60131 Ancona, Italy.
*e-mail: paolo@eealab.unian.it

Abstract

In this paper a critical review of gradient-based training methods for recurrent neural networks is presented including Back Propagation Through Time (BPTT), Real Time Recurrent Learning (RTRL) and several specific learning algorithms for different locally recurrent architectures. From this survey it comes out the need for a unifying view of all the specific procedures proposed for networks with local feedbacks, that keeps into account the general framework of recurrent networks learning: BPTT and RTRL. Therefore a learning method for local feedback network is proposed which combines together the best feature of BPTT, i.e. the lowest complexity, and of RTRL, i.e. the on-line operation, and includes as special case several specific algorithms already proposed, such as Temporal Back Propagation, Back Propagation for Sequences, Back-Tsoi algorithm and some others. In the general version, this new training method allows on-line efficient and accurate gradient calculation. It compares favourably with the previous algorithms in stability, speed/complexity trade off, accuracy.

1. Introduction

Internally static networks can be trained by the simplest algorithms: for the buffered Multi Layer Perceptron (MLP) with only input buffer (with no recursion) the standard Back Propagation (BP) should be used, while for the Narendra-Parthasarathy network [18], i.e. buffered MLP with input and output buffers, the so called "open loop" approximation of the standard BP is usually employed. It consists in opening the loop during the backward phase, feeding the network with the desired outputs instead of the true network outputs. In Infinite Impulse Response

+ This research was supported by the Italian MURST.

(IIR) adaptive filter theory this is the equation error approximation of the true output error approach [10], in neural network theory this is the teacher forced technique [2].

Extension of Back Propagation to recurrent networks was firstly proposed by F. Pineda and L. B. Almeida, e.g. [26] only in the case when the recurrent network behaviour relaxes to a fixed point. However, if a general temporal processing is needed, two main gradient-based learning approaches exist for recurrent networks [15,16,20]: Back Propagation Through Time (BPTT) [6,1,27,15] and Real Time Recurrent Learning (RTRL) [2,18,22,27,15].

BPTT is a family of algorithms which extends the BP paradigm to dynamic networks. There are two major points of view to understand what BPTT is. The first is an intuitive one: time unfolding of the recurrent network, i.e., for single layer single feedback delay fully recurrent networks one can think to the network state at time t as if it was obtained from the t-th layer output of a multilayer network with T layers, where T is the length of the sequence. The other point of view is a mathematical one and it is based on the Werbos theory of ordered derivatives [5]. Werbos provided a mathematical tool to rigorously compute the derivatives of a certain variable with respect to another one in complex structures described by ordered mathematical relations (for example a neural network).

Actually, with ordered derivatives it is possible to derive both BPTT and RTRL algorithms in the same framework [16,20]. The difference between BPTT and RTRL is in how the chain rule derivative expansion is applied. More specifically, during the learning phase, in BPTT signals and time flow in the reverse direction with respect to the forward phase whereas in RTRL they flow as in the forward calculations. Reversing the signal flow graph provides the great efficiency of BPTT but the necessary reversion of signal time scale makes it non-causal even if only one delay is present inside the network.

Therefore BPTT is local in space but not in time, is computationally simple but is non-causal; so it can be implemented only in batch mode. For on-line adaptation some approximations are needed, namely causalization and truncation of past history, as explained in [1,23,27] for fully recurrent neural networks.

Instead RTRL is local in time but not in space, computationally complex but intrinsically on-line. However even RTRL implements an approximated calculation of the gradient if the parameters are continually adapted since its true derivation would require constant weights [1,27].

In [27] Williams and Zipser report better performance and convergence rate for truncated BPTT than RTRL and explain this result stating that the history truncation approximation can be better than the approximation implemented in RTRL.

Recently Wan and Beaufayas [17] proposed a simple method to derive BPTT for discrete time dynamic neural networks composed of a general interconnection of weights, delays, additive units, differentiable non-linearities. This derivation can be carried out with simple transformations of the signal flow graph of the network itself; however the algorithm derived in this way is always non-causal and the authors did not address the question of on-line learning for networks with feedbacks.

On the contrary, several gradient-based learning algorithms have been presented for specific dynamic multilayer neural networks.

In [7] a learning algorithm, named "Temporal Back Propagation", was proposed by E. Wan. This is an on-line version of the batch mode BPTT approach [17]. However it can only be applied to the non-recurrent MLP with Finite Impulse Response (FIR) filter synapses [3,7,21,9], i.e. FIR-MLP often called Time Delay Neural Network (TDNN) [8].

Back Propagation for Sequences (BPS) is a learning algorithm proposed by Gori et al. [13,14,22,15] for both output and activation Local Feedback Multi Layered Networks (LF-MLNs) [14]. It is interesting because it is local both in time and in space, computationally simple and with small memory requirement; in fact it is only slightly more complex than standard BP. However it can be applied only to LF-MLN with no dynamic units in layers other than the first one. BPS basically is the classical backpropagation on the multilayer network with a recursive computation only inside each dynamic neuron. Due to the architectural constraints, this algorithm does not implement BPTT, but is somewhere between BP and RTRL. The same approch was proposed by Mozer in [24] that indipendently derived a quite similar algorithm named "Focused Back Propagation" for a locally recurrent network analogous to the Auto Regressive MLP (AR-MLP) [25]. BPS was rediscovered in [19] where was derived for a structure that is a particular case of the output feedback LF-MLN and was applied to control problems with good results.

In [3], a learning algorithm for MLP with IIR filter synapses [3,4,10,11,12] was proposed by A.D. Back and A.C. Tsoi. It is similar to BPS, implementing both a backpropagation and a recursive computation, but without any architectural restriction. However to avoid dynamic backpropagation, the authors propose a rough approximation of BPTT, using static backpropagation even through a dynamic neuron.

Similar learning algorithms are also Auto Regressive BP proposed by R.R. Leighton and B.C. Conrath [25] for the Auto Regressive MLP [25], and the algorithm in [28]. They are equivalent to Back-Tsoi algorithm since they also use instantaneous backpropagation without implementing the full BPTT backpropagation through a dynamic unit. So in the following of the paper we will call Back-Tsoi algorithm the method with instantaneous backpropagation and we will not refer anymore to the works in [25,28].

The unifying on-line method proposed in this paper, whose basic ideas were presented in [11,12], implements and combines together BPTT and RTRL paradigms for locally recurrent networks. Many algorithms can be derived by this method for locally recurrent networks: they implement an accurate (even if not exact, as usual for on-line training) computation of the gradient. The name that we will use is Causal Recursive Back Propagation (CRBP, not to be confused with Recurrent Back Propagation [26]) thus remembering the dual nature of the method: BPTT style formulas are used to backpropagate the error through the neurons and recursive computation of derivatives inside each neuron is implemented to calculate weights variations.

It is well known that RTRL and BPTT approaches are equivalent in batch mode operation [20]: they compute the same weights variations using different chain rule expansions. Since CRBP uses another expansion of the same derivatives, it becomes equivalent to them when working in batch mode (Recursive Back Propagation, RBP).

However the three methods are not equivalent in on-line mode. It must be stressed that in CRBP each local feedback is taken into account during adaptation with no history truncation for the coefficients of the same neuron, using recursive formulas instead of non-causal ones as in the BPTT approach.

In the following the Recursive Back Propagation batch learning method and its on-line version are derived for the MLP with IIR synapses; the formulas for LF-MLNs and AR-MLP can be derived in a similar way.

2. A Unifying Formulation for Learning Methods in Locally Recurrent Neural Networks

The notation that will be used, an extension of Widrow's notation, is summarized in the following:

M	number of layers in the network.
l	layer index. In particular l=0 and $l=M$ denote the input and output layer, respectively.
N_l	number of neurons of the l-th layer. In particular N_0 and N_M denote the number of inputs and outputs respectively.
n	neuron index.
t	time index. t=1,2, ... T. Where T is the length of the training sequence.
$x_n^{(l)}[t]$	output of the n-th neuron of the l-th layer, at time t. In particular n=0 refers to the bias inputs: $x_0^{(l)}=1$. Note that $\{ x_n^{(0)}[t]\}$, $n=1,\ldots,N_0$, are the input signals.
$L_{nm}^{(l)}-1$	order of the MA part of the synapse of the n-th neuron of the l-th layer relative to the m-th output of the (l-1)-th layer. $L_{nm}^{(l)}>=1$ and $L_{n0}^{(l)}=1$.
$I_{nm}^{(l)}$	order of the AR part of the synapse of the n-th neuron of the l-th layer relative to the m-th output of the (l-1)-th layer. $I_{nm}^{(l)}>=0$ and $I_{n0}^{(l)}=0$.
$w_{nm(p)}^{(l)}$	(p=0,1, ..., $L_{nm}^{(l)}-1$) coefficients of the MA part of the corresponding synapse. If $L_{nm}^{(l)}=1$, the synapse has no MA part and the weight notation becomes $w_{nm}^{(l)}$. $w_{n0}^{(l)}$ is the bias.
$v_{nm(p)}^{(l)}$	(p=1, ..., $I_{nm}^{(l)}$) coefficients of the AR part of the synapse. If $I_{nm}^{(l)}=0$ the synaptic filter is purely MA.
weight	either a w or v coefficient.
sgm(z)	activation function.
sgm'(z)	derivative of sgm(z).
$y_{nm}^{(l)}[t]$	synaptic filter output at time t relative to the synapse of n-th neuron, l-th layer and m-th input. $y_{n0}^{(l)}=w_{n0}^{(l)}$ is the bias.
$s_n^{(l)}[t]$	"net" quantity relative to the n-th neuron of the l-th layer at time t, i.e. the input to the corresponding activation function.

$d_n[t]$ $(n=1,\ldots,N_M)$ desired outputs at time t.

The forward phase at time t can be described by the following equations evaluated for $l=1,\ldots,M$ and $n=1,\ldots,N_l$:

$$y_{nm}^{(l)}[t]=\sum_{p=0}^{L_{nm}^{(l)}-1} w_{nm(p)}^{(l)} x_m^{(l-1)}[t-p]+\sum_{p=1}^{I_{nm}^{(l)}} v_{nm(p)}^{(l)} y_{nm}^{(l)}[t-p] \tag{1}$$

$$s_n^{(l)}[t]=\sum_{m=0}^{N_{l-1}} y_{nm}^{(l)}[t] \qquad x_n^{(l)}[t]=sgm(s_n^{(l)}[t]) \tag{2}$$

As in the static case, it holds:

$$\delta_n^{(l)}[t]=e_n^{(l)}[t]\,\mathrm{sgm}'(s_n^{(l)}[t]) \tag{3}$$

Therefore, using gradient descent method and the chain rule expansion:

$$\Delta w_{nm(p)}^{(l)}=\sum_{t=1}^{T}\Delta w_{nm(p)}^{(l)}[t+1] \quad , \quad \Delta w_{nm(p)}^{(l)}[t+1]=\mu\,\delta_n^{(l)}[t]\,\frac{\partial s_n^{(l)}[t]}{\partial w_{nm(p)}^{(l)}} \tag{4}$$

Similarly for the v weights we have:

$$\Delta v_{nm(p)}^{(l)}=\sum_{t=1}^{T}\Delta v_{nm(p)}^{(l)}[t+1] \quad , \quad \Delta v_{nm(p)}^{(l)}[t+1]=\mu\,\delta_n^{(l)}[t]\,\frac{\partial s_n^{(l)}[t]}{\partial v_{nm(p)}^{(l)}} \tag{5}$$

where

$$\frac{\partial s_n^{(l)}[t]}{\partial w_{nm(p)}^{(l)}}=x_m^{(l-1)}[t-p]+\sum_{r=1}^{I_{nm}^{(l)}} v_{nm(r)}^{(l)}\frac{\partial s_n^{(l)}[t-r]}{\partial w_{nm(p)}^{(l)}} \tag{6}$$

$$\frac{\partial s_n^{(l)}[t]}{\partial v_{nm(p)}^{(l)}}=y_{nm}^{(l)}[t-p]+\sum_{r=1}^{I_{nm}^{(l)}} v_{nm(r)}^{(l)}\frac{\partial s_n^{(l)}[t-r]}{\partial v_{nm(p)}^{(l)}} \tag{7}$$

in which the derivatives can be recursively computed.
The backpropagation through the layers can be derived by chain rule:

$$e_n^{(l)}[t]=\begin{cases} e_n[t] & \text{for } l=M \\ \displaystyle\sum_{q=1}^{N_{l+1}}\sum_{p=0}^{T-t}\delta_q^{(l+1)}[t+p]\,\frac{\partial y_{qn}^{(l+1)}[t+p]}{\partial x_n^{(l)}[t]} & \text{for } l=(M-1),\ldots,1 \end{cases} \tag{8}$$

where the partial derivatives are computed deriving expression (1):

$$\frac{\partial y_{qn}^{(l+1)}[t+p]}{\partial x_n^{(l)}[t]}=\left(\begin{cases} w_{qn(p)}^{(l+1)} & \text{if } 0\le p\le L_{qn}^{(l+1)}-1 \\ 0 & \text{otherwise}\end{cases}\right)+\sum_{r=1}^{\min(I_{qn}^{(l+1)},p)} v_{qn(r)}^{(l+1)}\frac{\partial y_{qn}^{(l+1)}[t+p-r]}{\partial x_n^{(l)}[t]} \tag{9}$$

These derivatives have a very interesting interpretation. Consider the expression of a generic causal linear filter output as the convolution of the input $x[\tau]$ with an impulse response $h[t,\tau]$ (in general time variant):

$$y[t]=\sum_{\tau=t_0}^{t} x[\tau]h[t,\tau]$$

where t_0 is the initial time instant. Differentiating we get:

$$\frac{\partial y[t+p]}{\partial x[t]} = h[t+p,t].$$

Obviously, if the filter is time invariant, the derivative does not depend on t but only on p and $h[t+p,t]=h[t+p-t]=h[p]$. This means that the derivative in (9) is the impulse response of the IIR filter. It is obtained through auto-regressive filtering of the sequence of the coefficients of the MA part with the AR part of the corresponding IIR synaptic filter. If the learning rate is small enough, also when on-line adaptation is performed, the derivative is slowly changing in time, i.e. with the t index in (9).

Therefore, for MLP with IIR synapses, expression (8) means that each back propagating error at layer l is a summation of all the *delta's* at the following layer filtered by the non-causal version of the respective IIR filter. The non-causal version of each filter can be obtained practically, convoluting with time reverted impulse response or time reverting the output of the filter giving the input in a reversed time scale.

The expressions from (1) to (9) constitute the Recursive Back Propagation algorithm for IIR-MLP.

As previously stated, the RBP algorithm is used only as an intermediate step in the derivation of CRBP. In fact, as shown by expression (8), the exact RBP algorithm is non-causal, since the $e_n^{(l)}$ at time t depends on the $\delta_q^{(l+1)}$ quantities, taken at future time instants. Therefore the weights update can only be performed in batch mode.

However the RBP algorithm, due to the recursive structure of expressions (6) and (7), can be easily approximated to obtain a very efficient on-line learning algorithm. The on-line approximation consists in three steps: (a) incremental instead of cumulative adaptation, (b) future convolution truncation, (c) causalization.

(a) Incremental instead of cumulative adaptation can be implemented using:

$$weight\_variation_{nm(p)}^{(l)}[t+1] = \Delta weight_{nm(p)}^{(l)}[t+1]$$

instead of the first expressions in (4) and (5), at each time step, where '*weight*' indicates either w or v .

(b) If a casualization is desired, a truncation of the future convolution is necessary, due to the infinite memory of the IIR synapses. The truncated formula is therefore:

$$e_n^{(l)}[t] = \begin{cases} e_n[t] & \text{for } l = M \\ \displaystyle\sum_{q=1}^{N_{l+1}} \sum_{p=0}^{Q_{l+1}} \delta_q^{(l+1)}[t+p] \; \frac{\partial y_{qn}^{(l+1)}[t+p]}{\partial x_n^{(l)}[t]} & \text{for } l = (M-1),\ldots,1 \end{cases} \qquad (10)$$

where Q_{l+1} is appropriately chosen.

(c) Then we have to introduce a suitable number of delays in the weight adaptation formulas in order to remove the non-causality. In other words:

$$weight^{(l)}[t+1] = weight^{(l)}[t] + weight\_variation^{(l)}[t+1-D_l]$$

where D_l is a suitable integer number. It follows that $D_l = \begin{cases} 0 & \text{if } l = M \\ \sum_{i=l+1}^{M} Q_i & \text{if } 1 \le l < M \end{cases}$

The causalised formula can be obtained from (10) reversing the order of the internal summation and issuing the variable change $t + Q_{l+1} \rightarrow \tau$, where τ is the current time instant (present).
For the sake of clarity, a diagram of CRBP is shown in Fig. 1.

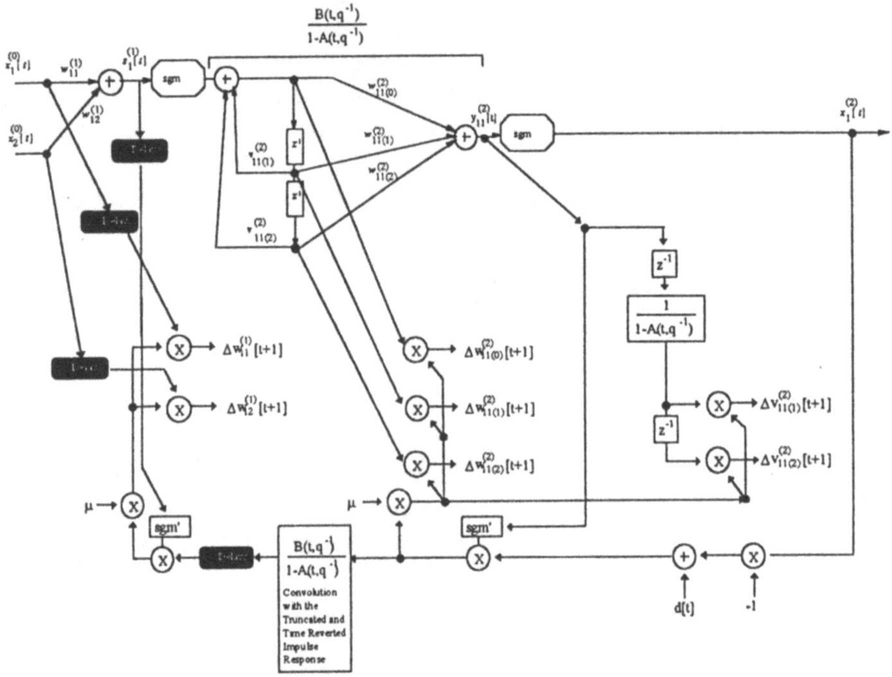

Fig. 1. The CRBP applied to an IIR-MLP example network (the bias terms are not shown). It is obtained assuming simplified recursive computation of derivatives. The Back-Tsoi approximation uses the same flow diagram but with a multiplication for $w_{11(0)}^{(2)}$ instead of the truncated IIR filtering and Q_2=0.

The causalisation and the on-line update, compared to the batch mode case, is not a strong approximation if the learning rate is small enough, because in this case the weights variation is small in the time interval of D_l instants. Instead the truncation approximation can be justified by the following property:

If a linear time invariant IIR filter is asymptotically stable (i.e. all the poles are inside the unit circle) then $\frac{\partial y[t+p]}{\partial x[t]} \to 0$ if $p \to \infty$ *where* $y[t]$ *is the output of the filter and* $x[t]$ *the input at time t.*

The proof can be done just considering that the derivative is the impulse response of the filter that must go to zero in the stable case. For the derivative to go to zero it is necessary and sufficient that the feedback coefficients in the calculation of (9) or the corresponding expressions for a locally recurrent network other than IIR-MLP, give poles inside the unit circle.

The condition $\frac{\partial y[t+p]}{\partial x[t]} \to 0$ if $p \to \infty$ where $y[t]$ is the output (or the *net*) and $x[t]$ an input of a recurrent neuron holds by definition for each neuron in IIR-MLP, activation-output feedback MLNs and AR-MLP in case each neuron exhibits forgetting behaviour. Instead in case of latching behaviour (possible only for output feedback MLN), that derivative does not go to zero and the corresponding linear system is unstable [14]. In this case, the truncation can be too strong an approximation.

It must be stressed that in CRBP each local feedback is taken into account during adaptation with no history truncation for the coefficients of the same neuron, using recursive formulas (6) and (7), instead of non-causal ones as in the BPTT approach.

The algorithm proposed by Back and Tsoi [3] that is the only on-line learning algorithm proposed specifically for the IIR-MLP, can be seen as a particular case of this approximation if a strong truncation of the summation is did: $Q_{l+1} = 0$ for each l. In this way the backpropagation is considering only the instantaneous influence of the IIR filter input to the output (the coefficient $w_{nm(0)}^{(l+1)}$). Hence in the scheme of Fig. 1, the truncated IIR filter should be replaced by a simple multiplication for $w_{11(0)}^{(2)}$. No causalization is needed (being D_l=0 for each l) and the algorithm is very simple. However we shall show that with the inclusion of only few additional memory terms in the backpropagation (Q_{l+1}>0) it is possible to reach much better stability and speed of convergence.

Also the BPS algorithm [13] can be obtained as particular case of CRBP when the architecture restriction that the dynamic units can only be placed in the first layer is given. The CRBP applied to the AR-MLP can be also viewed as a generalization of Mozer's and Leighton-Conrath's work [24,25]. Moreover if all the synapses contain only the MA part ($I_{nm}^{(l)}$=0 for each n,m and l), the architecture reduces to FIR-MLP and this algorithm reduces to the Temporal Back Propagation as in [7,9,21]. Obviously, if all the synaptic filters have no memory ($I_{nm}^{(l)}$=0 and $L_{nm}^{(l)}$=1 for each n,m and l), this algorithm becomes to standard on-line Back Propagation for the MLP.

3. Simulations

Many simulations were performed on IIR-MLP and activation-output feedback MLN while the AR-MLP was not implemented. For comparison purposes, also two traditional neural networks were tested, namely the static MLP with input and possibly output buffer, and the FIR-MLP. The results reported here refer to a problem of identification of non-linear dynamical system: a 16-PAM transmission channel [9].

The pulse shaping circuit transforms the discrete-time symbols stream $a[n]$ into a continuous-time signal $v(t)$ (PAM) by a filter with a raised-cosine shape and roll-off factor α . The signal $v[t]$ is then processed by the High-Power-Amplifier (HPA) which is modelled here by the following input-output relationship:

$$w[t] = \frac{2\, v[t]}{1 + v^2[t]} .$$

The peak power of the input signal $v[t]$ is set to the value of β dB (back-off factor), with β=0 dB being the normalised unit power. The HPA output $w[t]$ is corrupted by an additive white Gaussian noise $z[t]$, producing the final signal $y[t]$ with a given Signal-To-Noise ratio (SNR), see Fig 2. The overall system is clearly dynamic and non-linear.

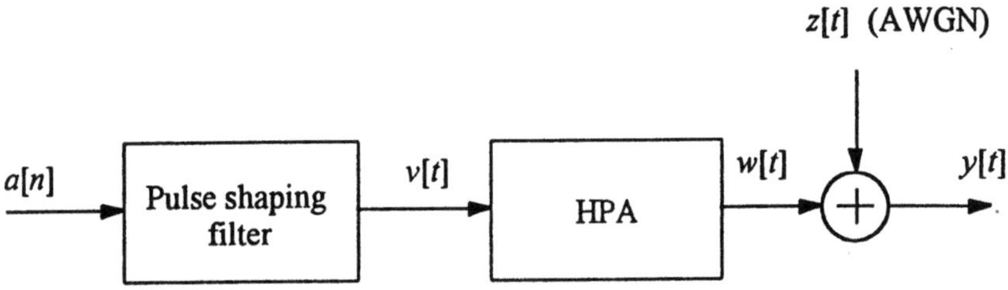

Fig. 2. Block diagram of the PAM transmission channel used in the simulations.

A neural network approach to equalise this system has already been proposed in the technical literature. In our experiment a neural network was used instead to identify a sampled version of the system. For this purpose, $\{a[n]\}$ was chosen to be a random sequence of 512 symbols drawn from a 16-symbols alphabet. The pulse shaping filter had a roll-off factor α=0.3, and the HPA back-off β was set to -2 dB. The noise level was very low: SNR=80 dB.

By using an over-sampling ratio of four at the output with respect to the symbol rate, the sequences $\{a[n]\}$ of 512 symbols and $\{y[t]\}$ of 2048 samples were used as the learning set and again the MSE was computed after all the 512 input symbols (epoch) were presented.

The number of delays for the five architectures (i.e. buffers lengths for the buffered MLPs, MA orders for the FIR-MLP, MA and AR orders for the locally recurrent networks) was chosen in order to obtain the best performance (approximately) for each network, while the total number of free parameter was fixed (40 parameters, bias included).

All the used networks had two layers, three hidden neurons with hyperbolic tangent activation function, and one linear output neuron. Three different learning algorithms were used: standard static backpropagation for buffered MLP, temporal backpropagation for FIR-MLP [7] and the proposed CRBP algorithm for the locally recurrent networks. The results are given in terms of Mean-Square-Error (MSE), expressed in dB, computed on the learning set after each epoch (after all the input-output samples were presented) and averaged over 20 runs, each with a different weights initialization.

First we verified that the locally recurrent MLPs perform much better than the two conventional MLPs in modeling the system and then we compared the new and the previous algorithms.

Fig. 3 shows that CRBP, is much faster, stable and also more accurate than the Back-Tsoi algorithm. A very small truncation parameter of CRBP is required to obtain good performance, while increasing it over a certain, small, range does not change the MSE appreciably.

From Fig. 4 it is evident that the averaged impulse response of the IIR filter in the IIR-MLP network goes to zero so the truncation approximation hypothesis is correct.

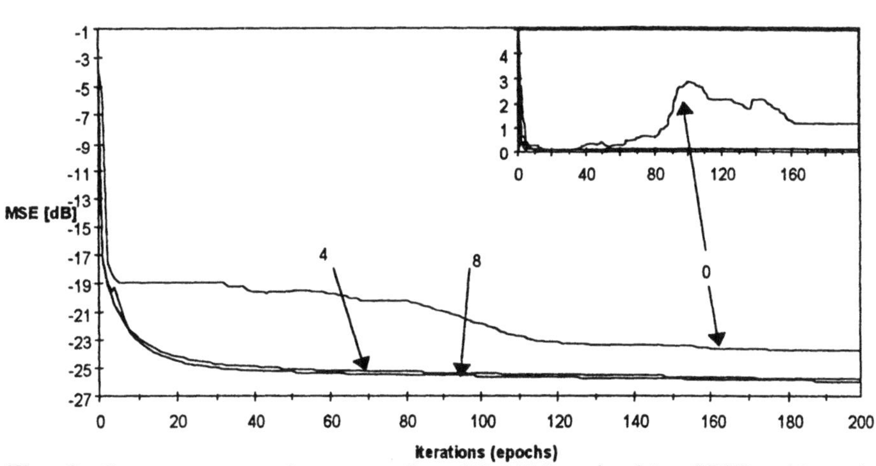

Fig. 3. Convergence performance of an IIR-MLP trained by CRBP with various values of the truncation parameter (Q_2; Q_2=0 gives the Back-Tsoi algorithm) on identifying the 16-PAM transmission system. The MA and AR orders were chosen respectively as 4 and 2 for both the hidden and output layers. Plots are averaged over 20 runs with different weight initializations. Momentum and Delta-Bar-Delta adaptive learning rate have been used. The variance on the 20 runs is shown on the top right.

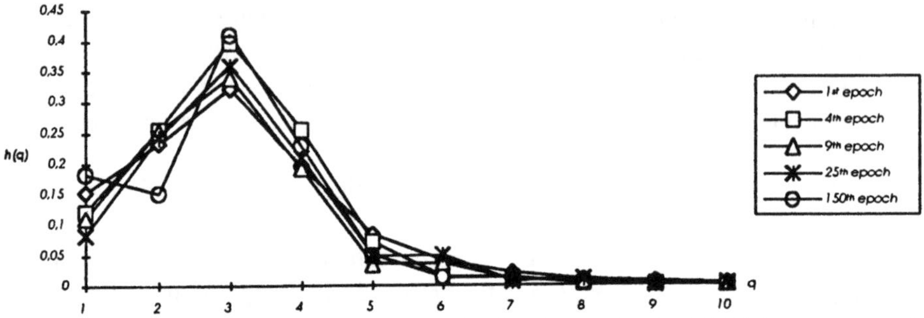

Fig. 4. Averaged Impulse Response of the IIR filters in the Multi Layer network identifying the P.A.M. system by the CRBP algorithm.

4. Conclusions

The increase in computational complexity between the Back-Tsoi algorithm [3] and CRBP is fairly low since, due to the recursion, the truncation parameter (Q_{l+1}) can be chosen quite small. In our simulations, we observed that the ratio between the execution times of CRBP and Back-Tsoi algorithm (one iteration) is less than 1.5, for all the architectures and parameter settings considered in the simulations.

A mathematical evaluation of complexity to compare CRBP with previous methods, in particular Back-Tsoi algorithm, can be carried out computing the number of multiplications and additions for one iteration of the learning phase. In the following, results for CRBP are reported in the significant special case of two layers IIR-MLP with bias and with MA-AR orders depending only on the layer index: M=2, $L_{nm}^{(l)}=L^{(l)}$, $I_{nm}^{(l)}=I^{(l)}$.

The number of multiplications ($M_{backward}$) of the backward phase (one iteration) is:

$$M_{backward} = 2(N_1+N_2)+N_1N_0\left(I^{(1)}+L^{(1)}(I^{(1)}+1)+(I^{(1)})^2\right)+$$

$$+N_2N_1\left(I^{(2)}+L^{(2)}(I^{(2)}+1)+(I^{(2)})^2+Q_2+1+\sum_{p=0}^{Q_2}\min(I^{(2)},p)\right)$$

The number of additions of the backward phase (one iteration) is:

$$A_{backward} = 2N_2+N_1N_0\left(I^{(1)}+L^{(1)}(I^{(1)}+1)+(I^{(1)})^2\right)+$$

$$+N_2N_1\left(I^{(2)}+L^{(2)}(I^{(2)}+1)+(I^{(2)})^2+Q_2+1+\sum_{p=0}^{Q_2}\min(I^{(2)},p)+\right.$$

$$\left.-\begin{cases} Q_2-L^{(2)}+1 & \text{if } Q_2>L^{(2)}-1 \\ 0 & \text{otherwise}\end{cases}\right)$$

The complexity of the Back-Tsoi algorithm is obtained choosing Q_2=0.

They must be added to the number of operations of the forward phase, always done before the backward phase.

The number of multiplications or additions of the forward phase (one iteration) is:

$$M_{forward} = A_{forward} = N_1 N_0 \left(L^{(1)} + I^{(1)}\right) + N_2 N_1 \left(L^{(2)} + I^{(2)}\right) .$$

By these formulas, substituting the configuration parameters of each of the IIR-MLP networks used in the simulations (only some reported here), and with Q_2=4, it is possible to get an averaged ratio $M_{CRBP}/M_{BackTsoi}$=1.20 and $A_{CRBP}/A_{BackTsoi}$=1.17, proving that the increase in complexity is quite small.

About the stability of the CRBP algorithm, in all the simulations we observed that, if the IIR network was initialised with stable synapses, the final result is a stable network as far as a small learning rate is used. A similar behaviour was exhibited by all the other locally recurrent architectures.

In conclusion, this work show that the locally recurrent MLPs can have superior modelling capabilities with respect to more traditional networks, namely MLP with external memory and FIR-MLP (or TDNN) for system identification. We described a general approach to derive on-line algorithms for locally recurrent networks and shown a new learning method, that, includes as special cases, the ones already known in literature. The algorithm derived by us has better stability and higher speed of convergence compared to the previous ones, as expected by the theoretical development and confirmed by simulations. Stability and speed of convergence are very important in real on-line applications, e.g. where time varying systems have to be tracked. The only drawback of the algorithm is a slight increase in complexity, which however can be easily reduced.

References

1. R.J. Williams, J. Peng. An efficient gradient-based algorithm for on line training of recurrent network trajectories. Neural Computation 2: 490-501, 1990.
2. R.J. Williams, D. Zipser. A Learning Algorithm for Continually Running Fully Recurrent Neural Networks. Neural Computation 1: 270-280, 1989.
3. A.D. Back, A.C. Tsoi. FIR and IIR synapses, a new neural network architecture for time series modelling. Neural Computation 3: 375-385, 1991.
4. A.C. Tsoi, A.D. Back. Locally recurrent globally feedforward networks: a critical review of architectures. IEEE Transactions on Neural Networks, vol. 5, no. 2, 229-239, March 1994.
5. P.J. Werbos. Beyond regression: New tools for prediction and analysis in the behavioural sciences. Ph.D. dissertation, Committee on Appl. Math., Harvard Univ., Cambridge, MA, Nov. 1974.
6. P.J. Werbos. Backpropagation through time: what it does and how to do it. Proceedings of IEEE, Special issue on neural networks, vol. 78, No. 10, pp.1550-1560, October 1990.
7. E.A. Wan. Temporal backpropagation for FIR neural networks. Proceedings of the International Joint Conference on Neural Networks, 1:575-580, 1990.
8. A. Waibel, T. Hanazawa, G. Hinton, K. Shikano, K.J. Lang. Phoneme recognition using time-delay neural networks. IEEE Trans. on Acoustic, Speech, and Signal Processing, Vol. 37, No.3, March 1989.
9. N. Benvenuto, F. Piazza, A. Uncini. Comparison of four learning algorithms for multilayer perceptron with FIR synapses. Proceeding of the IEEE International Conference of Neural Networks, 1994.
10. J.J. Shynk. Adaptive IIR filtering. IEEE ASSP Magazine, April 1989.
11. P. Campolucci, F. Piazza, A. Uncini. On-line learning algorithms for neural networks with IIR synapses. Proc. of the IEEE International Conference of Neural Networks, Perth, Nov. 1995.
12. P. Campolucci, A. Uncini, F. Piazza. Causal Back Propagation Through Time for Locally Recurrent Neural Networks. Proc. of the IEEE International Symposium on Circuits and Systems, Atlanta, May 1996.
13. Y.Bengio, R. De Mori, M.Gori. Learning the dynamic of speech with back-propagation for sequences. Pattern Recognition Letters, 13: 375-385, 1992.
14. P.Frasconi, M.Gori, G.Soda. Local Feedback Multilayered Networks. Neural Computation 4: 120-130, 1992.
15. B.A.Pearlmutter. Gradient Calculations for Dynamic Recurrent Neural Networks: A Survey. IEEE Trans. on Neural Networks vol. 6, no. 5, September 1995.
16. B. Srinivasan, U.R. Prasad and N.J. Rao. Backpropagation through Adjoints for the identification of Non linear Dynamic Systems using Recurrent Neural Models. IEEE Trans. on Neural Networks pp. 213-228, March 1994.

17. E.A.Wan, F.Beaufays. Diagrammatic Derivation of Gradient Algorithms for Neural Networks. Neural Computation 8: 182-201, 1996.
18. K.S. Narendra, K. Parthasarathy. Identification and control of dynamical systems using neural networks. IEEE Trans. on Neural Networks, vol. 1, pp.4-27, March 1990.
19. C.-C. Ku, K.Y.Lee. Diagonal Recurrent Neural Networks for Dynamic Systems Control. IEEE Trans. on Neural Networks vol. 6, no. 1, January 1995.
20. F.Beaufays, E.Wan. Relating Real-Time Backpropagation and Backpropagation-Through-Time: An Application of Flow Graph Interreciprocity. Neural Computation 6: 296-306, 1994.
21. A.D.Back, E.Wan, S.Lawrence, A.C.Tsoi. A unifying view of some training algorithms for multilayer perceptrons with FIR filter synapses. Proc. IEEE workshop on Neural Networks for Signal Processing, pp. 146-154, 1994.
22. B.A. Pearlmutter. Two New Learning Procedures for Recurrent Networks. Neural Networks Rev. vol. 3, no. 3, pp. 99-101, 1990.
23. J.L. Elman. Finding Structure in Time. Cognitive Science 14: 179-211, 1990.
24. M.C. Mozer. A Focused Back-propagation Algorithm for Temporal Pattern Recognition. Tech Rep. CRG-TR-88-3, University of Toronto, 1988 and Complex Systems 3: 349-381, 1989.
25. R.R. Leighton and B.C. Conrath. The Autoregressive Backpropagation Algorithm. Proc. International Joint Conference on Neural Networks, pp. 369-377, 1991.
26. L.B. Almeida. A learning rule for asynchronous perceptrons with feedback in combinatorial environment. Proc. International Conference on Neural Networks, vol. 2, pp. 609-618, 1987.
27. R.J. Williams, D. Zipser. Gradient-based learning algorithms for recurrent networks and their computational complexity. In Backpropagation: Theory, Architectures and Applications Y. Chauvin and D.E. Rumelhart, Eds. Hillsdale, NJ: Lawrence Erlbaum Associates, 1994.
28. T. Uchiyama, K. Shimohara, Y. Tokunaga. A modified leaky integrator network for temporal pattern recognition. Proc. of the International Joint Conference on Neural Networks, vol. 1, pp. 469-475, 1989.

SECTION 3

EDUARDO R. CAIANIELLO LECTURE

Employment of a Progressive Learning Neural Network for Identification and Control

Maurizio Cirrincione, Ph.D.

CE.RI.S.E.P.-C.N.R.
CEntro RIcerca Sistemi Elettrici di Potenza
Consiglio Nazionale delle Ricerche

viale delle Scienze, 90128 Palermo, Italy
phone (39) 91-484686, fax (39) 91-485555 ,
E-Mail nimzo@cerisep2.diepa.unipa.it

ABSTRACT

In this paper a direct inverse control scheme is presented, which is based on a clustering neural network, called Progressive Learning Network (PLN) because of its inherent capacity of learning on-line. .

After describing the PLN, the generalised and specialised inverse control schemes are introduced and then a method for using the PLN in this kind of control is shown. In particular a new version of this PLN is developed for the on-line control with specialised learning. This approach can control the whole system without having to use a very rich training set; moreover it is able to adapt itself on-line to new working conditions as it is based on an algorithm capable of varying the number of neurons of the hidden layer in order to learn examples that had not been presented previously or to forget rare situations. Numerical tests then follow to validate the control strategy.

INTRODUCTION

As it is known the use of neural control techniques has proved effective in most situations when it is not always easy to model the controlled system because of, e.g., nonlinearities, uncertainty of parameters, little available information about the controlled system and so on [1]. In particular these neural control techniques have proved most useful because of their capacity to learn through experience, to generalise, to be robust thanks to their inherent parallelism and to adapt themselves to any real-time variations of the controlled system. There are plenty of control architectures based on neural networks and most of them use supervised neural networks [2]. Among these the so-called adaptive inverse control schemes have been investigated [3][4] . As yet the most used architecture of neural networks used for this purpose has been that of the multi-layer perceptron trained with the backpropagation (BPN) algorithm [3][5], which however may present some problems in on-line learning and control. To overcome these problems it is shown here that a Progressive Learning Neural (PLN) network can make an on-line control, based on the above mentioned control scheme, due to its propriety of being able to solve system identification problems of nonlinear systems through a mechanism of progressive learning.

THE PROGRESSIVE LEARNING NETWORK (PLN)

The Progressive Learning Network (PLN) [6][7]works almost as the CPN (Counterpropagation network) but it allows incremental learning. This neural network is made up of three layers of neurons . The input and output layers, consisting of neurons with linear transfer function, have the task of normalising. The hidden layer is made up of competitive neurons and has no predefined dimensions. The number of its neurons is increased or decreased automatically according to the data amount progressively acquired by the neural network and to the required mapping accuracy. The PLN has two operating modes, *learning* and *recalling*, which can be started independently. Moreover there exists a *merging* algorithm aimed at regulating the distribution of the neurons in the hidden layer. The three operating modes are presented in the sequel.

A. Learning algorithm

Let $\mathbf{y} = \mathbf{f}(\mathbf{x})$ be a non-linear vector relationship (from R^m to R^n) to be mapped, from which a continuous flow of samples representing input-output pairs $(\mathbf{x}_i, \mathbf{y}_i)$ is extracted. The network parameters are:

m	dimension of the input layer	ρ_x	input space vigilance threshold
n	dimension of the output layer	ρ_y	output space vigilance threshold
K	dimension of the hidden layer (variable)	η	decay constant
$\mathbf{w}_k$	weight vector connecting the input layer to the k-th neuron of the hidden layer	ε	extinction threshold
$\mathbf{v}_k$	weight vector connecting the k-th neuron of the hidden layer to the output layer	λ	merging factor
s_k	real variable proportional to the number of samples identified by the k-th neuron of the hidden layer		

The parameters ρ_x, ρ_y, η, ε, λ are positive and real. Furthermore $\lambda < 1$ and $\eta < 1$. The number K of neurons of the hidden layer is initially set to zero. The index i stands for the i-th presented sample. The algorithm is as follows:

1) Present the first sample, let K=1 and assign the vectors representing the sample as weights of the first neuron: $\mathbf{w}_1 = \mathbf{x}_1$, $\mathbf{v}_1 = \mathbf{y}_1$, $s_1 = 1$. Let $i = 2$.

2) Present the i-th sample (x_i, y_i) and compute the K Euclidean distances D_k between the vector $\mathbf{x}_i$ and the weights $\mathbf{w}_k$ of the K neurons of the hidden layer.
3) Sort out the D_k's in increasing order and let k = 1.
4) If $D_k > \rho_x$ go to 7.
5) Compute the Euclidean distance H_k between $\mathbf{y}_i$ and $\mathbf{v}_k$ and verify that $H_k < \rho_y$. If the relation is satisfied update the weights of the k-th neuron according to:

$$W_K = W_K + \frac{X_K - W_{K-1}}{S_K + 1} \qquad V_K = V_K + \frac{Y_K - V_{K-1}}{S_K + 1} \qquad S_K = S_K + 1 + \eta$$

and go to 8, otherwise let k = k + 1.
6) If k < K go to 4.
7) Create a new neuron setting:
$K = K + 1$, $\mathbf{w}_K = x_i$, $\mathbf{v}_K = y_i$, $s_K = 1$.
8) For each k of the K neurons update $s_k = s_k - h$. If $s_k < \varepsilon$ delete the k-th neuron.
9) Let i = i + 1 and go to 2.

B. Merging algorithm

The aim of the merging algorithm is the reduction of those neuron pairs that have become too close in the previous phase. Its generic form is as follows:

1) Let i and j two neurons of the hidden layer.
2) Compute the Euclidean distance D_{ij} between the weights $\mathbf{w}_i$ and $\mathbf{w}_j$ of the i-th e j-th neurons.
3) If $D_{ij} > lr_x$ go to 8.
4) Compute the Euclidean distance H_{ij} between the weights $\mathbf{v}_i$ and $\mathbf{v}_j$.
5) If $H_{ij} > lr_y$ go to 8.
6) Update the i-th neuron according to:

$$W_i = W_i + S_i \frac{W_i - W_j}{S_i + S_j} \qquad V_i = V_i + S_i \frac{V_i - V_j}{S_i + S_j}$$

7) Delete the j-th neuron.
8) Choose a new i j pair of neurons and go to 1.

C. Recall algorithm

The recall algorithm is as follows:

1) Present the input vector $\mathbf{x}_i$.
2) Compute the K Euclidean distances D_k between the vector $\mathbf{x}_i$ and the weights $\mathbf{w}_k$ of the K neurons of the hidden layer.
3) Sort out the D_k's in increasing order and select the corresponding first P neurons.

4) Compute the estimated output $\mathbf{y}_i$ by: $y_i = \frac{\sum_{k=1}^{P} \frac{v_k}{D_k}}{\sum_{k=1}^{P} \frac{1}{D_k}}$

D. Comments

The number of neurons of the hidden layer is not to be determined a priori, but adapts automatically to the data presented. It depends on the learning parameters, mainly on the vigilance thresholds. Besides, the incremental learning of the PLN makes it particularly suitable for on-line applications, as in modelling systems with non stationary parameters.

The progressively added neurons of the hidden layer represent the centroids of the clusters in the input ($\mathbf{w}_k$) and output ($\mathbf{v}_k$) space. The vigilance thresholds ρ_x and ρ_y determine the radius of the clusters and therefore the resolution of the obtained mapping. The double threshold permits the separate evaluation of the distances in the input and the output space, increasing the resolution when similar $\mathbf{x}_i$'s map into different $\mathbf{y}_i$'s. The insertion of new samples into a cluster causes the centroid to displace inside its vector space. This displacement decreases as the number of samples classified into the cluster, measured by s_k, increases. If the decay constant η is set to a non zero value the s_k parameter of all non winning neurons is decreased of η on the presentation of a new sample. Therefore, under the assumption of a continuous flow of data to learn, the "stiffness " of the rarely winning neurons decreases, whereas the "stiffness" of the other neurons increases or reaches an equilibrium point. The neurons with a low s_k value are more easily displaced by new samples. They can be even deleted when s_k becomes less than the extinction threshold ε. The PLN tends to distribute its neurons uniformly, forming a regular grid whose meshes have a width which is roughly twice the vigilance threshold.

INVERSE CONTROL

The main idea of the inverse control is that of reproducing the inverse S^{-1} of the controlled system so as to eliminate the dynamics of the system S and thus to have the output u follow the input u_d closely when given the command y. (Fig. 1). The controller is usually adaptive and adjusts itself itself so as to optimise the performance of the overall system [4].

This method of control is generally called *direct inverse control* as it does not imply any identification of the controlled system.

However it is clear that such a method has some problems, such as those related to stability, casuality, invertibility, persistent excitation, parameter uncertainity, etc. Usually the direct inverse control follows two paths in order to learn the inverse of the system: the generalised learning and the specialised learning [5]. The control strategy based only on the generalised learning is called here generalised inverse control whilst that based on the specialised learning is called specialised inverse control.

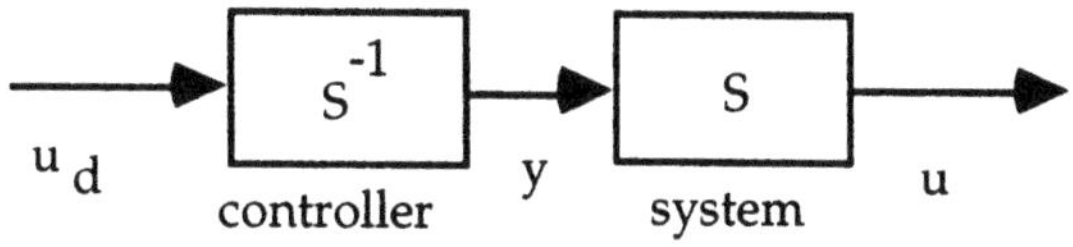

Fig. 1 Scheme of the inverse control

GENERALISED INVERSE CONTROL

The generalised inverse control comprises two phases. The *learning phase* , where the neural network identifies S^{-1} (fig 2) through the error ε between the input u to S and the output u' of the neural network, and the *productive phase* , where the trained neural network is used as a controller cascaded with the controlled system as shown in fig.2. It is clear that the neural network must be supplied with a very informative training set (persistent excitation principle) for the identification of the inverse system.

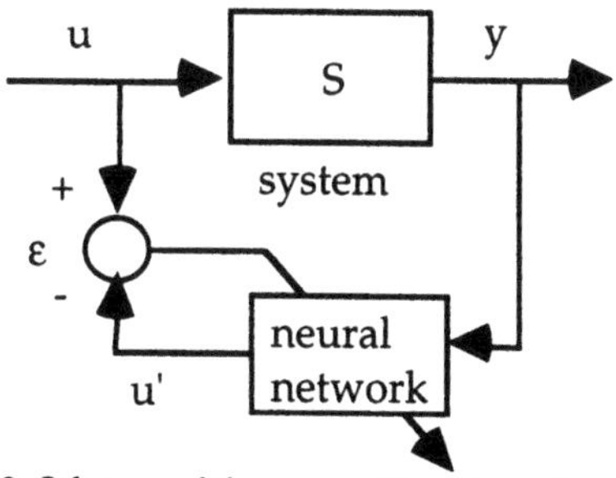

Fig. 2 Scheme of the generalised learning

However there exist some disadvantages, as this control strategy is not target oriented: choosing different u inputs does not at all assure that y outputs be in the domain of interest. This problem is tightly connected with that of persistent excitation. Moreover the controller is not able to follow any variation of the system or of the environment.

SPECIALISED INVERSE CONTROL

The *specialised inverse control* has the fundamental characteristic to carry out both the productive phase and the learning phase. The training of the neural controller happens in real time so that the control law adapts itself to variable conditions.

In fig. 3 the output error e_y between the actual output and the desired output is used to compute the variation of the control action performed by the neural controller with the aim of obtaining the best response of the system (fig.3). This computation is made by passing from the output error to the input error e_u (represented in the figure with the arrow of the signal through the system) and this requires the computation of the inverse of the Jacobian of the system.

The specialised learning allows the training of the neural network in the areas of y that are very interesting for the succes of the control; furthermore it is able to compute locally the inverse of the controlled system even if it is not globally one-to-one [3]. Finally this architecture is able to adapt itself to the possible variations of the input signal or to the variation of the parameters of the controlled system. Passing from the output error of the system to the input error (represented in the figure with the arrow of the signal through the system) requires, in every instant, the computation of the inverse of the Jacobian of the system

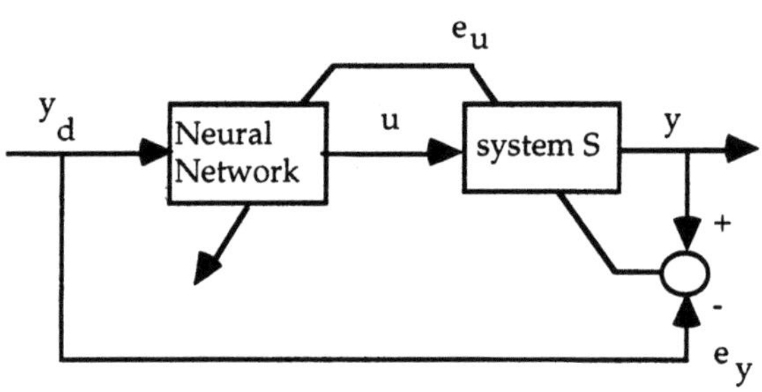

fig.3.Scheme of specialised learning

In particular when using the PLN algorithm the input to the neural network has been composed of

$$y_d(k+1) \qquad y_d(k) \qquad y_d(k-1)$$

$$y_d(k+1) - y_d(k) \qquad y_d(k) - y_d(k-1) \qquad y_d(k+1) - y_d(k-1)$$

The difference inputs are important as the PLN classifies the input data according to the Euclidean distance computed from the input vector and the weight vector **w**; therefore the sign of the difference supplies useful information for discriminating an acceleration phase from a deceleration one when there are similar numerical values.

The specialised phase of control is then as follows:

1)The PLN is trained with generalised learning (PLN as decsribed above)

2)The neuro-controller is put in cascade to the controlled system

3)$\omega_d(k+1)$ is given at the k-th instant,

4)$\Delta\omega(k) = E_\omega(k) = \omega_d(k)-\omega_s(k)$ is checked where $\omega_s(k)$ is the output of the system at the k-th instant due to the command u(k-1) and is compared with an accuracy threshold θ_ω.

5) If $\Delta\omega > \theta_\omega$, then the $\Delta\omega$ correction of the controller weights is backpropagated through the Jacobian J

$$\mathbf{\Delta u}(k-1) = E_v = \Delta\omega \, J^{-1}$$

where $\Delta \mathbf{u}(k-1) = E_V$ represents the error on the controller command given. The error $\Delta \mathbf{u}(k-1)$ on the command is the error that must be summed to $\mathbf{u}(k-1)$ to get an output $\omega(k)$ equal to the desired speed $\omega_d(k-1)$

6) $\mathbf{u}_{new}(k-1)= \mathbf{u}_{old}(k-1)+\Delta \mathbf{u}(k-1)$ is computed

7) The command obtained in the previous step is given to the PLN so as to be associated to the triplet $\omega(k)$ $\omega(k-1)$ $\omega(k-2)$ (Modified PLN, see below)

8) k=k+1 and go to step 3

For the *specialised learning* a **slightly modified PLN algorithm** has been used, as shown in the following paragraph. In this last algorithm the parameters are the same as those described in the above PLN , with the adding of the parameter K_X that represents the maximum number of neurons.

The index i stands for the i-th presented sample. K is initially set to zero. The algorithm is as follows:

1) Present the first sample, let K=1 and assign the vectors representing the sample as weights of the first neuron: $\mathbf{w}_1 = \mathbf{x}_1$, $\mathbf{v}_1 = \mathbf{y}_1$, $s_1 = 1$. Let $i = 2$.

2) Present the i-th sample $(\mathbf{x}_i, \mathbf{y}_i)$ and compute the K Euclidean distances D_k between the vector $\mathbf{x}_i$ and the weights $\mathbf{w}_k$ of the K neurons of the hidden layer.

3) Determine the kth neuron with minimum distance D_k (k=1...K) (winning neuron)

4) If $D_k > \rho_X$ go to 6.

5) Modify the weights and th conscience of the k-th neuron according to the following realtionships:

$$V_k = V_k + \frac{Y_k - V_k}{s_k + 1} \qquad s_k = s_k + 1$$

(The first of these equations makes the output weights of the k-th neuron approach the desired output in correspondance with input vector $\mathbf{x}_i$; the greater this getting closer, the less the winning neuron's conscience: thus it is inversely proportional to the frequency it wins.The 2nd equation updates the s_k factor, which is proportional to the number of times the neuron wins)

Go to 7

6) If $k < Kx$ create a new neuron

K=K+1;

or else create a new neuron instead of that which has won the fewest times. Let j be its index $\mathbf{w}_j = \mathbf{x}_i$, $\mathbf{v}_j = \mathbf{y}_i$, $s_j = 1$.

7) For each k of the K neurons, except the winning one, update $s_k = s_k - \eta$

8) go to 2.

The recall algorithm is the same as before, while no merging phase is present.

This modified algorithm has been necessary not to modify the initial set of weights of the neural network as produced by the generalised phase, otherwise the newly encountered examples could shift the weights of the neurons in a such a fashion that their distribution is not good any longer. For this reason the cumbersome merging phase has been omitted. Thus the initial "knowledge base" remains constant. On the contrary the **v** output weights do vary so as to get tuned to the new situations. For those situations that are quite far from those already learnt, new neurons are created. Thus the population of neurons increase in the specialised phase, as expected. An upper limit has been selected to avoid too many neurons: when this limit is reached and a new neuron is to be created, this is created in the place of that neuron whose conscience is the lowest, which means it has been used few times. This modified algorithm has not been used in the generalised phase as this phase aims at a global knowledge without any specific portion of the domain of interest; therefore fewer neurons suffice.

NUMERICAL RESULTS

The whole control system has been tested using the discrete model of a dc motor with separate excitation. In particular in the controlled system taken into account it has been assumed that the dc motor can be described by the following function

$$\omega(k+1) = F(\omega(k), \omega(k-1), v(k)) \qquad (1)$$

where v(k)= armature voltage [V] and ω(k)= angular speed [rad/s] at the k-th instant. This function is generally nonlinear. In [2] it is shown that (1) for such a system is invertible. The inverse function is

$$v(k) = G(\omega(k+1), \omega(k), \omega(k-1)) \qquad (2)$$

Based on (2) a neural network has been trained to learn this function. Therefore this network has 3 inputs and one output. However the function has been assumed a priori unknown and the task of the neural network is then that to associate the corresponding value of the command of armature voltage to every speed triplet.

For the simulations a dc motor of 1hp (746 W) has been considered with rated speed of 500 rounds/min (52.3 rad/s) and rated voltage of 240 V [2]. The nominal torque is then 746/52.3 = 14.3 Nm. A T sampling time of 50 ms has been used. The computing environments MATLAB® ver. 4.1 and SIMULINK® by MathWorks Inc. have been employed.

In fig. 4 the input voltage to the motor is shown during the generalised learning phase. This voltage has been applied in one iteration only. Of course its waveform should comply with the persistent excitation principle, earlier recalled. The motor has been forced to move with null load torque. The corresponding rotation speed has been recorded and then used for the generalised learning phase. Once finished this phase, a sinusoidal input reference speed has been given and the corresponding time response has been recorded (production phase of the generalised control), always considering a null torque load. In fig. 5 the response of the neural controlled system is drawn under these conditions; the bold line is the graph of the desired speed (it is a stairs function because of the sampling), while the thin line is the graph of the actual speed. The response would have been more correct, if more learning iterations had been carried out, but, as previously stated, in this phase an approximate control of the system is sufficient. The parameters adopted by the neural network in this generalised phase were : m=6; n =1; K =215; ρ_x = 0.018 ρ_y= 0.018; η=0.01; ε=0.001; λ=0.4; P=2. The choice of these parameters has been made heuristically.

After this phase the specialised learning phase has been started using the modified PLN algorithm. In this last case the heuristically chosen parameters have been the same as those shown earlier with K_x = 1500 and P=1.

The following figures show the operation of the electrical drive with different several load torques (C_r) and with different desired speed functions. As a first example a sawtooth waveform has been given with a load torque C_r= 0.004ω^2 [Nm].

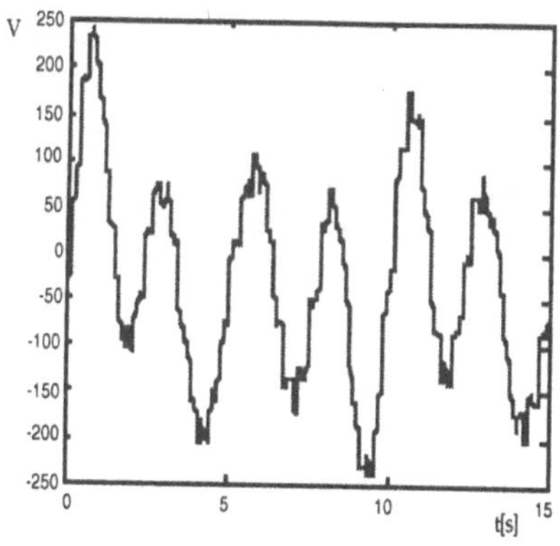

Fig. 4 Voltage supplied for the generalised learning phase

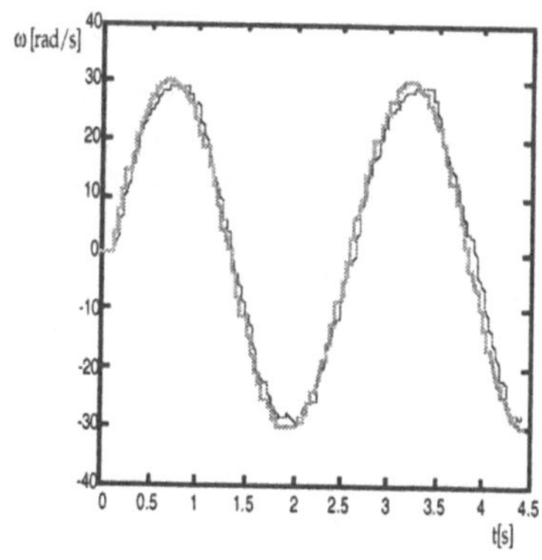

Fig.5 System response after generalised learning

The PLN network, as shown in fig. 6, settles quickly in this new load situation. Afterwards, under the same load torque, the function in fig. 7 has been given. In this case the network has come up against some difficulties to get used to this situation, but on the whole its performance has proved satisfactory at about 8s, as compared to that shown before 6s, thus showing a good adaptibility. It is necessary to remember that the PLN is faced with new situations which it has never encountered before. The number of neurons has increased up to 800 neurons.

Afterwards the control system has been given a sinusoidal waveform with a load torque of about 10 Nm (fig. 8). Also in this case the network has needed some iterations before adapting itself.

One has not to be taken aback by this great number of neurons, since the algorithm computation is not cumbersome. In particular the sorting of the algorithm can be substituted by the research of the minimum, since P=1. Obviously if P is greater, optimised sorting techniques can be used.

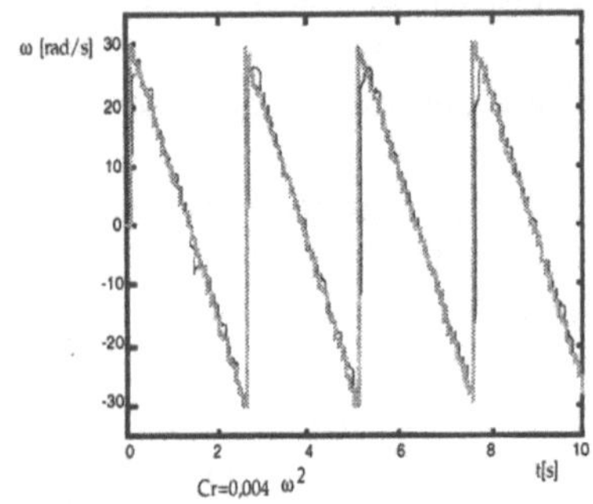

Fig..6 Performance of the system with a sawtooth input

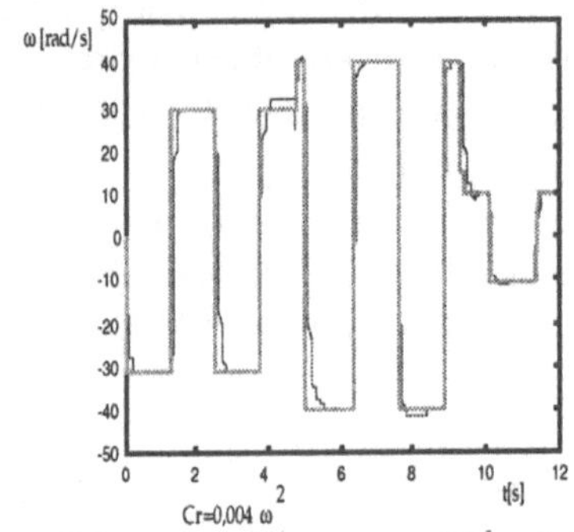

Fig..7 Sytem performance with a stairs waveform

Finally a severer load torque of $C_r = 0.02\omega^2$ Nm (in this last case the maximum torque is 18 Nm with 30 rad/s, i.e. greater than the rated torque; this means that such a torque cannot be supplied, but this case has only a theoretical meaning) has been given (fig. 9). In the second period the overshooting has already been eliminated. This overshooting is due to a reminiscence of different loads. In all simulations the maximum error was 5% of the rated speed, while the maximum root mean square error was 1.8 %.

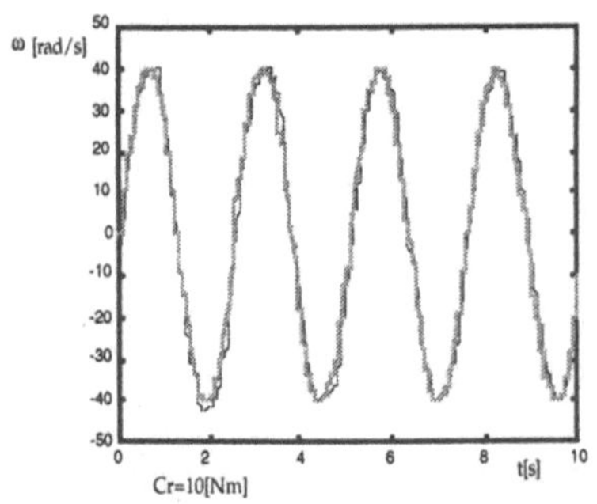

Fig.8 System performance with sinusoidal waveform

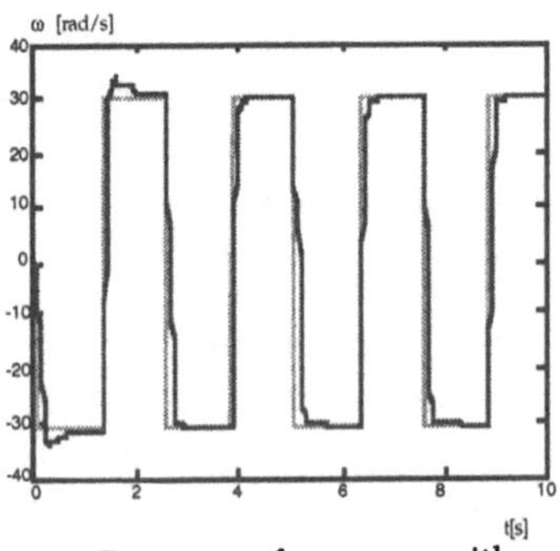

Fig. 9 Driver performance with $C_r = 0.02\omega^2$ Nm and square waveform

From all of these numerical tests it can be noticed that the sytem response is accurate also with load variations. The controller then adapts itself modifying its behaviour. Obviously sudden variations of the controlled system require some time for the control action to settle down.

CONCLUSIONS

In this work the utility of the PLN for control purposes has been analysed with particular reference to on-line inverse control. The on-line adaptability of the PLN permits a not very informative training pattern during the pre-phase of inverse identification carried out by the generalised learning. However the initial knowledge supplied by the generalised phase is necessary for stability problems and permits a quick tuning in the interest region of the reference. The specialised control using a PLN is in particular effective for the on-line learning of situations not yet known in spite of nonlinearities. Moreover it permits a robust control as the neurons which can fail are substituted for by newly born neurons. The specialised learning, as it acts locally, frees from the necessity to assume that the function is invertible, which is necessary for the generalised learning. Finally the fact that clustering techniques are used to classify inputs, permits to have an equiprobable distribution of samples so that rare situations can be accounted for. This is not the case for backpropagation neural networks, whose learning is heavily influenced by the probability distribution of the learning set.

REFERENCES

[1] Miller, Sutton,Werbos editors, *Neural networks for Control,* , MIT Press, Cambridge MA, 1992

[2] M. Cirrincione, *Diagnostica e controllo degli azionamenti elettrici con reti neurali* , Ph. D. Thesis, Palermo 1996.

[3] Sørensen O.: *Neural Networks in Control Applications* Ph.D Thesis, Aalborg University, Dept. Control Engineering , 1994

[4] Widrow B., Walach E.: *Adaptive Inverse Control,* Prentice-Hall, Englewood Cliffs, N.J., 1996

[5] Renders Jean-Michel:*Algorithmes génétiques et réseaux de neurones* Hermès Paris 1995

[6] Cirrincione G., Cirrincione M. Piglione F.: *A Clustering Neural Network for On-Line Learning in Power System.,* Neurap '95, Marseille, 13-15 December 1995

[7] G. Cirrincione, M.Cirrincione,F.Piglione:*Applicazione di una rete neurale ad apprendimento progressivo allo studio dei sistemi di potenza,* 96° riunione annuale AEI, Roma, 25-27 September 1995

ACKNOWLEDGMENTS

This work was supported by C.N.R. (Italian Research Council) and M.U.R.S.T. (Italian Ministry of University and Scientific and Tecnological Research

SECTION 4

MATHEMATICAL MODELS

What Size Needs Testing?

B. Apolloni
Department of Computer Science - University of Milan
Via Comelico 39-41, 20135 Milan, Italy

ABSTRACT. In spite of the general wisdom that much more examples need to test than to train a neural network, vice-versa we show that testing the approximation capability of a neural network generally demands smaller sample size than training it.
We move in an extended PAC learning framework and use some recent results in terms of sentry functions of a concept class to statistically proof our claims.

1.Introduction

PAC learning theory [6, 9] gives exact conditions for having that, given:

- a class G of functions g: R->R
- a loss function $\mathtt{l}(y,g(x))$
- a distribution law P on R and a sample $\Sigma=\{(X_1, g(X_1)),\ldots\ldots,(X_m, g(X_m))$
- a pair of real numbers ε and δ close to zero,

a function h is computable such that

$$P^{(m)}(E[\mathtt{l}(h(X,\Sigma),g(X))] \leq \varepsilon) \geq 1 - \delta,$$

where $P^{(m)}$ is the probability measure in the product space R^m.
One of these conditions concerns the sample complexity of the inference problem, and generally consists of upper and lower bounds on the size m of Σ. These bounds, that come from a clever and sophisticate theory [10], are however only seldom used by those people which want to learn h through a neural network. The actual size of the training set is of one or more order less than the size of Σ requested by the sample complexity, where this discrepancy can be attributed to the following inner limitations of the above theory:
1. the bounds on m constitute worst case results
2. the theory is not yet tailored to take into account the peculiarities of the neural network and of the learning algorithm.
Thus, we generally disregard the bounds, use a short training set to train the neural network and try to check the adequacy of this set by testing the inferred h on a new set of example (the test set). If the network (i.e. h) performs on the test nearby as well as on the training set we are satisfied and declare the learning task successful. To be safe, we are used to employ very large test sets mainly because their processing is relatively inexpensive and, of corse, more is better than less.
What news can testing gives us that we did not yet know from training? We answer this question in sect. 2 as it concerns boolean functions, after the question is framed in the sentry function theory [2]. In sect. 3 we extend our results to real functions. Our conclusion is that it is generally wasteful to use a test set larger than a training set, where a suitable ratio between the two sizes can be computed if some complexity parameters of the learning task are available.

2. Degrees of freedom in learning and checking a boolean function.

Let us start with the distribution free case and come us to consistent statistics.

Definition 1: Given a set **X** , a *class of formulas* or *class of concepts* **C** is a set of boolean functions c on **X**. These boolean functions are also called concepts c. By abuse of notation, we shall not make any distinction between c and its support, i.e. the set of elements x such that $c(x_i) = 1$. Therefore **C** can be also view as a set of subsets of **X**.

Willing infer an approximation h for c, let call it hypothesis, we distinguish inside the sample Σ a set of points which constitute the pivots around which to draw that hypothesis or other hypotheses equivalent in a proper metric space. Actually, they act as sentinels that forbid the expansion of c+h (symmetric difference between c and h). Thus, in figure 1 x_1 and x_2 outside c are sufficient to prevent that a larger circle non containing them includes c.
The remaining sampled points constitute then rear-guard which, if numerous and fairly scattered on **X**, give confidence that each pivot has been considered. Linking pivots, confidence and sample size allows us to bind the learning sample complexity.

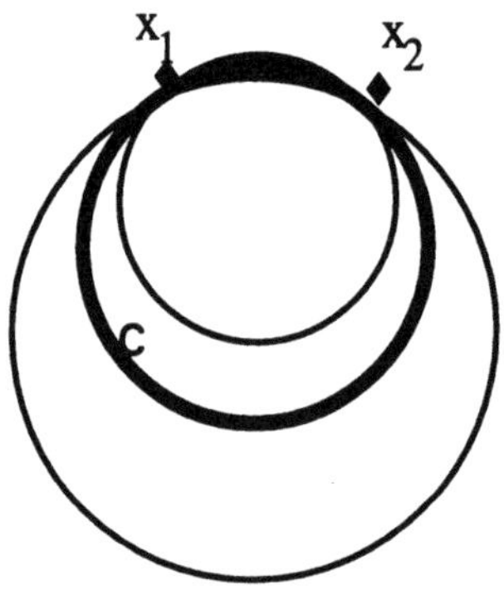

Figure 1 The two points x_1, x_2 are sufficient to sentinel c

Definition 2: Given a concept class **C** on **X**, an *outer sentry* function on **C** is a total function $\mathbf{S} : \mathbf{C} \cup \{\varnothing,\mathbf{X}\} \longmapsto 2^{\mathbf{X}}$ satisfying the following conditions:

(1) the elements of **S**(c) are outside c, i.e.: $c \cap \mathbf{S}(c) = \varnothing$.

(2) if $c_1, c_2 \in \mathbf{C}$, $c_2 \not\subseteq c_1$ and $c_1 \cup \mathbf{S}(c_1) \subseteq c_2 \cup \mathbf{S}(c_2)$ then $c_2 \cap \mathbf{S}(c_1) \neq \varnothing$.

(3) no $\mathbf{S}' \neq \mathbf{S}$ exists satisfying (1) and (2) and having the property that $\mathbf{S}'(c) \subseteq \mathbf{S}(c)$ for every c.

(4) whenever c_1 and c_2 are such that $c_1 \subset c_2 \cup \mathbf{S}(c_2)$ and $c_2 \cap \mathbf{S}(c_1) = \varnothing$, then the restriction of **S** to $\mathbf{C}-\{c_2\}$ is a sentry function on $\mathbf{C}-\{c_2\}$.

Terminology: $c^+ = c \cup \mathbf{S}(c)$. **S**(c) is the *outer frontier* upon **S** of c , their elements are called sentry points. c_2 is *sentinelled* by $\mathbf{S}(c_1)$ iff $c_2 \cap \mathbf{S}(c_1) \neq \varnothing$.

Remark 1: A frontier does not fully identify the sentinelled concept. A given concept class might admit more than one outer sentry function. Condition (4) prevent us from building sentry functions which are *unnatural*, where some sentry points of c_1 have the sole role of artificially increasing the elements of c_1^+ in order to prevent it from being included in another c_2. The mentioned conditions state that this role can be considered only a side effect of points which are primarily involved in sentinelling some formula.

Example 1:A possible frontier of an item c of the concept class **C** of of circle is shown in Fig. 1.

Example 2: Let us consider the class $\mathbf{B}_2$ of boolean forms on $\{0,1\}^2$:

$\mathbf{C}=\{0,1,x_1,x_2,x_1x_2\}$.

The related supports are:

	00	01	10	11
$c_1=0$	-	-	-	-
$c_2=x_1x_2$	-	-	-	+
$c_3=x_1$	-	-	+	+
$c_4=x_2$	-	+	-	+
$c_5=1$	+	+	+	+

Possible outer sentry function for **C** is:

$\mathbf{S}(c_1)=\{11\}$; $\mathbf{S}(c_2)=\{01,10\}$, $\mathbf{S}(c_3)=\{01\}$,$\mathbf{S}(c_4)=\{10\}$,$\mathbf{S}(c_5)=\varnothing$

Definition 3: We call *outer detail* $D_{\mathbf{C}}$ of a concept class **C** the maximum of the cardinalities of the frontiers of its concepts with respect to all possible sentry functions. In symbols, $D_{\mathbf{C}}=\max_{\mathbf{S},c}\#\mathbf{S}(c)$

Meaning by $d_{VC}(\mathbf{C})$ the Vapnik Chervonenkis dimension [10] of **C**, it holds:

Theorem 1[2] : For any concept class **C** , concept $c\in\mathbf{C}$, and sentry function **S**, the set $\mathbf{S}(c)$ is shattered by $\mathbf{C}\cup\{\varnothing,\mathbf{X}\}$. Thus: $D_{\mathbf{C}}\leq d_{VC}(\mathbf{C})+1$

Definition 4 – Given a probability measure P on **X** and a concept c, we denote by $\underline{X}^c{}_m$ a sampling which supplies *labelled sample* $\mathbf{X}^c{}_m$ consisting of m independent random pair $X_1,c(X_1)$, $X_2,c(X_2)$,..., X_m ,$c(X_m)$, and we call *example of size m* any specification $\mathbf{x}^c{}_m$ generated by $\underline{X}^c{}_m$. By a hypothesis H we mean any statistics on $\mathbf{X}^c{}_m$ which defines a random subset of **X**. For any given $\mathbf{x}^c{}_m$ the value h of H is said to be *consistent with* $\mathbf{x}^c{}_m$ if for every x_i, i=1,...,m, we have $c(x_i)=h(x_i)$. We denote by $\mathbf{H}\div c$ the set $\{(h\div c|h\in\mathbf{H})\}$, remember that $d_{VC}(\mathbf{C}\div c)=d_{VC}(\mathbf{C})$, and define $D_{\mathbf{H},\mathbf{C}}=\sup_c\{D_{\mathbf{H}\div c}\}$.

Definition 5 – Given a concept class **C** on **X**, by a *learning algorithm* we mean a function $\mathbf{A}$: $\{\mathbf{x}^c{}_*\}\longmapsto\{h\}$ such that: for every $0<\delta,\varepsilon<1$ there is an integer $m°>0$ such that for every labelled sampling $\underline{X}^c{}_m$ (i.e. every probability measure P on **X** and $c\in\mathbf{C}$) with $m\geq m°$, meaning $H=\mathbf{A}(\mathbf{X}^c{}_m)$, the probability $P_{error}=P(c(X)\neq H(X))$ is bounded by the probabilistical inequality:

$$P^{(m)}(P_{error}\leq\varepsilon)\geq 1-\delta.$$

If such a function exists, the class **C** is said to be *learnable*, ε and δ are called *accuracy parameters* of the learning algorithm, and the restriction of $\mathbf{A}$ to the set $\{(\mathbf{x}^c_m | m \geq m^\circ)\}$ is said to be a learning algorithm with accuracy parameters ε and δ for **C** .

The following results come by considering that the class $\{\mathbf{H} \div c\}$ of symmetric differences between the goal concepts c and the consistent hypotheses h's is sentinelled by substes of the labelled sample $\mathbf{X}^c_m$.
The results refer to the subfamily of *well-behaved* concept classes. This is a fine additional measurability property of a class **C** introduced by Shai Ben-David (see [5]). As a matter of fact almost all concept classes of concrete interest enjoy this property.

Lemma 1 (Basic Lemma) [2] Assume we are given:

— a set **X** and its probability measure P,

— a well behaved concept class **C** with $D_{\mathbf{C},\mathbf{C}} = \mu$,

— a labelled sampling $\underline{\mathbf{X}}^c_m$,

— a function $\mathbf{A}$: $\{\mathbf{x}^c_m\} \longmapsto \mathbf{C}$,

Consider the family of random sets $\{H_c = \mathbf{A}(\mathbf{X}^c_m),\}$ with c varying in **C**.

For a given c, let us denote by U_c the random variable given by the probability measure of $c \div H_c$.

Let $$I_\alpha(\mu, m-\mu+1) = 1 - \sum_{i=0}^{\mu-1} \binom{m}{i} \alpha^i (1-\alpha)^{m-i}.$$

Then, for each c in **C** and $0<\alpha<1$ $\qquad P^{(m)}(U_c \leq \alpha) \geq I_\alpha(\mu, m-\mu+1)$ (1)

Proof (sketch): Few technicalities apart (see the original proof for these details), by Definition 2, the event: " $U_c \leq \alpha$" coincides with the event: "there exists a subset B_α of **X** of measure α which contains the outer frontier of $c \div h$ and $c \div h$ itself", being $h = \mathbf{A}(\mathbf{x}^c_m)$, and this event is implied by the event " the number of points of $\mathbf{x}^c_m$ falling inside B_α is greater then the cardinality of the frontier of $c \div h$. Then, calling $U_c^+ = P(c \div H_c) + P(\mathbf{S}(c \div H_c))$, and denoting by small u the analogous probabilities when $\mathbf{X}^c_m$ is substituted by $\mathbf{x}^c_m$ and by n_α the number of those from among the sampled points which fall in B_α, N_α the analogous dealing with sample points:

a. $(u_c^+ \leq \alpha) \Leftrightarrow (c \div h_c \cup \mathbf{S}(c \div h_c) \subseteq B_\alpha) \Leftarrow (\mathbf{S}(c \div h_c) \subseteq B_{\alpha}") \Leftarrow (n_{\alpha}" \geq \#\mathbf{S}(c \div h_c))$
(2)

b. $P^{(m)}(U_c \leq \alpha) \geq P^{(m)}(N_\alpha \geq \#\mathbf{S}(c \div H_c)) \geq P^{(m)}(N_\alpha \geq \mu)$. $\square$

This lemma gives rise to the following theorem:

Theorem 2 [2] Given a well-behaved concept class **C** on **X** with $D_{\mathbf{C},\mathbf{C}} = \mu$ and a labelled sampling $\underline{\mathbf{X}}^c_m$, for $0 < \varepsilon, \delta < 1/2$, in case $m \geq \max \{ 2/\varepsilon \log(1/\delta), 5.5(\mu-$

1)/ε } any function $\mathfrak{A}$: $\{x^c{}_m\} \longmapsto C$ outputting consistent hypotheses is a learning algorithm with accuracy parameters ε and δ for **G**.
For any concept class **C** on **X** , with $d_{VC}(\mathbf{C}) \geq 17$, and any labelled sampling $\underline{X}^c{}_m$, if the probability measure P on **X** is unknown, the ratio ρ between maximum and minimum numbers of examples needed to learn **C** with accuracy parameters $0<\varepsilon<1/8$, $0<\delta<1/100$ is bounded by a constant.

Thus, for a training set $\mathbf{X}^c{}_m$, the actual degrees of freedom of H which guarantee the learning accuracy are around m- $D_{\mathbf{H}\div c}$, since the sentry points of c are sacrificed to bind c÷h. Stated in other words, h is consistent with the sentry points by construction and with the remaining sampled points by chance.

Fact 1: Once fixed h, if we check h on anther sample of size n, now the degree of freedom are exactly n. Namely, if h is consistent with the whole test set, then:

$$P^{(n)}(U_c \leq \alpha) \geq I_\alpha(1,n) \qquad (3)$$

Inequality (3) has the following operational meaning. Actually, in the lack of $D_{\mathbf{C},\mathbf{C}}$ the accuracy parameters ε and δ have a fuzzy more than a probabilistic meaning to the learner. For sample size large enough – so that for instance $I_\varepsilon(1,m) = 1-\delta$, with ε and δ low enough – if the learning algorithm produces a hypothesis h consistent with the sample we can count ourselves satisfied. The only doubt is that the actual degree of freedom are much lower than m or a non fair sample was drawn, so that our perception " zero errors over m" is misleading. But, if we test our hypotheses on m new example and account again zero errors, now the degrees of freedom are exactly m and we are confirmed on our perception. More formally, we get less than 1- $I_\varepsilon(1,m)$ the probability of assuming the measure of the symmetric difference c÷h ≤ε when this assumption is false. Said in other terms, (0,ε) is the confidence interval for the above measure at confidence level $I_\varepsilon(1,m)$.
Note that it is an excessive $D_{\mathbf{C},\mathbf{C}}$ at the basis of the well known overfitting phenomena.
Vice-versa, if our hypothesis is based on a poor sample we can not expect any improvement from testing.
This is the core of our claim.

Claim1: For a well-behaved concept class **C** on **X** and any - *known or unknown* - accuracy target (ε, δ) the ratio r between the cardinality n of the test set and m of the training set is at most 1.
In particular, in the simplifying assumption that the cardinality of the sentry sets equals $D_{\mathbf{C},\mathbf{C}}$ for every symmetric difference and sentry function, if the probability

measure P on **X** is unknown, then, for $D_{\mathbf{C},\mathbf{C}} = \mu$, $r \geq \frac{1}{1+\frac{\mu}{n}}$.

Proof: It is just an elementary algebra coming from imposing $P^{(m)}(U_c \leq \alpha)$ in (1) greater than $P^{(n)}(U_c \leq \alpha)$ in (3). □

Many variants can be discussed in different directions that leave conclusions essentially unchanged:

i. we have already perception of the learning task complexity, linked for instance to the complexity of the involved neural architecture [5], and increase m thereby. In this case disquisitions on testing and test set size [4,8] are needless.

ii. we use a special learning algorithm or are faced by a special distribution law. In this case, some sentinels can be spared, since some subset of the frontier of c is sufficient to prevent tangible enlargement of c÷h. Therefore the difference between sample size and number of degrees of freedom is lower than in the distribution free case.

Example 3: Let **X** be real plane, **C** the class of rectangles with edges parallel to the coordinate axes containing their origin, and P different from zero only in the first quadrant. It is easy to check that $D_{\mathbf{C},\mathbf{C}} = 4$, but we need at most 2 points to really bind, for this P, the symmetric differences.

iii. as usual in neural networks, we are satisfied with having only almost consistent hypotheses. Now, with reference to the Basic Lemma the key event is that B_α contains both the sentinels of $c \div H_c$ and the points which are mislabelled by h, necessarily falling in $c \div H_c$. Thus, denoting by ν the number of these points, the starting link in (2) is $(n_\alpha\text{"}\geq \#\mathbf{S}(c \div h_c)+\nu)$. Therefore, to obtain the degrees of freedom, also the number of mislabelled points is subtracted from the sample size.

iv. we decide of the learning success on the basis of number of testing errors (not necessarily equal to zero). This case can be solved in the same way as the previous one, since the same reasoning holds also for the testing set. Therefore, the number of degrees of freedom is obtained by subtracting the number of mislabelled points from the sample size.

v. we are interested to other accuracy parameters, different from probabilities ε and δ. In most cases it is just a matter of different error representations where the degrees of freedom do not depend from these representations.

3. Extensions to real functions.

The extension of PAC learning model to real functions did not have, after some base results (see for instance [7]), the same attention of the scientist community as in the case of boolean functions. Actually regression theory is so reach that the learning approach generally appears as needless as complex.
However, we will extend our sentry function approach to these functions just to argue about our main question.

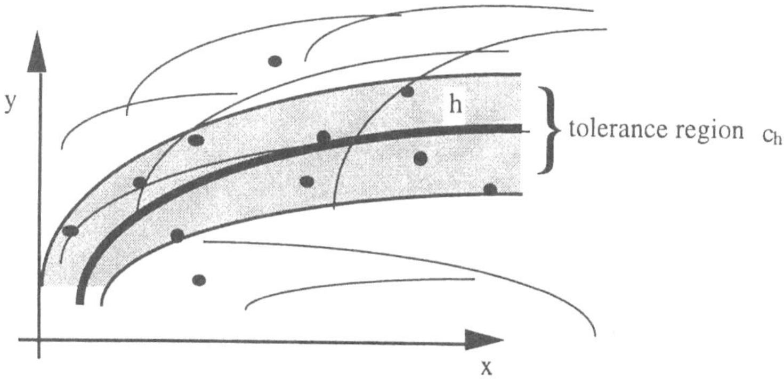

Figure 2. From among the family **F** of functions the learning algorithm selects a hypothesis h (bold line). This corresponds to selecting a tolerance region c_h from among a concept class **C**.

Then, given a family of functions **F**, and an element of the family f, let us consider a tolerance region containing some relevant fraction $1-\gamma$ of the sampled points (x_i,y_i), like in fig. 2. Look at the set of tolerance regions around the element of **F** as a concept class **C** and apply the results of the previous section. Thus, we obtain the following:

Theorem 3 Given a family **F** of functions on **X** and an associate class **C** of tolerance regions with $D_{\mathbf{C},\mathbf{C}} = \mu$ and a sampling $(\underline{X},\underline{Y})_m$, consider any function $\mathbf{A}$: $\{(\mathbf{x},\mathbf{y})_m\} \longmapsto \mathbf{F}$ outputting hypotheses containing at least a fraction $1-\gamma$ of sampled points, and define

$$1_l(h(x),f(x)) = \begin{cases} 1 \text{ if } (x,f(x)) \notin c_h \\ 0 \text{ otherwise} \end{cases}.$$

Then, for $0 < \varepsilon, \delta < 1/2$, in case $m \geq \dfrac{\max\left\{\frac{2}{\varepsilon}\log\left(\frac{1}{\delta}\right), 5.5\frac{(\mu-1)}{\varepsilon}\right\}}{1-\gamma}$,

$P^{(m)}(E[1_l(h(X),f(X))] \leq \varepsilon) \geq 1 - \delta$.

Proof: if follows directly from the Basic Lemma, taking into account the consideration of point iii. in the previous section, since $E[l(h(X),f(X))] = P((x,f(x)) \notin c_h)$. □

Finally, we can naturally extend the notion of sentry to the outer sentry function and related terminology as follows:

Definition 2': Given a concept class **C** on **X**, an *inner sentry* function on **C** is a total function $\mathbf{s}: \mathbf{C} \cup \{\emptyset, \mathbf{X}\} \longmapsto 2^{\mathbf{X}}$ satisfying the following conditions:

(1') the elements of **s**(c) are inside c. This means that, for every c in the domain of **s**, $c \cap \mathbf{s}(c) = \mathbf{s}(c)$

(2') if $c_1, c_2 \in \mathbf{C}$, $c_1 \not\subseteq c_2$ and $c_2 - \mathbf{s}(c_2) \subseteq c_1 - \mathbf{s}(c_1)$ then $\overline{c_2} \cap \mathbf{s}(c_1) \neq \varnothing$

(3') no $\mathbf{s}' \neq \mathbf{s}$ exists satisfying (1) and (2) and having the property that $\mathbf{s}'(c) \subseteq \mathbf{s}(c)$ for each c .

(4') whenever c_1 and c_2 are such that $c_2 - \mathbf{s}(c_2) \subset c_1$ and $\overline{c_2} \cap \mathbf{s}(c_1) = \varnothing$, then the restriction of **s** to $\mathbf{C}-\{c_2\}$ is a sentry function on $\mathbf{C}-\{c_2\}$.

c_2 is *sentinelled* by $\mathbf{s}(c_1)$ iff $\overline{c_2} \cap \mathbf{s}(c_1) \neq \varnothing$; $d_{\mathbf{C}} = \max_{\mathbf{s},c} \#\mathbf{s}(c)$

This allows us to consider a GE learning protocol [3] (see also [11]) where the training set is constituted, like in fig. 3, by triplets $(x,y, \lambda_f(x,y))$ where $\lambda_f(x,y)=1$ if $y \geq f(x)$, 0 otherwise. Taking into account that the difference between h and f gives rise to a symmetric–difference_like region - let us call *twist concept* - where the label attributed to the points by f and h are different, we can state the following theorem:

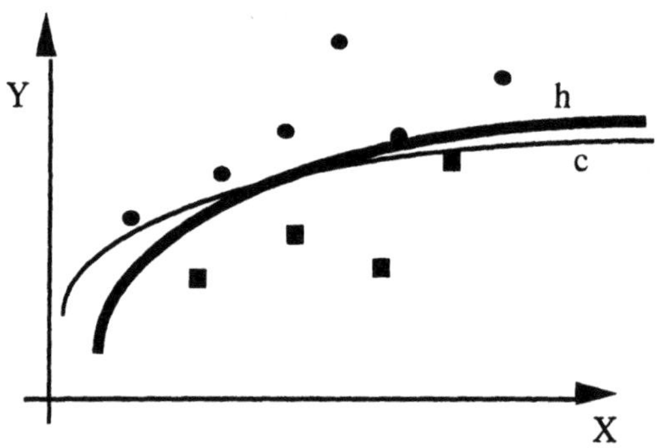

Figure 3: From the same class of function as in fig. 2 we draw a hypothesis h basing on

● = G(reater)E(qual) points and ■ = L(ower) points

Theorem 4 Given a family **F** of functions on **X** and an associate class **C** of twist concepts with $D_{\mathbf{C}} + d_{\mathbf{C}} = \mu$ and a GE sampling $(\underline{X},\underline{Y})^c{}_m$, consider any function $\mathcal{A} : \mathcal{A}: \{(\mathbf{x},\mathbf{y})^c{}_m\} \longmapsto \mathbf{F}$ outputting hypotheses consistent with the sample, and define

$$l_2(h(x),f(x)) = \begin{cases} 1 \text{ if } \lambda_h(x,y) \neq \lambda_f(x,y) \\ 0 \text{ otherwise} \end{cases}$$

Then, for $0 < \varepsilon, \delta < 1/2$, in case $m \geq \dfrac{\max\left\{\frac{2}{\varepsilon}\log\left(\frac{1}{\delta}\right), 5.5\frac{(\mu-1)}{\varepsilon}\right\}}{1-\gamma}$,

$P^{(m)}(E[l_2(h(X),f(X))] \leq \varepsilon) \geq 1 - \delta$.

Theorems 3 and 4, and extensions analogous to those in sect. 2, particularly apply to neural networks, where generally we try to fit the training set with a satisfying approximation. Though the notion of satisfying is generally fuzzy [1] , the following claim works useful:

Claim 2: For a function class **F** on **X** and any accuracy target (ε, δ) the ratio between the cardinality n of test set and m of the training set is at most 1.

References

[1] Apolloni B. (1992) *Design of Algorithms for Neural Networks. Supervised Learning.* Computers and artificial intelligence, vol. 5, 457-480, 1992.

[2] Apolloni B., Chiaravalli S. *PAC Learning of concept classes through the boundaries of their items.* J. Theoretical Computer Science, vol.172, 91-120, 1997.

[3] Apolloni B., C. Ferretti, G. Mauri, *Approximation of optimization problems and learnability* . Proc. of GAA 92,Roma,261-268, 1992.

[4] Barron A., *Neural networks approximation*, Procs. of 7th Yale Workshop on Adaprive and Learning Systems, pp.69-72, 1992.

[5] Baum E.,B., and D. Haussler, *What size net gives valid generalizations?*, Neural Comp. 1,151-160, 1989

[6] Blumer A., Ehrenfeucht A., Haussler D., Warmuth M., *Learnability and the Vapnik- Chervonenkis dimension*, J. of ACM 36, 929-965, 1989.

[7] D. Haussler, *Generalizing the PAC model for neural net and other learning applications.* Res. Rep. UCSC–CRL–89–30, University of California, Santa Cruz, 1989.

[8] Lawrence S, A.C. Tsoi and C.Lee. Giles, *Local minima and generalization*, Procs. ICNN, vol. 1, pp. 371-376, 1996.

[9] Valiant L.G. A theory of the learnable. *Communication of ACM* 27, 11 (1984), pp. 1134- 1142.

[10]Vapnik V.V. , *Estimation of dependences based on empirical data* ,Springer-Verlag N.Y.,1982.

[11]Vapnik V.V. , *The nature of Statistical Learning Theory* ,Springer-Verlag N.Y.,1982.

Entropy Based Comparison of Neural Networks for Classification

Sorin Draghici†

Vision and Neural Networks Laboratory, Wayne State University
431 State Hall, Detroit, 48202, MI, USA
E-mail: sod@cs.wayne.edu

Valeriu Beiu*

Los Alamos National Laboratory, Division NIS-1, Mail Stop D466
Los Alamos, NM 87545, USA
E-mail: beiu@lanl.gov

Abstract

This paper discusses some entropy based bounds for the case of real and limited integer weights neural networks. It is shown that a neural network using real weights can solve a dichotomy of $m = m_+ + m_-$ patterns using a number of bits less than $\max(m_+, m_-) \cdot n \{\lceil \log(D/d) \rceil + 2\}$ where n is the number of dimensions and D and d are the maximum and minimum distance between patterns in opposite classes, respectively. In the case of limited integer weights, it is shown that a neural network using integer weight in the range [-*p,p*] can solve a dichotomy of patterns in general positions with a number of bits greater than $\#bits > \min(m_+, m_-) \cdot n \cdot \lceil \log 2pD \rceil$.

1. Introduction

In recent years, multilayer feedforward neural networks (NN) have been shown to be very effective tools in many different applications [1, 2]. A natural and essential step in continuing the diffusion of these tools in our day by day use is their hardware implementation which is by far the most cost effective solution for large scale use. When the hardware implementation is contemplated, the issue of *the size* of the NN becomes crucial because the size is directly proportional with *the cost* of the implementation. In this light, any theoretical results which establish bounds on the size of a NN for a given problem is extremely important. In the same context, a particularly interesting case is that of the neural networks using limited integer weights. These networks are particularly suitable for hardware implementation because they need less space for storing the weights and the fixed point, limited

† Supported in part by the Michigan Space Grant Consortium

* On leave of absence from "Politehnica" University of Bucharest, Department of Computer Science, Spl. Independentei 313, RO-77206

precision arithmetic has much cheaper implementations in comparison with its floating point counterpart.

This paper presents an entropy based analysis which completes, unifies and correlates results partially presented in [3], [4], [5] and [6]. Tight bounds for real and integer weight neural networks are calculated.

2. Previous results

The problem to find the smallest *size* NN which can realize an arbitrary function given a set of m vectors (examples, or points) in n dimensions is not new. Many results have been obtained for NNs having a *threshold* activation function. This is probably due to the fact that this line of research was continuing on the rigorous results already obtained in the literature dealing with threshold logic from the mid 60s (see references in [7], [2]). Probably the first lower bound on the *size* of a threshold gate circuit for "almost all" n-ary Boolean functions was given by Neciporuk in 1964: $\text{size} \geq 2\left(2^n / n\right)^{1/2}$ [8]. Later, Lupanov has proven a very tight upper bound for the case in which depth=4: $\text{size} \leq 2\left(2^n / n\right)^{1/2}\left(1 + \Omega\left[\left(2^n / n\right)^{1/2}\right]\right)$ [9].

Similar existence exponential bounds can be found in [10], while in [11] a $\Omega\left(2^{n/3}\right)$ existence lower bound for arbitrary Boolean functions has been presented.

For classification problems, one of the first result was that a NN with only one hidden layer having m-1 nodes could compute an arbitrary dichotomy (sufficient condition). The main improvements are:

- Baum in [12] presented a NN with one hidden layer $\lceil m / n \rceil$ neurons capable of realizing an arbitrary dichotomy on a set of m points *in general position* in $\mathbf{R}^n$; if the points are on the corners of the n-dimensional hypercube (i.e., binary vectors), m-1 nodes are still needed;
- a slightly tighter bound was proven in [13]: only $\lceil 1 + (m-2) / n \rceil$ neurons are needed in the hidden layer for realizing an arbitrary dichotomy on a set of m points which satisfy a more relaxed topological assumption (only 'some' points are required to be *in general position*); also, the m-1 nodes condition was shown to be the least upper bound needed;
- Arai in [14] showed that m-1 hidden neurons are necessary for arbitrary separability (any mapping between input and output for the case of binary-valued units), but improved the bound for the two-category classification problem to *m/3* (without any condition on the inputs).

These results show that for binary inputs the *size* grows exponentially (as $m \leq 2^n$). Some existence lower bounds for the arbitrary dichotomy problem are (see [15]):

- a *depth*-2 NN requires at least $m/\lceil n\log(m/n)\rceil$ hidden neurons (if $m \geq 3n$);
- a *depth*-3 NN requires at least $2(m/\log m)^{1/2}$ neurons in each of the two hidden layer (if $m >> n^2$); this bound is identical to the one presented in [8] for $m = 2^n$;
- an arbitrarily interconnected NN without feedback needs $(2m/\log m)^{1/2}$ neurons (if $m >> n^2$).

Several other bounds for arbitrary Boolean functions can be found in [16]. All of these are: (i) revealing a gap between the upper and the lower bounds, thus encouraging research efforts to reduce (or even close) these gaps; (ii) suggesting that networks with more hidden layers might have a smaller *size*.

3. Theoretical considerations

3.1 Existence issues: Does a solution exist?

Before trying to establish any bounds for the necessary number of bits, one has to investigate whether the problem can be solved with the given tools. This issue is simpler in the case of the real weight networks. In this case, it is sufficient to show that a solution exists. Since the network uses real weights, if a solution exists, such a solution can be implemented[1] (because the hyperplanes can be placed in any position required by the solution). The issue becomes slightly more complicated for the case of limited precision integer weights. In such situation, the hyperplanes are restricted to only certain discrete positions. The answers to these questions are given by the following propositions.

Proposition 1

A set of patterns from two classes in *n* dimensions for which the minimum distance between two patterns of opposite classes is *d*, can always be separated using a uniform quantization of the space with elementary hypercubes of side $d/(k\sqrt{n})$ where k>1.

The proof is constructive and can be found in [3]. For space reasons, it will be omitted here. In [4], it is shown that the problem can always be solved even for the more convenient k=1.

---

[1] Note that this paper does not deal with the *training* i.e. the existence of *an algorithm* able to find a given solution. We are only interested in the possibilities of *a network* (or architecture). *A network* can solve a problem if and only if a solution exists, independently of the existence of *an algorithm* able to find this solution.

Proposition 2

Using integer weights in the range [$-p$, p], one can correctly classify any set of patterns for which the minimum distance between two patterns of opposite classes is $d_{\min}=1/p$.

The proof is based on induction on p and the number of dimensions n. Again, due to space limitations, the proof will be omitted here but can be found in [6].

3.2 Complexity issues: how big a network does one need in order to solve a given problem?

The interesting issue we have proposed to tackle is how complex should the network be for a given problem? Are there any bounds for the complexity of a network? In order to answer these questions, we must briefly discuss how we are going to measure the complexity of a network.

Many measures of complexity have been proposed. Among them, there are the *depth* (the number of edges on the longest input to the output path) and the *size* (the number of nodes). For VLSI implementation purposes, the *depth* can be put into correspondence with the delay and the *area* can be put into correspondence with the *area* of a VLSI chip. However, these measures are not the best criteria because the area of a neuron depends on the precision of its associated weights. Better criteria are the total *number of connections* [17, 18, 19, 20, 21] the total *number-of-bits* needed to represent the weights [22, 23] or *the sum of all the weights and thresholds* [24, 25, 26] The total *number of bits* is discussed further in [27, 25] etc. Keeping in mind that our ultimate goal is to build hardware implementations, we will adopt the total *number of bits* as an appropriate measure for the complexity of a neural network.

We shall now consider the case of a set of patterns of two classes with the minimum distance between two patterns from opposite classes $d=d_{\min}$ and we shall calculate some bounds on the number of bits necessary for both the case of real and limited integer weights.

Proposition 3

Let us consider the dichotomy of $m = m_+ + m_-$ examples from $\mathbf{R}^n$. Then, the number of bits necessary for the separation of the patterns (in general positions) using real weights is bounded by:

$$\#bits < \max(m_+, m_-)\cdot\left[n\cdot\left\lceil \log(D/d)\right\rceil + 2\right].$$

Proof

Find the examples (from the two classes) which are closest to one another: x_d, y_d (the distance between them is d). Translate the origin in x_d and rotate the axes such that x_d, y_d become the opposite corners of a hypercube. The side length is $l = d/\sqrt{n}$ and we can use it as a step to quantize the whole space. As there are no patterns situated at a distance smaller than d, it is certain that no hypercube will contain examples from opposite classes.

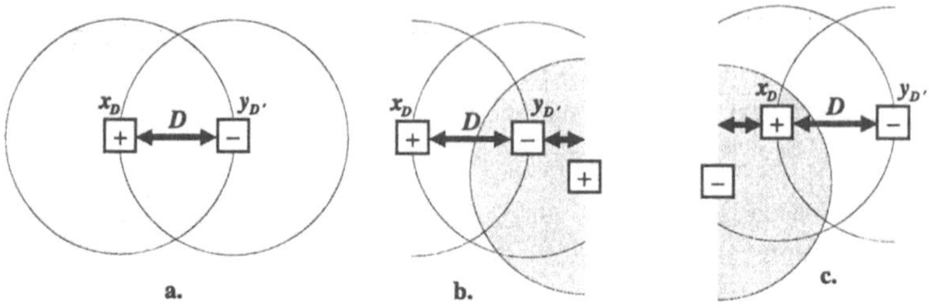

Fig. 1 Bounding the sub-space for a given set of examples

Because the largest distance between two patterns is D, there is a ball in $\mathbf{R}^n$ of radius D which contains all m examples (see Fig. 1). All the m_+ (respectively m_-) examples are contained inside a ball of radius D centered in that example from the opposite class which is used to determine the largest distance D: y_D and x_D. Furthermore, there are only three possible cases:

- all the examples are in the sub-space determined by the intersection of two balls; all m examples are inside the intersection of two balls of radius D;
- there are positive examples situated on the other side (with respect to x_D) of the hyperplane orthogonal to the segment x_Dy_D and containing y_D; select the furthest positive example and use it as the center of a third ball of radius D; all negative examples m_- are inside a subspace of the intersection of two balls of radius D;
- there are negative examples situated on the other side (with respect to y_D) of the hyperplane orthogonal to the segment x_Dy_D and containing x_D; now, all the m_+ examples are inside a sub-space of the intersection of two balls of radius D.

It is now clear that a bound on the number of bits can be obtained if one chooses to separate the least numerous class which contains minimum of m_- and m_+ patterns.

From [5], the volume of the intersection of two balls of radius r in $\mathbf{R}^n$, placed such that the center of each one is on the boundary of the other one, is $V(r,n) = 2\alpha(n-1)r^n \cdot a(n)$ where $\alpha(n) = \frac{\pi^{n/2}}{\Gamma(n/2+1)}$ is the volume of the unit ball in $\mathbf{R}^n$ and $a(n) = \frac{n-1}{n} \cdot a(n-2) - \frac{3^{(n-1)/2}}{n \cdot 2^n}$. Then, a bound on the number of bits can be calculated as $\#bits_{example} = \left\lceil \log\left(\frac{V(D,n)}{v_{hc}(d,n)}\right)\right\rceil = \left\lceil \log\left(\frac{2\pi^{(n-1)/2} D^n a(n) n^{n/2}}{d^n \Gamma[(n-1)/2+1]}\right)\right\rceil$.

From the same reference $\alpha(n) < \int_{\pi/6}^{\pi/2} \left(\sqrt{3}/2\right)^n d\theta = \left(\frac{\sqrt{3}}{2}\right)^n \cdot \frac{\pi}{3}$ and by using Stirling's formula $n! > \sqrt{2\pi n} \cdot (n/e)^n$ we obtain:

$$\#bits_{example} \le 1+\frac{n}{2}\log\pi-\frac{1}{2}\log\pi+n\log\frac{D}{d}+\log\pi-\log 3+\frac{n}{2}\log 3-n+$$
$$+\frac{n}{2}\log n-\frac{1}{2}\log\pi-\frac{1}{2}\log(n-1)-\frac{n-1}{2}\log(n-1)+\frac{n-1}{2}+\frac{n-1}{2}\log e$$

$$\#bits_{example} < \lceil n\log(D/d)+1.8396n\rceil < n\{\lceil\log(D/d)\rceil+2\}$$

We can choose M=max(m_-, m_+) so we make sure that the result is independent of the case chosen in Fig. 1 and, by multiplication with M, the proof is concluded.

Proposition 4

Let us consider a set of $m = m_+ + m_-$ patterns of two classes in the hypersphere of radius $D \le 1$ centred in origin of $\mathbf{R}^n$. Let us consider $d_{min}=1/p$ the minimum distance between two patterns belonging to different classes. Then, the number of bits necessary for the separation of the patterns (in general positions) using weights in the set $\{-p, -p-1, \ldots, 0, 1, \ldots, p\}$ is bounded by

$$\#bits > \min(m_+, m_-)\cdot n\cdot\lceil\log 2pD\rceil$$

Proof

From Proposition 2, it follows that one can divide the space using hyperplanes implemented with the given limited precision weights such that the maximum internal distance in any one region is less than $1/p$.

The proof of Proposition 2 is based on geometrical considerations which are illustrated in Fig. 2 and Fig. 3. Fig. 2 shows the hyperplanes which can be implemented with integer weights in the range [-3,3] (drawn in the square [-1,1]). There will be a certain number of 'large' volumes in which the maximum internal distance is 1/3-ε (1/p-ε in the general case) and a number of smaller volumes. Fig. 3 presents one of the 'large' volumes in 3D.

One can calculate the number of bits necessary for the representation of one example p_i as

$$\#bits_{p_i} = \lceil\log(V_{total}/V_{iv})\rceil$$

where V_{total} is the total volume of the problem and V_{iv} is the individual volume of the region which encloses (and separates) the pattern p_i. But all individual volumes are smaller or equal to the 'large' volumes which have the maximum internal distance $1/p$-ε (see [6]). In turn, this volume is convex (from construction) and therefore smaller than the volume V_{hs} of the hypersphere of diameter $1/p$. Therefore:

$$\#bits_{p_i} = \lceil\log(V_{total}/V_{iv})\rceil > \lceil\log(V_{total}/V_{hs})\rceil$$

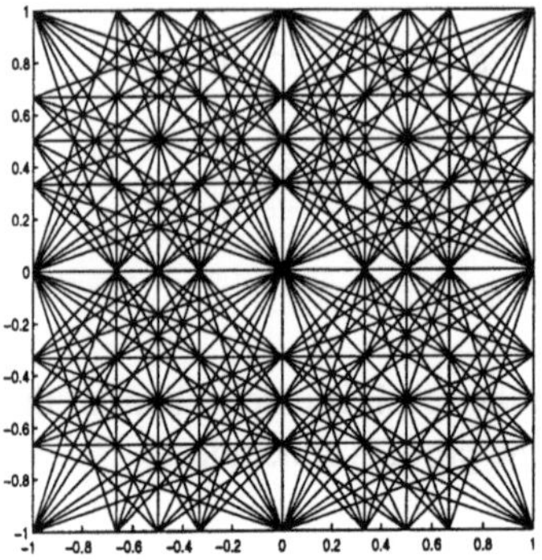

Fig. 2 The hyperplanes which can be implemented with integer weights in the range [-3,3] drawn in the square [-1,1].

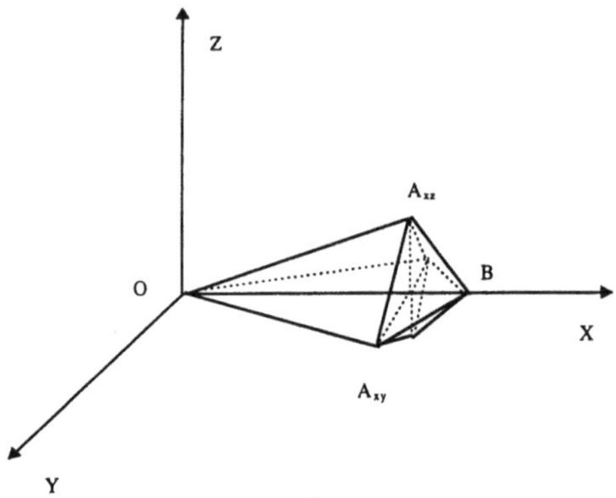

Fig. 3 The volume V^3 (in 3D). The largest distance between two points in this volume is OB along the x axis and is 1/p-ε.

For n even we have:

$$\#bits_{p_i} > \left\lceil \log \frac{V_{total}}{V_{hs}} \right\rceil = \left\lceil \log \frac{V_{total}}{\frac{\pi^{n/2}}{\Gamma(n/2+1)} d^n} \right\rceil = \left\lceil \log \frac{V_{total}}{\frac{\pi^{n/2}}{(n/2)!} d^n} \right\rceil$$

But, from hypothesis, all patterns are included in the sphere of radius D centered in the origin. Note that $1/2p<D<1$. The first inequality comes from the fact that $1/p$ is the minimum distance in-between two patterns and 2D is the diameter of the hypersphere containing all patterns. The second one is necessary because Proposition 1 was proved for the hypercube $[-1,1]^n$. In these conditions, V_{total} is the volume of the sphere of radius D and the bound can be written as:

$$\#bits_{p_i} > \left\lceil \log \frac{\frac{\pi^{n/2}}{(n/2)!} D^n}{\frac{\pi^{n/2}}{(n/2)!} d^n} \right\rceil = \left\lceil \log \frac{D^n}{d^n} \right\rceil = \left\lceil n \log \frac{D}{d} \right\rceil = \left\lceil n \log \frac{D}{\frac{1}{2p}} \right\rceil = \left\lceil n \log 2pD \right\rceil$$

By multiplying with $\min(m_+, m_-)$ i.e. the number of patterns in the smallest class, we obtain $\#bits > \min(m_+, m_-) \cdot n \cdot \lceil \log 2pD \rceil$. A similar expression can be obtained for n odd. QED.

This lower bound must not be interpreted as an absolute one. For a particular problem, when the patterns are in particularly favourable positions, more than one pattern from the same class can share the same volume and thus, the number of bits can be further reduced.

The upper bound holds even for the limited integer weight case. Therefore, for this case:

$$\min(m_+, m_-) \cdot n \cdot \{\lceil \log(D/d) \rceil\} < \#bits < \max(m_+, m_-) \cdot n \cdot \{\lceil \log(D/d) \rceil + 5/2\}.$$

4. Conclusions

This paper has addressed two issues. Firstly, it has been shown that both in the case of real and limited integer weights, the problem can always be solved. Then, based on the entropy of the data set, tight lower and upper bounds for the case of real and limited integer weights neural networks have been calculated.

Although the proof for the given bounds is constructive, the shape of the bounding space can not be easily used in practice because it is too expensive computationally. In practice, the simplest bounding space is a hypercube. By taking a hypercube of side lenght $2D$, the problem can be solved but the upper bound becomes

$$m\left\lceil \log\left[(2D^n)/(d/\sqrt{n})^n\right] \right\rceil < m\lceil 5n/2 + n\log(D/d) + (n\log n)/2 \rceil = O(mn\log n).$$

In other words, this has lead to a logarithmic increase on the upper bound.

5. Bibliography

1. Arbib, M.A. (ed.): The handbook of brain theory and neural networks, MIT Press, Cambridge, 1995
2. Fiesler, E., Beale, R. (eds.): Handbook of neural computation, E1.4: Digital Integrated Circuits and G: Neural Networks in Practice: Case Studies, Oxford Univ. Press, NY, 1996
3. Beiu, V., Entropy bounds for classification algorithms, Neural Network World, 6, No. 4, (1996), 497-505, IDG Press
4. Beiu, V., Taylor J.G., Direct synthesis of neural networks, Proc. MicroNeuro'96 (Lausanne, Switzerland), IEEE CS Press, Los Alamitos, CA, 1996, 257-264
5. Beiu, V., T. De Pauw, Tight bounds on the size of neural networks for classification problems, In: Biological and Artificial Computation: From Neuroscience to Technology, Lecture Notes in Computer Science, J. Mira, R. Moreno-Diaz, J. Cabestany (Eds.), p. 753-762, Springer Verlag, 1997
6. Draghici, S., Sethi, I.K., On the possibilities of the limited precision weights neural networks in classification problems, In: Biological and Artificial Computation: From Neuroscience to Technology, Lecture Notes in Computer Science, J. Mira, R. Moreno-Diaz, J. Cabestany (Eds.), p. 753-762, Springer Verlag, 1997
7. Beiu, V.,VLSI complexity of discrete neural networks, Gordon and Breach, 1997
8. Neciporuk, E.I., The synthesis of networks from threshold elements, Problemy Kibernetiki 11, 1964; 49-62. English translation in Automation Express 7 (1) 35-39 and 7 (2) 27-32
9. Lupanov, O.B., The synthesis of circuits from threshold elements, Problemy Kibernetiki 20, 109-140, 1973

10. Bruck,, J., Smolensky, R., Polynomial threshold functions, AC functions and spectral norms, Res. Rep. RJ 7410 (67387), 11/15/89, IBM Yorktown Heights, NY 1989. Also in SIAM J. Computing 21(1), 33-42, 1992
11. Siu, K.-Y., Roychowdhury, V., Kailath, T., Depth-size tradeoffs for neural computations, IEEE Trans. on Comp., 40 (12), 1991; 1402-1412
12. Baum, E.B., On the Capabilities of Multilayer Perceptrons, J. of Complexity 4. 193-215, 1988
13. Huang, S.-C., Huang, Y.-F., Bounds on the number of hidden neurons of multilayer perceptrons in classification and recognition, IEEE Trans. on Neural Networks 2 (1), 47-55, 1991
14. Arai, M. Bounds on the number of hidden units in binary-valued three-layer neural networks, NN 6 (6), 855-860, 1993
15. Hassoun, M.H., Fundamentals of artificial neural networks, MIT Press, Cambridge, MA, 1995
16. Paugam-Moisy, H., Optimisation des réseaux des neurones artificiels, Ph.D. thesis, Laboratoire de l'Informatique du Parallélisme LIP-IMAG, École Normale Supérieure de Lyon, 46 Allée d'Italie, 69364 Lyon, France, 1992
17. Hammerstrom, D., The connectivity analysis of simple associations - or - How many connections do you need?, NIPS'87, D.Z. Anderson (Ed.), Amer. Inst. Of Phys., New York, 338-347, 1988
18. Abu-Mostafa, Y.S., Connectivity vs. Entropy, NIPS'87, D.Z. Anderson(Ed), Amer. Inst. Of Phys., NY, 1-8, 1988
19. Klaggers, H., Soegtrop M., Limited fan-in random wired cascade-correlation learning architecture, MicroNeuro'93, D.J. Myers and A.F.Murray (Eds.), Univ.Ed Tech. Ltd., Edinburgh, 79-82, 1993
20. Phatak, D.S., Koren I., Connectivity and performance tradeoffs in the cascade-correlation learning architecture, IEEE Trans. NN's, 5(6), 930-935, 1994
21. Mason, R.D., Robertson W., Mapping Hierarchical Neural Networks to VLSI Hardware, Neural Networks, 8, 6, 905-913, 1995
22. Bruck, J., Goodman J.W., On the power of neural networks for solving hard problems, NIPS'87, D.Z. Anderson (Ed.), Amer. Inst. Of Phys., New York, 1988, 137-143 (also in J. of Complexity, 6, 129-135), 1990;
23. Williamson, R.C., e-Entropy and the complexity of feedforward neural networks, NIPS'90, R.P. Lippmann, J.E.Moody, D.S. Touretzky (Eds.), Morgan Kaufmann, San Mateo, CA, 946-952, 1991;
24. Beiu, V., Peperstraete, J., Vandewalle, J., Lauwereins, R., Comparison and threshold gate decomposition, in Myers, D.J., Murray, A.F.: MicroNeuro'93 (Edinburgh, UK), UnivEd Tech. Ltd., Edinburgh, 83-90, 1993;
25. Beiu, V., Neural Networks Using Threshold Gates: A Complexity Analysis of Their Area and Time Efficient VLSI Implementations, Ph.D. thesis, Katholieke Universiteit Leuven, 1994.
26. Beiu, V., Peperstraete, J., Vandewalle, J., Lauwereins, R., Area-time performnaces of some neural computations, in Borne, P., Fukuda, T., Tzafestas, S.G., Symp. On Signal Processing, Robotics and Neural Networks, GERF EC, Lille, 664-668, 1994
27. Denker, J.S., Wittner B.S., Network Generality, Training Required and Precision Required, NIPS'87, D.Z. Anderson (Ed.), Amer. Inst of Phys., New York, 219-222, 1988

A Hebbian model for Space Representation

Francesco Frisone   Pietro G. Morasso
DIST - University of Genova
Via Opera Pia 13, 16145 Genova, Italy
F: +39 10 3532154; E:friso@dist.dist.unige.it

Abstract

A Hebbian model for space representation based on two interacting Topology Representing Networks is proposed. Such a model make a 2-dimensional space representation of high dimensional data. The method is supported by the fact that this type of data-driven process of formation of connectivity patterns seems to be, from a biological point of view, both the most plausible and the most practical. The model is also supported by the observation that lattices are ways to map n-dimensional space into 2-dimensional one.

In the following, we support the heuristic validity of this model by means of a simulation study.

1 Introduction

In the problem of *representation* [3] the central question is how can an internal state of a system refer to anything at all in the external world.

The problem of representation is rarely discussed in cognitive psychology. Arguments put forward by [5] prompted cognitive scientists to contemplate the fact that not all representations are computationally equivalent. At the same time, it is generally taken for granted that a certain pattern of neuronal activity in someone's brain can represent the shape of a dog or the number 7.

Reviews in cognitive psychology tend to adopt extreme positions concerning representation, the upshot of which is that "we do not really understand our concepts of representation".

This paper instead of asking what is representation, it proposes a model of space representation of *information* from the "external world". The goal of the model is to develop an approximate representation in a self-organizing fashion.

2 Space representation and self-organizing maps

In a number of information processing tasks the problem which has to be solved efficiently can be reduced to a geometric problem which deals with the proximity of points in a metric space.

It is shown that simple Hebbian learning can result in the formation of a correct geometry representation [6]. Hebbian rule forms so-called *Delaunay triangulations* which play an important role in computational geometry for efficiently solving proximity problems.

Most popular self-organizing models represent input space arranging the neurons (by means a Hebbian learning rule) on a regular lattice that become a topographic representation of the stimulus space. In this way the representation is implemented by means of a *codebook*. From this point of view the problems of the space representation becomes a problem of optimal tessellation or tiling of a quantized hyper-surface.

Our method starts from a completely different approach: the input space representation is codified in the lateral connections established between neurons by means a Hebbian rule. The method is supported by the fact that this type of data-driven process of formation of connectivity patterns seems to be, from a biological point of view, both the most plausible and the most practical [10]. It makes sense to assume that the connections initially have random weights, within a predetermined range, and later on self-organize according to a Hebbian process to form global order: this is in agreement with a general underlying ecological pressure on brain formation [2, 8, 9] towards (i) minimization of volume and (ii) maximization of connectivity. The method it is also based on the observation that lattices are ways to map n-dimensional space into 2-dimensional one [1] .

The space representation is obtained directly by the self-organizing learning of two *Topology Representing Network* (TRN) [7]. TRN is a self-organizing neural network whose property is to be "perfectly topology preserving". The focal-point is the following:

> *the number of the connections that each neuron has established with other neurons at the end of the learning phase is considered as representative of the intrinsic dimensionality of input data close to the neuron itself* [4].

From this point of view the space representation become a problem of optimal wiring.

3 The Model

Let us consider a computational map as a graph of n *processing elements* operating in parallel on a common afferent signal $\vec{x} \in \mathcal{M}_s \subset \Re^n$:

$$\mathcal{M} = (\mathcal{P}, \mathcal{A}) \tag{1}$$

where $\mathcal{P} = \{\tilde{p}_i : i = 1, \ldots, n\}$ is a set of PE and $\mathcal{A} = \{a_{ij} : i, j = 1, \ldots, n\}$ is the symmetrical connection matrix ($a_{ij} = a_{ji} = 1$ if $\tilde{p}_i$ and $\tilde{p}_j$ are connected; $a_{ij} = 0$ otherwise). Each processing element is defined by two quantities (or prototype vectors):

$$\tilde{p}_i = \{\vec{\pi}_i^y; \vec{\pi}_i^x\} \tag{2}$$

where $\vec{\pi}_i^y \subset \Re^2$ is the neuron position vector in the map, and $\vec{\pi}_i^x \subset \Re^n$ is its associated weight vector. Each PE has a selective response on a receptive field, described by an activation function $U_i^x(\vec{x})$ that is maximized by a preferred input $\vec{x} = \vec{\pi}_i^x$, i.e. the *prototype* vector 'stored' in that PE.

The prototypes in the model are trained by means of a Hebbian rule:

$$\Delta\vec{\pi}_i = \epsilon \cdot e^{\frac{-k_i}{\lambda}}(\vec{x} - \vec{\pi}_i) \quad i = 1 \ldots n \tag{3}$$

$$\Delta a_{ij} = -\gamma a_{ij} + \begin{cases} 1 & \text{if } \| \vec{x} - \vec{\pi}_i \| \leq \| \vec{x} - \vec{\pi}_j \| \leq \| \vec{x} - \vec{\pi}_k \| \quad \forall k = 1 \ldots n \\ 0 & \text{otherwise} \end{cases} \tag{4}$$

where ϵ, k_i, λ are learning parameters and γ is a decay factor. Two types of input data are used: one is generated artificially ($\vec{y} \in \mathcal{M}_c \subset \Re^2$) and expresses the computational map frame and the other ($\vec{x} \in \mathcal{M}_s \subset \Re^n$) is relayed from outside the computational map as a common input stimulus. We also assume that the map frame is a 2-dimensional manifold $\mathcal{M}_c$ given by a uniform distribution of data $\vec{y}$ and stimuli are a distribution of data $\vec{x}$ on a n-dimensional manifold $\mathcal{M}_s$.

The learning is subdivided into two phases:

1. We train the first TRN that we associate with $\vec{\pi}^y$ prototype vectors and so we build the map frame (in others words we arrange the neurons on a two dimensional lattice);

2. We set $\vec{\pi}_i^x = \vec{\pi}_i^y \; \forall i$ (setting to 0 the $n-2$ features) and then we train the second TRN associated with $\vec{\pi}^x$ prototype vectors. As a consequence the network becomes a topographic representation of the stimuli, in the sense that similar stimuli are projected onto units adjacent in the network and vice versa.

The matrix $\mathcal{A}$ is common for both TRNs. In this way the matrix obtained after the learning maps the topology of the stimuli in a two dimensional lattice. In more details,

we can say that a stimulus vector $\vec{x} \in \mathcal{M}_s$ is mapped to the map neuron position $\vec{\pi}_i^y$, the attached vector $\vec{\pi}_i^x$ of which is closest to $\vec{x}$ (see Figure 1). The mapping from $\mathcal{M}_s$ to the map is neighborhood preserving, i. e. if similar stimuli are close within the manifold $\mathcal{M}_s$, are mapped to prototypes which are adjacent within the map. We mean that two prototypes $\vec{\pi}_i^y$ and $\vec{\pi}_j^y$ are adjacent if $a_{ij} = 1$ (and this even if $\vec{\pi}_i^y$ and $\vec{\pi}_j^y$ are not close [1] in the computational map frame).

A computational map transforms a vector $\vec{x}$ into a vector of activation values $U^x \in [0,1]^N$; several PEs are active at any time, i.e the map implements a *population coding* scheme. The value of $\vec{x}$ or *population vector* can be estimated from a given set of activations as: $\vec{x}_{est} = \sum_i \vec{\pi}_i^x U_i^x$.

[1] We leave the definition of "closely" of $\vec{\pi}_i^y$ and $\vec{\pi}_j^y$ in an Euclidean space, to the reader's intuition.

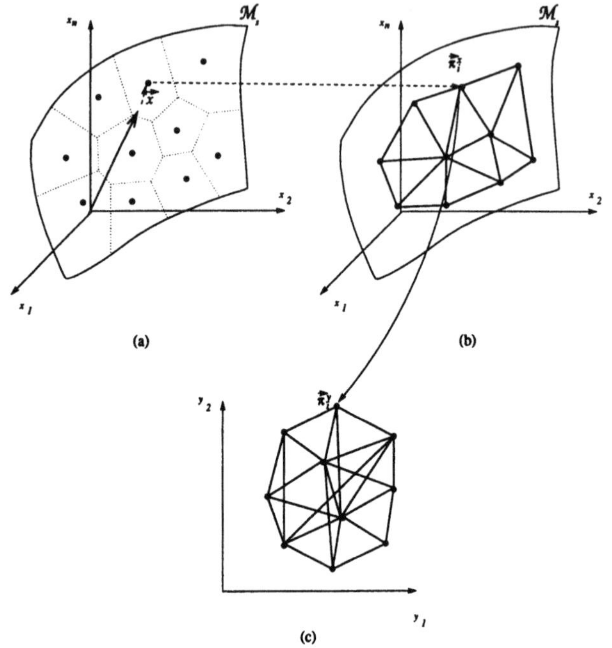

Figure 1: The mapping from $\mathcal{M}_s$ to the computational map. (a) a distribution of data on the intrinsic manifold $\mathcal{M}_s$ in the n-dimensional stimuli space and its vector quantization: $\vec{x}$ is a generic data point; (b) the first TRN: the prototype vector $\vec{\pi}_i^x$ closest to $\vec{x}$; (c) the second TRN: the map neuron position vector $\vec{\pi}_i^y$ attached to the vector $\vec{\pi}_i^x$.

4 Simulations results

The simulations are structured as follows: The prototype vectors $\vec{\pi}^y$ are initialized randomly. The first TRN is trained with a training set consisting of a uniform distribution within a circle (it represent a simplified computational map frame). After learning the prototype are arranged on a lattice (typically a 2D triangular grid, with 6 neighbors per prototype, see Figure 2).

Further step is to train the second TRN with the stimuli. The stimulus $\vec{x}$ (embedded in a 3D space) is obtained randomly sampled from an input source with an uniform distribution $p(\vec{x})$. After learning the prototype vectors $\vec{\pi}^x$ are a *topographic representation* of the stimulus space. As a consequence of the second training the first TRN is modified as regards the connections which have grown to the pattern of figure 3. The relation of the connections modification of the first TRN to the training of the second TRN is the matrix $\mathcal{A}$, that is shared by the two TRN. After the second training the first TRN is a topologically continuous representation of the 3D stimulus space.

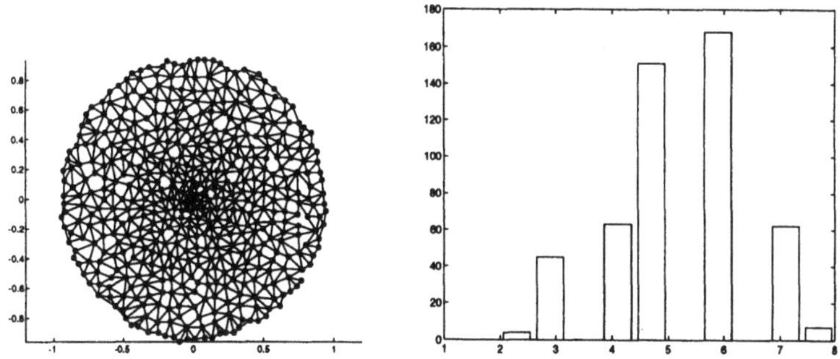

(a) (b)

Figure 2: The first TRN. (a) The lattice of prototype vectors $\vec{\pi}^y$ before training the second TRN; (b) the connections histogram: it represents how many prototypes have n connections.

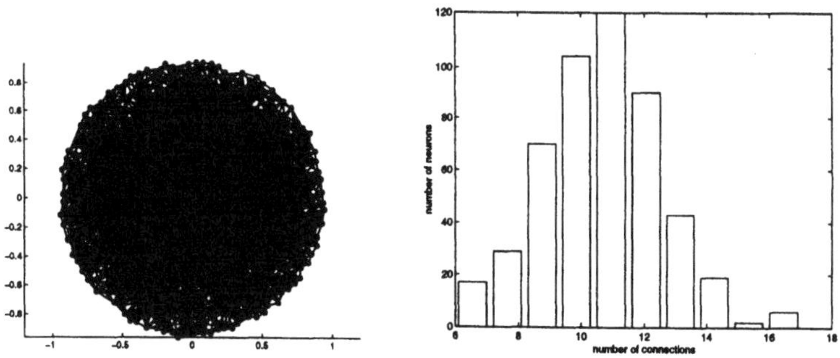

(a) (b)

Figure 3: The first TRN. (a)the modified lattice of prototype vectors $\vec{\pi}^y$ after have trained the second TRN; (b) the connections histogram.

5 Conclusions

A computational map model which is based on two TRN that interact by means of a matrix has been described. The experiments tested the validity of the model and show that this model is a *topologically continuous* representation of stimuli. Many regions in the brain are known to be topographic representations of stimuli (e.g. sensory areas). The human brain contains ten million kilometers of wiring, and there are various ways in which this very considerable length of fibers can be organized: different topologies and physical packing strategies might be used. In this paper we have shown a biological plausible way to organize wiring in order to represent efficiently n-dimensional stimuli.

Different sensory or motor schemas might be characterized by different *firing patterns* serving as a code for an item from an individual's memory. Memory recall may consist of the creation of a spatiotemporal sequence of neuron firings, probably one similar to that present at the time of the input to memory.

References

[1] V. Braitenberg. *Vehicles - Experiments in Synthetic Psychology.* MIT Press, Cambridge, MA, 1984.

[2] C. Cherniak. Component placement optimization in the brain. *Journal of Neuroscience*, 14:2418–2427, 1994.

[3] R. Cummins. *Meaning and mental representation.* MIT Press, Cambridge, MA, 1989.

[4] F. Frisone, F. Firenze, P. Morasso, and L. Ricciardiello. Application of Topology-Representing Networks to the Estimation of the Intrinsic Dimensionality of Data. In *ICANN95- Int. Conf. on Artificial Neural Networks*, volume 1, pages 323–327, Paris, October 1995.

[5] D. Marr. *Vision.* W. H. Freeman, San Francisco, CA, 1982.

[6] T. Martinetz. Competitive Hebbian Learning Rule forms perfectly topology preserving maps. In S. Gielen and B. Kappen, editors, *ICANN93- Int. Conf. on Artificial Neural Networks*, Amsterdam, 1993.

[7] T. Martinetz and K. Schulten. Topology Representing Networks. *Neural Networks*, 3:507–522, 1994.

[8] G. J. Mitchison. Neuronal branching patterns and the economy of cortical wiring. *Proc. of the Royal Society*, B:151–158, 1991.

[9] G. J. Mitchison. Axonal trees and cortical architecture. *Trends in Neurosciences*, 15:122–126, 1992.

[10] J.M.J. Murre and Sturdy D.P.F. The connectivity of the brain: multi-level quantitative analysis. Technical report, University of Amsterdam, Medical Research Council - Applied Psychology Unit, Amsterdam, 1994.

Sequences of Discrete Hopfield's Networks for the Maximum Clique Problem

G. Grossi

Dipartimento di Scienze dell'Informazione
Università degli Studi di Milano
via Comelico, 39 - 20135 Milano Italy

Abstract We propose here a neural approximation technique for the Maximum Clique problem. The core of the method consists of a sequence of Hopfield's networks that, in polynomial time, converge to a state representing a clique for a given graph. Some experiments made on the DIMACS benchmark show that the approximated solutions found are promising. Finally, the possibility to extend this technique to other **NP**-hard problems and to implement it onto neural hardware are discussed.

Keywords Maximum Clique problem, constrained optimization, Hopfield's networks.

1 Introduction

Computing the size of the largest clique in a graph G (MAX CLIQUE problem) is one of the first problems shown to be **NP**-complete [6]. More recently, Feige et al. [3] showed that even approximating this problem within a constant factor is **NP**-hard. In particular, if $\mathbf{P} \neq \mathbf{NP}$, no polynomial time algorithm can approximate MAX CLIQUE within a factor $n^{\frac{1}{4}}$, where n is the number of vertices of the graph [2].

This problem is frequently encountered in such diverse domains as cluster analysis, informations retrieval, computer vision, to name just a few and turns out to be intimately related to a number of others difficult graph problems. Despite the negative results on the approximability, for its theoretical and practical relevance, many researchers have suggested heuristics that in some case yield "satisfactory" sub-optimal solutions [5].

In this paper a polynomial time technique for approximating MAX CLIQUE based on discrete Hopfield's networks [4] is presented. Since MAX CLIQUE is a problem with constraints on the solutions, i.e., not all the elements of the search space represent valid solutions, the Hopfield's model can turns out to be inefficient. To overcame this, we propose a method that consists of building a finite sequence of networks where the energy function of the $(t+1)$-th network is the energy function of the t-th network augmented by a penalty factor depending on the number of violated constraints. At each step there are two alternating phases, one of evolution and one of updating of the weights. We can show that this iterative process lead to a feasible solution that locally maximizes the objective function of the problem.

Some interesting features of this method are:

1. the search space is finite, differently from most of the constrained optimization technique that work on continuous space;
2. the number of neurons of each network is equal to the number of vertices of the graph;
3. the absolute value reached by the weights, during the process, is bounded by the number of vertices.

As far as the computational complexity analysis it is possible to show that the number of networks in the sequence is bounded by the number of pairs of distinct vertices non connected in the graph multiplied by the degree of the graph.

The algorithm has been experimented on graphs of different size collected in the benchmark of the second DIMACS implementation challenge, whose purpose was to find effective approximation algorithms for some **NP**-hard problems. The results on the benchmark are comparable with the best found by others algorithms presented to the challenge.

The paper is organized as follows. In the next Section we formally characterize the constraints of the problem by means of Boolean formulae. In Section 3 we present the neural approximation algorithm, where some heuristics on the DIMACS benchmark are given in Section 4. Finally, in Section 5, we discuss how to address future work.

2 Preliminaries and Logical Definition of Constraints

Let $G = \langle V, E \rangle$ be an arbitrary undirected graph, where $V = \{1, \ldots, n\}$ is the set of vertices and $E \subseteq V \oplus V$ (not ordered pairs) is the set of edges. Two distinct vertices i and j are called *adjacent* if they are connected by an edge; a *clique* of G is a subset of V in which every pair of vertices is adjacent. A clique is called *maximal* if it is not subset of another clique, and the highest-cardinality maximal clique is called *maximum*. The *Maximum Clique* problem (MAX CLIQUE) is to find a maximum clique in a given graph G. The *adjacent matrix* of G is the matrix $A = (a_{ij})$ where $a_{ij} = 1$ if $\{i, j\} \in E$ and, $a_{ij} = 0$ otherwise.

Let $X_G = \{x_1, \ldots, x_n\}$ be a set of Boolean variables associated with G. A *literal* over X_G is either a variable $x_i \in X_G$ or its negation $\overline{x}_i$, a ***k-clause*** c is a disjunction of k literals, and a ***k-term*** t is a conjunction of k literals. By an assignment on X_G we mean a function $\sigma : X_G \rightarrow \{0, 1\}$; the literal x_i is said to be true (false) under the assignment σ if $\sigma(x_i) = 1$ ($\sigma(x_i) = 0$) and the literal $\bar{x}_i$ is said to be true (false) if $\sigma(x_i) = 0$ ($\sigma(x_i) = 1$). A clause c is said to be satisfied by the assignment σ on X_G if and only if at least one of its literals is true while a term t is said to be satisfied by σ on X_G if and only if all its literals are true.

For a set $S \subseteq V$, let us define its *characteristic vector* χ^S as:

$$\chi_i^S = \begin{cases} 1, & \text{if } i \in S; \\ 0, & \text{otherwise.} \end{cases}$$

An assignment σ on X_G uniquely identifies the subset S of G whose characteristic vector $\chi^S = (\sigma(x_1), \ldots, \sigma(x_n))$. With Clique_G we denote the set of all assignments that correspond to cliques in G.

Let's consider the following set of 2-clauses that we call the *set of constraints* of the instance G

$$\mathsf{C}_G = \{\overline{x}_i \vee \overline{x}_j : \{i,j\} \notin E\}.$$

Observe that if $\{i,j\} \notin E$ then any assignment that does not satisfy the clause $\overline{x}_i \vee \overline{x}_j$ cannot belong to Clique_G; moreover

Proposition 1. *Let $G = \langle V, E\rangle$ be an undirected graph and let C_G be the set of constraints of G. Then, an assignment σ satisfies the boolean formula*

$$\psi = \bigwedge_{c \in \mathsf{C}_G} c \tag{1}$$

if and only if $\sigma \in \mathsf{Clique}_G$.

Let's consider now the following set of 2-term

$$\mathsf{T}_G = \{x_i \wedge x_j : \{i,j\} \in E\}.$$

Notice that if σ is an assignment corresponding to a clique of k vertices, then $\frac{k(k-1)}{2}$ terms of T_G are satisfied by σ.

The example in Figure 1 help to clarify the previous definition.

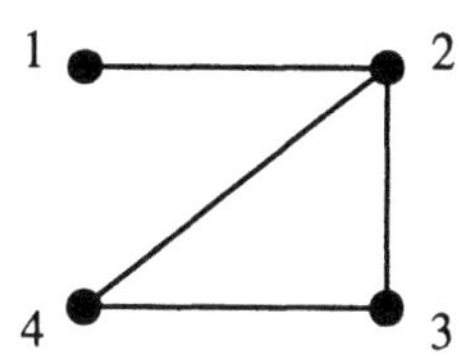

Figure1. Graph $G = (V,E)$, where $V = \{1,2,3,4\}$ and $E = \{\{1,2\},\{2,3\},\{2,4\},\{3,4\}\}$. The sets C_G, T_G and Clique_G for this graph are: $\mathsf{C}_G = \{(\overline{x}_1 \vee \overline{x}_3), (\overline{x}_1 \vee \overline{x}_4)\}$, $\mathsf{T}_G = \{(x_1 \wedge x_2), (x_2 \wedge x_3), (x_2 \wedge x_4), (x_3 \wedge x_4)\}$ and $\mathsf{Clique}_G = \{0011, 0110, 0101, 1100, 0111\}$. The assignment 0111 satisfies all the 2-clauses of C_G and the maximum number of 2-terms of T_G, i.e. 3 of 4.

In the next section we present an approximation algorithm, based on discrete Hopfield's networks, that finds suboptimal solutions for a given instance G maximizing the number of 2-terms of T_G without violating the constraints in C_G.

3 A Neural Algorithm Based on the Hopfield's Model

Given a graph G, let's introduce, for each variable $x_i \in X_G$, a variable $y_i = 2x_i - 1$ that assumes values on the set $\{-1, 1\}$. Moreover, let's define: for each 2-term $x_i \wedge x_j$ the polynomial

$$f_{\text{AND}}(y_i, y_j) = y_i + y_j + y_i y_j \ ,$$

and for each 2-clause $\overline{x}_i \vee \overline{x}_j$ the polynomial

$$f_{\text{OR}}(y_i, y_j) = -y_i - y_j - y_i y_j \ .$$

The mappings of the functions f_{AND} and f_{OR} is given in the Table 1.

Table1. Mapping of the functions f_{OR} and f_{AND}.

x	y	f_{OR}	f_{AND}
1	1	-3	3
-1	1	1	-1
1	-1	1	-1
-1	-1	1	-1

Let's consider then the following quadratic functions $\Psi : \{-1,1\}^n \to \mathbb{Z}$ and $\Omega : \{-1,1\}^n \to \mathbb{Z}$, defined as

$$\Psi(y_1, \ldots, y_n) = \sum_{x_i \wedge x_j \in \mathsf{T_G}} f_{\text{AND}}(y_i, y_j) = \sum_{i \neq j} a_{ij} y_i y_j + \sum_i u_i y_i \ , \tag{2}$$

$$\Omega(y_1, \ldots, y_n) = \sum_{\overline{x}_i \vee \overline{x}_j \in \mathsf{C_G}} f_{\text{OR}}(y_i, y_j) = \sum_{i \neq j} (a_{ij} - 1) y_i y_j - \sum_i v_i y_i \ , \tag{3}$$

where u_i is the number of vertices adjacent to the vertex i and $v_i = n - u_i - 1$ is the number of vertices nonadjacent to i. For each $\mathbf{y} \in \{-1,1\}^n$ we call $\sigma_{\mathbf{y}}$ the corresponding assignment for the variable in X_G, i.e. $\sigma_{\mathbf{y}}(x_i) = \frac{y_i + 1}{2}$. An interesting property of Ω is that its maximum value is $|\mathsf{C_G}|$ (cardinality of the set $\mathsf{C_G}$), and $\Omega(\mathbf{y}) = |\mathsf{C_G}|$ if and only if $\sigma_{\mathbf{y}} \in \mathsf{Clique_G}$. Differently, on the set $\{\mathbf{y} \in \{-1,1\}^n : \sigma_{\mathbf{y}} \in \mathsf{Clique_G}\}$ the maximum value of Ψ is found in correspondence of those assignments that identify a maximum clique of G.

In this setting, solving the MAX CLIQUE problem can be reduced to solving the following integer quadratic program:

$$\begin{aligned} &\text{maximize} \quad \Psi(\mathbf{y}) = \mathbf{y}^T A \mathbf{y} + \mathbf{u} \cdot \mathbf{y} \\ &\text{subject to} \quad \Omega(\mathbf{y}) = |\mathsf{C_G}| \ . \end{aligned} \tag{4}$$

Here we give a polynomial time technique of finding an approximate solutions for (4), based on a sequence of discrete neural network $\{\mathcal{R}_k\}_{k\geq 0}$.

The network $\mathcal{R}_k$ of the sequence is an Hopfield's network (with asynchronous dynamic); the neurons $\{1,\ldots,n\}$ represent the vertices of G and they assume state in $\{-1,1\}$. The energy function Φ_k of the network $\mathcal{R}_k$ is obtained as follows:

1. $\Phi_0(\mathbf{y}) = \Psi(\mathbf{y}) + \Omega(\mathbf{y})$;
2. let $\{\tilde{\mathbf{y}}^{(k)}\}_{k>0}$ a sequence of elements of $\{-1,1\}^n$ in which $\tilde{\mathbf{y}}^{(k)}$ is the attractor of the network $\mathcal{R}_k$ initialized with $\tilde{\mathbf{y}}^{(k-1)}$, while $\tilde{\mathbf{y}}^{(0)}$ is the attractor of the network $\mathcal{R}_0$ initialized with $(1,\ldots,1)$, and let ${\mathsf{C}_\mathsf{G}}^{(k-1)}$ be the set of 2-clauses in C_G not satisfied by the assignment $\sigma_{\tilde{\mathbf{y}}^{(k-1)}}$ corresponding to $\tilde{\mathbf{y}}^{(k-1)}$, then:

$$\Phi_k(\mathbf{y}) = \Phi_{k-1}(\mathbf{y}) + \sum_{\overline{x}_i \vee \overline{x}_j \in {\mathsf{C}_\mathsf{G}}^{(k-1)}} f_{\mathrm{OR}}(y_i, y_j). \tag{5}$$

This approximation method, consisting of two alternating phases, evolution and updating of the weights, can be simulated by the following algorithm:

RECURSIVE-HOPFIELD-NETS

Input: a graph $G = (V, E)$;

T_G := $\{x_i \wedge x_j : \{i,j\} \in E\}$;
C_G := $\{\overline{x}_i \vee \overline{x}_j : \{i,j\} \notin E\}$;
$\mathcal{R}_0$:= Hopfield's net with energy $\Phi_0(\mathbf{y}) = \Psi(\mathbf{y}) + \Omega(\mathbf{y})$;
$\tilde{\mathbf{y}}^{(0)}$:= attractor of $\mathcal{R}_0$ initialized with $(1,\ldots,1)$;
${\mathsf{C}_\mathsf{G}}^{(0)}$:= set of 2-clauses of C_G not satisfied by $\sigma_{\tilde{\mathbf{y}}^{(k)}}$;
k := 0;

while $\left[\bigwedge_{c \in \mathsf{C}_\mathsf{G}} c \quad \text{on } \sigma_{\tilde{\mathbf{y}}^{(k)}} \text{ is FALSE}\right]$ **do**

k := $k+1$;
$\mathcal{R}_k$:= $\Phi_k(\mathbf{y}) = \Phi_{k-1}(\mathbf{y}) + \sum_{\overline{x}_i \vee \overline{x}_j \in {\mathsf{C}_\mathsf{G}}^{(k-1)}} f_{\mathrm{OR}}(y_i, y_j)$;
$\tilde{\mathbf{y}}^{(k)}$:= attractor of $\mathcal{R}_k$ initialized with $\tilde{\mathbf{y}}^{(k-1)}$;
${\mathsf{C}_\mathsf{G}}^{(k)}$:= set of 2-clauses of C_G not satisfied by $\sigma_{\tilde{\mathbf{y}}^{(k)}}$;

Output: a maximal Clique S of G such that $\chi^S = \sigma_{\tilde{\mathbf{y}}^{(k)}}$.

The convergence of the previous algorithm is assured by the following

Theorem 2. *Let $G = \langle V, E \rangle$ be an undirected graph, X_G be the set of associated Boolean variables, and let* $\mathsf{Clique_G}$ *be the set of assignments on X_G that correspond to cliques of G. Let $\{\tilde{\mathbf{y}}^{(k)}\}_{k \geq 0}$ be a sequence of elements of $\{-1, 1\}^n$ such that $\tilde{\mathbf{y}}^{(k)}$ is an attractor of the Hopfield's network $\mathcal{R}_k$ with energy function* (5), *then:*

1. *the sequence $\{\tilde{\mathbf{y}}^{(k)}\}_{k \geq 0}$ is finite;*
2. *the last element of the sequence $\tilde{\mathbf{y}}^{(f)}$ correspond to an assignment $\sigma_{\tilde{\mathbf{y}}^{(f)}} \in$* $\mathsf{Clique_G}$*;*
3. *the clique represented by $\tilde{\mathbf{y}}^{(f)}$ is a maximal clique.*

As far as the computational complexity analysis it is possible to show that the number of networks in the sequence $\{\mathcal{R}_k\}_{k \geq 0}$ is bounded by $m \cdot \omega(G)$, where m is the number of pairs of distinct vertices non connected in the graph and $\omega(G)$ the degree of the graph.

4 Experimental Results

The algorithm RECURSIVE-HOPFIELD-NETS (RHN for short) has been experimented on graphs of different size collected in the benchmark of the second DIMACS implementation challenge, that took place in 1993. The purpose of this challenge was to find effective optimization and approximation algorithms for the problems MAX CLIQUE, GRAPH COLORING, and SATISFIABILITY.

The results of the simulations are summarized in Table 2. The first column (Graph) contains the name of the instance; the second (Vertices) the number of vertices n; in the third column (RHN) the results of the algorithm RHN are presented, and in the last column the best results, obtained by all participants to the challenge, are reported.

The times required by the algorithm RHN ranges from few seconds for the smallest instances to some minutes for the largest ones. The analysis of the worst case time complexity is very hard because it depends on two factors that are not simple to calculate: the length of the sequence of the Hopfield's networks and the number of the complete updating cycles that each network requires to evolve from the initial state to the equilibrium state. Also an analytical solution for the average case analysis is difficult to find, so we can give only some results on the average number of network updating cycles obtained by simulations. To this purpose we have experimentally estimated the expectation of the number of network updating cycles and we have found that it is about 3 updating cycles, independently on the size of the network. So we can conclude that each network evolves very quickly on average.

5 Concluding Remarks

In this paper we describe an approximation technique and show that its performances are promising. Besides the performances, there are at least two

Table2. Results on the DIMACS benchmark instances. The second column reports the results found by the algorithm RHN, while the third column list the best results of all participants (with star if optimality is proved). We write in bold the values of the second column if they coincide with the best achieved in the challenge.

Graph	Vertices	RHN	Best Result
MANN_a27	378	125	126*
MANN_a45	1035	340	345*
Hamming-1	64	**4**	4*
Hamming-2	64	**32**	32*
Hamming-1	256	**16**	16*
Hamming-2	256	**128**	128*
Hamming	1024	35	40
p.hat300-1	300	**25**	25*
p.hat300-2	300	34	36*
p.hat500-1	500	**9**	9*
p.hat500-2	500	49	49 ÷ 50
p.hat500-3	500	**36**	36*
Johnson28	28	**4**	4*
Johnson70	70	**14**	14*
Johnson120	120	**8**	8*
Johnson496	496	**16**	16

other perspectives that make interesting this method and that we briefly recall in the following.

1. This method can be easily generalized to obtain a discrete optimization technique for solving other **NP**-hard problems with constraints on the solutions. There are indeed a lot of problems whose constraints and whose objective functions can be characterized as for MAX CLIQUE, and then reduced to a quadratic program of the form (4). For instance, an immediate transformation can be given for the MAX WEIGHTED CLIQUE problem, considering the weight w_{ij} from the units i and j in a graph G as the number of occurrences of the 2-term $x_i \wedge x_j$ in the set T_G.
2. On the bases of our previous work [1], and for the inherent simplicity of the schema of the algorithm, it is not difficult to design a uniform family of circuits of small size and depth and implement it on programmable devices.

6 Acknowledgments

I wish to thank Alberto Bertoni and Paola Campadelli for encouraging this work, giving useful suggestions and for carefully readings the paper.

References

1. M. A. Alberti, A. Bertoni, P. Campadelli, G. Grossi, and R. Posenato. A Neural Circuit for the Maximum 2-Satisfiability Problem. In Mateo Valero and Antonio Gonzalez, editors, *Euromicro Workshop on Parallel and Distributed Processing*, pages 319–323, Los Alamitos, CA, January, 25–27 1995. EUROMICRO, IEEE Computer Society Press.
2. M. Bellare, O. Goldreich, and M. Sudan. Free bits, pcps and non-approximability - towards tight results. In *Technical Report TR95-024, Electronic Colluquium on Computational Complexity*, 1996.
3. U. Feige, S. Goldwasser, S. Safra L. Lovàsz, and M. Szegedy. Approximating clique is almost np-complete. In *Proceedings of the 32nd Annual IEEE Symposium on the Foundations of Computer Science*, pages 2–12, 1991.
4. J.J. Hopfield. Neural networks and physical systems with emergent collective computational abilities. In *Proceedings of the National Academy of Sciences*, pages 2554–2558, 1982.
5. D.S. Johnson and M. Trick. Dimacs series in discrete mathematics and theoretical computer science. In *Cliques, Coloring, and Satisfiability: Second DIMACS Implementation Challange*. in press.
6. R.M. Karp. *Reducibility among Combinatorial Problems*, pages 85–103. Complexity of Computer Computations. Plenum Press, New York, 1972.

Rates of Approximation of Multivariable Functions by One-hidden-layer Neural Networks

Věra Kůrková *

Institute of Computer Science, Prague, Czechia

Abstract

We investigate rates of approximation of multivariable functions by one-hidden-layer neural networks with a general hidden unit function. Under mild assumptions on hidden unit function we derive upper bounds on rates of approximation (measured by both the number of hidden units and the size of parameters) in terms of various norms of the function to be approximated and its higher order moduli of continuity.

1 Introduction

Although neural networks of many types can approximate continuous or $\mathcal{L}_p$ multivariable functions (see e.g. [14], [16]), as the accuracy of approximation increases one may require an arbitrarily large number of hidden units and the size of the network parameters may also grow or decrease without bound. Thus rate of approximation of a function by feedforward networks from a given class depends on both the number of hidden units and the size of their parameters.

The question whether this "universal approximation property" can be achieved even with parameters bounded from above was answered by Hornik [7]. The complementary task is to characterize functions that can be approximated with any accuracy by only varying parameters while the number of hidden units remains fixed. We proved in [9] that for Heaviside perceptron networks there are no additional functions than functions exactly computable by such networks for which this way of approximation is possible. On the other hand, several authors described sets of functions that can be approximated in this way by networks with smooth hidden unit functions (see e.g. [5]). Recently, dependence of approximation error on the number of hidden units has become better understood. Jones [8] introduced a recursive method of estimating error of incremental approximation and together with Barron proposed to apply it to neural networks. Combining this method with Fourier representation Barron [2] derived upper bounds on rates of approximation by sigmoidal perceptron networks as a function of hidden units. Following Barron and Jones, several authors derived such upper bounds for networks of various types (see e.g. [15], [4], [13]).

In this paper, we investigate rates of approximation of multivariable functions by one-hidden-layer neural networks with a general hidden unit function. Under mild assumptions on the hidden unit function, we derive upper bounds on rates of approximation (measured by both the number of hidden units and the size of parameters) in terms of various norms of the function to be approximated and its higher order moduli of continuity.

*This work was partially supported by GA AV grant A2030602 and KBN grant 8T11A02311.

2 Complexity of functions with respect to universal neural network classes

In this paper we examine approximation of continuous functions by one-hidden-layer networks with a single linear output unit. Such networks compute functions of the form $\sum_{i=1}^{n} w_i \phi(\mathbf{y}_i, \mathbf{x})$, where n corresponds to the number of hidden units, $w_i \in \mathcal{R}$, $i = 1, \ldots, n$, to *output weights* and $\phi : \mathcal{R}^{p+d} \rightarrow \mathcal{R}$ to the type of hidden units with $\mathbf{y}_i \in \mathcal{R}^p$ representing their parameters and $\mathbf{x} \in \mathcal{R}^d$ input vectors ($\mathcal{R}$ denotes the set of real numbers). We call such networks *ϕ-networks*. For example, for *perceptrons* with an activation function $\psi : \mathcal{R} \rightarrow \mathcal{R}$, the number of parameters p equals $d+1$ and $\phi((\mathbf{v}, b), \mathbf{x}) = P_\psi(\mathbf{v}, b, \mathbf{x}) = \psi(\mathbf{v} \cdot \mathbf{x} + b)$, where $\mathbf{v} \in \mathcal{R}^d$ is an *input weight* vector and $b \in \mathcal{R}$ is a *bias*. For *radial-basis-function* (RBF) units with a radial (even) function $\psi : \mathcal{R} \rightarrow \mathcal{R}$ $\phi((\mathbf{v}, b), \mathbf{x}) = B_\psi(\mathbf{v}, b, \mathbf{x}) = \psi(b\|\mathbf{x} - \mathbf{v}\|)$, where $\mathbf{v} \in \mathcal{R}^d$ is a *centroid*, $b \in \mathcal{R}$, $b > 0$, is a *width* and $\|.\|$ denotes the Euclidean norm on $\mathcal{R}^d$.

For a subset $J \subseteq \mathcal{R}^d$, a function $\phi : \mathcal{R}^{p+d} \rightarrow \mathcal{R}$ representing a type of a computational unit, n positive integer and $a_l, a_u > 0$ we denote by $\mathcal{F}(\phi, J, n, a_l, a_u)$ the set of all functions from J to $\mathcal{R}$ of the form $\sum_{i=1}^{n} w_i \phi(\mathbf{y}_i, \mathbf{x})$, where $w_i \in \mathcal{R}$ and $\mathbf{y}_i \in \mathcal{R}^p$ such that for all $i = 1, \ldots, n$ $\|\mathbf{y}_i\| \leq a_u$ and for all pairs $i \neq i'$ $a_l \leq |y_{ij} - y_{i'j}|$ for all $j = 1, \ldots, p$. When either n or a_l and a_u or both n and a_l and a_u are not bounded we will use notation $\mathcal{F}(\phi, J, *, a_l, a_u)$, $\mathcal{F}(\phi, J, n, *, *)$ or $\mathcal{F}(\phi, J, *, *, *)$, resp. We will abbreviate $\mathcal{F}(\phi, J, *, *, *)$ by $\mathcal{F}(\phi, J)$. For $J \subseteq \mathcal{R}^d$ we denote by $(\mathcal{C}(J), \|.\|_{\mathcal{C}(J)})$ and $(\mathcal{L}_p(J), \|.\|_p)$ (for $p \in [1, \infty]$) standard normed linear spaces of continuous functions with supremum norm and spaces of $\mathcal{L}_p$ functions, resp.

For a fixed $J \subseteq \mathcal{R}^d$ and a normed linear space $(\mathcal{X}, \|.\|)$ of functions on J with a norm $\|.\|$ consider *rate of approximation* of a function f by ϕ-networks as a mapping $\varepsilon_{f,\phi} : \mathcal{N}_+ \times \mathcal{R}_+^2 \rightarrow \mathcal{R}_+$ defined by $\varepsilon_{f,\phi}(n, a_l, a_u) = \inf\{\|f - h\|; h \in \mathcal{F}(\phi, J, n, a_l, a_u)\}$ ($\mathcal{N}_+$ denotes the set of positive integers and $\mathcal{R}_+$ the set of non-negative real numbers). When infimum is taken over sets $\mathcal{F}(\phi, J, *, a_l, a_u)$, $\mathcal{F}(\phi, J, n, *, *)$ or $\mathcal{F}(\phi, J)$ we will use notation $\varepsilon_{f,\phi}(*, a_l, a_u)$, $\varepsilon_{f,\phi}(n, *, *)$ or $\varepsilon_{f,\phi}(*, *, *)$, resp. Thus if $\varepsilon_{f,\phi}(*, *, *) = 0$ then f is in the closure of $\mathcal{F}(\phi, J)$ with respect to the topology induced by $\|.\|$.

A class of ϕ-networks has the *universal approximation property* with respect to either continuous or $\mathcal{L}_p$ functions if for all compact subsets of $\mathcal{R}^d$ of any dimension d for any function f from $(\mathcal{C}(J), \|.\|_{\mathcal{C}})$ or $(\mathcal{L}_p, \|.\|_p)$, resp., $\varepsilon_{f,\phi}(*, *, *) = 0$. Many classes of networks are known to poses this property (see e.g., [14], [16]). Each class of ϕ-networks having the universal approximation property determines on the corresponding normed linear space of multivariable functions a hierarchy of complexity partially ordered by $\preceq$ defined by $f \preceq h$ if $\varepsilon_{f,\phi} \leq \varepsilon_{h,\phi}$.

We showed in [9] that when both the number of hidden units and network parameters are bounded then for many types of feedforward networks there is a choice of network parameterization (not necessarily unique) producing an approximation of any continuous function achieving the minimal error. Such classes of networks are said to have the *best approximation property*. More precisely, for any compact $J \subset \mathcal{R}^d$, ϕ bounded and continuous and $f \in \mathcal{C}(J)$ $\varepsilon_{f,\phi}(n, a_l, a_u) = \min\{\|f - h\|_{\mathcal{C}}; h \in \mathcal{F}(\phi, n, a_l, a_u)\}$.

3 Rates of approximation depending on the size of parameters

Various authors ([5], [9]) listed examples of functions that can be approximated with any accuracy by networks with a fixed number of hidden units, i.e. for which $\varepsilon_{f,\phi}(n,*,*) = 0$ for some positive integer n. The following general approach includes all such cases.

Let $\mathcal{C}^q(\mathcal{R}^p)$ denotes the set of all functions on $\mathcal{R}^p$ for which all iterated partial derivatives of order at most q exist and are continuous, $\mathcal{C}^\infty(\mathcal{R}^p)$ denotes the set of functions with continuous partial derivatives of all orders. For a function $f \in \mathcal{C}^q(\mathcal{R}^p)$, $s \in \{1,\ldots,q\}$ and $j \in \{1,\ldots,p\}$ denote by $D_j^{(s)} f$ the partial derivative of order s with respect to the j-th variable, and for $s = 0$ define $D_j^{(0)} f = f$. We write D_j instead of $D_j^{(1)}$. For a multiindex $\mathbf{s} = (s_1,\ldots,s_p) \in \mathcal{N}^p$ let $|\mathbf{s}| = \sum_{j=1}^p s_j$ and for a finite set P let $|P|$ denotes the number of its elements.

For $\phi \in \mathcal{C}^\infty(\mathcal{R}^{p+d})$, $s \in \mathcal{N}$, $r \in \mathcal{N}_+$ denote by $\mathcal{D}(\phi, J, r, s)$ the set of all linear combinations of r functions obtained using partial differential operators of order at most s acting on $\phi(\mathbf{y},\mathbf{x}) = \phi(y_1,\ldots,y_p,x_1,\ldots,x_d)$ with respect to the first p variables $y_1,\ldots,y_p$. More precisely, $\mathcal{D}(\phi, J, r, s)$ is the set of all functions $f : J \to \mathcal{R}$ of the form $f(\mathbf{x}) = \sum_{i=1}^m \sum_{\mathbf{s}\in P_i} a_{i\mathbf{s}} D_1^{(s_1)} \ldots D_p^{(s_p)} \phi(\mathbf{y}_i, \mathbf{x})$, where $m \in \mathcal{N}_+$, for every $i = 1,\ldots,m$ $\mathbf{y}_i \in \mathcal{R}^p$, $P_i \subset {\mathcal{N}_+}^p$ is finite and $\sum_{i=1}^m |P_i| \leq r$, for every $\mathbf{s} \in P_i$ $a_{i\mathbf{s}} \in \mathcal{R}$ and $|\mathbf{s}| \leq s$. Note that since we allow $\mathbf{s} = \mathbf{0}$, $\mathcal{F}(\phi, J, n, *, *) \subseteq \mathcal{D}(\phi, J, n, 0)$. Let $\mathcal{D}(\phi, A) = \cup\{\mathcal{D}(\phi, A, r, s); s \in \mathcal{N}, r \in \mathcal{N}_+\}$.

The following theorem is a reformulation of our result proved in [12].

Theorem 3.1 *Let d, p, r be positive integers, s be a non-negative integer, $\phi \in \mathcal{C}^\infty(\mathcal{R}^{p+d})$ and $J \subset \mathcal{R}^d$ be compact. Then for every $f \in (\mathcal{D}(\phi, J, r, s), \|.\|_C)$ $\varepsilon_{f,\phi}(r(s+1)^p, *, *) = 0$.*

Thus, if a hidden unit function, ϕ, is smooth, for each linear combination of iterated partial derivatives of ϕ with respect to its parameters f we have $\varepsilon_{f,\phi}(n,*,*) = 0$ for a sufficiently large n depending polynomially on the sum of orders of all the terms and exponentially on the dimension of parameter space. Hence such function f can be approximated with any accuracy by networks with only n hidden units. However, notice that a sequence (indexed by $m \in \mathcal{N}_+$) of networks with fixed nember of hidden units approximating an iterated partial derivative $D_1^{(s_1)} \ldots D_p^{(s_p)} \phi$ have output weights growing of order $\mathcal{O}(m^s)$, where $s = |\mathbf{s}|$, and the differences between hidden unit parameters decreasing of order $\mathcal{O}(\frac{1}{m})$. Thus for large m such approximating functions are from $\mathcal{F}(\phi, J, (s+1)^p, a_l, a_u)$ with a_l of order $\frac{1}{m}$ and a_u of order m^s. Implementation of such networks might not be feasible for large m. On the other hand, if m is small enough to allow implementation, then the achievable approximation error might not be sufficiently accurate.

For $f \in \mathcal{D}(\phi, J)$ we can estimate the decrease of the error of approximation $\varepsilon_{f,\phi}(n,.,.)$ in dependence of size of parameters in terms of higher order moduli of continuity of $\phi(.,\mathbf{x})$. Recall that for a function $h \in (\mathcal{C}^\infty(J), \|.\|_C)$ and a positive integer s the *s-th order modulus of continuity* $\omega_{h,s}$ is a function $\omega_{h,s} : \mathcal{R}_+ \to \mathcal{R}_+$

such that for every $\delta \in \mathcal{R}_+$ $\omega_{h,s}(\delta) = \sup\{\|\Delta^s_{\mathbf{u}}(h,.)\|_C; \mathbf{u} \in \mathcal{R}^d, \|\mathbf{u}\| \leq \delta\}$, where $\Delta^s_{\mathbf{u}}(h,\mathbf{y}) = \sum_{i=0}^{s} \binom{k}{i} h(\mathbf{y} + i\mathbf{u})$.

If a hidden unit function does not satisfy a special type of recursion and the ratio between change of output weights and differences between hidden unit parameters is polynomial then the only functions that can be approximated by networks with a fixed number of hidden units are the functions described above, i.e. linear combinations of iterated partial derivatives of the hidden unit function with respect to its parameters. The remaining two cases (when hidden unit function satisfies this special condition and when this ratio is exponential) both lead to situations where we cannot infer anything about limits of sequences of functions computable by networks with fixed number of hidden units (for more details and proofs see [12]).

4 Rates of approximation depending on the number of hidden units

Using ideas from projection pursuit method Jones [8] derived a quite general tool for estimating rates of approximation in Hilbert spaces. The following is a version of Jones' result slightly improved by Barron [2, p.934]. If $(\mathcal{X}, \|.\|)$ is a normed linear space then by *cl* we denote the closure in the topology induced on $\mathcal{X}$ by the norm $\|.\|$ and by *conv* the convex hull.

Theorem 4.1 (Jones-Barron) *Let $(\mathcal{X}, \|.\|)$ be a Hilbert space, B a positive real number and $\mathcal{G}$ a subset of $\mathcal{X}$ such that for every $g \in \mathcal{G}$ $\|g\| \leq B$. Then for every $f \in cl\ conv\ \mathcal{G}$, for every $c > B^2 - \|f\|^2$ and for every positive integer n there exists f_n that is a convex combination of n elements of $\mathcal{G}$ such that $\|f - f_n\|^2 \leq \frac{c}{n}$.*

To apply this theorem to neural networks, Barron [1] introduced a concept of a variation of a function with respect to a set of characteristic functions, in particular variation with respect to half-spaces. In [10] we generalized this concept to a variation with respect to a family of functions. Let d be a positive integer and $(\mathcal{X}, \|.\|)$ be a normed linear space. For a subset $\mathcal{G}$ of $\mathcal{X}$ containing at least one non-zero element and a positive real number B let $\mathcal{G}(B) = \{wg; g \in \mathcal{G}, |w| \leq B\}$. For $f \in \mathcal{X}$ define *variation of f with respect to $\mathcal{G}$* (or *$\mathcal{G}$-variation*) by $V(f,\mathcal{G}) = \inf\{B \in \mathcal{R}_+; f \in cl\ conv\ \mathcal{G}(B)\}$. Note that if the set over which the infimum is taken is empty then $V(f,\mathcal{G}) = \infty$. The concept of $\mathcal{G}$-variation depends on the choice of a norm $\|.\|$ with respect to which the closure is taken; to simplify the notation we only write $V(f,\mathcal{G})$. We showed in [10] that (i) the infimum in the definition of $\mathcal{G}$-variation is always achieved, (ii) $V(.,\mathcal{G})$ is a norm on $\{f \in \mathcal{X}; V(f,\mathcal{G}) < \infty\}$, (iii) for every $f \in \mathcal{X}$ $\frac{\|f\|}{\sup_{g\in\mathcal{G}} \|g\|} \leq V(f,\mathcal{G})$. Together with Hlaváčková and Savický we derived in [6] the following geometric characterization of variation ($\mathcal{G}^\perp$ denotes the orthogonal complement of $\mathcal{G}$).

Theorem 4.2 *Let $(\mathcal{X}, \|.\|)$ be a Hilbert space and $\mathcal{G}$ be its subset such that $\mathcal{G} \neq \{0\}$. Then for every $f \in \mathcal{X}$ $V(f,\mathcal{G}) = \sup_{h\in\mathcal{X}-\mathcal{G}^\perp} \frac{|f\cdot h|}{\sup_{g\in\mathcal{G}} |g\cdot h|}$.*

In particular, when f is not orthogonal to $\mathcal{G}$ then $V(f,\mathcal{G}) \geq \frac{\|f\|}{\sup_{g\in\mathcal{G}} |<f,g>|}$. Thus functions that are "almost orthogonal" to $\mathcal{G}$ have large $\mathcal{G}$-variation.

Reformulating Jones-Barron's theorem in terms of $\mathcal{G}$-variation, we get an upper bound on rate of approximation by convex combinations of n elements of $\mathcal{G}$ of the form $\sqrt{\frac{c}{n}}$, where $c > (V(f,\mathcal{G}) \sup_{g\in\mathcal{G}} \|g\|)^2 - \|f\|^2$. Using this theorem to estimate error of approximation by *linear* instead of *convex* combinations we can replace $\mathcal{G}$ by $\mathcal{G}(\alpha) = \{\alpha(g)g; g \in \mathcal{G}\}$, where $\alpha : \mathcal{G} \to \mathcal{R}$ is any mapping. Jones-Barron theorem gives the smallest upper bound for α minimizing the product $V(f,\mathcal{G}(\alpha)) \sup_{g\in\mathcal{G}} \|\alpha(g)g\|$. We showed in [10] that this product is minimal for $\alpha_0(g) = \frac{1}{\|g\|}$. Denoting $\mathcal{G}^0 = \{\frac{g}{\|g\|}; g \in \mathcal{G}\}$ we get the following corollary of Jones-Barron's theorem.

Corollary 4.3 *Let $(\mathcal{X}, \|.\|)$ be a Hilbert space and $\mathcal{G}$ a subset of $\mathcal{X}$. Then for every $f \in \mathcal{X}$ with $V(f,\mathcal{G}^0) < \infty$, for every $c > V(f,\mathcal{G}^0)^2 - \|f\|^2$ and for every positive integer n there exists f_n that is a linear combination of n elements of $\mathcal{G}$ such that $\|f - f_n\|^2 \leq \frac{c}{n}$.*

For a hidden unit function $\phi : \mathcal{R}^{p+d} \to \mathcal{R}$ and a compact $J \subset \mathcal{R}^d$ let $\mathcal{G}_\phi = \{\phi(\mathbf{y},.) : J \to \mathcal{R}; \mathbf{y} \in Y\}$. Then for every $f \in (\mathcal{L}_2(J), \|.\|_2)$ this corollary implies that $\varepsilon_{f,\phi}(n,*,*) \leq \sqrt{\frac{V(f,\mathcal{G}_\phi^0)^2 - \|f\|_2^2}{n}}$ for every $n \in \mathcal{N}_+$.

To derive upper bounds on rates of approximation of multivariable functions by neural networks using this corollary we need to estimate $\mathcal{G}_\phi$-variation for ϕ representing standard neural network hidden unit functions. When a function can be represented by an integral equation corresponding metaphorically to a neural network with a continuum of hidden units we can use the following bound on variation derived together with Kainen and Kreinovich in [13].

Theorem 4.4 *Let d, p be positive integers, $J \subseteq \mathcal{R}^d$ and $f \in (\mathcal{C}(J).\|.\|_\mathcal{C})$ be any function which can be represented as $f(\mathbf{x}) = \int_Y w(\mathbf{y})\phi(\mathbf{x},\mathbf{y})d\mathbf{y}$ where $Y \subseteq \mathcal{R}^p$, $w \in \mathcal{C}(Y)$ is compactly supported, and let $\mathcal{G}_\phi = \{\phi(.,\mathbf{y}) : J \to \mathcal{R}; \mathbf{y} \in Y\}$. Then $V(f,\mathcal{G}_\phi) \leq \int_Y |w(\mathbf{y})|d\mathbf{y}$.*

Note that the integral equation assumed as the hypothesis of this theorem is called a *linear integral equation of the first kind with the kernel* ϕ and that f is called an *integral transform* of w. Thus $\mathcal{G}_\phi$-variation (with respect to the topology of uniform convergence) of an integral transform of w is bounded from above by the $\mathcal{L}_1$-norm of w. Barron [2] used Fourier representation corresponding to perceptron networks with cosine activation function and from bounds on rates of approximation by networks of this type, derived estimates for sigmoidal perceptron networks by approximating cosine by sigmoidal. Together with Kainen and Kreinovich we obtained in [13] tighter estimates using an integral formula with $\phi(\mathbf{y},\mathbf{x}) = \vartheta(\mathbf{e}\cdot\mathbf{x} + b)$, where ϑ denotes the Heaviside activation function. Using our integral formula, variation of any sufficiently smooth function can be estimated by the $\mathcal{L}_1$-norm of a weighting function w corresponding to flow of order d of f through hyperplanes.

DeVore et al. [3] proved that when parameters of approximating neural networks with n hidden units are chosen in a *continuous* dependence on the function to be approximated then one can always find smooth functions for which the number of hidden units needed to guarantee a given approximation error is growing exponentially with the input dimension d. In [6] we derived exponential (of order $\mathcal{O}(2^{7d/8})$) lower bounds on variation with respect to half-spaces for real-valued functions of d Boolean variables. Continuous extensions of such functions to $[0,1]^d$ provide examples of functions with variation with respect to half-spaces growing exponentially with d. For such functions, Corollary 4.3 gives an upper bound on approximation by Heaviside perceptron networks which grows exponentially with the number of variables.

References

[1] A. R. Barron. Neural net approximation. In **Proceedings of the 7th Yale Workshop on Adaptive and Learning Systems** (pp. 69–72), 1992.

[2] A. R. Barron. Universal approximation bounds for superposition of a sigmoidal function. **IEEE Transactions on Information Theory**, 39(3):930–945, 1993.

[3] R. DeVore, R. Howard and C. Micchelli. Optimal nonlinear approximation. **Manuscripta Mathematica**, 63:469–478, 1989.

[4] F. Girosi and G. Anzellotti. Rates of convergence for radial basis function and neural networks. In **Artificial Neural Networks for Speech and Vision** (pp. 97–113). Chapman & Hall, London, 1993.

[5] M. Gori, F. Scarselli and A. C. Tsoi. Which classes of functions can a given multilayer perceptron approximate? In **Proceedings of the ICNN'96** (pp. 2226-2231), IEEE, 1996.

[6] K. Hlaváčková, V. Kůrková and P. Savický. Representations and rates of approximation of real-valued Boolean functions by neural networks (manuscript).

[7] K. Hornik. Some new results on neural network approximation. **Neural Networks**, 6:1069–1072, 1993.

[8] L. K. Jones. A simple lemma on greedy approximation in Hilbert space and convergence rates for projection pursuit regression and neural network training. **Annals of Statistics**, 20:608–613, 1992.

[9] V. Kůrková. Approximation of functions by perceptron networks with bounded number of hidden units. **Neural Networks**, 8:745–750, 1995.

[10] V. Kůrková. Dimension-independent rates of approximation by neural networks. In **Computer-Intensive Methods in Control and Signal Processing: Curse of Dimensionality** (pp. 261–270), Birkhauser, Boston, 1997.

[11] V. Kůrková. Incremental approximation by neural networks. In **Dealing with Complexity: A Neural Network Approach**. Springer, London, 1997 (in press)

[12] V. Kůrková. Trade-off between the size of weights and the number of hidden units in feedforward networks. Technical Report ICS-96-495.

[13] V. Kůrková, P.C. Kainen and V. Kreinovich. Estimates of the number of hidden units and variation with respect to half-spaces. **Neural Networks**, 1997 (in press).

[14] H. N. Mhaskar and C. A. Micchelli. Approximation by superposition of sigmoidal and radial basis functions. **Advances in Applied Mathematics**, 13:350–373, 1992.

[15] H. N. Mhaskar and C. A. Micchelli. Dimension-independent bounds on the degree of approximation by neural networks. **IBM Journal of Research and Development**, 38:277–284, 1994.

[16] J. Park and I. W. Sandberg. Approximation and radial-basis-function networks. **Neural Computation**, 5:305–316, 1993.

Energy Functional and Fixed Points of a Neural Network

Leonid B. Litinsky
Institute for High Pressure Physics Russian Academy of Sciences
Troitsk, Russia

6.06.97

Abstract

A dynamic system, which is used in the neural network theory, Ising spin glasses and factor analysis, has been investigated. The properties of the connection matrix, which guarantee the coincidence of the set of the fixed points of the dynamic system with the set of local minima of the energy functional, have been determined. The influence of the connection matrix diagonal elements on the structure of the fixed points set has been investigated.

1 Introduction

We define a neural network as a dynamic system of n spin variables (*spins*) which can take one of two values:

$$\sigma_i = \{\pm 1\}, \quad i = 1, 2, \ldots, n. \tag{1}$$

The spins are connected by a symmetric connection matrix $J = (J_{ij})$:

$$J_{ij} = J_{ji}, \quad i, j = 1, 2, \ldots, n.$$

The local potential

$$h_i(t) = \sum_{j=1}^{n} J_{ij}\sigma_j(t) \tag{2}$$

with which the network acts on spin i, determines solely the value of spin i at time $t + 1$:

$$\sigma_i(t+1) = \begin{cases} \sigma_i(t), & \text{if} \quad h_i(t)\sigma_i(t) \geq 0 \\ -\sigma_i(t), & \text{if} \quad h_i(t)\sigma_i(t) < 0 \end{cases} \tag{3}$$

The state of the network as a whole is described by a *configuration vector* $\vec{\sigma}$, whose coordinates are given by Eq.(1). In what follows, Greek letters will be used to designate configuration vectors.

We want to investigate the set of the so called *fixed points* of the network, i.e. such states $\vec{\sigma}^*$, that for all coordinates σ_i^* have:

$$\sigma_i^* h_i \geq 0, \quad i = 1, 2, \ldots, n. \tag{4}$$

Besides the neural network theory, the mathematical model (1)-(3) is also used in the factor alalysis [1] and in the Ising spin glass theory [2]. The neural network theory makes use of a physical concept of the *energy of the state* $\vec{\sigma}$, which is defined as

$$E(\vec{\sigma}) = -\frac{1}{n}\sum_{i=1}^{n}\sigma_i h_i = -\frac{1}{n}\sum_{i,j=1}^{n} J_{ij}\sigma_i\sigma_j. \tag{5}$$

It is very important, both from the physical point of view and the ability of the network to have content-addressable memory [2], that the energy of the state would be a decreasing function on every step of the network evolution. And, moreover, the fixed points must be the local minima of the energy functional (5).

In the second section, we obtain the conditions under which a connection matrix J guarantees the fulfillment of the above mentioned requirements. It has been found that the Hebb connection matrix as well as the connection matrices which are used in physical problems possess the necessary property. But this is not the case for the projection matrix [3]. As a result, a network with such a connection matrix has a set of fixed points which is wider than the set of the local minima of the energy functional (5). In the third section, we show how the situation for a network with a projection matrix can be improved.

Notations. In what follows, a network with a connection matrix J is called a J-network. We denote by $FP(J)$ the set of all fixed points of the J-network. A configuration vector which is a fixed point of a network will have a superscript "*":

$$\vec{\sigma}^* \in FP(J).$$

We denote by $LM(J)$ the set of the local minima of the energy functional (5). To examine the local minima of the functional (5), we introduce a topology on the set of configuration vectors: the set of n configuration vectors $\vec{\sigma}^{(l)}$ which are the nearest to the vector $\vec{\sigma}$ in the sense of the Hamming distance will be called a *vicinity* of the state $\vec{\sigma}$:

$$\vec{\sigma}^{(l)} = (\sigma_1, \sigma_2, \ldots, -\sigma_l, \ldots, \sigma_n), \quad l = 1, 2, \ldots, n.$$

In other words, the state $\vec{\sigma}^{(l)}$ from the vicinity of the state $\vec{\sigma}$ differs from the latter by the opposite value of the lth spin only,

$$\vec{\sigma} \in LM(J) \Leftrightarrow E(\vec{\sigma}) \le E(\vec{\sigma}^{(l)}), \quad l = 1, 2, \ldots, n.$$

Finally, a matrix with zero diagonal elements will be marked by the superscript "0":

$$J^{(0)} \Leftrightarrow J_{ii} = 0, \quad i = 1, 2, \ldots, n.$$

2 On the role of the diagonal elements

Theorem 1

1. The set of the local minima of the energy functional (5) does not depend on the value of the diagonal elements of the connection matrix:

$$LM(J) = LM(J + A),$$

where

$$A = diag\{a_{11}, a_{22}, \ldots, a_{nn}\} \tag{6}$$

and all the elements a_{ii} are arbitrary real numbers.

2. For a connection matrix $J^{(0)}$ with zero diagonal elements, the set of the fixed points coincides with the set of the local minima of the energy functional

$$FP(J^{(0)}) = LM(J^{(0)}). \tag{7}$$

3. Let all the elements a_{ii} of the diagonal matrix (6) be positive, then

$$FP(J^{(0)} + A) \supseteq FP(J^{(0)}) \supseteq FP(J^{(0)} - A). \tag{8}$$

The proof of Theorem 1: Let's write the energy of the state $\vec{\sigma}$, extracting the contribution of the lth spin. Up to the positive factor we obtain:

$$E(\vec{\sigma}) \propto -\sum_{i,j\neq l} J_{ij}\sigma_i\sigma_j + J_{ll} - 2\sigma_l h_l. \tag{9}$$

The state $\vec{\sigma}$ will be the local minimum of the energy functional if and only if the system of the inequalities (10) is fulfilled for all states $\vec{\sigma}^{(l)}$ from the vicinity of the state $\vec{\sigma}$:

$$E(\vec{\sigma}^{(l)}) - E(\vec{\sigma}) \propto \sigma_l h_l - J_{ll} = \sigma_l \sum_{j\neq l} J_{lj}\sigma_j \geq 0, \quad l = 1, 2, \ldots, n. \tag{10}$$

It is evident that the inequalities (10) do not depend on the values of the diagonal elements. The conditions of their fulfillment are defined by the off-diagonal part of the matrix J. By this the first item of the Theorem is proved. Moreover, it follows from the inequalities (10) that for nonnegative J_{ll} any local minimum of the energy functional is also a fixed point of the network:

$$LM(J) \subseteq FP(J) \text{ when } J_{ll} \geq 0, \quad l = 1, 2, \ldots, n. \tag{11}$$

Then, let a state $\vec{\sigma}^*$ be a fixed point of the network: $\sigma_l^* h_l \geq 0, \quad l = 1, 2, \ldots, n$. With the help of Eq.(9) we obtain:

$$E(\vec{\sigma}^{(l)}) - E(\vec{\sigma}^*) \propto \sigma_l^* h_l - J_{ll} \begin{cases} \geq & 0, \text{ if } J_{ll} = 0 \\ ? & 0, \text{ if } J_{ll} > 0 \\ > & 0, \text{ if } J_{ll} < 0 \end{cases}$$

In other words, for nonpositive J_{ll} any fixed point of the network is a local minimum of the energy functional:

$$LM(J) \supseteq FP(J) \text{ when } J_{ll} \leq 0, \quad l = 1, 2, \ldots, n. \tag{12}$$

Combined with the proved first item of the Theorem, Eqs. (11) and (12) justify the correctness of Eqs. (7) and (8). Thus, the proof of the Theorem is finished.

In fact, to some extent the Theorem 1 permits regulating the set of the fixed points of the network. Let's explain this statement. If the matrix $J^{(0)}$ is transformed by the diagonal matrix A, $J(A) = J^{(0)} + A$, then in accordance with the Theorem 1, the set of the local minima of the energy functional is not changed. But this transformation affects the set of the fixed points of the $J(A)$-network. Indeed, if all the matrix elements a_{ii} are positive, the set of the $J(A)$-network fixed points extends as compared with $FP(J^{(0)})$. The last is true due to the appearance of the new fixed points which are not the local minima. If, on the contrary, all the matrix elements a_{ii} are negative, the set of the fixed points of the $J(A)$-network narrows as compared with $FP(J^{(0)})$: some states, remaining, as they were, the local minima of the energy functional, cease to be the fixed points.

The last statement allows to suggest a simple method for the elimination of the unnecessary fixed points of the network. Let's formulate it in the form of a theorem.

Theorem 2

Let the fixed points of a $J^{(0)}$-network be numbered in such a way that

$$E(\vec{\sigma}^{(1)} \leq E(\vec{\sigma}^{(2)} \leq \ldots \leq E(\vec{\sigma}^{(k)} < E(\vec{\sigma}^{(k+1)} \leq \ldots$$

(to simplify the writing, here we omit the superscript "*" in the notations of the fixed points). Let A be a diagonal matrix whose elements are defined by the equalities

$$a_{ii} = \min_{l=1,k} \sigma_i^{(l)} h_i(\vec{\sigma}^{(l)}), \quad i = 1, 2, \ldots n, \tag{13}$$

where $h_i(\vec{\sigma})$ is the potential (2) which acts on the ith spin in the $J^{(0)}$-network. Then

$$FP(J^{(0)} - A) = \{\vec{\sigma}^{(1)}, \vec{\sigma}^{(2)}, \ldots, \vec{\sigma}^{(k)}\}.$$

The proof of Theorem 2: Since all a_{ii} from Eq. (13) are positive, the set of the $(J^{(0)} - A)$-network fixed points, due to Theorem 1, can be only narrower in comparison with the set $J^{(0)}$-network fixed points. And from the definition (4) of a fixed point, it follows that the state $\vec{\sigma}^{(l)}$ will be a $(J^{(0)} - A)$-network fixed point if and only if the system of the inequalities

$$\sigma_i^{(l)} h_i(\vec{\sigma}^{(l)}) - a_{ii} \geq 0, \quad i = 1, 2, \ldots, n \tag{14}$$

is fulfilled. When the definition (13) is taken into account, it is evident that for any fixed point $\vec{\sigma}^{(l)}$ with the $l \leq k$ the system of the inequalities (14) is fulfilled. Consequently, the first k states of the $\vec{\sigma}^{(l)}$ are the $(J^{(0)} - A)$-network fixed points. On the other hand, by proceeding from Eq.(5) for the energy and taking into account that the $J^{(0)}$-network fixed points are strictly ordered with respect to the energy increase, it is easy to see that at least for one of the coordinates of the state $\vec{\sigma}^{(l)}$ with $l > k$, the inequalities (14) are not fulfilled. Consequently, the states $\vec{\sigma}^{(l)}$ with $l > k$ are not the $(J^{(0)} - A)$-network fixed points.

Remark. From Eq.(9) it can be easily shown that even under the sequential dynamics the evolution of a network with a connection matrix whose diagonal elements are negative can be accompanied by the energy increase. As a result, even under the sequential dynamics limit cycles can be formed for such a network! From this point of view, the connection matrices with negative diagonal elements are absolutely nonphysical. But Theorem 2 gives a simple and effective method to eliminate high energy fixed points. In some cases this method can be very useful. In particular, it is well-known [3, 4, 5], that for a network with the projection connection matrix the energies of the spurious fixed points are larger then the energies of the memorized patterns. Consequently all such spurious fixed points can be easily eliminated with the help of Theorem 2.

3 Projection connection matrix

1). Let

$$\vec{\xi}^{(l)} = (\xi_1^{(l)}, \xi_2^{(l)}, \ldots, \xi_n^{(l)}), \quad l = 1, 2, \ldots, p, \tag{15}$$

be p preassigned configuration vectors which we would like to have as a network fixed points (such vectors are usually called the *memorized patterns*). It is known [3], that it can be easily done if a matrix P of orthogonal projection onto the linear subspace $\Lambda_{<\vec{\xi}^{(1)}, \vec{\xi}^{(2)}, \ldots, \vec{\xi}^{(p)}>}$, spanned by the p memorized patterns $\vec{\xi}^{(l)}$, is taken as a connection matrix. The matrix P is symmetric and nilpotent one: $P^T = P, \quad P^2 = P$. Besides, by definition $P\vec{\xi}^{(l)} = \vec{\xi}^{(l)}, \quad l = 1, 2, \ldots, p$. Consequently, the vectors $\vec{\xi}^{(l)}$ are not only the fixed points of the P-network, but provide the global minimum of the energy functional (5):

$$E(\vec{\xi}^{(l)}) = -\frac{(P\vec{\xi}^{(l)}, \vec{\xi}^{(l)})}{n} = -1, \quad l = 1, 2, \ldots, p.$$

But, it is known from experience, that, as a rule, the P-network has additional fixed points which are called *spurious* fixed points. Their number is much larger that for the network with Hebb's connection matrix. And the worst is that not all the P-network fixed points are the local minima of the energy functional [5]. Theorem 1 helps to clarify the situation.

2). For simplicity we assume that p memorized patterns $\vec{\xi}^{(l)}$ are linearly independent vectors. We introduce a rectangular $(p \times n)$- matrix Ξ whose rows are memorized patterns $\vec{\xi}^{(l)}$:

$$\Xi = \begin{pmatrix} \xi_1^{(1)} & \xi_2^{(1)} & \ldots & \xi_n^{(1)} \\ \xi_1^{(2)} & \xi_2^{(2)} & \ldots & \xi_n^{(2)} \\ \ldots & \ldots & \ldots & \ldots \\ \xi_1^{(p)} & \xi_2^{(p)} & \ldots & \xi_n^{(p)} \end{pmatrix} \tag{16}$$

Then the matrix of the orthogonal projection onto the subspace $\Lambda_{<\{\vec{\xi}^{(l)}\}_1^p>}$ is

$$P = Y\Xi, \tag{17}$$

where Y is the $(n \times p)$-matrix that is pseudoinverse of the matrix Ξ. Apropos of the construction of pseudoinverse matrices, see [3, 4]. We only want to mention, that the columns of the matrix Y are n-dimensional vectors $\vec{y}^{(l)}$ such that $(\vec{y}^{(l)}, \vec{\xi}^{(l')}) = \delta_{ll'}$, where $\delta_{ll'}$ is the Kronecker symbol; $\vec{y}^{(l)}$ are also the linearly independent vectors.

The diagonal elements of the matrix P are positive. Indeed, they are equal to the squares of the projections onto the subspace $\Lambda_{<\vec{\xi}^{(1)},\vec{\xi}^{(2)},\ldots,\vec{\xi}^{(p)}>}$ of the n-dimensional Cartesian unit vectors $\vec{e}^{(i)} = (0,\ldots,1,\ldots,0)$:

$$P_{ii} = (P\vec{e}^{(i)}, \vec{e}^{(i)}) = \| P\vec{e}^{(i)} \|^2 = d_i^2, \quad i = 1,2,\ldots,n. \tag{18}$$

The values d_i^2 must be nonzero, otherwise the vectors $P\vec{e}^{(i)} = \sum_{j=1}^{p} \xi_i^{(j)} \vec{y}^{(j)}$, which are the sums of the linearly independent vectors, would be zero. Then, according to Theorem 1, the set of the P-network fixed points will really be wider than the set of the local minima of the energy functional.

If instead the P-network we consider the $P^{(0)}$-network,

$$P^{(0)} = P - D, \text{ where } D = diag\{d_1^2, d_2^2, \ldots, d_n^2\} \tag{19}$$

only the local minima of the energy functional will be the fixed points of the $P^{(0)}$-network. Since the memorized patterns provide the global minimum of the energy functional, they will necessarily be the $P^{(0)}$-network fixed points. In addition, the $P^{(0)}$-network has no nonphysical fixed points, i.e. those which are not the local minima of the energy functional.

Let's show that the set of the $P^{(0)}$-network fixed points has a structure which resembles the structure of the set of the fixed points for Hopfield's model [4].

Theorem 3

All n neurons can be enumerated in such a way that all the $P^{(0)}$-network fixed points will be of a "piecewise constant" kind:

$$\vec{\sigma}^* = (\underbrace{\varepsilon_1, \varepsilon_1, \ldots, \varepsilon_1}_{n_1}, \underbrace{\varepsilon_2, \varepsilon_2, \ldots, \varepsilon_2}_{n_2}, \ldots, \underbrace{\varepsilon_v, \varepsilon_v, \ldots, \varepsilon_v}_{n_v}), \tag{20}$$

where $\varepsilon_i = \{\pm 1\}$. The number v, the composition and the dimension n_i of constant sign intervals are defined uniquely by the memorized patterns matrix Ξ (16).

The proof of Theorem 3. For simplicity we assume that the number of the neurons n is much larger than the number of the memorized patterns p. For definiteness, we assume that $n > 2^p$. Then it is evident that not all n p-

dimensional column-vectors

$$\vec{\xi_i} = \begin{pmatrix} \xi_i^{(1)} \\ \xi_i^{(2)} \\ \vdots \\ \xi_i^{(p)} \end{pmatrix}, \quad i = 1, 2, \ldots, n \tag{21}$$

of the matrixΞ will be different. Some of them will be repeated [1]. Let's assume that n column-vectors $\vec{\xi_i}$ break up into v groups. Each group consists of some identical vectors: n_1 identical vectors belong to the first group; n_2 identical vectors belong to the second group and so on. And $n_1 + n_2 + \ldots + n_v = n$. Without loss of generality it may be assumed that the neurons of the network can be numbered in such a way that the matrix Ξ will have a form:

$$\Xi = \begin{pmatrix} \xi_1^{(1)} & \ldots & \xi_1^{(1)} & \xi_2^{(1)} & \ldots & \xi_2^{(1)} & \ldots & \xi_v^{(1)} & \ldots & \xi_v^{(1)} \\ \xi_1^{(2)} & \ldots & \xi_1^{(2)} & \xi_2^{(2)} & \ldots & \xi_2^{(2)} & \ldots & \xi_v^{(2)} & \ldots & \xi_v^{(2)} \\ \ldots & \ldots & \ldots & \ldots & \ldots & \ldots & \ldots & \ldots & \ldots & \ldots \\ \xi_1^{(p)} & \ldots & \xi_1^{(p)} & \xi_2^{(p)} & \ldots & \xi_2^{(p)} & \ldots & \xi_v^{(p)} & \ldots & \xi_v^{(p)} \end{pmatrix} \tag{22}$$

It was shown in [4] that when the projection matrix P acts onto the configuration vector $\vec{\sigma}$ the result is

$$P\vec{\sigma} = \sum_{l=1}^{p} m^{(l)}(\vec{\sigma})\vec{\xi}^{(l)},$$

where $m^{(l)}(\vec{\sigma})$ depends only on the state $\vec{\sigma}$. If $\vec{\sigma}^*$ is a fixed point of the $P^{(0)}$-network, its coordinates σ^* must satisfy the system of equations:

$$sign(P\vec{\sigma}^* - D\vec{\sigma}^*) \equiv sign\left(\sum_{l=1}^{p} m^{(l)}(\vec{\sigma}^*)\xi_i^{(l)} - d_i^2\sigma_i^*\right) = \sigma_i^*, \quad i = 1, 2, \ldots, n. \tag{23}$$

With respect to the form of the matrix Ξ (see Eq.(22)), it is easy to understand that, for example, for the first n_1 values of the subscript i all the sums $\sum_{l=1}^{p} m^{(l)}(\vec{\sigma}^*)\xi_i^{(l)}$ are the same: $\sum_{l=1}^{p} m^{(l)}(\vec{\sigma}^*)\xi_i^{(l)} = M, \quad i = 1, 2, \ldots, n_1$. ¿From here it immediately follows, that the first n_1 coordinates of the fixed point $\vec{\sigma}^*$ must be equal. Indeed, let's contrarily assume that, for example, $\sigma_1^* = 1$ and $\sigma_2^* = -1$. Then from Eqs. (23) it follows that two inequalities

$$\begin{cases} M \geq d_1^2 \\ -M \geq d_2^2 \end{cases}$$

have to be fulfilled simultaneously. But this is impossible.

Consequently, the first n_1 coordinates of the $P^{(0)}$-network fixed point are equal to one another. Similarly, it can be proved that the next n_2 coordinates

[1] The p-dimentional column-vectors $\vec{\xi_i}$ (21) are labelled with subscripts in contrast to the n-dimensional memorized patterns $\vec{\xi}^{(l)}$ (15), which are labelled with superscripts.

of the fixed point are equal to one another too, and so on up to the equality among the last n_v coordinates. The Theorem is proved.

3). Thus, the $P^{(0)}$-network possesses some attractive properties. Namely, all the memorized patterns will necessarily be its fixed points. Moreover, all the fixed points are, firstly, the local minima of the energy functional; secondly, they are of "piecewise constant" kind given by Eq. (20). It is known [4, 6] that the last two of the above mentioned properties are also typical for the fixed points of the Hopfield model, that is, for a network with the Hebb connection matrix. In our following discussions we will have in mind either the $P^{(0)}$-network, or the Hopfield model.

While Eq.(20) is only the necessary condition for a configuration to be a fixed point of a network, it restricts sufficiently the circle of the "applicants". Let's provide some estimates.

If v is the number of *different* column-vectors of the matrix Ξ and q is the number of the fixed points of the related network, it is clear that $q \leq 2^v$. Next, when the number of the memorized patterns p is given, a natural estimate for v is: $v \leq 2^p$. But, as it was shown in [4], actually we have:

$$q \leq 2^{2^{p-1}}. \tag{24}$$

Eq. (24) restricts the number of the fixed points from above. It is easy to verify that when $p = 2$, the inequality (24) transforms into the equality, and q just equals 4. But even for $p = 3$ the right-hand side of Eq.(24) is 16, and in [4] it was shown that for $p = 3$ the maximum possible number of the network fixed points is 14. This result coincides with the one of [7]. Other estimates for the fixed points number can be found in [8, 9, 10] .

Partially this work was supported by RFBR grant No. 95-01-01191.

References

[1] L.B.Litinsky. Neural network and factor analysis. Neural Network World 1996; 6:325-330.

[2] E.Domany, J.L. van Hemmen and K.Schulten (Eds.). Models of neural networks. Springer-Verlag, Berlin, 1991.

[3] L.Personnaz, I.Guyon and G.Dreyfus. Collective computational properties of neural networks: new learning mechanisms. Phys. Rev. A 1986; 34: 4217-4228.

[4] L.B.Litinsky. Direct calculation of the stable points of a neural network. Theor. and Math. Phys. 1994; 101: 1492-1501.

[5] I.Kanter, H.Sompolinsky. Associative recall of memory without errors. Phys. Rev. A 1987; 35: 380-392.

[6] A.A.Vedenov, A.A.Ezhov et al.. Structure of patterns in associative memory models. In: Neural Networks - Theory and Architecture, A.V. Holden and V.I. Kryukov (Eds.), Manch. Univ. Press, pp. 169 - 186, 1991.

[7] P.Baldi. Symmetries and learning in neural network models. Phys. Rev. Lett. 1987; 59: 1976 - 1978.

[8] P.Baldi, S.S.Venkatesh. Number of stable points for sipn-glass and neural networks of high orders. Phys. Rev. Lett. 1987; 58: 913 - 916.

[9] P.Baldi. Neural networks, orientations of the hypercube, and algebraic threshold functions. IEEE Trans. on Inform. Theory 1988; 34: 523 - 530.

[10] P.Kuhlman, J.K.Anlauf. The number of metastable states in the projection rule neural network. J. Phys. A: Math., Gen. 1994; 27: 5857 - 5870.

A Distribution-Free VC-Dimension-Based Performance Bound

Davide Mattera
Dipartimento di Ingegneria Elettronica
Università degli Studi di Napoli "Federico II"
Napoli, Italy

Francesco Palmieri
Dipartimento di Ingegneria Elettronica
Università degli Studi di Napoli "Federico II"
Napoli, Italy

Abstract

We report a new bound to the joint probability that both the approximation error between the a binary function learned by the input/output examples and the target binary function is larger than ϵ and the empirical error on the examples is smaller than a fixed not-null fraction of ϵ. The given bounds are independent of the probability distribution on the input space and improve some existing results on generalization abilities of an adaptive binary function.

1 Introduction

The ability to perform generalization is one of the most important properties of connectionist networks and has been the subject of a considerable research effort, mostly through experimental studies. Theoretical rather than experimental analysis of generalization is important if we wish to obtain results that are representative of a complete class of networks.

Let us consider a set X (sample space), a generic probability density $\mu(X)$ and a set of functions $\mathcal{F}$, called the hypothesis space, defined on X with values in $Y = \{0,1\}$: $\mathcal{F} = \{f : X \to Y\}$. We select one binary function $\overline{f}$, the so-called target function, not necessarily belonging to $\mathcal{F}$. A quantity of interest is the "error probability" (or "approximation error") e_f, defined as the probability measure of the subset of X on which f and $\overline{f}$ give different classification. Usually all we know about the target function $\overline{f}$ is its value on a finite set of i.i.d. training examples $\{(\mathbf{x}_1, \overline{f}(\mathbf{x}_1)), \ldots, (\mathbf{x}_m, \overline{f}(\mathbf{x}_m))\}$. One expects that, if the frequency of errors observed on the training set is small and the training set is large enough, the approximation error will be sufficiently small.

One of the most effective techniques for tackling the analysis of the generalization is provided by Vapnik's theory of minimization of the empirical risk.

The theory is very general (in particular it is valid for any probability density $\mu(X)$) and very appealing, even though the bounds so far proposed in the literature are generally considered to be rather crude. However, there are indication that the general results may not be so crude on small sample sizes if compared to known asymptotic results [1].

In this paper we report new results for the binary functions case on the scenario where the trained system (e.g., neural network) may exhibit, after learning, a small but non null fraction of errors ν_f^m. Such a situation is common in the applications and it may depend on: (1) a neural network that does not have enough degrees of freedom; (2) an inaccurate training algorithm; (3) noise on the examples. Moreover, the results we obtain in this paper for the case of binary functions can be straightforwardly extended to some general real functions learning scenarios [2, 3].

The paper is structured as follows. In Section 1 we review previous results on the topic and in Section 2 the new bounds are proposed. In Section 3 we present a comparison between the results of the Section 1 and 2. To avoid useless repetition we give most of the necessary definitions here.

Definitions:

(i) m = # of examples in the training set.

(ii) $e_f = \mu\{f(\mathbf{x}) \neq \overline{f}(\mathbf{x})\}$ = error probability on X.

(iii) ϵ = the approximation parameter $(0 < \epsilon < 1)$.

(iv) ν_f^m = fraction of errors on the training set.

(v) $\mu^m(\cdot)$ = probability density of the m-tuple of the examples $\{\mathbf{x}_1, \ldots, \mathbf{x}_m\}$.

(vi) $\Pi(\mathbf{x}_1, \ldots, \mathbf{x}_m)$ = # of dichotomies realizable by the network on the examples $\{\mathbf{x}_1, \ldots, \mathbf{x}_m\}$.

(vii) $\Pi(m) = \max_{\{\mathbf{x}_1,\ldots,\mathbf{x}_m\}} \Pi(\mathbf{x}_1, \ldots, \mathbf{x}_m)$ = "growth function ", i.e. maximum number of dichotomies realizable by the network on all possible choices of m examples from X.

(viii) d = Vapnik-Chervonenkis (VC) dimension of the set of binary functions $\mathcal{F}$, i.e. the maximum value of m such that $\Pi(m) = 2^m$.

(ix) $$u(\alpha) = \begin{cases} 1 & \alpha \geq 0 \\ 0 & \alpha < 0 \end{cases} \quad \text{(Step function)}.$$

(x) $h_2(p) = -p \cdot log_2 p - (1-p) \cdot log_2(1-p)$ (Binary Entropy).

2 Previous Results

2.1 Upper Bounds on the error probability

The results so far appeared in the literature[1] are based on the following result of Vapnik [4]: suppose that the desired function $\overline{f}$ is identically null (i.e., $\overline{f}(\mathbf{x}) = 0$

[1] In [4] the following bound valid for a generic (non necessarily small) error ν_f^m on the training set is given:

for every $\mathbf{x} \in X)^2$:

$$\mu^m \left\{ \sup_{f \in \mathcal{F}} \frac{e_f - \nu_f^m}{e_f^{\frac{1}{q}}} > \eta \right\}$$

$$\leq 8 \cdot \Pi(2m) \cdot \exp(-\frac{1}{4}\eta^2 \cdot m^{2-\frac{2}{q}}) \qquad 1 < q \leq 2, \ 0 < \eta < 1. \qquad (1)$$

In [6] observing that the conditions $\nu_f^m \leq (1-\gamma^{'})e_f$ and $e_f > \epsilon$ imply that $\frac{e_f - \nu_f^m}{e_f^{\frac{1}{q}}}|_{q=2} \geq \gamma^{'}\sqrt{\epsilon}$, where $0 < \gamma^{'} < 1$, the following corollary of (1) holds

$$\mu^m \left\{ \sup_{f \in \mathcal{F}} u(T_1 - m \cdot \nu_f^m)e_f > \epsilon \right\} \leq a{\cdot}\Pi(2m){\cdot}\exp(-\frac{1}{4}\gamma^{'2}\epsilon{\cdot}m) \triangleq p_1 \quad (2)$$

with $T_1 = m \cdot (1-\gamma^{'})e_f$ and $a = 8$.

The bound (2) has been improved in [2] with $a = 4$; in [3] it is reported that a can be reduced to $a = 2$ and also to $a = 1$ if ϵm is integer. Clearly by setting $\gamma^{'} = 1$ we have a bound for the scenario with zero training errors. Unfortunately, for this case bound (2) is looser than the best bounds obtained [5]. The expression we will propose in the following generalizes directly one of the better bounds for the scenario with zero training errors.

We reiterate that the existing results and the ones we propose in this paper give an upper bound on the *joint* probability that both the approximation error is larger than ϵ and the empirical error is smaller than $(1-\gamma^{'})\epsilon$. These hold also if the desired funtion $\overline{f}$ does not belong to the class of functions $\mathcal{F}$. However, in practice one needs a bound to the *conditional* probability p that generalization error is smaller than ϵ when the empirical error resulting from the training algorithm is smaller than $(1-\gamma^{'})\epsilon$. To bound p with p_1 (defined in (2)), we need to assume the marginal probability p_a that the function provided by the training algorithm has an empirical error smaller than $(1-\gamma^{'})\epsilon$ to be equal to one. If this assumption is ***a priori*** not reasonable, a correct bound to p is, of course, the ratio of p_1 and p_a.

$\mu^m\{\sup_{f \in \mathcal{F}} |\nu_f^m - e_f| > \epsilon\} \leq 4 \cdot \Pi(2m) \cdot \exp\{-\frac{m\epsilon^2}{8}\}$. In [5] an improvement of this bound is given but the dependence on ϵ^2 in the exponent remains. Therefore, it is looser than the bound (2) proposed for the case of small training error and it will not be considered in this paper. However, it is more general than the bounds we consider in this paper since it does not need any ***a priori*** assumption to be applied in practice.

[2]Even though equation (2) refers to an identically null desired function, the result is fully applicable to any scenario simply by replacing X with the cartesian product $Y = X \times \{0,1\}$ [6] with a new set of functions on Y that are zero only on the points $y = (x, b)$ with $f(x) = b$. Because this new set of function can be shown to have the same growth function $\Pi(m)$ of the first set of functions $\mathcal{F}$, theorem (2) and its improved version (5) proposed by us in this paper can be utilized to approximate a stochastic function on X with a deterministic function of $\mathcal{F}$. The quantity e_f becomes the probability of the subset of Y that disagrees with f and ν_f^m is the fraction of the examples that disagree with f. This learning framework is usually called Agnostic PAC (Probably Approximately Correct) learning.

2.2 Bounds for the minimum number of examples

In [6] it is shown that the bound on the probability in (2) with $a = 8$ is smaller than δ if

$$m \geq \max\left(\frac{32}{\epsilon} \cdot log_e(\frac{8}{\delta}), \frac{64 \cdot d}{\epsilon} \cdot log_e(\frac{64}{\epsilon})\right) \quad . \tag{3}$$

In [2] (3) is refined by showing that the bound on the probability in (2) with $a = 4$ is smaller than δ if

$$m \geq \frac{1}{\gamma'^2 \epsilon(1-\sqrt{\epsilon})}\left(4 \cdot log_e(\frac{a}{\delta}) + 6 \cdot d \cdot \log_e\left(\frac{4}{\gamma' \frac{4}{3}\epsilon}\right)\right) = m_1(\epsilon, \gamma', \delta) \ . \tag{4}$$

To derive these bounds, the well-known Vapnik inequality $\Pi(m) \leq \left(\frac{em}{d}\right)^d$ on the growth function is utilized. The results so far appeared in literature and the ones proposed in the following are valid under light technical conditions [6].
Example. Suppose we are running an experiment on m examples on which we are able to obtain 3% of errors on the training set ($\nu_f^m = 0.03$) and we want to bound the probability that the generalization error is larger than 10% ($\epsilon = 0.1$), for a class of functions with $d = 20$. Simply by rewriting the argument of the LHS of (2) as $\sup u\left(e_f - \frac{v_f^m}{1-\gamma'}\right) e_f > \epsilon$, we have that the event $\sup\ e_f > 0.1$ requires to fix $\gamma' = 0.7$. Therefore, to choose the value of m such that the probability that both the training error is smaller than 3% and the generalization error is larger than 10% is bounded by $\delta = 10^{-2}$, we use (4) with $a = 1$, obtaining $m = 15465$.

3 Proposed Bounds

Let us define the following function $g(\epsilon, \gamma)$:

$$g(\epsilon,\gamma) \stackrel{\triangle}{=} \frac{1}{2}\left(\frac{1}{2-\epsilon(1+\gamma)}\right)^{\gamma} \cdot 2^{(1+\gamma)h_2(\frac{\gamma}{\gamma+1})} \quad .$$

The bound (2) can be improved as follows:

$$\mu^m\left\{\sup_{f\in\mathcal{F}} u(T_1 - m \cdot \nu_f^m)e_f > \epsilon\right\} \leq 2 \cdot \Pi(2m) \cdot \{g(\epsilon,\gamma)\}^{\epsilon m - 1} \stackrel{\triangle}{=} p_2 \quad , \tag{5}$$

in which now $T_1 = \gamma\epsilon(1-\frac{1}{b}) \cdot m$, $\forall b > 1$, provided that $m \geq \frac{b}{\epsilon}$, $0 < \gamma < 1$ and $\epsilon \leq \epsilon_1(\gamma)$ where

$$\epsilon_1(\gamma) \stackrel{\triangle}{=} \min\left[\frac{1}{1+\gamma}, \frac{0.22}{\gamma}, \frac{2 - 2^{\frac{1+\gamma}{\gamma}h_2\left(\frac{\gamma}{\gamma+1}\right) - \frac{1}{\gamma}}}{1+\gamma}\right] \quad . \tag{6}$$

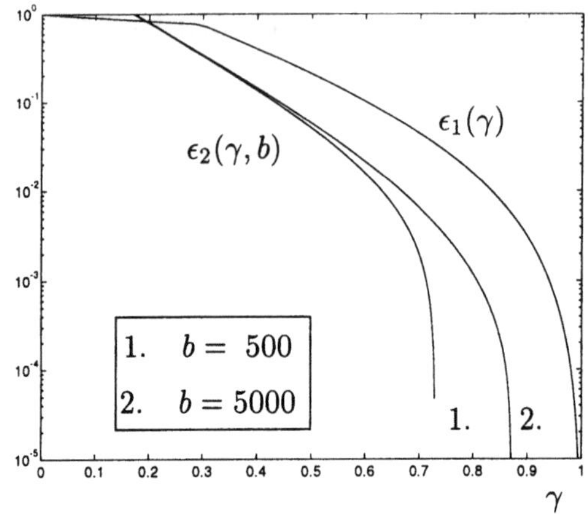

Figure 1: The behavior of ϵ_1 and ϵ_2 versus γ for $b = 5000$ and $b = 500$ and $a = 1$.

The quantity $\epsilon_1(\gamma)$ is depicted in fig. 1. The bound p_2 on the probability of incorrect generalization given in (5) is smaller than δ if

$$m \geq \frac{d\ log_e\left(\dfrac{2}{\epsilon\ r\ log_e \dfrac{1}{g(\epsilon,\gamma)}}\right) + log_e \dfrac{1}{g(\epsilon,\gamma)} + log_e(\dfrac{2}{\delta})}{\epsilon(1-r) log_e \dfrac{1}{g(\epsilon,\gamma)}} = m_2(\epsilon, \gamma, \delta) \quad ,(7)$$

for any $0 < r < 1$ (it seems from a small number of trials that a good choice for r is 0.1).

Moreover, for the case in which the new introduced bound doesn't hold (i.e., when $\epsilon > \epsilon_1(\gamma)$), it is useful to refine the bound (4) from (2); the probability p_1 is smaller than δ if

$$m \geq \frac{4\ d\ log_e\left(\dfrac{8}{\gamma'^2 \epsilon\beta}\right) + 4\ log_e(\dfrac{a}{\delta})}{\gamma'^2 \epsilon(1-\beta)} = m_3(\epsilon, \gamma', \delta) \quad , \tag{8}$$

with β chosen equal to 0.097. To clarify the usage of (5) and (7) let us discuss the following example.

Example. Suppose we are running an experiment as in Section 1. Simply by rewriting the argument of the LHS of (5) as $\sup u\left(\epsilon - \dfrac{v_f^m}{\gamma(1-b^{-1})}\right) e_f > \epsilon$, we have that the event sup $e_f > 0.1$ requires to fix γ and b such that the argument of the step function is larger or equal to zero and $b \leq m\epsilon$. Therefore, to choose the value of m such that the probability that both the training error

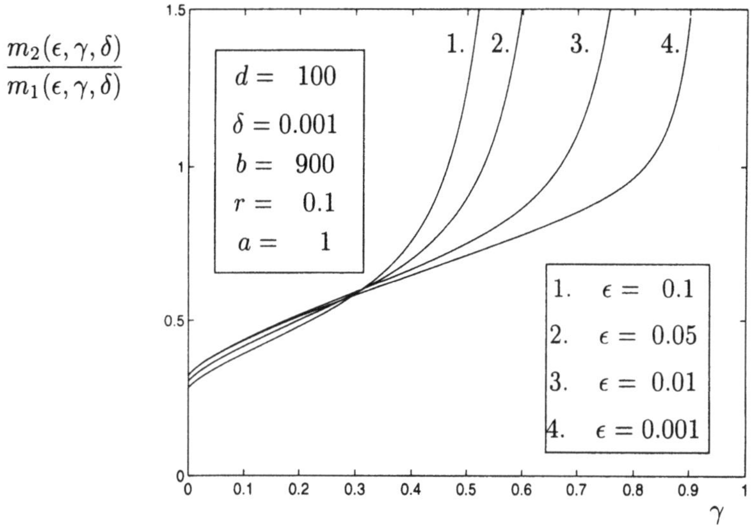

Figure 2: The behavior of the ratio between m_2 and m_1 versus γ for some values of the parameters.

is smaller than 3% and the generalization error is larger than 10% is bounded by $\delta = 10^{-2}$, we start fixing $\gamma = 0.3$, obtaining, by (7), $m' = 9073$; then we fix b and γ such that $b \leq m'\epsilon$ and $\gamma \geq \dfrac{\nu_f^m}{\epsilon(1-b^{-1})}$ and, again by (7), the required m: $b = 908$, $\gamma = 0.3 + 3 \cdot 10^{-4}$ and $m = 9090$.

4 Comparison with the Previous Bounds

To compare the proposed bounds p_2 (5) with the previous best bound p_1 (2), we fix $\gamma' = 1 - \gamma(1 - \frac{1}{b})$; it can be shown that, if

$$\epsilon < \frac{2 - 2^{\left\{\frac{1+\gamma}{\gamma} h_2\left(\frac{\gamma}{\gamma+1}\right) - \frac{1}{\gamma}\right\}} \cdot \left(\frac{4}{a}\right)^{\frac{1}{b\gamma}} \cdot e^{\frac{[1-\gamma(1-\frac{1}{b})]^2}{4\gamma}}}{1+\gamma} \triangleq \epsilon_2(\gamma, b),$$

we have $p_2 < p_1$. Fig.1 shows the behavior of the curve $\epsilon_2(\gamma, b)$ versus γ for $b = 500$ and $b = 5000$ and $a = 1$; in fact, the dependence of ϵ_2 on b is not very important. Note that there are a number of situations in which the new bound is better than p_1.

To compare the proposed bound $m_2(\epsilon, \gamma, \delta)$ for the minimum number of examples in (7) versus the previous bound $m_1(\epsilon, \gamma', \delta)$, we again fix $\gamma' = 1 - \gamma(1 - \frac{1}{b})$. Fig. 2 shows the behavior of the ratio $\dfrac{m_2(\epsilon,\gamma,\delta)}{m_1(\epsilon,\gamma,\delta)}$ versus γ for different values of ϵ and some fixed values of the other parameters (in particular we choose $b = 900$ since $\epsilon \cdot m_2(\epsilon, \gamma, \delta) > 900$ for all the chosen values of ϵ even if $\gamma = 0$). Fig. 2 confirms that, when γ grows, the proposed bound on m is better than the previous one until $\epsilon_2(\gamma, b) > \epsilon$ and that the proposed bound m_2 becomes not useful when ϵ is close to $\epsilon_1(\gamma)$.

Moreover, it can be noted that in the proposed bound m_3, differently from the existing one m_1, is not present the factor $\frac{1}{1-\sqrt{\epsilon}}$ responsible for the increasing of m_1 when ϵ is sufficiently large. Therefore, the improvement is considerable for values of ϵ such that the other proposed bound m_2 is not valid.

5 Conclusions

We have given new bounds on the joint probability that the generalization error is larger than ϵ and the training error is smaller than another non-null fixed value smaller than ϵ. Moreover, an upper-bound is given on the number of examples which assures than this joint probability is smaller than a fixed value δ.

The approach presented here is heavily based on Vapnik's approach to the generalization bound theorems where we have tried to give our best attempt to improve the approximations on the combinatorial formulas. The proposed formulas compare well with previous results appeared in the literature.

References

[1] Cherkassky, V., Mulier, F. and Vapnik, V., Comparison of VC-Method with Classical Methods for Model Selection, *Proceedings of the 1996 World Congress on Neural Networks*, pp. 957-962, 1996.

[2] Anthony, M. and Shawe-Taylor, J. , A Result of Vapnik with Applications, *Discrete Appl. Math.*, Vol. **47**, pp. 207-217, 1993.

[3] Hole, A., Vapnik-Chervonenkis Generalization Bounds for Real Valued Neural Networks, *Neural Computation*, Vol. 8, pp. 1277-1299, 1996.

[4] Vapnik, V. N., *Estimation of Dependences Based on Empirical Data*, Springer-Verlag, 1982.

[5] Parrondo J.M.R. and Van den Broeck C., Vapnik-Chervonenkis Bounds for Generalization, *Journal of Physics. a*, Vol. 26 (9), pp. 2211-2223, 1993.

[6] Blumer, A., Ehrenfeucht, A., Haussler, D. and Warmuth, M.K., Learnability and the Vapnik-Chervonenkis Dimension, *J. ACM*, Vol. 36(4), pp. 929-965, 1989.

ATTRACTOR NEURAL NETWORKS AS MODELS OF SEMANTIC MEMORY

Eliano Pessa Maria Pietronilla Penna

ECONA - Centro Interuniversitario di Ricerca sull' Elaborazione Cognitiva nei Sistemi Naturali e Artificiali
c/o Dipartimento di Psicologia, Università di Roma "La Sapienza" Via dei Marsi, 78 , 00185 Roma, Italy, Tel: +39-6-49917631, Fax: +39-6-4451667

ABSTRACT

We introduce a particular Attractor Neural Network (ANN) with a learning rule able to store sets of patterns with a two-level ultrametric structure, in order to model human semantic memory operation. Our simulations show that this model is able to reproduce a particular quantitative feature of this operation observed in experiments with human subjects, i.e. the correlation between high values of the prototypicity of exemplars of a given concept and low values of recognition reaction times for phrases asserting that the same exemplars belong to this concept. This shows that ANNs can be considered as good candidates for modelling some features of human semantic memory.

1. Introduction

In Cognitive Psychology traditionally long-term memory is viewed as composed by two different subsystems: *episodic memory* and *semantic memory* [8]. The former stores events of past experience, and its operation is evidenced through context-dependent tasks, such as the recall of suitable lists of items previously memorized. The latter, on the contrary, stores concepts and relationships between concepts, and enters into play when we deal with context-independent tasks, such as the ones requiring some amount of reasoning or of utilization of abstract knowledge. There were many attempts, in the past, to model semantic memory through suitable *semantic networks*, whose nodes were associated to single concepts, and whose connection lines were chosen to represent semantic links between concepts [3]. However, these models were unable to account for many experimental findings relative to human subjects' behavior in context-independent tasks [5]. For this reason during the Eighties the interest in these topics declined.

The advent of models based on Attractor Neural Networks (ANNs) [1] gave rise, however, to new possibilities in order to represent in a better way the network-like properties of semantic memory. To this regard, the most attractive ANNs appear to be the ones based on learning rules designed to memorize sets of patterns embedded in an ultrametric structure [4], [7]. Such a term denotes a situation in which data are organized like nodes in a tree, in such a way that all descendant nodes, branching from a given ancestor node, have the same distance from this latter. Within the context of ANNs generally the distance between two patterns is measured through the amount of their overlap. An ultrametric data structure has some resemblance with the cognitive organization of concepts within human semantic memory. We could, to this regard, identify ancestors with superordinate concepts (or classes), and descendants with subordinate concepts (or exemplars). We remark, on the other hand, that ANNs with learning rules designed to store set of patterns with ultrametric structure suffer from many drawbacks, such as : 1) the existence of spurious attractors, and 2) the limited memory capacity. Moreover, when using such

ANNs to model the operation of human semantic memory, we encounter a further difficulty, i.e. 3) how to find a suitable coding of superordinate and subordinate concepts, like the ones used in everyday life, in such a way as to comply with the constraints imposed by ultrametricity on the form of codes associated to "ancestors" and "descendants" patterns. In this paper we will propose a particular model of a two-level semantic memory (i.e. containing only one level of superordinate "ancestors" concepts and one level of subordinate "descendants" concepts), in order to solve problems associated to 1) and 3). Our model is based on: a) the introduction of units with probabilistic activation functions, characterized by a suitable "temperature" parameter; b) a suitable form of coding of superordinate and subordinate concepts, able to assure only a partial satisfaction of ultrametricity constraints. In order to test model's performance, we tried to simulate human subjects' behavior in a classical experiment on semantic memory, based on the recognition of truth or falsity of suitable propositions asserting a connection between a superordinate and a subordinate concept. The results of our simulations evidenced that the model was able to reproduce an experimental effect, observed in human subjects, i.e. the correlation between high values of prototypicity of subordinate concepts and low values of recognition reaction times [2], [3]. This shows that it is convenient to use ANNs to model semantic memory operation, at least in experimental paradigms such as the one quoted before.

2. The model

As we said before, when we deal with sets of patterns characterized by a two-level hierarchical structure of ultrametric type, a fundamental constraint is that all descendants of a given ancestor must have the same overlap with the ancestor itself. In the model we adopted all patterns were coded through binary vectors (whose components are +1 or -1). It is possible to show [1][7] that, if we denote by $x_i^{(s)}$ the binary vector coding the s-th ancestor pattern (i=1,...,N), and by $y_i^{[r(s)]}$ the binary vector coding the r-th descendant of the s-th ancestor, in order to store the ultrametric structure constituted by a set of ancestors together with their respective descendants one must use a suitable generalization of Hebb law. To this regard, we introduced a monolayered network of units with binary outputs, totally interconnected, whose connection weights w_{ij} were determined, as a function of the whole set of patterns to be stored, through [4]:

$$w_{ij} = (1/N)\Sigma_s x_i^{(s)} x_j^{(s)} [1+(1/\delta)\,\Sigma_{r(s)}(\eta_i^{[r(s)]}-a^{(s)})(\eta_j^{[r(s)]}-a^{(s)})] \quad , \qquad (1)$$

where

$$\eta_i^{[r(s)]} = x_i^{(s)}\, y_i^{[r(s)]} \quad , \qquad (2)$$

δ is a suitable parameter, and N is the number of units belonging to the network. Here $a^{(s)}$ denotes the overlap between a generic descendant of the s-th ancestor and the ancestor itself. By definition, the value of this overlap should be the same for all descendants of a given ancestor. As usual, all patterns, both the ones associated to ancestors and the ones associated to descendants, are coded in such a way as to be characterized by a zero mean value.

In this way, semantic memory was contained within the structure of network connection weights. As usual, retrieval dynamics was coincident with the free evolution of network activation state, with fixed connection weights, starting from an initial state coincident with the retrieval pattern. In order to avoid the presence of spurious attractors in retrieval dynamics, we introduced a probabilistic activation law for the network units, by defining the probability $Pr(z_i)$ of the binary output z_i of the i-th unit, in the usual fashion, as:

$$Pr(z_i) = (1/2)(1 + tgh(\beta\, P_i\, z_i)) \ , \qquad (3)$$

where $\beta = 1/T$, the symbol T denoting a parameter called "temperature". P_i denotes, in turn, the conventional activation potential of the i-th unit. In these conditions also the retrieval dynamics has a stochastic character and the equilibrium state must be defined in such a way as to take into account its possible fluctuations. It can be shown [4] that, if this dynamics is of sequential type and the condition:

$$\delta > 1 - a^{(s)} \qquad (4)$$

is satisfied for every value of s, then we can find a suitable critical value T_c of temperature (and a corresponding definition of the equilibrium state) such that, when $T > T_c$, the only equilibrium states are constituted by ancestor patterns.

In order to use such a network to store superordinate and subordinate concepts, like the ones we think are contained within human semantic memory, we coded each concept through a suitable list of properties, in such a way that the activation of each network unit was associated to the presence of a particular property. Thus, the distinction between superordinate and subordinate concepts was represented only through the different properties associated to the concepts themselves. Moreover, the hierarchical conceptual structure to be stored was contained directly within the choice of which patterns should be considered as ancestors, and which patterns as descendants, in order to compute the connection weight values through (1). On the other hand, such a procedure gave rise to a difficulty: in practical cases, the condition of ultrametricity (according to which all descendants of a given ancestor have the same overlap with the ancestor itself) was very difficult to satisfy. For this reason we modified this model, by introducing in (1), at the place of $a^{(s)}$, the average value of the overlaps between each different descendant of the s-th ancestor and the ancestor itself.

3. The simulation.

The aim of our simulation was the one of reproducing an experimental situation used to study semantic memory operation through human subjects performance. In it to the subject is presented a proposition asserting a particular connection between a given descendant (i.e. a particular exemplar) and a given ancestor (i.e. a general concept), like "a canary is a bird". The subject's task is to answer "yes" or "not" (in an equivalent way, "true" or "false") as fastly as possible. Generally subject's reaction time is the measured dependent variable.

Our simulation was organized into four successive steps. In the first one all patterns, both ancestors and descendants, were coded through a suitable list of properties. We show two examples relative to one of the coding schemata we used in the following Tables I (containing the code of a descendant) and II (containing the code of an ancestor).

	not at all	a little	very much	sometimes	bias	bias
beaked	-1	-1	+1	-1	+1	+1
feathered	-1	-1	+1	-1	+1	+1
oviparous	-1	-1	+1	-1	+1	+1
winged	-1	+1	-1	-1	+1	+1
biped	-1	-1	+1	-1	+1	+1
tailed	+1	-1	-1	-1	+1	+1
has retractile claws	+1	-1	-1	-1	+1	+1
whiskered	+1	-1	-1	-1	+1	+1
eared	+1	-1	-1	-1	+1	+1
runs	-1	+1	-1	-1	+1	+1
flies	-1	+1	-1	-1	+1	+1
swims	+1	- 1	-1	-1	+1	+1
hunts the prey	-1	+1	-1	-1	+1	+1
can see in the dark	+1	-1	-1	-1	+1	+1
carnivorous	-1	+1	-1	-1	+1	+1
smells	+1	-1	-1	-1	+1	+1

Table I Coding of the subordinate concept “hen”.

	not at all	a little	very much	sometimes	bias	bias
beaked	-1	-1	+1	-1	+1	+1
feathered	-1	-1	+1	-1	+1	+1
oviparous	-1	-1	+1	-1	+1	+1
winged	-1	- 1	+1	-1	+1	+1
biped	-1	-1	+1	-1	+1	+1
tailed	-1	-1	-1	+1	+1	+1
has retractile claws	+1	-1	-1	-1	+1	+1
whiskered	+1	-1	-1	-1	+1	+1
eared	+1	-1	-1	-1	+1	+1
runs	-1	- 1	-1	+1	+1	+1
flies	-1	- 1	-1	+1	+1	+1
swims	+1	- 1	-1	-1	+1	+1
hunts the prey	-1	- 1	-1	+1	+1	+1
can see in the dark	- 1	-1	-1	-1	+1	+1
carnivorous	-1	- 1	-1	+1	+1	+1
smells	+1	-1	-1	-1	+1	+1

Table II Coding of the superordinate concept “bird”

From each binary matrix associated to a given concept a binary vector was obtained by reading the matrix in a given order (starting from upper left element, row by row). Besides, these patterns were memorized according to the rule (1), in which each overlap was replaced by the average overlap. In the second phase the retrieval dynamics was triggered by the presentation of a particular descendant, to be identified with the initial state of this dynamics. During network evolution we monitored the overlap between the instantaneous state of the network and this descendant and the one between the instantaneous state and its ancestor. We did many run, by varying the values of parameters T and δ, in order to find the values of these parameters granting for an overcoming, at some time step, of the overlap with the descendant, initially very high, by the overlap with the ancestor, initially very low. In the third phase, one found the most suitable values of T and δ, we registered, for each descendant (chosen as initial state of retrieval dynamics), the number of time steps needed for observing such an overcoming. This number was considered as a measure of the *prototypicity* of the descendant taken into consideration. In the fourth phase the retrieval dynamics was subdivided in two successive sub-phases. In the first one, triggered by the initial presentation of a particular descendant, each unit received as inputs both the usual ones coming from the outputs of the other network units, and also a supplementary input given by the value of the corresponding component of the ancestor pattern. In the second one, this supplementary input was eliminated, and we monitored, as before, the two overlaps between the network instantaneous state and, respectively, the descendant and its ancestor. The number of time steps needed to observe an overcoming of the overlap with the descendant by the overlap with the ancestor was interpreted as corresponding to *recognition reaction time* in corrispondence to the presentation of a phrase asserting that the given descendant was an exemplar of the given ancestor.

As regards the coding of the descendants and of the ancestors, as it is possible to see from Table I, we introduced a general list of possible properties, each one, in turn, characterized by different grades, or intensities, like "not at all", "a little", ,"very much", "sometimes present". In this way each pattern was associated to a matrix, each row of which was corresponding to a particular property. We put +1 at the crossing of a particular row and a particular column if this pattern was characterized by the property corresponding to this row with an intensity corresponding to this column. In the contrary case we put -1. As regards ancestor patterns, we put always +1s in the column corresponding to the intensity "sometimes present" (or an equivalent expression) at the crossings with all rows associated to properties characterizing some exemplars of the class represented by the ancestor, but not all exemplars. To each matrix derived through the method described before we added a suitable number of columns containing only +1 values in order to grant for a satisfaction of the zero average value condition. From each matrix thus obtained we derived a vector by reading the matrix elements following a suitable order.

4. Results and discussion.

We did two different simulations, one with only one ancestor ("bird") and 6 particular descendants, and the other with three different ancestors ("vehicles", "weapons", and "animals"), each one with 25 different descendants. In both cases we found, as most suitable parameter values, δ = 2 and T = 0.8. As the retrieval dynamics was probabilistic in character, we did, for each particular descendant, 10 different simulations, averaging the results. In the first simulation all patterns were coded through 96-components vectors, whereas in the second one we used 135-

components vectors. We found that the number of time steps required to observe an overcoming of the overlap with the descendant by the overlap with the ancestor was, for each descendant, always lesser in the fourth simulation phase than in the third simulation phase. Typical values of this number were of the order of a thousand steps for 135-components vectors, and of some hundred steps for 96-components vectors. By measuring the prototypicity degree through the difference between the maximum allowable evolution time and the time required for observing the overcoming of the overlap with the descendant by the overlap with the ancestor, we found in the first simulation a Bravais-Pearson correlation coefficient, between the prototypicity degree of the descendant and the reaction time (measured as described in previous paragraph), of -0.32. In the second simulation this correlation coefficient was -0.36. These data are to be compared with the value of -0.41 found by McCloskey [6] in experiments with human subjects.

Our findings seem to suggest that ANNs are able to model a particular quantitative feature of semantic memory operation. We claim, however, that the problem of the limited memory capacity remains still unsolved. According to us, it cannot be dealt with by adopting the framework of learning rules based on a total interconnection, such as (1). Further generalizations of ANNs models are needed to model other important features of human memory operation.

References

1. Amit D. Modeling Brain Function. The World of Attractor Neural Networks. Cambridge University Press, Cambridge, 1989.
2. Chang T.M. Semantic memory: Facts and models. Psychol.Bull 1986; 99: 199-220;
3. Collins A. and Loftus E.F. A spreading activation theory of semantic processing.Psychol.Rev. 1975; 82: 407-428.
4. Feigelman M.V. and Ioffe, L.B. The augmented models of associative memory: asymmetric interaction and hierarchy of patterns. Int.J.Mod.Phys. 1987; B1: 51-60.
5. Johnson-Laird P.N., Herrmann D.J. and Chaffin R. Only connections: A critique of semantic networks. Psychol.Bull. 1984; 96: 292-315.
6. McCloskey M. The stimulus familiarity problem in semantic memory research. J.of Verbal Learning and Verbal Behavior. 1980; 19: 485-502.
7. Parga N. and Virasoro M.A. The ultrametric organization of memories in a neural network. Journal de Physique 1986; 47: 1857-1864.
8. Tulving E. Episodic and semantic memory. In E.Tulving and E.Donaldson (eds) Organization of memory. Academic Press, New York, pp. 382-404, 1972.

SECTION 5

PATTERN RECOGNITION AND ROBOTICS

Image Reconstruction Using A Hierarchical RBF Network Architecture

N.A. Borghese[1], G. Ferrigno[2] and S. Ferrari[1,2]
1 Istituto Neuroscienze e Bioimmagini, CNR, Via Mario Bianco, 9 20131 Milano, Italy - borghese@inb.mi.cnr.it
2 Dipartimento di Bioingegneria, Politecnico di Milano, Fondazione ProJuventute, Via Gozzadini, 7, 20148 Milano, Italy

Abstract. In this paper a new RBF architecture is presented. The Gaussian units are arranged in a set of hierarchical grids, which form the hidden layers. Each layer, is characterised by a certain variance and spacing between the units. The first layer gives a coarse approximation of the surface, while the other (higher) layers approximate the residual error at decreasing scales. The Gaussian units in the higher layers are inserted only where the residual error is higher than a predefined threshold making the overall error uniformly small. A proper value of the variance for the units in each layer is computed from the spacing between the Gaussians in that layer. The weights are determined through a local maximum a-posteriori estimate carried out on the available data. The 3D reconstruction of a human face starting from a sparse set of 3D data points through this architecture is reported.

1 Introduction

In this paper, the reconstruction of a continuous surface starting from a set of 3D points not equally sampled is addressed. A valuable solution is represented by RBF Gaussian networks which have the following analytical shape [1, 2]:

$$z = s(\mathbf{x}) = \sum_{k=1}^{M} \mathbf{w}_k g(\mathbf{x}; \mathbf{c}_k, \Sigma_k) \tag{1}$$

where z is the height of the surface and $\mathbf{x}$ and $\mathbf{c}_k$ belong to the plane on which the surface is defined. The parameters to be determined are: the number of the Gaussian units, M, their position $\{\mathbf{c}_k\}$ and covariance $\{\Sigma_k\}$ and the value of the weights $\{\mathbf{w}_k\}$. Global optimal solutions based on minimising cost functions [1] greatly suffer from local minima; and hybrid procedures are usually preferred (e.g. [3, 4, 5]). In these procedures, to which our architecture belongs, the network parameters can be subdivided into two sets: the *structural parameters* (the number of Gaussians, their position and covariance) and the *synaptic weights* (the network weights). Different algorithms are used to set the value of the parameters belonging to the two sets. In this approach gridding of the input space simplify the estimation of the structural parameters [2] and, considerations on linear filtering theory allows to substitute the local maximum a-posteriori estimate of s($\mathbf{x}$) in the grid crossings to the weights [7].

2 Setting the value for the variance

A RBF network with equally spaced units can be seen as the convolution of a Gaussian kernel with the sequence of the weights and as a low-pass filter. When the Gaussians are taken radially symmetric, the kernel can be written as:

$$g(\mathbf{x};\mathbf{c}_k,\Sigma_k)=g(\mathbf{x};\mathbf{c}_k,\sigma_k) \tag{2}$$

where a single parameter, σ_k, can be substituted to the 2 x 2 covariance matrix, Σ_k. The kernel can now be expressed as the product of two Gaussians with the same standard deviation, σ, one for each of the two orthogonal axes in the plane allowing to reduce the discussion to the monodimensional case without loosing generality. RBF analytical formulation (Eq. 1) has the following interpretation in the Fourier domain:

$$s(x)=\sum_{k=1}^{M} w_k \frac{e^{-\frac{(x-x_k)^2}{\sigma^2}}}{\sqrt{\pi}\sigma} = W(\nu_j)G(\nu) \tag{3}$$

where $W(\nu_j)$ and $G(\nu)$ are the Fourier Transform respectively of the sequences of the weights $\{w_k\}$ and of the Gaussian function g(.). The Fourier Transform of the Gaussian, $G(\nu)$, is itself a Gaussian:

$$G(\nu) = e^{-\pi^2\sigma^2\nu^2} e^{-2\pi j\nu c} = |G(\nu;\sigma)| e^{-2\pi j\nu_c} \tag{4}$$

The normalisation factor $\sqrt{\pi}\sigma$ in equation (3) was necessary to get $|G(\nu)| = 1$ in the proximity of the origin (ν=0, DC component of the spectrum).

The value of σ regulates the low-pass filtering capabilities of g(.): the greater the value of σ the smaller is the cut-off frequency. Ideally $G(\nu)$ should be equal to 1 for all the frequencies which constitute s(**x**) (the Pass Band defined as the interval $[0\ \nu_M]$) and 0 outside this interval. This is not realisable by the Gaussian or any other real filter and some approximation should be tolerated. Given δ_1 as the maximum attenuation in the Pass Band, the value of σ can be computed consequently as:

$$\sigma_{Max} \leq \frac{\sqrt{-\ln \delta_1}}{\pi \nu_M} \tag{5}$$

The value of δ_1 adopted here is $\sqrt{2}/2$ (attenuation equal to -3dB). If a value of σ below σ_{Max} were chosen, the highest frequency components of s(**x**) would be filtered out. A lower limit to the value of σ is given by the spacing between the Gaussian units. In fact, if σ were too low, aliasing in the frequency domain occur as two Gaussians might overlap consistently. From the theoretical point of view, aliasing cannot be avoided using Gaussian functions because their support is not finite; nevertheless, fixing a maximum frequency content above which the contribution of the Gaussians can be neglected, a lower bound for σ can be determined as:

$$\sigma_{min} \geq \frac{\sqrt{-\ln \delta_2}}{\pi \nu_s/2} \tag{6}$$

where δ_2 is set as the value for which the amplitude of the Gaussian function in the frequency domain, is equal to 10^{-3}. ν_s is the sampling frequency, equivalent to the inverse of the spacing between two consecutive Gaussians. Following filtering theory, as far as the value of σ in the Gaussian satisfies the two relationships (5) and (6), a good reconstruction of s(**x**) can be obtained by substituting the value of the surface, s(.), sampled in the grid crossings, s_k, to the weights. Equation (2) becomes:

$$s(\mathbf{x})=\sum_{k=1}^{M} w_k \frac{e^{-\frac{(\mathbf{x}-\mathbf{x}_k)^2}{\sigma^2}}}{\sqrt{\pi}\sigma} = \sum_{k=1}^{M} s_k \frac{e^{-\frac{(\mathbf{x}-\mathbf{x}_k)^2}{\sigma^2}}}{\sqrt{\pi}\sigma} \Delta\mathbf{x}_k \tag{7}$$

3 Estimating the value of the weights

The above result is interesting but cannot be directly applicable to our problem where the data points are not equally spaced. A solution proposed here is based on a local maximum a-posteriori estimate of $s_k=s(\mathbf{x}_k)$ carried out on the data points. This is based on the assumption that the value of a data point is closer to s_k, the closer is the point to $\mathbf{x}_k$. This suggests to weight the data points in the neighbourhood of $\mathbf{x}_k$ by a function decreasing with the distance of that point from $\mathbf{x}_k$. Assuming this weighing function Gaussian, the following MAP estimator of s_k is obtained:

$$s(\mathbf{x_k}) = \frac{\sum_{r=1}^{R} s_r e^{-\frac{(\mathbf{x}_r - \mathbf{x}_k)^2}{\sigma_w^2}}}{\sum_{r=1}^{R} e^{-\frac{(\mathbf{x}_r - \mathbf{x}_k)^2}{\sigma_w^2}}} \tag{8}$$

where as "neighbourhood" of $\mathbf{x}_k$ is somehow arbitrary taken the region, R, inside two meshes: $\mathbf{x}_k \pm d\,\mathbf{x}_k$ ($d\,\mathbf{x}_k = \mathbf{x}_{k+1} - \mathbf{x}_k$). The value of σ_w has been taken equal to $\sigma/2$ to avoid filtering of the data.

4 Hierarchical gridding

This approach is somehow rigid as it allows only one value for the variance (and for the cut-off frequency) over all the input space. This is undesirable in many situations where the frequency content is different in different regions of the input space. When a single variance is used for the entire image, σ should be chosen small enough to reconstruct the finest details, although these may occur in few regions of the input space. The consequence is a thick gridding with a loss of resources and possibly overfitting in some regions.

A better solution is to distribute more Gaussian units in those regions where they are effectively required (highest frequency) and to use less Gaussians in the others. This has been achieved using a hierarchical approach where the Gaussian units are distributed in different layers, each having its own grid spacing and a characteristic variance. The first layer will output a rough approximation of the surface at high scale (large value of σ); the other layers will contribute with the definition of the finest details by adding Gaussians units at lower scales (cf. Fig. 2).

In each layer, the Gaussian units are inserted in the crossing of the grids only when the residual error in its neighbourhood (defined as for Eq. 8) exceeds a certain threshold. The residual is measured with respect to the input data set for the first layer and with respect to the residual in the previous layer for the additional layers: these contribute incrementally to the reconstruction of the function $s(\mathbf{x})$. It should be remarked that with this kind of architecture, the obtained residual error is lowered uniformly under the predefined threshold.

5 Results

The 3D reconstruction of a human face is here reported. It has been achieved starting from a set of N = 9370 3D data points sparsely sampled through the ELITE system

[8] and a laser pointer, and reported in Figure 1. A RBF hierarchical structure reported in this paper, with four layers has been used. The number of the Gaussians of each layer, their standard deviation and the residual error at the output of each layer are reported in Table I.

The position of the Gaussians each layer is reported in Figures 2. The incremental contribution of each layer is reported in Figures 3.

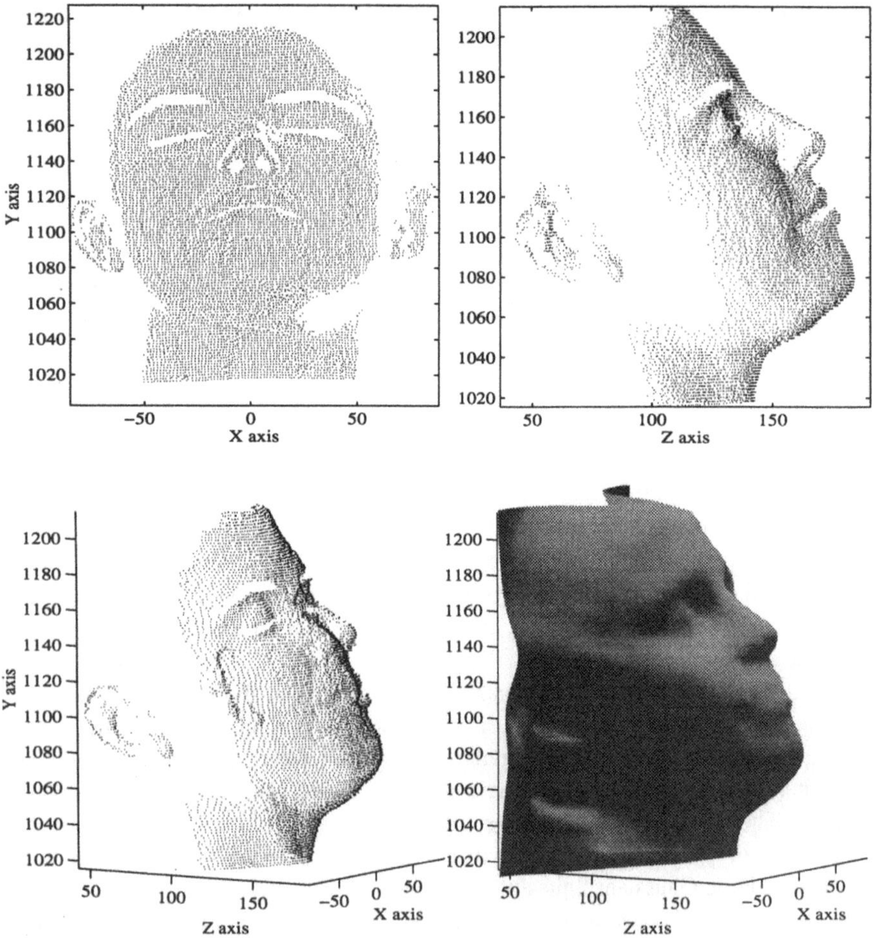

Fig. 1. The 9370 points which constitute the input data set. These points have been created over the face by means of a laser pointer and surveyed by a pair of TVcameras. The surface obtained with the algorithm described in this paper is reported in the bottom right panel.

6 Conclusion

Although in a preliminary stage, this architecture is promising as it combines a high degree of flexibility, given by the hierarchical allocation of the Gaussian units, to a direct computation of the parameters. Overall it represents a fast method for computing a value of the RBF network parameters close to their optimum, at least on parallel machines.

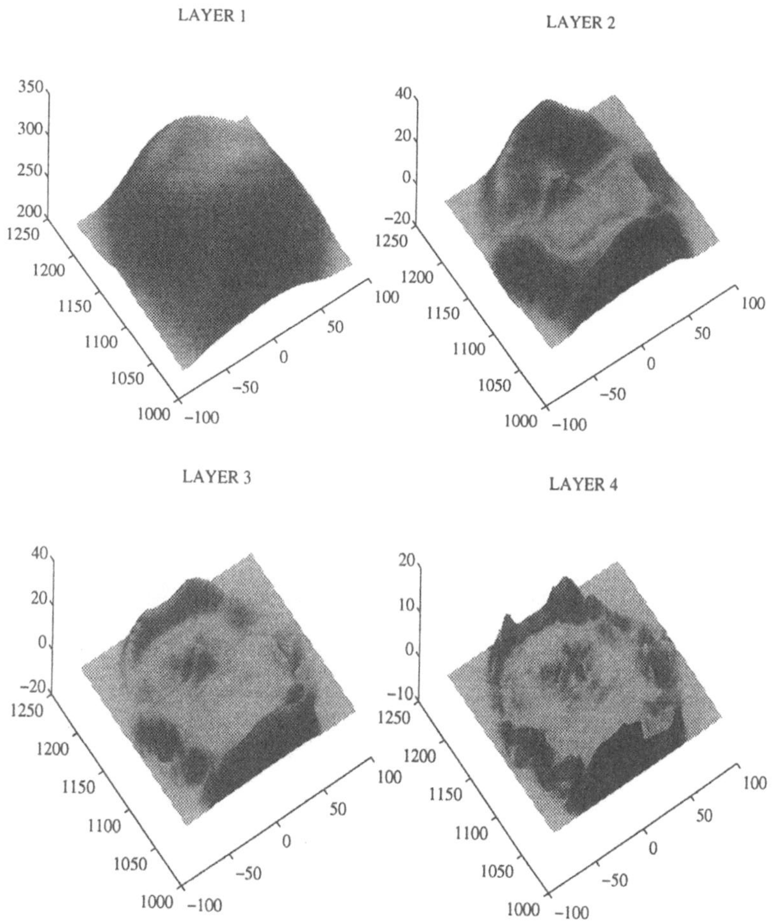

Fig. 2. The output of each layer of the network is reported.

References

1. F. Girosi, M. Jones and T. Poggio, Regularization Theory and Neural Networks Architectures, *Neural Computation* 7 (1995) 219-269.
2. R.M. Sanner and J.E. Slotine, Gaussian Networks for Direct Adaptive Control, *IEEE Trans. on Neural Networks* 3(6) (1992) 837-863.
3. T. Kohonen, *Self-Organizing Maps* (Springer-Verlag Berlin 1995).
4. J. Platt, A Resource-Allocating Network for Function Interpolation, *Neural Computation* 3 (1991) 213-225.
5. J. Moody and C. Darken, Fast-learning in networks of locally-tuned processing units, *Neural Computation,* 1(2) (1989) 281-294.
6. D.S. Broomhead & D. Lowe, Multivariable functional interpolation and adaptive networks, *Complex Systems* 2, (1988) 321-355.

7. Borghese N.A. and Ferrari S. Hierarchical RBF networks and local parameter estimate, *submitted to NeuroComputing*.
8. G. Ferrigno, N.A. Borghese, A. Pedotti, "*Pattern Recognition in 3D Automatic Human Motion Analysis*", *ISPRS J. Photogrammetry Remote Sensing*, 45 (1990), pp 227-246.

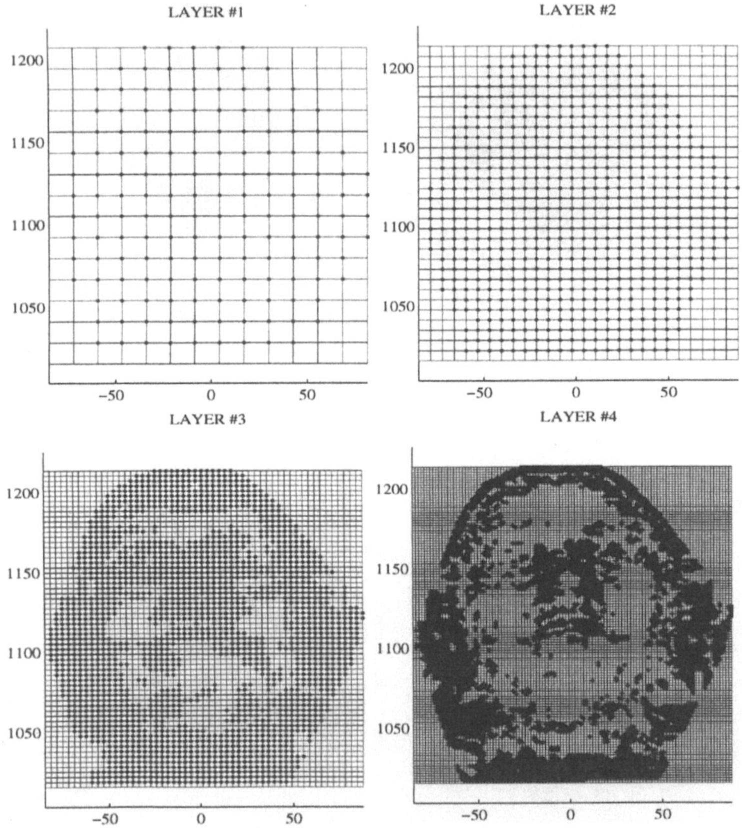

Fig. 3. The position of the Gaussians is reported for each layer as a dot at the grid crossings.

Table I

#layer	mse	# of Gaussians	$\nu_{cut\text{-}off}$ [Hz]	σ [mm]
1	197.4	158/224	10	18.74
2	39.72	639/896	20	9.37
3	9.362	1967/3465	40	4.685
4	2.396	4567/13625	80	2.342

Tab. 1. For each layer, k, the mean reconstruction error produced by the network by using the first k layers is reported along with the number of Gaussian inserted in that layer with their $\nu_{cut\text{-}off}$ and σ.

Word Recognition by MLP-based Character Spotting and Dynamic Programming

F. Camastra[◇] - E. Cepollina[♣] - A.M. Colla[◇]

[◇] Elsag Bailey - Un'Azienda Finmeccanica S.p.A

Via G. Puccini, 2 - 16154 Genova (ITALY)

[♣] Dip. Informatica e Scienze dell'Informazione, Università di Genova

Via Dodecaneso, 33 - 16146 Genova (ITALY)

Abstract

This paper describes a method for handprinted word recognition, with the following characteristics: traditional pre-processing (relevant to single characters, obtained by word segmentation) is replaced by pre-processing based on piecewise normalization applied at whole words; feature extraction and character classification by MLP are performed in a sliding window fashion; the output string is matched with an ASCII word vocabulary by Dynamic Programming with the Levenshtein distance; a list of word candidates is issued. Afterwards, when the language is formally known, an appropriate parser can be applied to full Sentence Recognition. Tests on a medium size vocabulary show extremely promising results.

1 Introduction

A method for **handprinted word recognition** is presented, with the following characteristics:

- *no traditional preprocessing* (segmentation into characters, deslanting, size normalization);
- *whole word preprocessing* based on baseline straightening and piecewise normalization;
- feature extraction and character classification by MLP performed on a *sliding window* which scans the word image; the output is a string of character hypotheses;
- the output string is matched with a word vocabulary (ASCII) by the *Levenshtein distance*; a list of word candidates is issued;
- when a *grammar* can be defined, this method can be used to generate word hypotheses for **sentence recognition**.

The paper presents the performance obtained by our method on "Natural Language-like" sentences with a medium size Italian vocabulary. The results obtained in preliminary tests are extremely promising, both at word and at sentence level.

2 General recognition scheme

This work was partially inspired by previous work on recognition without explicit segmentation into characters [1, 2, 3]. However, it aims at developing a general sentence recognition system, possibly not confined to hand*printing*.
The sentence recognition scheme is based on a ***bottom-up strategy*** : information is first extracted at low (image) level, in the form of character hypotheses, then lexical knowledge is applied to obtain candidate word sequences, to which grammatical knowledge can be finally applied. Character hypotheses are generated by a process which avoids traditional image segmentation, by scanning the word image with a *sliding window*. At each positioning of the window, feature extraction and neural-based classification are performed. We can call this approach **character spotting**: characters are simultaneously located and recognized within the word. This approach was successfully applied to Automatic Speech Recognition [4], and can be adapted to cursive handwriting as well, provided a robust set of primitives (graphemes, sub-graphemes and grapheme groups) is defined. Character recognition is error prone, due to the uncertain location of units; lexical information intervenes to overcome this problem.
Instead of character recognition, central to the system is **word recognition**, to which both character classification and lexical knowledge concur.

3 The word recognition method

3.1 Word level pre-processing

In traditional recognition approaches, the basic unit to be detected and classified is the *character*. The written lines are segmented into characters by several different methods. Character-level preprocessing consists of deslanting and size normalization. In our approach (Figure 1), where there is no explicit segmentation into characters, *word* is the typical basic unit, and preprocessing comprises noise filtering and baseline straightening. *Noise filtering* can consist of the following: point noise filtering, removal of fixed structures, contour smoothing, filling or reconstruction of small areas impaired by the image acquisition process. *Baseline straightening* is performed by estimating the inferior line or word guideline (baseline); this can be modelled by one or more contiguous line segments. The baseline is straightened by progressive vertical shifts of pixel columns. This procedure is simpler than deslanting, which typically implies rotation.
The straightened word is then segmented into regions *("pseudo-characters")* either completely connected or composed of connected parts with overlapped projections. Each "pseudo-character" is then separately normalized, either to a standard size, or to a standard height while maintaining the original aspect ratio; the normalization type is chosen according to the latter. Finally the word image is rebuilt by joining the normalized "pseudo-characters".

3.2 Character level measure

Character spotting is performed by feature extraction and MLP-based classification within a fixed size *sliding window* scanning horizontally the normalized

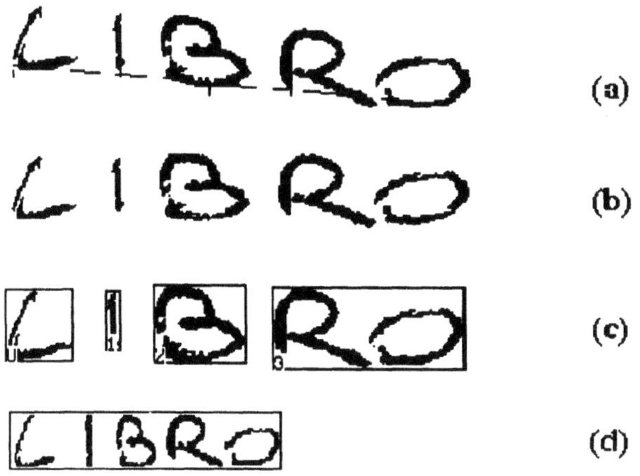

Figure 1: *Original image with estimated baseline (a), straightened image (b), segmentation into "pseudo-characters"(c), and word rebuilding after piecewise normalization (d).*

word image (Figure 2). Scanning is carried out in two alternate modes: a *sacchadic mode*, where the window "jumps" from pseudo-character to pseudo-character, and an *exhaustive mode*, where the window shifts continuously (i.e. with regular speed) within the current pseudo-character. At each window position a *measure operation* is performed, consisting in the following: a vector of features [8] for character representation is generated, and a 26-class MLP classifier [5, 6], trained on isolated uppercase handprinted characters both from NIST and Elsag's proprietary databases, is fed with the feature vector. The MLP output is *symbolic*, i.e., when the class with the highest response is scored above a given threshold, the ASCII symbol corresponding to that class is issued; otherwise, a "don't know" symbol ("_") is produced. When the pseudo-character width is identical to the window size, only one measure is taken; the output symbol is replicated a number of times proportional to the window size. This way the symbolic output string is homogeneous over all the pseudo-characters, both those likely to be real characters and those composed of more characters, where more symbols are issued. The sequence of character hypotheses is then filtered to remove incongruities (such as a spurious symbol in the middle of a sequence of identical characters).

3.3 Lexical analysis

Lexical analysis is performed by a typical *Dynamic Programming* scheme [10] based on the *Levenshtein distance* (see [7] and references). Both the output of the measure process and all the reference words in the lexicon are represented by ASCII strings.

If X is the unknown string, and Y is the reference string, the Levenshtein distance is thus computed:

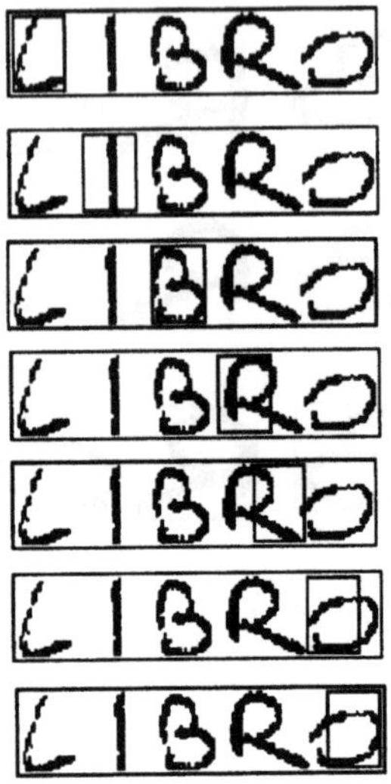

HYPOTHESES FROM THE NEURAL NET CLASSIFIER:
*L*I*B*_RR_N_UY_O_J*

Figure 2: *Sliding window for character spotting performing both sacchadic (four pseudo-characters: see Fig.1) and exhaustive (in the last pseudo-character) scanning.*

$$D(X,Y) = \sum_{i=1,\ldots,N} d(x_i, y_{k(i)})$$

$$d(x_i, y_{k(i)}) = min \begin{pmatrix} subs(x_i, y_{k(i)_S}), \\ subs(x_i, y_{k(i)_D}) + dup(y_{k(i-1)}), \\ subs(x_i, y_{k(i)_C}) + canc(y_{k(i-1)+1}) \end{pmatrix}$$

$$k(i) = \begin{cases} k(i)_D = k(i-1) & (DUP) \\ k(i)_S = k(i-1)+1 & (SUBS) \\ k(i)_C = k(i-1)+2 & (CANC) \end{cases}$$

Here $subs(a,b)$ represents the penalty for substituting symbol a with b; $dup(a)$ and $canc(a)$ the penalties for duplicating or cancelling symbol a.
The unknown word is recognized as the reference in the lexicon with the minimum distance. Alternatively, a list of word hypotheses can be issued. Each hypothesis is scored with the computed distance value from the unknown word.

4 Experimental results

4.1 Word recognition

The test image database consists of **handprinted** sentences (uppercase only) written by several writers (so far, 35). Each writer produced ten sentences on a white A4 paper sheet, with no format constraints, but the limitation that *one sentence must be contained in one single line.* The instructions for the writers

	% Correct Words
TOP	81.12% (1053)
Top 3	89.7% (1164)
Top 5	91.3% (1185)
Top 10	93% (1208)

Table 1: *Experimental results on handprinted word recognition (test set 1298 words, lexicon size 629).*

	% Correct Sentences
TOP	64% (151)
Top 3	70.8% (167)
Top 5	75% (177)
Top 10	80% (189)

Table 2: *Experimental results on full sentences (test set 236 sentences, average perplexity 27).*

were the following:

- Simple sentences with the following general structure:
  < **SENTENCE** > ::=
  < **SUBJECT** > < **VERB** > (< **COMPLEMENT** > | < **ADVERB** >)
- "AND" conjunctions are allowed.
- Italian or English. No restrictions on lexicon.

The images were acquired by means of a black and white scanner at 300 dpi resolution; each image was segmented to produce ten sentence images in TIFF format. As a whole 350 sentence images were obtained, corresponding to a 52-word English lexicon and a 629-word Italian lexicon. Tests were performed on a subset consisting of 236 Italian sentences (for a total of 1298 words), representative of almost all the writers. The sentences not admissible according to the above grammar were discarded. The results in terms of percentage of correctly recognized words are summarized in Table 1.

4.2 Sentence recognition

Sentence recognition is based on a *LR(1) (Left-to-Right-1)* parser [9], apt to parse "Natural Language-like" sentences, as the ones making up our database. The input to the parser is the sequence of word hypotheses, scored with the normalized Levenshtein distance. The overall score for a sentence is the sum of the scores of all the words in the sentence. The parser checks grammatical concordance in some cases (i.e. articles and nouns, present tense conjugation). The output is an ordered list of *sentence hypotheses.*
Table 2 summarizes the results obtained on the above mentioned test set, in terms of *completely correct* sentences, i.e. where all the words are correctly recognized.

5 Conclusions

In this paper we presented a word recognition system based on MLP-based character spotting and word matching by dynamic programming.
Character spotting avoids some problems due to explicit segmentation and traditional character preprocessing. The use of lexical knowledge is very important to achieve good recognition performance.
The method can be employed as the bottom end of a sentence recognition system. Preliminary results obtained by a very simple parser are quite promising. By improving the features used for character representation and/or by further training a MLP classifier on a larger set of examples we expect to obtain even better results.
Conspicuous computation resources are required for the measure process. Therefore a VLSI implementation could be advisable.

Acknowledgements

We wish to acknowledge Riccardo Cecinati (Elsag Bailey) for helpful discussions and support in the test database generation, and Paolo Venturini (DIBE University of Genova) for providing part of the preprocessing algorithms.

References

[1] Matan CJ., Burges C., Le Cun Y. and Denker JS. Multi-digit recognition using a space displacement neural network. In: Advances in Neural Information Processing Systems, vol. 4, pp. 488-495, 1991

[2] Martin G. and Rashid M. Recognizing overlapping hand-printed characters by centered-object integrated segmentation and recognition. In: Advances in Neural Information Processing Systems, vol. 4, pp. 504-511, 1991

[3] Keeler J. and Rumelhart DE. A self-organizing integrated segmentation and recognition neural net. In: Advances in Neural Information Processing Systems, vol. 4, pp. 496-503, 1991

[4] Scagliola C., Carossino A., Colla AM. et al. Real-Time Large Vocabulary Word Recognition via Diphone Spotting and Multiprocessor Implementation. Speech Comm. 1988; 7: 389-396

[5] Hertz J., Krogh A. and Palmer RG. **An Introduction to Neural Computation**. Addison-Wesley, 1991

[6] Colla AM. and Pedrazzi P. Single and Coupled Neural Handprinted Character Classifiers. In: M. Marinaro and P.G. Morasso (Ed.s), ICANN 94 - Proc. of the Int. Conf. on ARTIFICIAL NEURAL NETWORKS. Sorrento (Italy), vol. II, pp. 969-972, Springer-Verlag, 1994

[7] Cepollina E. Metodi avanzati per il riconoscimento del manoscritto. Tesi di Laurea in Scienza dell'Informazione (M. Sci. Thesis in Computer Science). DISI Univ. di Genova, 1996

[8] Pedrazzi P. and Colla AM. Simple Feature Extraction For Handwritten Character Recognition. In: Proc. IEEE 1995 Int. Conference on Image Processing ICIP-95. Washington, vol. III, pp. 320-323, 1995

[9] Aho AV. and Ullman JD. **Principles of Compiler Design**. Addison-Wesley, Reading (USA), 1978

[10] Sakoe H. and Chiba S. Dynamic Programming algorithm Optimization for Spoken Word Recognition. IEEE Trans. ASSP-26, 1, pp. 43-49, 1978

Video Data Compression Using Multilayer Perceptrons

Sergio Carrato

D.E.E.I., University of Trieste, v. Valerio, 10, 34100 Trieste, Italy
e-mail: carrato@ipl.univ.trieste.it
tel: +39 40 6767147; fax: +39 40 6763460

Summary. In this paper, we present a neural network-based approach to the problem of video compression. In particular, an MPEG-like encoder is proposed, in which a novel scheme is proposed for a very low cost motion compensation of the frames which lie in between I or P frames. To code the error information of the *inter* coded frames, several multilayer perceptron are utilised, which operate on both two- and three-dimensional data.

Simulation results are also presented, which show the peculiar characteristics of the proposed approach.

1. Introduction

Recently, several contributions have appeared in the literature concerning the use of Multilayer Perceptrons (MLP) for both image [1][2] and video [3] coding. Generally, a Multi-Layer Perceptron (MLP) with one hidden layer is used as a compander (compressor-expander) of the images; its structure is characterised by the same number of input and output nodes and a lower number of nodes in the hidden layer. During the training phase, different images (actually subdivided into blocks) are fed into the input layer and the network adapts its weights to reproduce the same images at the output nodes with minimum error. After this phase, the net is able to code the data: when the original image is fed into the input layer, its compressed version is available at the output of the hidden nodes and it can be recovered with its original dimensions at the output layer.

In the present paper we propose a new approach to the problem of video coding, where several MLPs operate both on 2- and 3-dimensional data in order to reduce both spatial and temporal redundancy.

2. Algorithm description

The block diagram of the proposed coder is presented in Fig. 2.1, where it may be seen that the frames to be coded are grouped in three classes, I, P, and A, which will be defined in the following.

The proposed algorithm operates on a data structure, reported in Fig. 2.2, which is quite similar to that used in MPEG [4][5], where the image sequence is partitioned in Group Of Pictures (GOPs).

The first frame of each GOP is coded *intra* (I frame); we use a standard transform-based technique followed by zig-zag scanning and entropy coding. In each GOP there are also several frames which are predicted using block-based motion compensation [6], and are called P frames: the first P frame is predicted

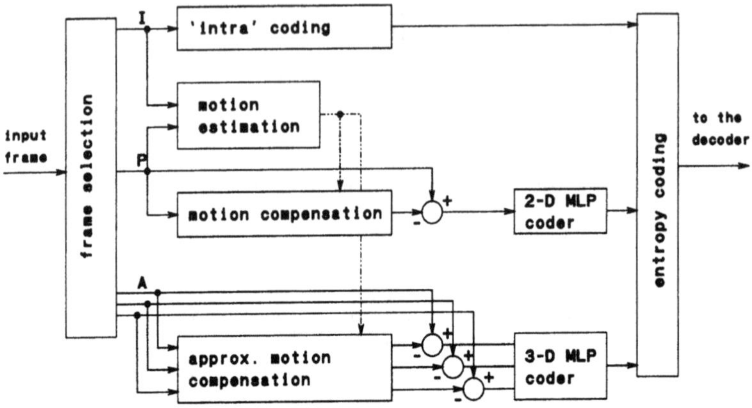

Figure 2.1. Block diagram of the proposed algorithm, which uses two MLPs to code the error images of motion compensated frames.

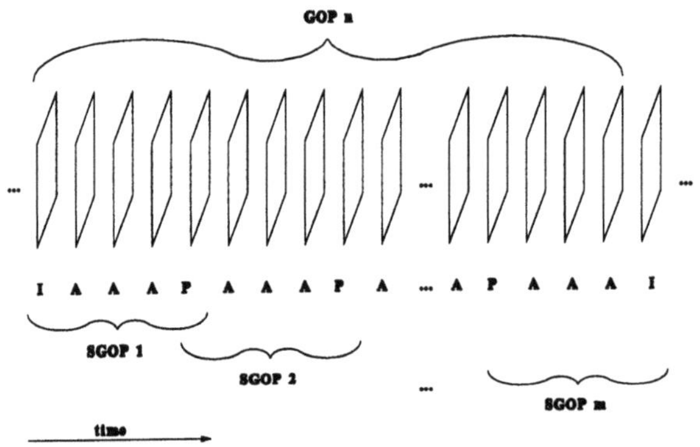

Figure 2.2. Structure of a Group of Pictures (GOP). The I frames are *intra* coded; P frames are motion predicted, while A frames are approximated using interpolated motion vectors.

with reference to the I frame, the second P-frame with reference to the first one, and so on.

The main difference with respect to MPEG deals with the remaining frames, which in MPEG are called B frames and are predicted using bidirectional motion compensation (i.e. with reference to both a preceding and a successive frame), so that the transmission of the corresponding motion vectors is needed. In our coding scheme, in turn, in order to reduce the total bit rate we build a first approximation of these frames by exploiting the already available motion vectors between the nearest preceding and successive I or P frame, so that we obtain an approximate prediction with almost no additional bit rate[1].

Again with reference to Fig. 2.2, let us define Small Group Of Pictures, SGOP, a set of frames in between two I or P frame, extremes included; let also call A frames the frames of the SGOP, extremes excluded. The first SGOP of a

[1] More precisely, some overhead is needed only for the last SGOP of each GOP, because in this case motion vectors have to be computed even though its last frame is actually the I frame of the following GOP and consequently is *intra* coded.

GOP is constituted by the I frame, several A frames, and the first P frame; the second SGOP has two P frames as extremes, while the last SGOP is formed by the last P frame, several A frames, and the I frame of the following GOP.

As already mentioned, in order to predict the A frames of a given SGOP, we exploit the fact that the motion vectors from the first to the last frame of the SGOP are available. If we suppose that the motion velocities are reasonably constant in the time interval between the first and the last frame of the SGOP, we can estimate the motion between the first frame of the SGOP and each A frame by interpolating the motion vector of the last frame, i.e. by scaling it according to the position of each A frame in the SGOP (Fig. 2.3).

In our implementation, we subdivided each SGOP in four SGOPs, and we used SGOPs composed of 5 frames.

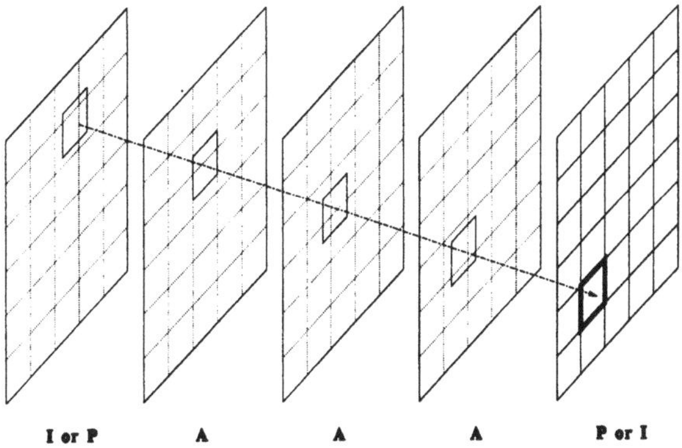

Figure 2.3. Example of motion compensation using interpolated motion vectors for the A frames.

In order to improve the image quality, of course at the expense of a higher bit rate, it is useful to code and transmit the difference between the actual and the motion compensated P and A frames. The error in the P frames could be coded using a conventional DCT-based approach, as done e.g. in MPEG2 [4]. In turn, we use an MLP which yields in the hidden layer a compressed version of the data; the approach is similar to the one proposed e.g. in [1], but in this case error images (i.e., essentially zero mean data) are coded instead of normal ones. It has to be noted that DCT is commonly used for this kind of images [5][7], even though their statistics are not guaranteed to match those needed for an efficient DCT coding. MLPs have shown to be able to efficiently code normal images, and should be capable of adapting their performances to signals with different statistics. We subdivide each error image into square blocks (8×8 pixels in our implementation) and the blocks are processed by a suitably trained MLP.

Also the difference between the actual and the reconstructed A frames can be considered and processed, again in order to improve the image quality. Of course, these error images could be processed similarly to what is done for the P frames. In turn, due to the fact that these images share the same kind of approximate motion compensation, we propose to consider all the A frames in a SGOP (three in our simulations) simultaneously, by coding the errors of spatially close pixels in the different images together. More precisely, we partition each image into square blocks (8 × 8 pixels in our simulations) and we group the blocks belonging to different frames, thus obtaining three-dimensional *macroblocks*, in our case of 8 × 8 × 3 pixels. Similarly to what has been done with the P frames, these macroblocks are then processed by another 2-layer MLP, which again is able to provide in the hidden layer a compressed version of the data. Following this approach it is possible to exploit the residual redundancy in the data after the approximate motion compensation.

3. Simulation results

Several experiments have been performed using the luminance component of standard progressive sequences in CIF format (352 × 288 pixels), in order to test the proposed algorithm. Motion compensation has been performed using a standard block matching technique with ± 16 search range; information related to the motion vector has been entropy coded.

3.1 MLPs dimensions and training

As already explained, one MLP is devoted to the coding of error images related to P frames. As usual [8], a sigmoid with bias has been used as activation function for each node. For what concerns the number of hidden nodes, we found 5 (i.e., a compression ratio equal to 12.8) to be a reasonable compromise between quality of the output image and amount of data to be transmitted to the receiver.

The 64 × 5 × 64 MLP has been trained with 12 P frames taken from the sequence 'Miss America', using the standard backpropagation algorithm [8] with exponentially decreasing learning factor and fixed (= 0.9) momentum.

During the test phase, the signal at the hidden nodes has been quantised using a 16 level linear quantiser; this is not an optimal choice, and has been applied here only for reasons of simplicity; the resulting data have been entropy coded.

A similar approach has been followed for the MLP dedicated to the compression of the errors in the A frames. In this case, the dimensions of the MLP are $192 \times h_3 \times 192$, being 8 × 8 × 3 the size of the input and output data and h_3 the number of hidden nodes. Also in this case, a good compromise between image quality and data rate experimentally yields to a value $h_3 = 12$, which corresponds to a compression ratio equal to 16. All the other details are similar to those related to the MLP used for the P frames.

To have an idea of the results of the training phase, in Fig. 3.1 the networks outputs are reported when each hidden node is successively excited. The training duration was 100 epochs. These images represent a sort of 'basis' of the subspaces found by the MLPs (they would actually be the bases if the neuron activation functions were linear), so that the MLPs are able to reconstruct at their output those images which are nonlinear combinations of these basic patterns.

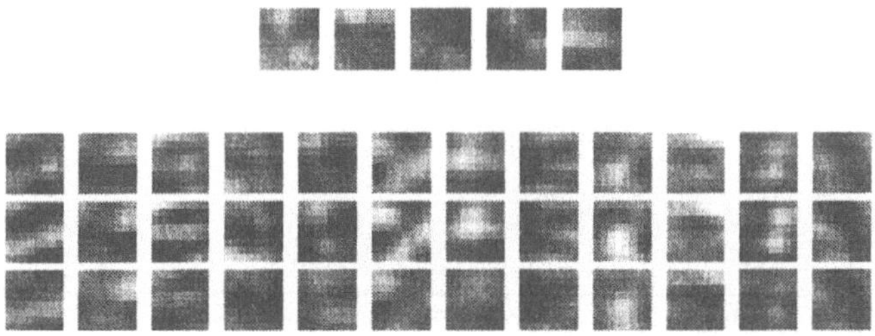

Figure 3.1. Images obtained exciting individually each hidden node of the two-dimensional (top) and three-dimensional (bottom) MLPs.

3.2 Simulation results

In Fig. 3.2, the PSNR and the bit rate are reported for 4 GOPs of the sequence 'Miss America', with MLP-based error coding for both the P frames and the A frames. Mean PSNR and bit rate are 33.3 dB and 0.09 bpp, respectively. As an example, one frame of the original and of the processed sequence are reported in Fig. 3.3. The frame shown is the central one of the last SGOP of the first GOP, and has one of the lower PSNR's in all the sequence, 31.6 dB.

In the bit rate plot, the four 'bit sources' are reported (together with the total), namely the coding of the I frames, the motion vectors, the errors in the P frames, and the errors in the A frames, respectively. In order to show the relative weight of these different kind of data, each of them has been 'distributed' over all the frames it contributes to. More precisely, the bits required to code the I frame are evenly divided over all the frames of the SGOP, because the quality of the I frames also determines those of both P and A frames; similarly, the bits needed for both the motion vectors and the P error frames of each SGOP are considered to refer to both the P and the A frames of the same SGOP; finally, the coding of the A frames errors only relates to A frames.

It may be noted that the proposed system yields both subjectively and objectively good image quality at reasonably low bit rates, so that it can be considered as an interesting approach to video coding for videotelephony and multimedia applications.

References

1. G. W. Cottrell, P. Munro, and D. Zipser, "Image compression by back propagation: an example of extensional programming," in *Models of cognition: a review of cognition science* (N. E. Sharkey, ed.), NJ: Norwood, 1989.
2. M. Mougeot, R. Azencott, and B. Angeniol, "A study of image compression with backpropagation," in *NATO ASI Series, Vol. F 68, Neurocomputing* (F. F. Soulie and J. Herault, eds.), Berlin Heidelberg: Springer-Verlag, 1990.
3. K. I. Diamantaras and S. Y. Kung, "Compressing moving pictures using the APEX neural principal component extractor," in *Proc. 1993 IEEE Workshop on Neural Networks for Signal Processing*, (Linthicum Heights, MD), pp. 321–330, Sept. 1993.
4. ISO/IEC, "Coding of moving pictures and associated audio." ISO/IEC JTC 1/SC 29 WG 11, MPEG 92/No 245, July 1992.
5. L. Chiariglione, "The development of an integrated audiovisual coding standard: MPEG," *Proceedings of the IEEE*, vol. 83, pp. 151–157, Feb. 1995.

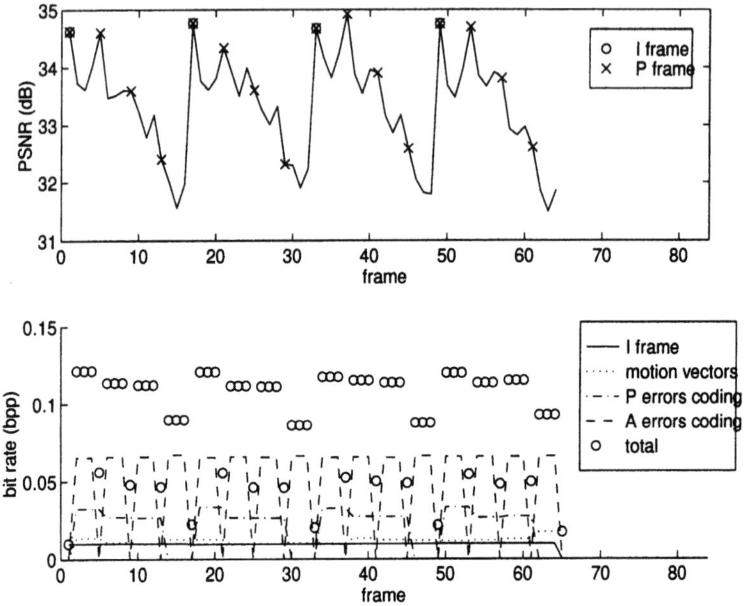

Figure 3.2. PSNR and bit rate versus frame number for 64 frames of the sequence 'Miss America', coded by the proposed algorithm. Mean PSNR and bit rate are 33.3 dB and 0.09 bpp, respectively.

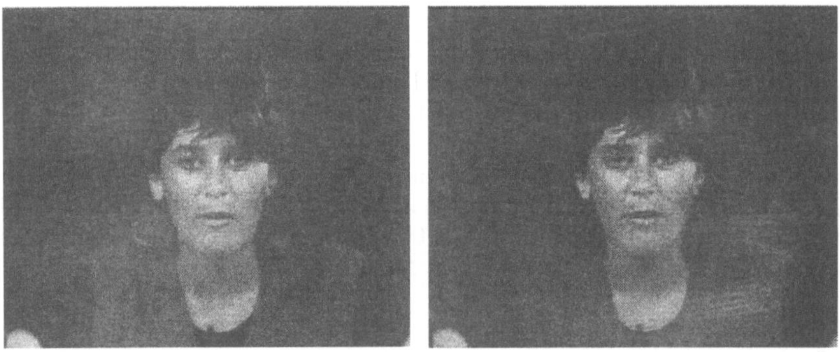

Figure 3.3. Original(left) and reconstructed (right) 15th frame of the sequence 'Miss America'.

6. J. R. Jain and A. K. Jain, "Displacement measurement and its application in interframe image coding," *IEEE Trans. Commun.*, vol. COM-29, pp. 1799–1806, Dec. 1981.
7. M. Rabbani and P. W. Jones, *Digital Image Compression Techniques.* Bellingham, Washington: SPIE Optical Engineering Press, 1991.
8. R. P. Lippmann, "An introduction to computing with neural nets," *IEEE ASSP Magazine*, pp. 4–21, Apr. 1987.

Speeding Up Neural Network Execution: An Application To Speech Recognition

F. Mana, D. Albesano, and R. Gemello
CSELT - Centro Studi E Laboratori Telecomunicazioni
Via G.Reiss Romoli, 274
10148 Torino (ITALY)
Tel: +39-11-2286258
Email: mana@cselt.it

Abstract - In recent years, many papers have addressed the problem of speeding up neural network execution, most of them trying to reduce network size by weight and neuron pruning, and others making use of special hardware. In this paper we propose a new, different method[1] able to reduce the computational effort needed to calculate the output activity of a neural network. The suggested technique can be applied to a wide class of connectionist models for processing of slow varying signals (for example: vocal, radar, sonar and video signals). In addition, neither specialized hardware nor big quantities of additional memory are required. For each neuron of the network, the method suggests comparing its activation value at a certain moment with the corresponding activation value computed at the previous net forward computation: if no change occurred the neuron does not perform any computation, otherwise it propagates to the connected neurons the difference of its two activations multiplied by its outcoming weights. The proposal is verified in a speech recognition framework on two main tasks with two different neural network architectures. The results show a drastic reduction of the execution time on both the neural architectures and no significant changes in recognition quality.

1 Introduction

Multi-layer Perceptron (MLP) networks are widely diffused in the industrial applications of neural networks (NN). Therefore, it is important, from an engineering point of view, to design and test methods to improve their execution efficiency. Until now, the problem of speeding up NN execution has been investigated following two different approaches. The first one regards hardware implementation where connectionist models are built directly on VLSI chips (using both analog and digital technology) exploiting their inherent parallelism to the utmost [8][5]. The second

[1] Patent pending

direction regards speeding up NN execution indirectly reducing the network architecture and size [7][6].

In this paper we describe the difference forward propagation; a method suitable for reducing the amount of computation needed at each net execution [3]. The method is based on a well known concept in engineering, i.e. the concept of propagation of differences. In this work it has been applied to the forward computation of MLP networks, obtaining a relevant saving of computation time by means of a parsimonious use of the computation performed in previous executions. At the beginning of each sequence, the network is properly initialized to keep into account the static information. Then, for each item of the sequence, only the differences in time of the unit activations are propagated through the network. This method is described in detail in chapter 2, while in chapter 3 the method is tested on two real speech recognition tasks using two different network architectures. Despite this paper shows an application to standard MLP for speech recognition, the method functions potentially for a wide class of neural networks as well (e.g. Hopfield and RBF), and can be applied to many signal processing tasks such as audio and video recognition, radar and sonar trace analysis, and so on.

2 The Method

In this section we introduce the method we propose to speed up the neural network forward computation. For the sake of simplicity we describe it considering the case of a MLP network, however the method is very general. Let us consider $net_i(t)$ the input at time t for a generic unit i and consider $\Delta o_j(t+1)$ the variation at time t+1 of the activation of unit j connected by an incoming weight to the i-th unit. We can introduce $\Delta o_j(t+1)$ variation in the standard net definition for MLP and obtain:

$$\begin{aligned} net_i(t+1) &= \Sigma_j\, w_{ij}(o_j(t)+\Delta o_j(t+1)) + bias_i = \\ &= \Sigma_j\, w_{ij} o_j(t) + \Sigma_j\, w_{ij}\Delta o_j(t+1) + bias_i = \\ &= net_i(t) + \Sigma_j\, w_{ij}\Delta o_j(t+1). \end{aligned} \tag{1}$$

where: $\Delta o_j(t+1) = o_j(t+1)-o_j(t)$. This formula points out how a variation on the activation of unit u_j will influence the activation of unit u_i at time t+1 ($net_i(t+1)$) with respects to the previous activation value $net_i(t)$. At this point, it is possible to realize the forward computation by means of the propagation through the net of the difference of the unit activation $\Delta o_j(t+1)$ instead of the activation value $o_j(t+1)$. Since at the very first execution (t=0) no previous information is available, we use the standard forward computation based on the propagation of the activation value in order to initialize the net data structure. In more detail we set all input values to 0 and with the first execution we propagate through the net bias values. After that, for each forward computation of the net we use the following algorithm:

```
ForEach input unit u_j
    o_j (t)= x_j(t)
    Compute the input difference: Δo_j(t) = o_j(t)-o_j(t-1)
    If (Δo_j(t) ≠ 0)
        ForEach weight w_ij outcoming from unit u_j to unit u_i
            Incrementally update net_i value: net_i(t) = net_i(t) + w_ij Δo_j(t)
        End
End
ForEach hidden unit u_j
    Compute the unit activation: o_j(t) = SIGM(net_j(t))
    Compute the difference: Δo_j(t) = o_j(t)-o_j(t-1)
    If (Δo_j(t) ≠ 0)
        ForEach weight w_ij outcoming from unit u_j to unit u_i
            Incrementally update net_i value: net_i(t) = net_i(t) + w_ij Δo_j(t)
        End
End
ForEach output unit u_j
    Compute the unit activation o_j(t) = SIGM(net_j(t))
End
```

Looking in more detail at the proposed algorithm, some considerations must be done. The first one concerns the choice of carrying out the computation visiting the weights outcoming from a unit instead of the weights incoming to a unit. The motivation of this implementative choice is that when the unit activation difference is computed, it is possible to check if changes must be propagated or not. If the unit activation difference is null, no changes must be propagated, thereby we do not consider its outcoming weights and the computation goes on to the next unit. This saving of computation is the core of the method: the reduction of the number of operations is achieved by skipping all the weights outcoming from the units with unchanged activations and the final execution time is comparable with that of a smaller network. The second regards memory requirements: no significative extra-memory is required; in fact, the only data structures used are the vectors that contain $net_j(t)$ and $o_j(t-1)$. At a generic iteration at time t, it is implicitly assumed that the vector net(t) inherits its values from net(t-1), while $o_j(t)$ is stored into a temporary variable, and after the computation of $\Delta o_j(t)$ it is saved as $o_j(t-1)$. In practice, the algorithm requires a unique data structure "net" that is initialized (net(0)) and then maintains its values from an iteration to the next one. During the iteration its values are incrementally updated by the propagation of differences.

The main advantage of the forward computation based on the propagation of differences relies on the capability to optimally use, when $\Delta o_j(t)=0$, the computations performed in the previous executions. However, if activation values are real numbers, $\Delta o_j(t)$ can never be exactly 0.0; so, it is necessary to quantize the activation values, in order to allow the $\Delta o_j(t)=0$ condition to happen.

The simplest thing to do is to perform a linear quantization of the codomain of the activation function. The number of finite different values assumed by $o_j(t)$ depends on the step of quantization of the codomain. Quantization takes place for every hidden unit activation function whereas for input and output layers it is not performed. Quantization allows the method to work, but potentially introduces an error on the output $o_j(t)$. However experimental results point out how the quantization is possible without great reduction in output accuracy because the approximation introduced is largely compensated by the distributed computation. The accuracy of the network computation in solving a given task and the execution time depend on the number of steps involved in the quantization: accuracy of net outputs increases with the number of quantization steps, whereas maximum of speed up is achieved using the minimum number of steps. For this reason, a tuning of the quantization step is necessary in order to find the best compromise between fast execution and performance requirements.

3 Experimental Results

A lot of experimental activity was performed in order to investigate, on real domains, the behavior of the proposed method. The speed up of the forward computation at different values of the quantization step and the variation of the accuracy of the network computation were evaluated on two different speaker independent speech recognition tasks, allowing the proposed method to work with different neural network architectures: a connected digit recognition task, for voice dialing or credit card codes recognition, and a continuous speech recognition task for voice information access, both over the Italian public switched telephone network.

The data pre-processing technique consisted of a Mel-based spectral analysis followed by a Discrete Cosine Transform to obtain Cepstral coefficients. Together with the cepstral coefficients, the value of the logarithm of the total energy of each frame was retained as it provides some information about distinguishing the voiced parts of the speech input from the unvoiced ones. First order derivatives and second order derivatives of the log energy and of the 12 cepstral coefficients were computed at each frame, resulting in 39 parameters each 10 msec.

In both the tasks, we used the Recurrent Neural Automata(*) (RNA), a specific architecture for speech recognition devised in 1992 and described in [1] and [2]. The connectionist models were trained using the standard backpropagation algorithm as described in [2] where word boundary detection, time alignment and classification are computed at the same time as a single optimization problem and tested in a connected/continuous framework [4] based on dynamic programming.

Figures 3.1 and 3.2 report the results we obtained using the testing data bases. In the case of the connected digit task we have 2467 credit card codes, 16 digits long, while in the case of the continuous task we have 928 spontaneous sentences (2371 total words) collected by naive speakers and recorded during a field trial of the system. All the experiments were conducted on a SUN Sparc 20 computer; they differed from each other according to the testing data set and the value of the sigmoid codomain quantization parameter that assumed values from 5 to 50 with a step of 5 (x-axis in the figures).

(*) Patent pending

The results are espressed in term of three parameters: WA, SRR and RTR. The WA line reports the word accuracy i.e. the percentage of single word recognition, the line SRR is about the sentence recognition rate i.e. the percentage of fully recognized sequences, and finally the RTR line reports the real time ratio i.e. how much CPU time is required to recognize one second of speech.

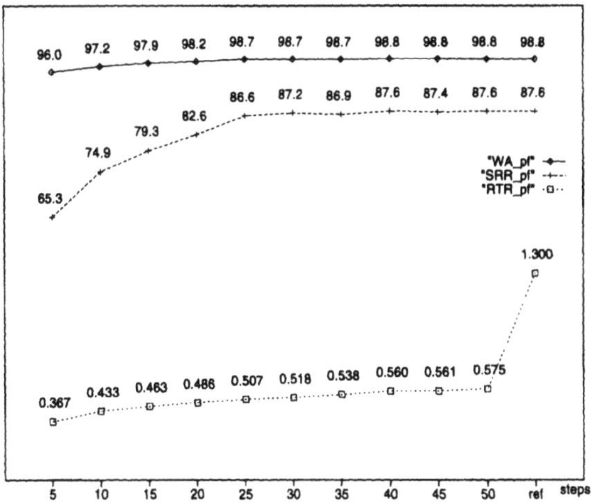

Fig.3.1 - The behaviour of the method working on the connected task

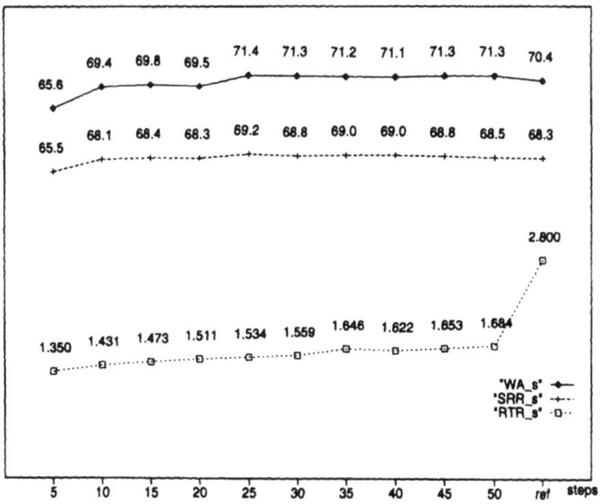

Fig.3.2 - The behaviour of the method working on the continuous task

4 Conclusions

In this paper we have proposed a new method to speed up the neural network forward computation. The method is quite general and is based on the re-use of the computations performed in the previous forward computations. The proposed algorithm propagates, from input to output units, the activation differences instead of the activation absolute values, so allowing to skip the propagation for units with no appreciable activation difference. In order to exploit the method and achieve an effective reduction of execution time, it is necessary to perform a quantization of the activation function codomain. The method has been verified empirically in a speech recognition framework using the MLP model with different architectures. Analyzing the results we achieved a reduction of the computation requirement of about 1/3 on our on-line speech recognizer running over a SUN Sparc 20.

References

1. D. Albesano, R. Gemello and F. Mana, "*Isolated Word Recognition with Recurrent Network Automata*", Proc. IJCNN 92, Baltimore, June 1992.
2. D. Albesano, R. Gemello, and F. Mana, "*Recurrent Network Automata for Speaker Independent Connected Digit Recognition*", Proc. WCNN 95, Washington D.C., July 1995.
3. D. Albesano, R. Gemello, and F. Mana, *"Speeding up Neural Network Execution: An Application to Speech Recognition"*, Proc. of IEEE Workshop on Neural Networks for Signal Processing; Kyoto, September 1996.
4. L. Fissore, R. Pieraccini et alii, "*Syntax driven recognition of connected words by Markov Models*", Proc. ICASSP 84, San Diego, March 1984.
5. D. E. Johnson, J. S. Marsland and W. Eccleston, "*Neural Network Implementation Using a Single MOST Per Synapse*", IEEE Transactions on Neural Networks, Vol. 6, N 4, July 1995.
6. X. Liang and X. Wang, "*Information Crosswise Propagation (CP) Learning in Multilayer Perceptrons - A Novel Way to Neuron Pruning*", Proc. WCNN 95, Washington D.C., July 1995.
7. A. Malinowski, D. A. Miller and J. M. Zurada, "*Reconciling Training and Weight Suppression: New Guidelines for Pruning - Efficient Training*", Proc. WCNN 95, Washington D.C., July 1995.
8. J. Van der Spiegel, C. Donham et alii, "*Large Scale Analog Neural Computer with Programmable Architecture and Programmable Time Constants for Temporal Pattern Analysis*", Proc. ICNN 94, Orlando (FL), June 1994.

Periodicity Analysis of Unevenly Spaced Data by Means of Neural Networks

M.Rasile
INFM, unita' di Salerno
84081 Baronissi (SA) Italia

L.Milano
Dipartimento di Scienze Fisiche, Universita' di Napoli "Federico II"
and Istituto Nazionale di Fisica Nucleare sez. Napoli
Mostra d'Oltremare, Pad. 20, I-80125 Napoli, Italia

R.Tagliaferri
Dipartimento di Informatica ed Applicazioni "R.M. Capocelli",
Universita' di Salerno and INFM. unita' di Salerno
84081 Baronissi (SA) Italia
Corresponding author E-mail robtag@dia.unisa.it

G.Longo
Osservatorio Astronomico di Capodimonte
80131 Napoli Italia

Abstract

Periodicity analysis of unevenly collected data is a relevant issue in several scientific fields. In astrophysics, for example, we have to find the fundamental period of light or radial velocity curves which are unevenly sampled observations of stars. Classical spectral analysis methods are unsatisfactory to face the problem. In this paper we present a neural network based estimator system which performs well the frequency extraction in unevenly sampled signals. It uses a unsupervised Hebbian nonlinear neural algorithm to extract, from the interpolated signal, the principal components which, in turn, are used by the MUSIC frequency estimator algorithm to extract the frequencies. The neural network is tolerant to noise amplification due to interpolation and, above all, to blank time window in the data. We benchmark the system on realistic and real signals with the Periodogram.

1 Introduction

The more sensitive instrumentation and observational techniques become, the more frequently we find variable signals in time domain that previously were believed to be constant. Research for possible periodicities in the signal curves is then a natural consequence, when not an important issue. One of the most relevant problem concerning the techniques of periodic signal analysis is the way in which data are collected: many time series are collected at unevenly sampling rate. In this paper we will propose a new way to approach the problem using neural networks.

2 Spectral analysis and unevenly spaced data

2.1 Introduction

Periodicity analysis of noisy signals is a relevant topic in all scientific fields, such as astrophysics, geology, and so on. [2, 4].

We can formulate the problem in this way: a physical variable X is measured at discrete times t_i; the time series $\{X(t_i)\}$ can be seen as the sum of a signal and random errors: $X_i = X(t_i) = X_s(t_i) + R(t_i)$. The problem, then, is to estimate the fundamental frequencies of the signal [2, 4, 5, 12, 14]. The physical variable X can be either measured at uniform time steps, leading to an evenly sampled signal, or at unevenly spaced time steps, leading to uneven sampling [2, 8, 22]. In the first case there exist a lot of valid tools to solve the problem, based on Fourier analysis [12, 14, 18]. On the other hand, in the case of uneven sampling, classical techniques cannot be effectively used [2, 8, 22]. The best solution may be the interpolation of data to obtain an evenly sampled signal. However, this is not always working due to the interpolation amplification of the noise and to the sensitivity of Fourier technique to it [9]. There are other techniques used in specific areas [6, 13]: however, none of them faces directly the problem, so that they are not truly reliable. The most used tool for periodicity analysis of evenly or unevenly sampled signals is the Periodogram [22]; therefore we will refer to it to evaluate our system.

2.2 Periodogram and its variations

The Periodogram (P), is an estimator of the signal energy in the frequency domain [5, 12, 14, 18].

2.2.1 Scargle's Periodogram

This tool is a variation of the classical P. It was introduced by J.D. Scargle [22] for these reasons: 1) data from instrumental sampling are often not equally spaced; 2) due to P inconsistency [12, 14, 18], we must introduce a selection criterion for signal components.

In fact, in the case of even sampling, the classical P has a simple statistic distribution: it is exponentially distributed for Gaussian noise. In the uneven sampling case the distribution becomes very complex. However, Scargle's P has the same distribution of the even case [22]. Its definition is:

$$P_x(f) = \frac{1}{2}\frac{[\sum_{n=0}^{N-1} x(n)\cos 2\pi f(t_n - \tau)]^2}{\sum_{n=0}^{N-1}\cos^2 2\pi f(t_n - \tau)} + \frac{[\sum_{n=0}^{N-1} x(n)\sin 2\pi f(t_n - \tau)]^2}{\sum_{n=0}^{N-1}\sin^2 2\pi f(t_n - \tau)} \quad (1)$$

where

$$\tau = \frac{1}{4\pi f} \frac{\sum_{n=0}^{N-1} \sin 4\pi f t_n}{\sum_{n=0}^{N-1} \cos 4\pi f t_n}$$

and τ is a shift variable on the time axis, f is the frequency, x is the data vector, $\{t_n\}$ is the observation series.

2.3 Modern spectral analysis

Frequency estimation of narrow band signals in Gaussian noise is a problem related to many fields [12, 14]. Since the classical methods of Fourier analysis suffer from statistic and resolution problems, then newer techniques based on the analysis of the signal autocorrelation matrix eigenvectors were introduced [12, 14].

2.3.1 Spectral analysis with eigenvectors

Let us assume to have a signal with p sinusoidal components (narrow band). The p sinusoids are modelled as a stationary ergodic signal, and this is possible only if the phases are assumed to be indipendent random variables uniformly distributed in $[0, 2\pi)$ (see [12, 14]). To estimate the frequencies we exploit the properties of the signal autocorrelation matrix (a.m.) [12, 14]. The a.m. is the sum of the signal and the noise matrices; the p principal eigenvectors of the signal matrix allow the estimate of frequencies; the p principal eigenvectors of the signal matrix are the same of the total matrix.

3 PCA Neural Nets

3.1 Introduction

Principal Component analysis (PCA) is a widely used technique in data analysis. Mathematically, it is defined as follows: let $\mathbf{C} = E(\mathbf{x}\mathbf{x}^T)$ be the covariance matrix of L-dimensional zero mean input data vectors $\mathbf{x}$. The i-th principal component of $\mathbf{x}$ is defined as $\mathbf{x}^T \mathbf{c}(i)$, where $\mathbf{c}(i)$ is the normalized eigenvector of $\mathbf{C}$ corresponding to the i-th largest eigenvalue $\lambda(i)$. The subspace spanned by the principal eigenvectors $\mathbf{c}(1), \ldots, \mathbf{c}(M), (M < L))$ is called the PCA subspace (of dimensionality M) [16, 17]. PCA's can be neurally realized in various ways [1, 7, 15, 16, 19, 21]. The PCA network used by us is a one layer feedforward neural network which is able to extract the principal components of the stream of input vectors. Typically, Hebbian type learning rules are used, based on the one unit learning algorithm originally proposed by Oja[16]. Many different versions and extensions of this basic algorithm have been proposed during the recent years; see [10, 11, 16].

3.2 Linear, robust, nonlinear PCA Neural Nets

The structure of the PCA neural network can be summarized as follows [10, 11, 16]: there is one input layer, and one forward layer of neurons totally connected to the inputs; during the learning phase there are feedback links among neurons, that classify the network structure as either hierarchical or symmetric. After the learning phase the network becomes purely feedforward. The hierarchical case leads to the well known GHA algorithm [11, 21]; in the symmetric case we have the Oja's subspace network [16].

PCA neural algorithms can be derived from optimization problems, such as variance maximization and representation error minimization [10, 11]. We can generalize these problems to nonlinear problems, getting nonlinear algorithms (and relative networks); see also [10, 11]. These have the same structure of the linear ones: either hierarchical or symmetric. These learning algorithms can be further classified in: robust PCA algorithms and nonlinear PCA algorithms. We define robust PCA so that the objective function grows less than quadratically [10, 11]. The nonlinear learning function appears at selected places only. In nonlinear PCA algorithms all the outputs of the neurons are nonlinear function of the responses.

3.2.1 Robust PCA algorithms

In the robust generalization of variance maximization, the objective function $f(t)$ is assumed to be a valid cost function [10, 11], such as $\ln\cos(t)$ e $|t|$. This leads to the algorithm:

$$\mathbf{w}_{k+1}(i) = \mathbf{w}_k(i) + \mu_k g(y_k(i))\mathbf{e}_k(i), \qquad \mathbf{e}_k(i) = \mathbf{x}_k - \sum_{j=1}^{I(i)} y_k(j)\mathbf{w}_k(j) \tag{2}$$

In the hierarchical case we have $I(i) = i$. In the symmetric case $I(i) = M$, the error vector $\mathbf{e}_k(i)$ becomes the same $\mathbf{e}_k$ for all the neurons, and eq.(2) can be compactly written as:

$$\mathbf{W}_{k+1} = \mathbf{W}_k + \mu\mathbf{e}_k g(\mathbf{y}_k^T) \tag{3}$$

where $\mathbf{y} = \mathbf{W}_k^T\mathbf{x}$ is the instantaneous vector of neuron responses. The learning function g, derivative of f, is applied separately to each component of the argument vector.

The robust generalization of the representation error problem [10, 11], with $f(t) \leq t^2$, leads to the stochastic gradient algorithm :

$$\mathbf{w}_{k+1}(i) = \mathbf{w}_k(i) + \mu(\mathbf{w}_k(i)^T g(\mathbf{e}_k(i))\mathbf{x}_k + \mathbf{x}_k^T\mathbf{w}_k(i) g(\mathbf{e}_k(i))) \tag{4}$$

This algorithm can be again considered in both hierarchical and symmetric cases. In the symmetric case $I(i) = M$, the error vector is the same $(\mathbf{e}_k)$ for all the weights $\mathbf{w}_k$. In the hierarchical case $I(i) = i$, eq.(4) gives the robust counterparts of principal eigenvectors $\mathbf{c}(i)$.

3.2.2 *Approximated Algorithms*

The first update term $\mathbf{w}_k(i)^T g(\mathbf{e}_k(i))\mathbf{x}_k$ in eq.(4) is proportional to the same vector $\mathbf{x}_k$ for all weights $\mathbf{w}_k(i)$. Furthermore, we can assume that the error vector $\mathbf{e}_k$ should be relatively small after the initial convergence. Hence, we can neglet the first term in eq.(4) and this leads to:

$$\mathbf{w}_{k+1}(i) = \mathbf{w}_k(i) + \mu y_k(i) g(\mathbf{e}_k(i)) \tag{5}$$

3.2.3 *Nonlinear PCA Algorithms*

Let us consider now the nonlinear extensions of PCA algorithms. We can obtain them in a heuristic way by requiring all neuron outputs to be always nonlinear in the equation (2) (see [10, 11]). This leads to:

$$\mathbf{w}_{k+1}(i) = \mathbf{w}_k(i) + \mu g(y_k(i))\mathbf{b}_k(i), \quad \mathbf{b}_k(i) = \mathbf{x}_k - \sum_{j=1}^{I(i)} g(y_k(j))\mathbf{w}_k(j) \quad \forall i = 1, \ldots, p \tag{6}$$

4 The neural network based estimator system

The process for periodicity analysis can be divided in the following steps:

- **Preprocessing**

We first interpolate the data and then calculate and subtract the average pattern to obtain zero mean process [10, 11].

- **Neural computing**

The fundamental learning parameters are: **1)** the initial weight matrix; **2)** the number of neurons, that is the number of principal eigenvectors that we need, equal to twice the number of signal periodicities (for real signals); **3)** ϵ, i.e. the threshold parameter for convergence ; **4)** α, the nonlinear learning function parameter; **5)** μ, that is the learning rate.

We inizialize the weight matrix $\mathbf{W}$ assigning the classical small random values. Otherwise we can use the orthonormalized first patterns of the signal as the columns of the matrix: experimental results show that the latter technique speeds up the convergence of our neural estimator (n.e.). However, it cannot be used with anomalously shaped signals, such as stratigraphic geological signals.

Experimental results show that α can be fixed to : 1., 5., 10., 20. Moreover, the learning rate μ can be also decreased during the learning phase, but we fix it between 0.05 e 0.0005 [10, 11, 16].

- **Frequency estimator**

We exploit the frequency estimator **Multiple Signal Classificator**. It takes as input the weight matrix columns after the learning. The estimated signal frequencies are obtained as the peak locations of the following function [12, 14]:

$$P_{MUSIC} = \log\left(\frac{1}{1 - \sum_{i=1}^{M} |\mathbf{e}_f^H \mathbf{w}(i)|^2}\right)$$

where $\mathbf{w}(i)$ is the i–th weight vector after learning, and $\mathbf{e}_f^H$ is the pure sinusoidal vector : $\mathbf{e}_f^H = [1, e_f^{j2\pi f}, \ldots, e_f^{j2\pi f(L-1)}]^H$.

When f is the frequency of the i–th sinusoidal component, $f = f_i$, we have $\mathbf{e} = \mathbf{e}_i$ and $P_{MUSIC} \to \infty$. In practice we have a peak near and in corrispondence of the component frequency. Estimates are related to the highest peaks.

5 Experimental results

5.1 Introduction

In this section we show the performance of the neural based estimator system using realistic and real data. Realistic and real data come from astrophysics. Specifically, realistic data are light curves and radial velocity curves simulations, while the real signal is a light curve in the Johnson's system [2].

We have to spend few words about the differences of behaviour among the neural algorithm models elicited by the experiments. Nonlinear algorithms are more complex than robust ones; they are relatively slower in converging, with higher probability to be caught in local minima, so their estimates results are sometimes not reliable. So we restrict our choice to robust models. Moreover, symmetric models require more effort in finding the right parameters to achieve convergence than the hierarchical ones. The performance, however, are comparable [20].

Therefore the model used in the following is that of eq.(2) in the hierarchical case with learning function $g_2(t) = sgn(t)\log(1 + \alpha|t|)$.

5.2 Realistic data

Here we present a set of realistic signals generated from light curve and radial velocity curve models from astrophysics [23].

We can see that there are wide time windows in which we do not know the data at all (see figures 1,3,5), and each signal is unevenly sampled between two consecutive windows [23].

The signals are divided in the natural segments of data and then interpolated.

The analysis is difficult since the shape of the signal, above all the shortness of data windows, limits the pattern dimension and therefore the goodness of the learning.

In figures 1,3,5 for each signal we present the total set of points and one data window. Then we show the estimate of the n.e. applied to the whole data set, the estimate of P on the largest data subset (window) and the estimate of P on the whole data set (this does not bring any information as we can see from the figures 2,4,6). The set of realistic signals are representative of two classes of eclipsing binary light and radial velocity curves (i.e. a contact and a semi-detached system). The simulations are quite realistic either concerning the unevenly spaced data for chunk of observations, or for the great time interval between different chunks, including several elapsed periods of the system [23]. We compare the neural network based estimator with the P on these signals, and the results are shown in tables 5.1, 5.2, 5.3, and figures 2,4,6.

We show the experiments on a radial velocity curve (see figures 3 and 4).
Signal parameter: period= 0.36 days, noise variance= 0.05.
Neural algorithm parameter: $\alpha = 10.$, $\mu = 0.0001$, $g_2(t) = sgn(t)\log(1 + \alpha|t|)$, number of points in each pattern= 90
Scargle parameters: $Tapering = 30\%$, $p_0 = 0.01$.

Algorithm	Estimate
Neural algorithm	0.3690
Periodogram	0.3247

Tab.5.1: Estimate results on realistic signal 1.

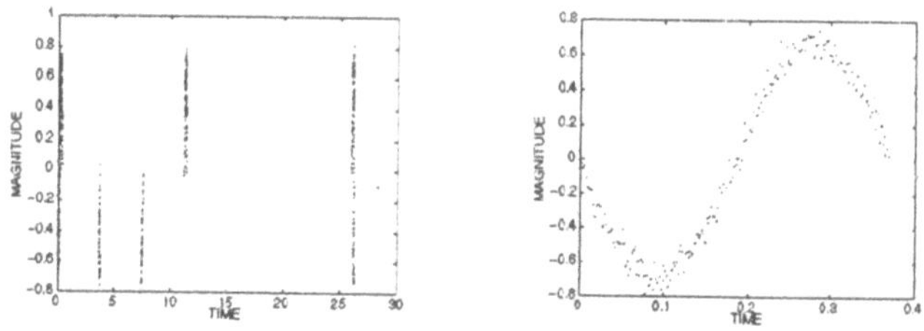

(a) (b)

Figure 1: Realistic signal 1 - (a) Total signal: radial velocity curve (b) First window of signal 1

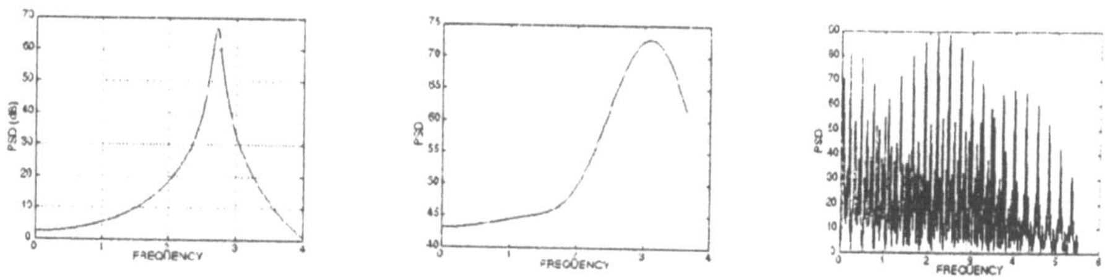

(a) (b)

(c)

Figure 2: Realistic signal 1 - (a) Neural Estimate (whole set) (b) P Estimate (first window) (c) P Estimate (whole set)

We show the experiments on a radial velocity curve with a different period (see figures 3 and 4).

Signal parameter: period= 0.86 days, noise variance= 0.05.

Neural algorithm parameter: $\alpha = 10.$, $\mu = 0.0001$, $g_2(t) = sgn(t)\log(1 + \alpha|t|)$, number of points in each pattern= 90

Scargle parameters: $Tapering = 30\%$, $p_0 = 0.01$.

Algorithm	Estimate
Neural algorithm	0.9000
Periodogram	0.7874

Tab.5.2: Estimate results on realistic signal 2.

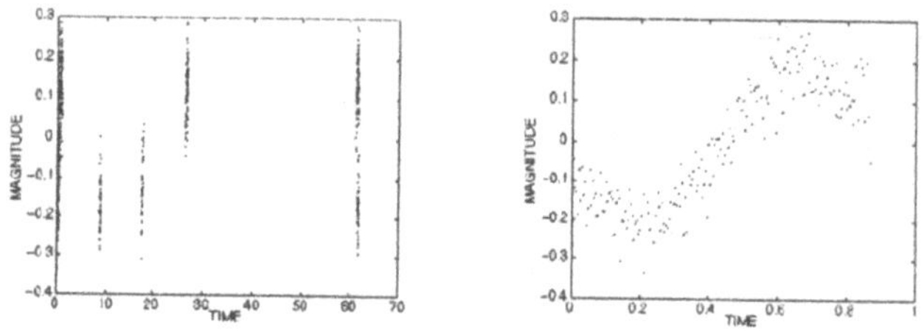

(a) (b)

Figure 3: Realistic signal 2 - (a) Total signal: radial velocity curve (b) First window of signal 2

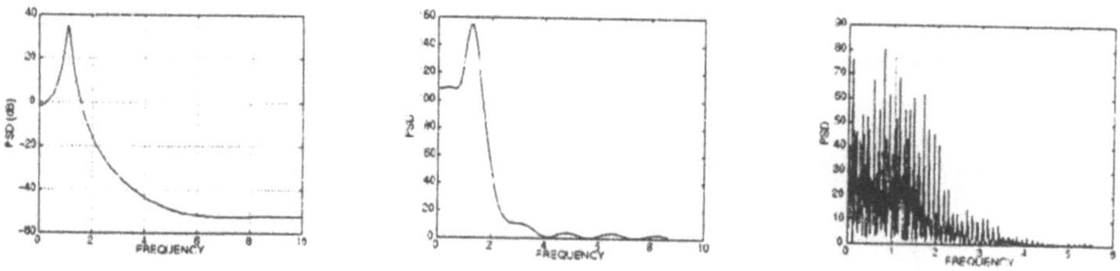

(a) (b)

(c)

Figure 4: Realistic signal 2 - (a) Neural Estimate (whole set) (b) P Estimate (first window) (c) P Estimate (whole set)

We show the experiments on a light curve with the same period of the previous realistic curve (see figures 5 and 6).

Signal parameter: period= 0.86 days, noise variance= 0.05.

Neural algorithm parameter: $\alpha = 10.$, $\mu = 0.0001$, $g_2(t) = sgn(t)\log(1 + \alpha|t|)$, number of points in each pattern= 90

Scargle parameters: $Tapering = 30\%$, $p_0 = 0.01$.

Algorithm	Estimate
Neural algorithm	0.8403
Periodogram	2.6709

Tab.5.3: Estimate results on realistic signal 3.

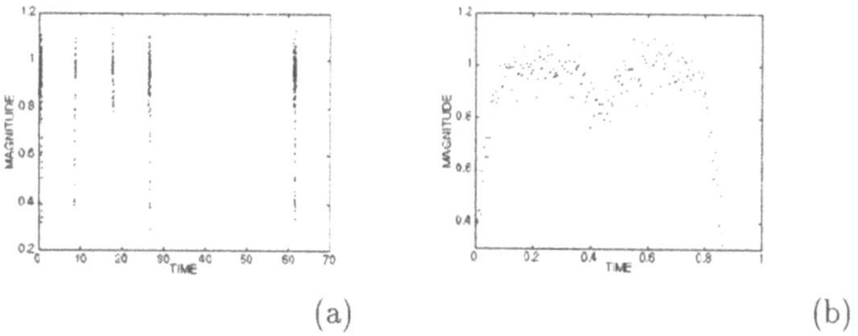

Figure 5: Realistic signal 3 - (a) Total signal: light curve (b) First window of signal 3

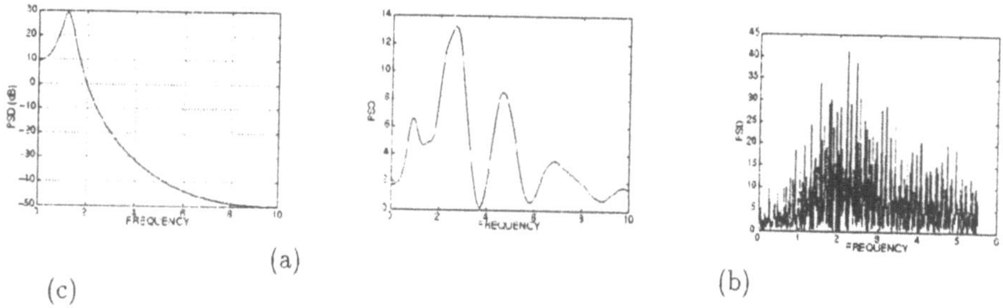

Figure 6: Realistic signal 3 - (a) Neural Estimate (whole set) (b) P Estimate (first window) (c) P Estimate (whole set)

5.3 Real data

The signal we used for the test phase is a light curve in the Johnson's system [2] for the U Pegasi star.

Experimental parameters for the n.e. are: $\alpha = 20.0$; $\mu = 0.0001$; $\epsilon = 0.001$; learning function $g(t) = sgn(t)\log(1 + \alpha|t|)$. The analysis is difficult because of the complex shape of the signal which limits the pattern dimension and therefore the goodness of the learning (see figure 7). The period found by the n.e. is expressed in Julian Days and is in agreement with results cited in literature [3]. The fundamental frequency is 5.4 $1/JD$. Scargle's P does not bring any information if we use the whole set of unevenly spaced data, due to

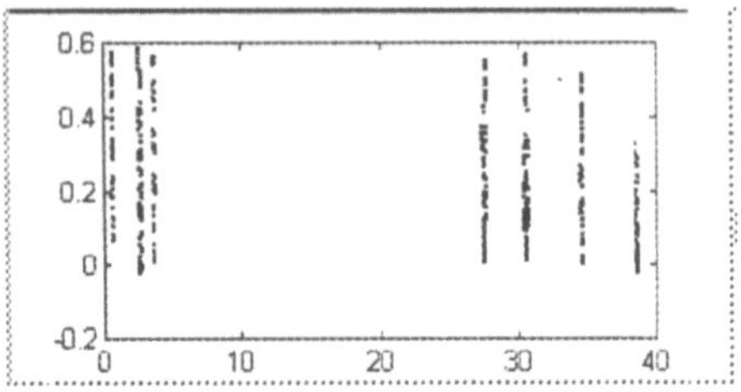

Figure 7: Light curve of U Pegasi

the time windows (see Fig.8(b)). We are forced to apply the P only on the largest subset of consecutive points, but we obtain a poor estimate since we ignore the remaining information. Results are shown in figure 8 and table 5.4.

Algorithm	Estimate
Neural algorithm	0.18516
Periodogram	0.1923

Tab.5.4: Estimate results on real light curve signal from U Pegasi star .

Figure 8: U Pegasi (a) Neural Estimate (b) P Estimate (whole set) (c) P Estimate (single subset)

6 Conclusions

We have realized and experimented a new method for spectral analysis for unevenly sampled signals based on three phases: preprocessing, extraction of principal eigenvectors and estimate of signal frequencies. This is done, respectively, by interpolation, nonlinear PCA neural networks, and *Multiple Signal Classificator* algorithm. First of all, we have shown that neural networks are a valid tool for spectral analysis.

However, above all, what is really important is that neural networks, as realized in our neural estimator system, represent a new tool to face and solve a problem tied with data acquisition in many scientific fields: the unevenly sampling scheme.

Experimental results have shown the validity of our method as an alternative to Periodogram, and in general to classical spectral analysis, expecially in presence of the lackness of complex statistics and high error probability. Moreover, for unevenly sampled data, our system offers great advantages with respect to Periodogram. First of all, it allows us to use a simply and direct way to solve the problem, such as the interpolation. Last, but not least, the neural network is insensitive to blank time windows present in the data, and allows to exploit the whole set of sampled points to extract the signal frequencies.

7 Acknowledgments

This work has been partially supported by IIASS, MURST 40% "*Metodologie e tecniche di progettazione per sistemi eterogenei basati su architetture neurali* " unit of Salerno and by the Italian Space Agency.

The authors would like to thank Prof. Oja for his kind suggestions.

References

[1] Baldi P., Hornik K., Neural networks for principal component analysis: learning from examples without local minima, Neural Networks, 2, (7), 53-58, 1989.

[2] Barone F., Milano L., Russo G., A new method of spectral analysis of unevenly spaced astrophysical data. I. The single-period case, The Astrophysical Journal, 421, 284-302, 1994.

[3] Binnendijk L., The light variation and Orbital Elements of U Pegasi, The Astronomical Journal, 65, (2), 1960.

[4] Brescia M., D'Argenio B., Ferreri V., Longo G., Pelosi N., Rampone S., Tagliaferri R., Neural net aided detection of astronomical periodicities in geologic records, Earth Planetary Science and Letters, 139, 33-45, 1996.

[5] Deeming T. J., Fourier analysis with unequally-spaced data, Astrophysics and Space Science, 36, 137-158, 1975.

[6] Ferraz-Mello S., Estimation of periods from unequally spaced observations, The Astronomical Journal, 86, (4), 1981.

[7] Jutten C., Herault J., Blind separation of sources, partI: an adaptive algorithm based on neuromimetic architecture, Signal Processing, 24, (1), 1-10, 1991.

[8] Horne J. H., Baliunas S. L., A prescription for period analysis of unevenly sampled time series, The Astrophysical Journal, 302, 757-763, 1986.

[9] Horowitz L. L., IEEE Trans., ASSP-22, 22, 1974.

[10] Karhunen J., Joutsensalo J., Representation and separation of signals using nonlinear PCA type learning, Neural Networks, 7, 113-127, 1994.

[11] Karhunen J., Joutsensalo J., Generalization of principal component analysis, optimization problems, and neural networks, Neural Networks, 8, 549-562, 1995.

[12] Kay S. M., Modern spectral estimation: theory and application, Englewood Cliffs: Prentice-Hall, 1988.

[13] Lomb N. R., Least-squares frequency analysis of unequally spaced data, Astrophysics and Space Science, 39, 447-462, 1976.

[14] Marple S. L., Digital spectral analysis with applications, Englewood Cliffs: Prentice-Hall, 1987.

[15] Oja E., A simplified neuron model as a principal component analyzer, Journal of Mathematical Biology, 15, 267-273, 1982.

[16] Oja E., Ogawa H., Wangviwattana J., Learning in nonlinear constrained Hebbian network, Artificial neural networks, T. Kohonen et al. Ed.s, Amsterdam: North-Holland, 385-390, 1991.

[17] Oja E., Karhunen J., Wang L., Vigario R., Principal and independent components in neural networks - recent developments, Seventh Italian Workshop on Neural Networks, Vietri 1995, M.Marinaro & R.Tagliaferri Ed.s, Singapore: World Scientific Pu., 16-35, 1996.

[18] Oppenheim A. V., Schafer R. W., Digital signal processing, Prentice-Hall, 1965.

[19] Plumbley M., A Hebbian/anti Hebbian network which optimizes information capacity by orthonormalizing the principal subspace, in Proc. IEE Conf. on Artificial Neural Networks, Brighton, UK, 86-90, 1993.

[20] Rasile M., Milano L., Tagliaferri R., Longo G., Neural Networks for periodicity analysis of unevenly spaced data, Proceedings of the 1997 International Conference on Neural Networks ICNN'97, N. B. Karayiannis et al. Ed.s, Piscataway, NJ: IEEE, 2257-2262, 1997.

[21] Sanger T. D., Optimal unsupervised learning in a single-layer linear feedforward network, Neural Network, 2, 459-473, 1989.

[22] Scargle J. D., Studies in astronomical time series analysis; statistical aspects of spectral analysis of unevenly spaced data, The Astrophysical Journal, 263, 835-853, 1982.

[23] Wilson R. E., Devinney E. J., ApJ, 166, 605-614, 1971.

Computational Maps for Articulatory Speech Synthesis

Vittorio Sanguineti Pietro G. Morasso
DIST - University of Genova
Via Opera Pia 13, 16145 Genova, Italy
F: +39 10 3532154; E:sangui@.dist.unige.it

Abstract

A computational model for bi-directional coordinate transformations is demonstrated, which is based on two topologically organized computational maps and exploits their intra- and cross-connections for generating smooth trajectories. The model has been applied to speech motor control in order to study the linkage between vocal tract geometry and sound. It can simultaneously fit experimental trajectories in the formant and articulator spaces, respectively, and it is shown that in the generation of continuous sequences of vowels, the computed trajectories of the vocal tract can account for redundancy resolution, and accommodate different speaking rates and levels of stress.

1 Attractor computational maps

Let us consider a neural architecture, consisting of a number of processing elements (PEs) with a lattice of lateral connections; at a given time instant, such a map is characterized by (i) an internal *state* or pattern of activation, U_i^x, $i = 1, \cdots, N$, corresponding to the population vector $\vec{x}_{est} = \sum_i \vec{\pi}_i^x U_i^x$ and determined by the local pattern of connectivity; (ii) an external *input* field E_i^x. Let the dynamics of each PE be described by the following equation:

$$\tau \frac{dV_i^x}{dt} + V_i^x = c_p \sum_j C_{ij}^x U_j^x + c_e E_i^x \cdot V_i^x \tag{1}$$

where V_i^x is a local state variable, τ, c_p and c_e are positive constants. Dynamics is characterized by the combination of lateral excitation (positive connection weights C_{ij}), self-inhibition (determined by $1/\tau$), and gating/shunting inhibition. In particular, the output function $U_i^x = g_i(\vec{V}^x) = V_i^x / \sum_j \sum_k C_{jk}^x V_k^x$ has the effect of a *gating inhibition*, responsible for a competitive dynamics, as the lateral intra-connections are all equal and excitatory ($C_{ij}^x = 1$ if $j \in \mathcal{N}^x(i)$). The second term on the right-hand side has the effect of a *shunting* interaction, in which the external input, E_i^x, is weighted by the present state, V_i^x.

Elsewhere[6] the dynamic behavior of this model is discussed in detail. In summary, if the external inputs are non-zero and the initial state is characterized by a local peak of activation, the peak 'migrates' toward the PE in the map for which E_i^x has its maximum value.

There is a simple way to associate a 'semantics' to such an architecture. In particular, the map can be interpreted as a 'spatial representation' of a given physical quantity, $\vec{x} \in \mathcal{X}$, if each PE f in the map corresponds to a specific value or prototype $\vec{x} = \vec{\pi}^x(f)$ (and viceversa), and the lateral connections reflect the topology of $\mathcal{X}$ – that is, 'similar' prototypes correspond to adjacent (i.e. directly connected) PEs on the map and, viceversa, adjacent PEs correspond to 'similar' prototypes. This assimilates computational maps to Topology-Representing Networks (TRNs), for which a learning algorithm has been demonstrated[5] . In addition, the activation field (and in general any scalar field) can be interpreted as representing a specific value of $\vec{x}$. In particular, the following value of $\vec{x}$ or *population vector* can be inferred from the activation field: $\vec{x}_{est} = \sum_i \vec{\pi}_i^x U_i^x$.

It has been shown[6] that the activation dynamics of Eq. 1 causes the population vector to follow a trajectory that (i) reflects the topology of the lateral connections (i.e. that of X), and (ii) is smooth and displays a bell-shaped velocity profile. These properties suggest that this neural architecture can be exploited to generate trajectories in the space $\mathcal{X}$, provided that the lateral connections of the map reflect its topology. A simple extension of the TRN algorithm also allows to represent relationships among different spaces by means of cross-connections between individual maps (one for each space).

2 Articulatory speech synthesis

A spoken message is the acoustic outcome of a sequence of elementary gestures, each corresponding to a particular phoneme or group of phonemes[4] . Invariance studies have shown that vowels are well identified in the frequency domain by the position of a small number of peaks (typically 5) in the short-time power spectrum: they are called *formants* and correspond to natural frequencies or poles in the frequency response of the vocal tract. The same invariance studies show that stop consonants are not very well described in this way, and are better characterized by specifying the position of *constrictions*, i.e. local minima of the vocal tract profile. A computational architecture for the generation of speech motor plans can be schematically represented as shown in Fig. 1. It consists of three interconnected maps: (i) a proximal articulatory map, representing the space $\mathcal{X}$ of geometric configurations of the vocal tract; (ii) a distal acoustic map, accounting for the acoustic behaviors (typically vowels or vowel-like consonants) which can be expressed in the frequency domain of formants; (iii) a distal constriction map, accounting for other acoustic behaviors (typically consonants) which are better expressed as constrictions in the vocal tract.

The training phase. The available training set contained acoustic and geometric data obtained from a male french speaker, pronouncing VVV and VCV sequences. All together, the dataset covers about 100 sec of speech and for teaching the acoustic computational map we only considered the acoustic part (the iconic part of the dataset was used for learning the articulatory map). Only the first and second maps could be trained with the available experimental data, but the computational architecture is perfectly suitable for

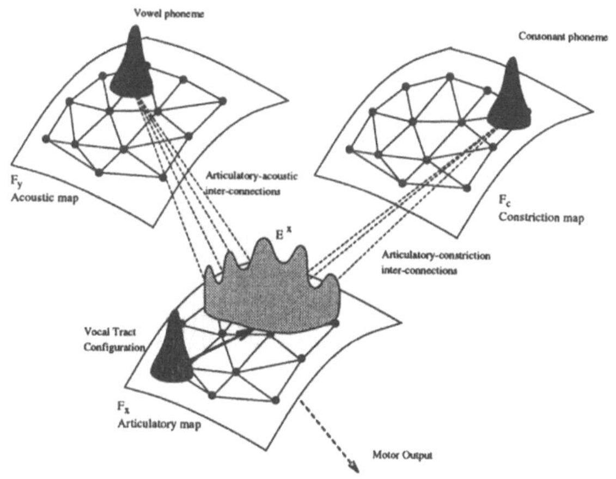

Figure 1: A computational architecture for the control of speech movements. $\mathcal{F}_x$: articulatory map; $\mathcal{F}_y$: acoustic map; $\mathcal{F}_c$: constriction map

dealing simultaneously with two or more distal maps. Therefore, the distal vector is restricted to the acoustic component: $\vec{y} = [F_1\, F_2\, F_3\, F_4\, F_5]^T$, whereas the configuration of the vocal tract was characterized by means of the following 10 parameters[1] : Lip Height (LH), Lip Protrusion (LP), Jaw Height (JH), Tongue Body (TB), Tongue Dorsum (TD), Tongue Advance (TA), Larynx Elevation (LY), Velum Height (VH), Lips Vertical (LV). Each computational map was separately trained by means of Hebbian, self-organizing techniques. In particular, the TRN algorithm [5] was used for adapting the prototype vectors (or centers of their receptive fields) of the neurons of the map (1000 for the articulatory map, and 500 for the acoustic one) and to grow and prune the lateral connections. The above is known to provide a good approximation of the Delaunay triangulation of the underlying manifold, pruned according to the constraint of topology representation.

Representation of acoustic and articulator space. The trained maps exhibit interesting structural characteristics, which can be analyzed in order to understand the topology and shape of the articulatory and acoustic manifolds. The issue of dimensionality was addressed under the hypothesis of a fixed relation between connectivity of the map and dimensionality of the manifold. In fact, it has been shown [3] that topologically continuous lattices behave like regular sphere packings [2] of the same dimension and, in particular, the mean number of intra-connections equals the *kissing number* $k(n)$ for that dimension (the number of spheres that are in contact or "kiss" a given one). In other words, from the kissing number it is possible to infer the lattice dimension and such number can be estimated by the histogram of lateral connections.

We computed the histogram of lateral connections of the trained articulatory map, which is shown in Fig. 2 (left). The average number of connections is 25.35 and the histogram peaks at 26, consistently with the kissing number of a 4-dimensional manifold which is equal to 24. The histogram for the

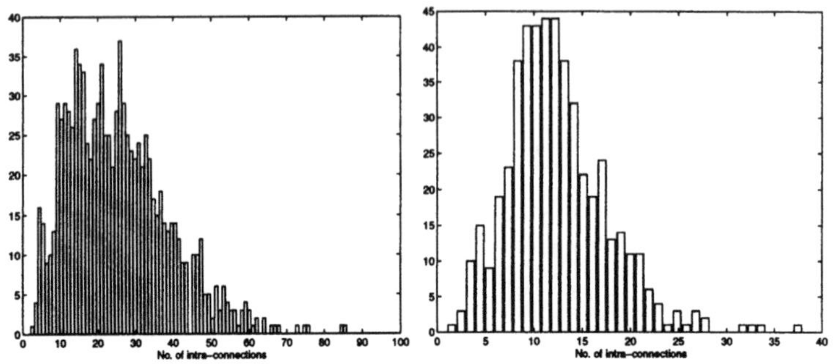

Figure 2: Distribution of intra-connections after learning in the articulatory map (left), and in the acoustic map (right).

acoustic map is shown in Fig. 2 (right). In the case of the acoustic map (see Fig. 2, right), the average number of intra-connections is 12.22 and the peak of the histogram is reached at 11-12 connections: this is consistent with a 3-dimensional manifold because the kissing number in 3D is 12. Moreover, a secondary smaller peak is present at a value of 5, which is close to the kissing number of a 2-dimensional manifold, which is 6: this is consistent with the fact that the boundary of a 3-dimensional manifold is generally 2-dimensional.
Generation of VV sequences. As a simulation study of the computational model outlined in the previous section, let us consider the problem of generating articulatory commands related to sequences of vowels. In this case the planning system is reduced to the dynamic interaction of two computational maps. As regards the acoustic map, the first topic we need to face is the representation of the vowel targets in the sequence. The acoustic variability of vowels in speech samples suggests that they can be simply described by a Normal distribution, with a well determined mean value (a point $\vec{y}^i$ in formant space) and a "small" variance. This means that each vowel phoneme V^i can be represented by means of unimodal potential field in acoustic space: $E^y_{V^i}(\vec{y})$. A possible mechanism for chaining different vowels in a sequence is to have different fields (one for each vowel target) and to modulate them by means of weighting time functions $f(t)$, appropriately shifted in time: $E^y_{V^i}(\vec{y},t) = E^y_{V^i}(\vec{y}) \cdot f(t-t_i)$. This function must be bell-shaped, with a limited time support, in order to capture the concept of *dominance*, a notion that has received some support by the experimental investigation of speech sequences, performed at different rates [4]. If different fields are modulated by delayed, but possibly overlapped, weighting functions it is then possible to establish a time-varying global field which induces smooth trajectories in the acoustic space: $E^y_{glob}(\vec{y},t) = \sum_i E^y_{V_i}(\vec{y}) f(t-t_i)$. Let E^y_j denote the value of the global distal field 'sensed' by the j-th neuron in the map. The formation of the motor plan is automatically driven by the projection of the global acoustic field onto the articulatory map via the cross-connections $E^x_i(t) = C^{xy}_{ij} E^y_j(t) / \sum_k C^{xy}_{kj} E^y_j(t)$ because it excites the map-wide dynamics described by Eq. 1. In figure 3 the above technique was applied for fitting VVV sequences of the training set. The trajectory of formants was extracted from

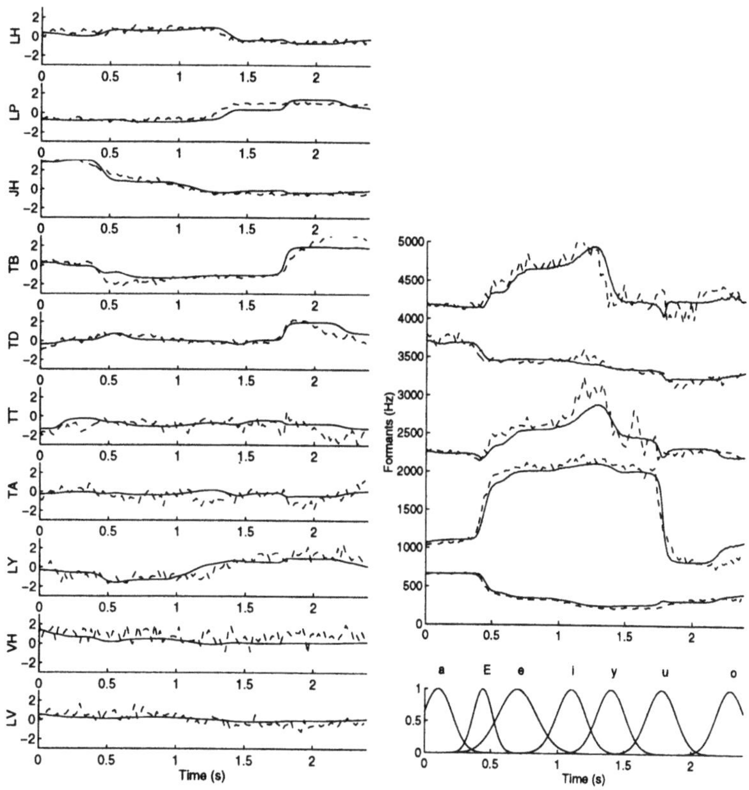

Figure 3: Articulatory commands (left) and corresponding formants (bottom) for the sequence /aɛeiyuo/. Dashed line: experimental data. Continuous line: model simulation. The target fields are modulated by 7 Gaussians $f(t)$, centered on the *transitions* observed in the time course of formants (right, bottom). Parameters of the simulation: $\tau = 50$ ms, $c_p = 10$, $c_e = 30$

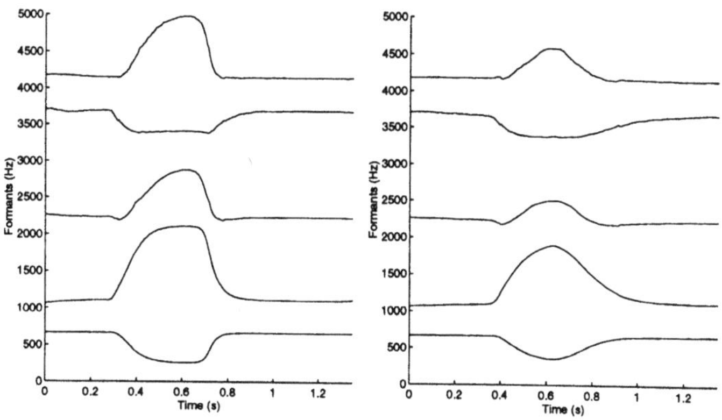

Figure 4: Simulation of /aia/ sequence displaying the phenomenon of vowel reduction. Stressed ($\tau = 0.05$ s, left) and unstressed ($\tau = 0.15$ s, right) conditions, same speaking rate

the data by means of signal processing techniques and the time course of the 10 articulators was computed by estimating (via a model-driven relaxation process) the best fit of each frame in the sequence. In the fitting, the transition time, duration, and position of each phonemic field had to be estimated. All the rest was obtained by integrating the dynamic system. The figure clearly shows that the two interacting networks (500 + 1000 neurons) are powerful enough to reproduce the experimental data.

Flexibility of the model. It should be noted that the model is able to synthesize a given sequence at different speaking rates and under different stress conditions: speaking rate is controlled by simply scaling the distances in time among consecutive target fields, whereas the level of stress can be controlled by varying the time constant τ of the map relaxation equation 1. To illustrate this aspect, the same sequence, /aia/, was simulated with different values of τ, corresponding to different stress conditions, by keeping constant the speaking rate. The results are shown in Fig. 4: in the unstressed case the full /*i*/ has become more like a /e/. The model can be extended to more complex sequences, including consonants, by taking into account that different from vowels, consonants have remarkably invariant features in the articulatory space; thus consonantal phonemes might be specified as fields on an additional map in a *space of constrictions.* In this framework, VCV sequences can arise from the interaction of the articulatory map with both the acoustic and the constriction map, as indicated in the computational architecture of fig. 1.

References

[1] P. Badin, B. Gabioud, D. Beautemps, T. Lallouache, G. Bailly, S. Maeda, J. P. Zerling, and G. Brock. Cineradiography of VCV sequences: articulatory-acoustic data for a speech production model. In *International Conference on Acoustics*, pages 349–352, Trondheim, Norway, 1995.

[2] J. H. Conway and N. Sloane. *Sphere packings, lattices and groups.* Springer-Verlag, New York, NY, 2 edition, 1993.

[3] F. Frisone, F. Firenze, P. Morasso, and L. Ricciardiello. Application of Topology Representing Networks to the estimation of the intrinsic dimensionality of data. In *International Conference on Artificial Neural Networks*, Paris, France, 1995.

[4] A. Löfqvist. Speech as audible gestures. In W. J. Hardcastle and A. Marchal, editors, *Speech Production and Speech Modelling*, NATO ASI Series, pages 289–322. Kluwer, Dordrecht, NL, 1990.

[5] T. Martinetz and K. Schulten. Topology Representing Networks. *Neural Networks*, 7(3):507–522, 1994.

[6] P. Morasso and V. Sanguineti, editors. *Self-Organization, Computational Maps and Motor Control.* Elsevier Science Publ., 1997.

A Neural Solution for a Mobile Robot Navigation into Unknown Indoor Environments Using Visual Landmarks

Salvatore Vitabile
DIE - Dipartimento di Ingegneria Elettrica, University of Palermo
Viale delle Scienze, 90128 Palermo, Italy

Francesco Bianco
DIE - Dipartimento di Ingegneria Elettrica, University of Palermo
Viale delle Scienze, 90128 Palermo, Italy

Filippo Sorbello
DIE - Dipartimento di Ingegneria Elettrica, University of Palermo
Viale delle Scienze, 90128 Palermo, Italy

Abstract

In this paper we present a neural solution for a mobile robot navigation into unknown indoor environments by using landmarks. Robot navigation task is implemented by two groups of processes based on MLP neural networks classifiers: a Low Level Vision System performs obstacle avoidance and corridor following, while an High Level Vision System extracts landmarks contents and performs goal directed navigation. A path-planner manages the two navigation systems and interacts with the robot hardware. The proposed solution is very strong and flexible and can be used to drive a mobile robot in real indoor environments. In the paper experimental results are also reported.

1 Introduction

Autonomous mobile robot navigation into indoor unknown environments using only visual inputs is topic of great interest in vision and robotics communities. Robot motion and trajectory involves different tasks ranging from high level goal oriented tasks to low level indoor corridor following and obstacle avoidance. Goal directed navigation can be a result of a path-planner actions that determines on-line the optimal path from current position to the target. Simultaneously low level tasks, mainly related to robot control and navigation, can be better accomplished by appropriate behaviours which react to measured spatial situation without long delay of reasoning. Landmarks, designed in order to be easily traceable from a CCD colour camera on the robot head, can be used to drive the robot in the navigation task into indoor environments[7]. Planning methods require global information about the environment so an efficient and fast vision system must be designed. Many application in vision-guide mobile robotics are based on strong models or geometric representations of the external robot environment [1, 2, 3]. Other works use odometer and sonar sensors to extract useful information for robot navigation [4]. In this paper we present a robot path-planner based on neural techniques to process the only robot input data: a RGB colour image. The proposed solution is able to build a qualitative, topological map of real indoor environment and to locate and construe landmarks in order to extract useful information for robot indoor navigation. A feed-forward neural networks solution is very attractive because it realizes a very good compromise between recognition rate, recognition speed and memory resources. In particular, Multilayer Perceptrons are widely used for classification problems. The capability to approximate boundary surfaces of arbitrary complexity make the MLP universal classifiers [5]. Furthermore MLP neural network has been implemented on embedded chip using standard VLSI technologies [6]. The next section introduces the proposed solution with the adopted strategies. Section 3 is about the performance of the designed system together with some preliminary experimental results on a set of real images supplied by the robot camera.

2 The proposed solution

The Robot Path-Planner is the main component of the proposed solution. It receives from the human operator the string command about the robot destination goal and consequently it chooses the properly actions for the robot goal directed navigation into real indoor environments on the basis of the vision process results. Robot vision process is based on neural networks classifiers to perform vision processes at different levels of abstraction on robot image in order to extract useful information for robot navigation. The use of simple pre-processing techniques, the appropriate chosen of the training set, the choice of opportune activation functions and a learning procedure based on Powell's conjugate gradient optimization algorithm are the main ingredients of a recipe that yields results very interesting in terms of both recognition rate and speed for the adopted MLP classifiers. The block scheme of the proposed solution is showed in figure 1.The Robot Vision System (RVS) is based on two groups of processes: a Low Level Vision System (LLVS) implements obstacle avoidance and corridor following while an High Level Vision System (HLVS) extracts landmarks contents to supply information for the goal directed navigation. The LLVS is based on a MLP neural network in order to build a depth map from a single robot colour image of the indoor environment. Furthermore the LLVS is able to trace robot trajectory inside the built depth map image following the median line of the floor free zones. The HLVS uses an algorithm based on colour filter and on Hough transform in order to segment and extract useful information for robot goal directed navigation. The useful information are contained in a rectangular green landmark with an alpha-numerical string and a directional or position symbol. Both symbols and alpha-numerical string are successively recognized by two MLP neural networks. On the basis of both LLVS and HLVS results, the Robot Path-Planner gives commands for the robot

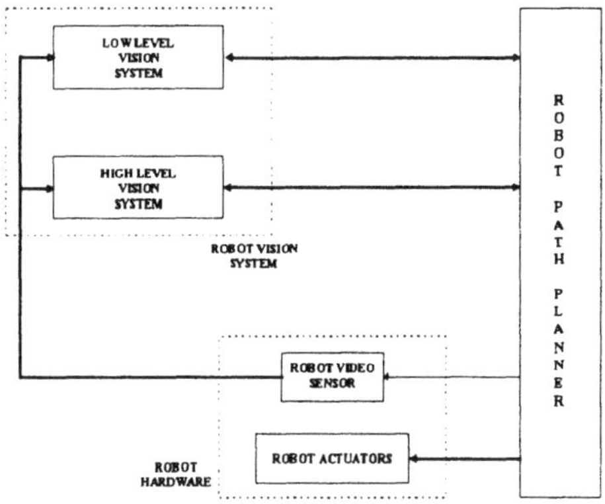

Figure 1: Block scheme of the proposed solution: the Robot Path Planner manages in a properly way. The Robot Vision System to supply commands to the robot actuators and the robot camera

goal destination..

2.1 The Low Level Vision System

The Low Level Vision System is able to classify a robot colour image of the real indoor environment in free floor zones and obstacle zones. The LLVS algorithm is developed in three sequential phases. In the first phase a MLP neural network performs the environment image classification building a binary image in which a black zone is related with a free floor zone while a white zone is related with an obstacle or wall zone. Starting from the obtained binary image, the LLVS is able to build the depth map of the start image. In the last phase the LLVS supplies trajectory inside the built depth map image. The dimension of the robot RGB image is 256*240 pixel, so we adopted a pre-processing technique to reduce the neural input data dimension. The robot image is divided into 240 sub-images of 16*16 pixels. Each 16*16 sub-image is codified with 192 floating points (64 for each RGB component) which value is the average value of a set of 2*2 pixels in the 16*16 sub-image. Thus the 192 floating point values are used as inputs of the MLP neural classifier. The related output is a binary 16*15 matrix in which low level value is joined to a free floor zone, while the high level value is joined to a no free floor zone. The obtained binary image is used to build the radial depth map that gives the distance to the nearest obstacle for each column of the image since the image columns correspond to the directions in ground plane. The depth map represents the empty space before the robot, so the LLVS can calculate the average point for each row of the depth map. The sequence of the average points is the robot's trajectory in the analyzed image. In the figure 2 are showed two examples of real robot indoor environment with the related obtained images.

2.2 The High Level Vision System

The HLVS is able to locate, segment and analyze a visual landmarks inside a robot colour image in order to obtain commands for robot destination goal [7]. We use a green rectangular zone as landmark with a black uppercase characters sequence and directional or position symbols inside it. The directional symbols can be a black directional arrow to drive the robot into indoor environment or a black square to locate a robot destination point. In the first phase the robot RGB image is processed applying a green colour filter that extracts all green zone from the image. The obtained image is subject to noise, so a noise cleaning mask is applied to reduce the noise isolated points. We use also the Inner boundary tracing algorithm to locate and erase the extended noise zone if their extension is lower than a prefixed user threshold. Finally the extraction process of the rectangular landmarks zone is based on Hough transform. Landmark's symbols extraction is based on a simple algorithm to exploit the projection of every symbol on a Cartesian system hit on the bottom left vertex of the image. The extracted symbols (both characters and directional symbols) are recognized by two MLP neural networks after a pre-processing technique to conform their dimension [7].

3 Experimental results

We tested the proposed algorithm for the perceptual aspect of a mobile robot navigation in indoor environment. We tested our solution on a sequence of still images supplied by the color camera of our Real World Interface B12 mobile robot. Robots environment is the networks of corridors of the 3rd floor of the CSAI Lab in the University of Palermo. The MLP neural networks have the topology 64-64-26 for the printed uppercase characters recognition, 64-5-3 for the directional or position symbol recognition and 192-5-2 for the indoor environment image classification. Networks are trained off-line starting with randomly chosen initial weight values. The neural networks' training set consist of 500 real robot images for indoor environment classification task, of 2,340 elements for uppercase characters recognition task and more than 100 elements for directional symbols recognition task. Landmarks detection rate, symbol recognition rate and environment images recognition rate are very high so the mobile robot can interact actively with the environment by means of the information that are present in the real environment using the same signs to transmit the information to human being.

4 Conclusion

Indoor environment luminance must be adequate and landmarks colour must be in contrast to environment background, so the landmark can be detected by robot to extract useful information for its navigation. The luminance environment is important for the indoor environment images classification even if the

MLP neural classifier has good generalization capabilities. Experimental results show that the proposed solution is very strong to luminance variation and noise so it can be used with real indoor environments. Besides our approach is very flexible and adaptable: it is very simple to increase symbols number to create a language to drive a robot into indoor environments or to train off-line the MLP neural networks for different floor background. Future research activities in this field will be aimed at increasing the speed of the whole perceptual system for a real time floors classification and landmarks detection.

Acknowledgments

Authors would like to tank G.A.M. Gioiello and G. Vassallo for their contributed to MLP software simulator development.

References

[1] E.D. Dickmanns, B.D. Mysliwets: Recursive 3D Road and relative ego-state recognition, IEEE Trans. on P. A. and M. I., 14:199-213, 1992.

[2] E.D. Dickmanns, B.D. Mysliwets, T. Christians: An Integrated spatio-Temporal approach to automaticvisual guidance of autonomous vehicles, IEEE Trans. on S. Man and Cybernetics, 20:1273-1284, 1994.

[3] R.A. Brooks: Solving the Find-Path Problem by Good Representation of Free Space, IEEE Trans. on S. Man and Cybernetics, 13:190-197, 1983.

[4] H. Beom H. Cho: A sensor based obstacle avoidance controller for a mobile robot using fuzzy logic and neural networks, Proc. IEEE International Conf. on Intelligent Robot and System, 1470-1475, 1992.

[5] M. Gioiello, A. Tarantino, F. Sorbello, G. Vassallo: Simple Techniques For An Efficient Recognition Of Handwritten Characters Using A Mlp, Journal of Intelligen Systems Vol 6, nos 3-4, 199-220, 1996.

[6] M. Gioiello, F. Sorbello, G. Vassallo: A new fully digital neural network hardware architecture for binary valued pattern recognition, Proc. of the International Conference on Signal Processing Applications and Technology (ICSPAT) Boston, 701-718, 1992.

[7] S. Vitabile, F. Bianco, F. Sorbello: A Solution for a Mobile Robot Navigation into Unstructured Environments, Proc. of 30th Inter. Symp. on Automotive Technology and Automation, Florence - Italy,133-140, 1997.

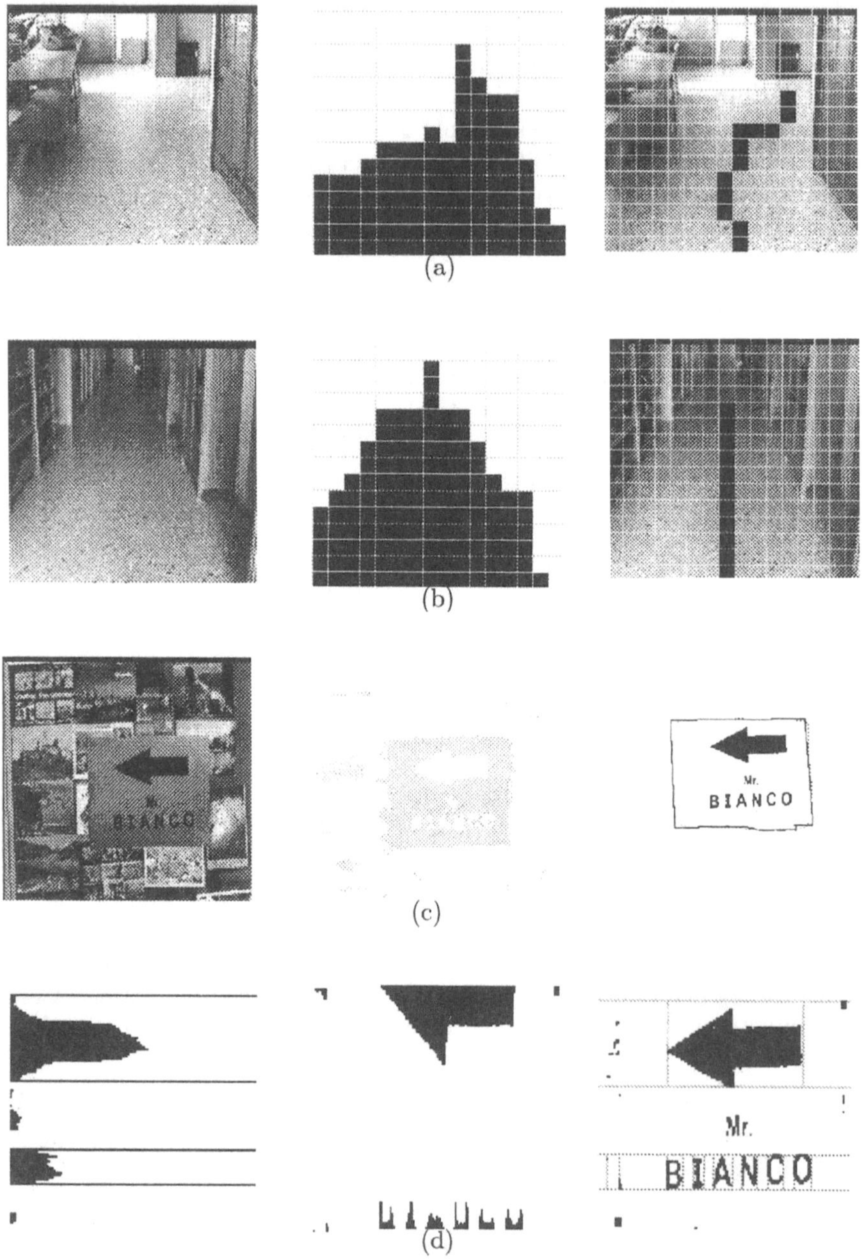

Figure 2: In a) and b) two examples of LLVS performances: on the first column the robot camera image, on the second column the image obtained after the neural classification phase, on the third column the robot trajectory in the environment; c) the different phases of the HLVS for landmark extraction from the whole environment image; d) the different phases of the HLVS landmarks contents extraction.

SECTION 6

APPLICATIONS

An Application of the Bootstrap 632+ Rule to Ecological Data

C. Furlanello [1], S. Merler[1,2], C. Chemini[2], and A. Rizzoli[2]

[1] Istituto per la Ricerca Scientifica e Tecnologica,
38050 Povo - Trento,
{furlan,merler}@irst.itc.it,

[2] Centro di Ecologia Alpina, Trento
38040 Viote del Monte Bondone - Trento,
{chemini,rizzoli}@cea.itc.it,

Abstract

We applied the novel bootstrap 632+ rule to choose tree-based classifiers trained for modeling the risk of parasite presence in a host population of ungulates. The method is designed to control overfitting: compact classification trees (CART) are selected using a nonlinear combination of the resubstitution error and the standard bootstrap error estimate. Model selection based on the 632+ rule offers a gain over cross-validation for CART models. The tree classifier selected by the new rule for this application favourably compared with standard multivariate GLIM models.
Keywords: bootstrap 632+, model selection, classification and regression trees.

1 Introduction

Producing the simplest classification model with the smallest prediction error on new observations requires to optimally balance reduction of error on the training material with control of overfitting. An improved bootstrap schema has been recently proposed for model selection in classification problems [1]. The novel bootstrap 632+ procedure combines the standard bootstrap error estimate with the resubstitution error, using a measure of overfitting as regularization coefficient. In [2], we showed on synthetic and real data that the method may be used to correctly estimate the error rate needed for evaluation of CART (classification and regression tree) models. The CART approach provides an algorithm for building a finite sequence of tree models of increasing complexity [3], where model complexity is linked to the cardinality of the partition of the pattern space obtained from the leaves of the tree classifier. The optimal complexity index may be selected by searching for the minimal error estimate on the admissible models. It is mandatory to use a prediction error estimate, as CART is prone to overfitting the training data. The idea is to apply the 632+ rule instead of the cross-validation estimate typically applied within CART pruning procedures. The basic notion of CART model selection with estimates from the bootstrap family is introduced in Section 2.

In this paper, we discuss performance of the new method on a model of infestation of roe deer (*Capreolus capreolus*) by the tick Ixodes ricinus. As the tick supports the epidemiology of Lyme disease (*Borrelia burgdoferi*) and TBE virus in Italy [4, 5], it is important to provide a model of this host-parasite association to introduce appropriate pest management technologies. In Section 3, we will show that the classification tree chosen according to the 632+ rule outperformed the basic CART algorithm in predicting presence of ticks on the roe deer datasets, avoiding overfitting or bias effects of alternative bootstrap methods. The CART developed with 632+ procedure is compared with a standard generalized linear model (GLIM). Finally, the optimal CART model for the deer population is shown to be consistent with the geographical mesoscale model developed in [6].

2 Tree-based Classifiers and the Bootstrap 632+ Rule

Tree-based classifiers are potentially prone to overfitting, thus training must focus on estimates of out-of-sample error to obtain regularized models which will generalize well on novel data. Cross-validation and bootstrap over the training set are typically applied with CART for error estimation and model selection [3]. Cross-validation provides a low bias solution, at the cost of significant variability for discontinuous error functions [1, 7]; bootstrap methods may smooth over possible discontinuity of the error function, but the standard bootstrap is upwardly biased. Suppose indeed that values $x_1, \ldots, x_n \overset{i.i.d.}{\sim} F$ are observed and let the empirical distribution function $\widehat{F}$ be defined assigning probability $1/n$ to each value $x_1, \ldots, x_n$. Let Err be the true error rate and $\overline{err}$ the resubstitution error; the idea is to estimate the parameter Err from the expected value $E_F[\overline{err}(x_1, \ldots, x_n)]$ considering expectation over *bootstrap replicates* of the original sample, i.e. samples $\mathbf{x}^* = \{x_1^*, \ldots, x_n^*\}$ of size n extracted *with replacement* from $\widehat{F}$. In practice, B bootstrap samples $\mathbf{x}^{*^b}$ are generated from the original data and for each of them a misclassification error R^{*^b} is computed over the data points *not* included in $\mathbf{x}^{*^b}$. The bootstrap estimate is finally obtained by averaging over the replicate samples:

$$R^{(boot)} = \frac{1}{B} \sum_{b=1}^{B} R^{*^b}. \tag{1}$$

The probability that a data point appears in the bootstrap sample is $1 - (1 - 1/n)^n \approx .632$ (for $n > 40$). Thus, for n sufficiently large, approximately a fraction of $.368\,n$ data are replaced by duplicate points. Given a prediction rule constructed over the bootstrap sample, the prediction error will likely be larger for points that are not extracted by the replication procedure and the bootstrap estimate in (1) results upward biased by construction. An adjustment was proposed in [8] with the *bootstrap 632* estimate

$$R^{(632)} = .368\,\overline{err} + .632\,R^{(boot)} \tag{2}$$

Variable	*Value*
Altitude	200–2350 m
Age	1–5
Weight	7–25
Roe deer density	2.7–21.8 head/100 ha

Table 1: Predictor variables

where the weighted contribution of the training set error $\overline{err}$ was introduced to correct the upward bias in $R^{(boot)}$. However, the bootstrap 632 estimator may become overly optimistic for highly overfitting rules. In this case $\overline{err}$ may become close to vanish, and a downward bias is observed.

The *bootstrap 632+* estimate of the error rate has been proposed in [1] as a less biased compromise between $\overline{err}$ and $R^{(boot)}$. Let γ be the expected error rate for independent pattern and class labels, estimated as $\widehat{\gamma} = \sum p_l(1 - q_l)$, where p_l and q_l are respectively the prior and posterior probability of class l [1, 2]. This no-information error rate may be used to define the *relative overfitting rate*:

$$\widehat{R} = \frac{R^{(boot)} - \overline{err}}{\widehat{\gamma} - \overline{err}}. \tag{3}$$

When $\overline{err} \leq R^{(boot)} \leq \widehat{\gamma}$, $\widehat{R}$ ranges from 0 (which corresponds to no overfitting) to 1. The definition in [1] includes the cases of $\widehat{R} < 0$ or $\widehat{R} > 1$, for which values $\widehat{R} = 0$ or $\widehat{R} = 1$ are respectively assigned. The bootstrap 632+ estimator may thus be defined introducing non-fixed weighting for the resubstitution and bootstrap error rates in (2):

$$R^{(632+)} = (1 - \widehat{w})\,\overline{err} + \widehat{w}\,R^{(boot)} \tag{4}$$

where

$$\widehat{w} = \frac{0.632}{1 - 0.368\,\widehat{R}}. \tag{5}$$

Note that by definition $R^{(632+)}$ ranges from $R^{(632)}$ (no overfitting) to $R^{(boot)}$ (maximum relative overfitting). The technique is indeed designed to put greater weight on $R^{(boot)}$ in problems in which the overfitting is significant.

3 Understanding the *b*632+ Rule: Application

In Europe, the chief vector of the agents of Lyme disease is the tick *Ixodes ricinus* [5]. Roe deer could be reasonably considered the most important wild large mammalian host supporting *I. ricinus* life cycle, and a natural tracer for detecting its distribution and abundance. In the first two weeks of September 1994, 534 male roe deers harvested in 56 game districts of the Province of Trento were examined for ticks. Occurrence of ticks was recorded on a total of 301 specimens. Predictor variables and value ranges are listed in Table 1.

In accordance with the methodology of [9], the results listed in Table 2 were obtained as an average of twenty iterations of the procedure which follows:

CART				GLIM
boot	*b632*	*b632+*	*CV*	
19.4	21.9	19.1	20.0	23.2

Table 2: Average test set errors

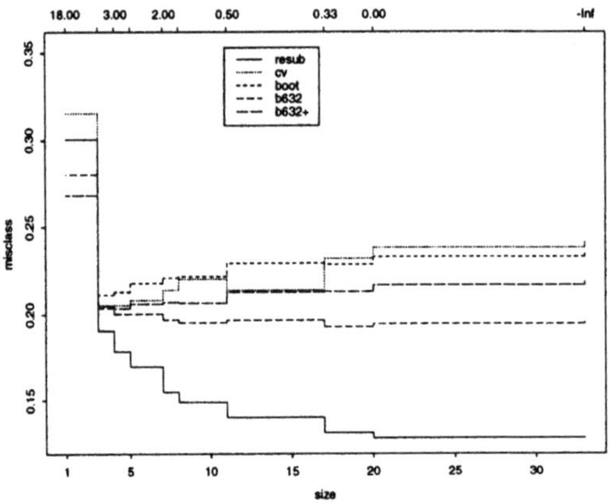

Figure 1: Roe deer data set. A comparison of different error estimates for CART, parameterized by the regularization coefficient (horizontal scale, top) or by the number of terminal nodes (horizontal scale, bottom).

i. Select a training set of 90% of the available data and set the remainder aside as a test set.

ii. Develop a maximal tree and the sequence of subtrees on the current training set. For each one of the model selection procedures, estimate errors and select optimal classification trees.

iii. Test the selected trees on the remaining data.

The table includes the average error of a standard GLIM model. A collection of results typical of step ii. is given in Figure 1, where the different estimates are compared for increasing values of the regularization parameter, i.e. for decreasing numbers of terminal nodes. For each model the bootstrap estimates were computed for $B = 50$ replicated experiments. The minimum of the $R^{(632+)}$ estimate is achieved for $\alpha = 3$ corresponding to a tree with only 3 terminal nodes. The bootstrap 632 rule is instead not able to recover from the minimum of the resubstitution error achieved in correspondence to the maximal tree solution. A behavior typical of the bias-variance tradeoff is visible in Figure 2, where the resubstitution error and the relative overfitting rate estimate $\widehat{R}$

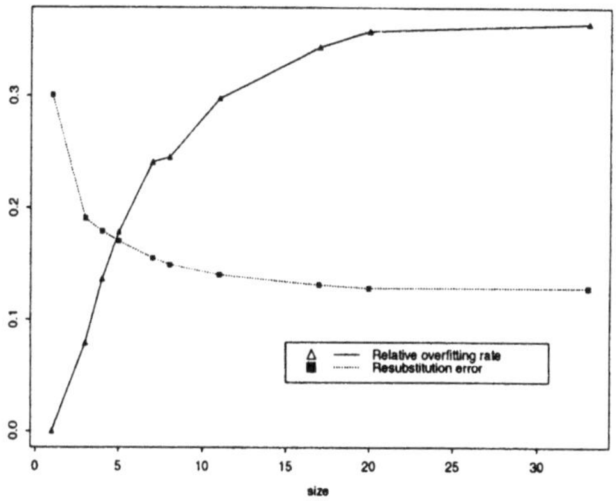

Figure 2: Roe deer data set. Relative overfitting rate and resubstitution error *vs* the number of terminal nodes.

are plotted versus the tree size. The introduction of $\widehat{R}$ allows to balance the contribution of out-of-sample and resubstitution errors in definition (4).

From a tick ecologist's perspective, the CART model highlighted altitude and host density as the two variables which appear to have the greatest effect on host infestation, with presence decreasing above 1125 m a.s.l. and with roe deer density below 8.5 head/100 ha. Results are consistent with previous work on mesoscale distribution of the parasite, for which a discriminant value of 1094 m a.s.l. had been obtained [6]. The average prediction error of CART according to the 632+ rule favorably compares with the generalized linear classification model, with a relative improvement of 18%.

4 Conclusions

The study on the roe deer data appears to confirm the previous results of [2]. The new method is able to overcome the limits of the standard and the 632 bootstrap procedures. A compact subtree has been selected, with an estimate of model prediction error not upwardly biased as with the standard bootstrap. The use of the bootstrap 632+ rule for model selection in this problem is one of the first real applications of the method. Model prediction error for the selected CART compared favorably with that estimated by the standard method.

Collaboration with G. Nicolini is gratefully acknowledged.

References

[1] B. Efron and R.J. Tibshirani. Cross-validation and the bootstrap: Estimating the error rate of a prediction rule. Technical Report 176, Standford Univ., May 1995.

[2] S. Merler and C. Furlanello. Selection of tree-based classifiers with the bootstrap 632+ rule. *Biometrical Journal*, 39(2):1–14, 1997.

[3] L. Breiman, J. Friedman, R. Olshen, and C. Stone. *Classification and Regression Trees*. Wadsworth and Brooks/Cole, Pacific Grove CA, 1984.

[4] D. Bassetti, A. Cristofolini, G. De Venuto, C. Costanzi, C. Chemini, M.G. Ciufolini, L. Nicoletti, S. Percopo, and P. Verani. Studi sulla diffusione del TBE virus in Trentino. *Riv. Med. Trentina*, 31:57–67, 1993.

[5] C. Chemini, G. Nicolini, A.P. Rizzoli, and C. Genchi. Alcuni dati preliminari sull'ecologia e il ruolo patogeno della zecca Ixodes ricinus in Trentino. *Riv. Med. Trentina*, 31:51–56, 1993.

[6] S. Merler, C. Furlanello, C. Chemini, and G. Nicolini. Classification Tree Methods for Analysis of Mesoscale Distribution of Ixodes Ricinus (Acari: Ixodidae) in Trentino, Italian Alps. *Journal of Medical Entomology*, 33(6):888–893, 1996.

[7] B.D. Ripley. *Pattern Recognition and Neural Networks*. Cambridge University Press, 1996.

[8] B. Efron. Estimating the error rate of a prediction rule: some improvements on cross-validation. *J. Amer. Statist. Assoc.*, 78:316–331, 1983.

[9] Leo Breiman. Bagging predictors. *Machine Learning*, 26(2):123–140, 1996.

ARE HYBRID FUZZY-NEURAL SYSTEMS ACTUALLY USEFUL IN PLASMA ENGINEERING?

F.C.Morabito and M.Campolo

DIEMA, University of Reggio Calabria,
Faculty of Engineering, Via E.Cuzzocrea, 48
I-89127 Reggio Calabria, Italy
Tel.:+39-965 875224 - Fax:+39-965 875247
E-Mail: morabito@csiins.csii.unirc.it
http://www.ing.unirc.it/

Hybrid techniques are investigated as potential solutions of practical control problems in plasma engineering. A novel plasma shape identification procedure based on both Neural Network (NN) and Fuzzy System (FS) approaches is proposed. The concept of *Fuzzy Curves* (FCs) is firstly introduced to reduce the size of the available pattern of measurements (inputs of the procedure). The mapping between the reduced input pattern and the corresponding set of parameters describing the plasma (outputs of the procedure) is then approximated by a FS whose bank of rules is directly extracted from the relevant FCs. A fast NN is finally trained to learn the estimation error of the fuzzy block. The final processor is capable of improving the rapidity of the identification in real time, which is an important goal for control. As a by-product, the designed Fuzzy-Neural System reduces the extrapolation problems typically encountered when using NN models.

1. INTRODUCTION

For controlling the discharge evolution of the plasma column in a tokamak nuclear fusion reactor, a fast analysis of data coming from magnetic sensors located along the mechanical structures facing the plasma is required. The aim is to determining a set of parameters describing the underlying physical model. This is commonly carried out by using an approximate model of the experiment. The basic input-output nonlinear mapping is implemented by a NN or a similar expansion in terms of different "hidden node" functions [1, 2]. Some magnetic diagnostics (flux loops and field probes) provide the pattern of raw data from which any algorithm is started.

For future reactors, the determination of the optimal number and location of the sensors is also an important issue. In this paper, the concept of Fuzzy Curve (FC) is adopted for ranking the input variables in order to select the most relevant ones for plasma identification [3]. Each record of the training data base includes either measurements from experimental discharges or from a numerical code simulating the plasma evolution, and the corresponding plasma parameters as defined by the physical model. The FCs are also used to get, by inspection, some insights about the model structure. It is indeed possible to synthesize a very approximate model of the underlying physical phenomenon by manipulating the symbolic rules which can be extracted from the previous step. The resulting FS can be used for getting an immediate idea of the time evolution of the discharge (this can be useful, for example, for an earlier prediction of an anomalous event).

In addition, by using an adaptive approach in varying the fuzzy membership function (FMF) parameters, the fuzzy model resulting from learning can be given back to experts for further analysis and interpretation.

2. THE PLASMA ENGINEERING PROBLEM

The variables of interest are approximated as functions of the magnetic measurements whose shape and type are not known in advance. The standard approach in deriving the relationships between the inputs and the outputs is to guess a sort of dependency among the variables and then to determine the coefficients of the expansion by means of a procedure of optimization. The typical criterion is to match the model against a data base of previously available example patterns. We use here a data base of 3154 cases which have been generated by using a numerical code based on the ASDEX-Upgrade tokamak configuration [2]. The database includes patterns by four possible plasma column configurations (inner and outer limiter, upper and lower X-point). Details of the problem, the configuration and the identification problem are beyond the scope of the present work and can be found elsewhere [1, 2]. The input vector of the procedure is a set of samples of the same underlying flux (or field) function. It is thus rather expected that the various inputs are correlated data. Furthermore, different measurements can have an impact on different output parameters. For the feedback control problem, it would be of interest to know which inputs are relevant for the estimation of each output. This study can start from a high number of candidate measurements among which to determine the optimal number and location. In this paper, a nonlinear procedure based on FC concept is proposed for the input relevance assessment. An additional difficulty in treating the ASDEX-Upgrade database derives from the fact that the plasma column can assume four different configurations during the evolution of the discharge. The interpolation of the global database, i.e. that including patterns of all configurations, is a difficult problem, in that the mapping shows first derivative discontinuities at the transition between configurations. The common solution to this problem is to make separate regressions for different plasma categories. This, in turn, may imply difficulties related to the different accuracies of the four regressors. Figure 2.1 shows the distribution of the horizontal minor radius, a, of the plasma column within the database. It is clearly seen that the inverse problem is strongly ill-posed and that the first two (limiter) configurations shows much of the variance of the output. While the NN regressor finds most difficult regressing the limiter databases, from a physical viewpoint it is easy to explain the wide variance of these configurations.

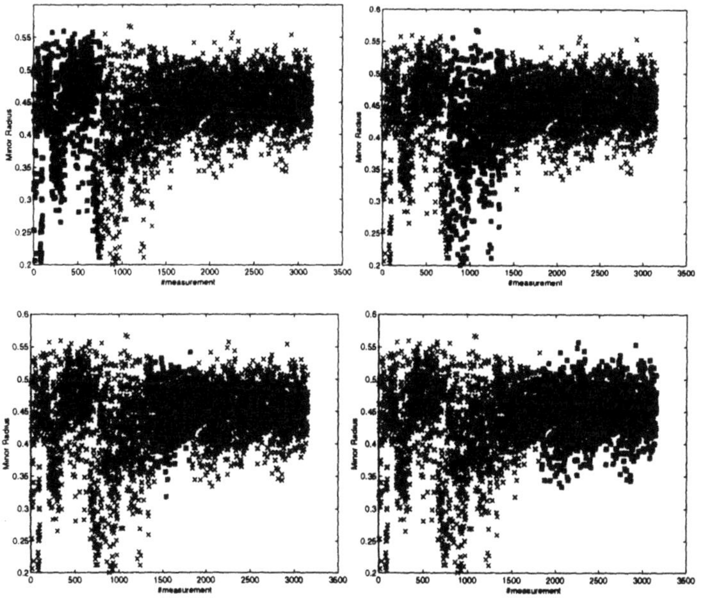

Figure 2.1. Distribution of the relevant output variable (horizontal minor radius) among the 3154 example cases. Crosses and circles highlight the patterns for the different configurations.

This imply that an expert may suggest rules for interpreting the problems, which will be represented as fuzzy rules in the FS framework. This physical information could be of help in reducing the problem ill-posedness. In this paper, the fuzzy rules will be directly determined by using the FCs. Of course, the model could take benefit from adding some expert rules.

3. THE FUZZY-NEURAL IDENTIFICATION PROCEDURE

In the following, the concept of the fuzzy curves for a Multiple-Input Single-Output (MISO) system is explained. The input of the model are the flux and field measurements from magnetic sensors, x_i (i=1,..., N), and the output, y, is the horizontal minor radius, a, of the plasma column. The goal of the procedure is to determine which inputs are the most relevant among the N possible candidates.

We assume that m training data are available, thus x_{ik} (k=1,..., m) represent the ith coordinate of the m training patterns. The *fuzzy curve* is defined as follows:

$$c_i(x_i) = \sum_k \Phi_{ik}(x_i)\, y_k / \sum_k \Phi_{ik}(x_i) \quad k=1, \ldots, m,$$

where $\Phi_{ik}(x_i) = exp\,[-((x_{ik} - x_i)/\sigma)^2]$ is a Gaussian function. We take σ as a fraction (about 20%) of the range for the corresponding input measurement within the data base. It can be noted that the fuzzy curve shape and range are influenced by the choice of the standard deviation parameter, σ. We have heuristically studied the impact on the model of the choice of σ [5].

Each database example is treated as a fuzzy rule of the type:

$$\text{IF } x_i \text{ is } \Phi_{ik}(x_i) \text{ THEN } y \text{ is } y_k$$

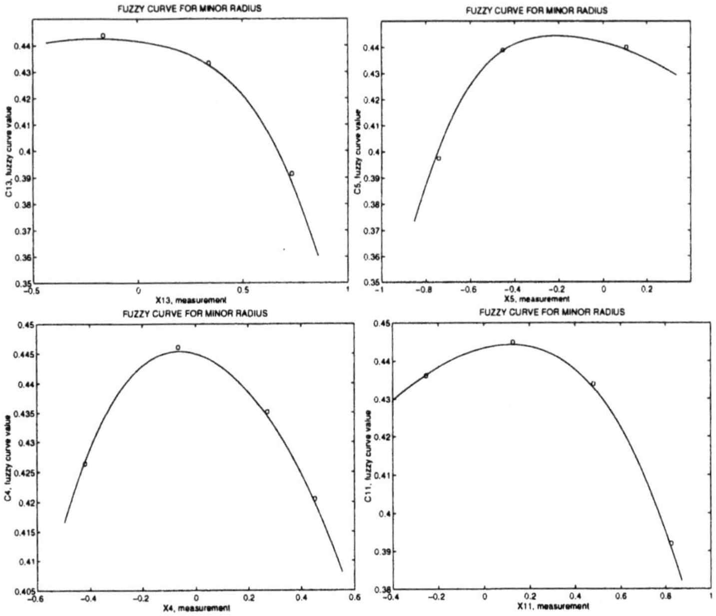

Fig.3.1 - Examples of fuzzy curves for *a* (minor radius) and extraction of fuzzy rules (circles).

for each (x_i, y) input-output pair of variables. Each membership function Φ_{ik} is drawn so that $\Phi_{ik}=1$ coincides with the point (x_{ik} , y_k).

The fuzzy curve, c_i , which describes a given input-output relationship, is inspected to determine the relative importance of the input with respect to the identification of the corresponding output parameter. The parameter of interest is scarcely influenced by the input value if the related fuzzy curve is nearly flat.
A global quality measurement of the input relevance is directly obtained by the FC as a *figure of merit* defined as the range of the fuzzy curve, ($c_{i\ max}$ - $c_{i\ min}$). This range is typically a fraction of the range spanned by the corresponding output variable, y, on the whole data set of examples. Figure 3.1 shows some examples of FCs for the plasma minor radius, *a* . Figure 3.2 reports a plot of the figure of merit determined starting from the fuzzy curves vs. the corresponding input measurements for *a*. It is clear that various inputs weight differently for different configurations.

The FS here used is based on global figure of merit curve. The idea is to gain some knowledge which could be of help in reducing the ill-posedness of the global problem by putting constraints on the mapping.

The importance of a sensor is judged not only on the basis of the figure of merit but also on the shape of the curve. The presence of peaks and valleys is indeed associated to possible fuzzy rules which will be used in the fuzzy inference procedure to build a first guess identification model.

Once the best inputs have been determined, the procedure foresees the design of a simplified identification model starting from the corresponding FCs. This is carried out by estimating the number of rules which cover the whole range of each FC, which is related to both the maximum and minimum and the shape of the FC. We decide to cover the FC input and output range by using Membership Functions (MFs) of the Gaussian type. These functions are centered on regularly spaced point

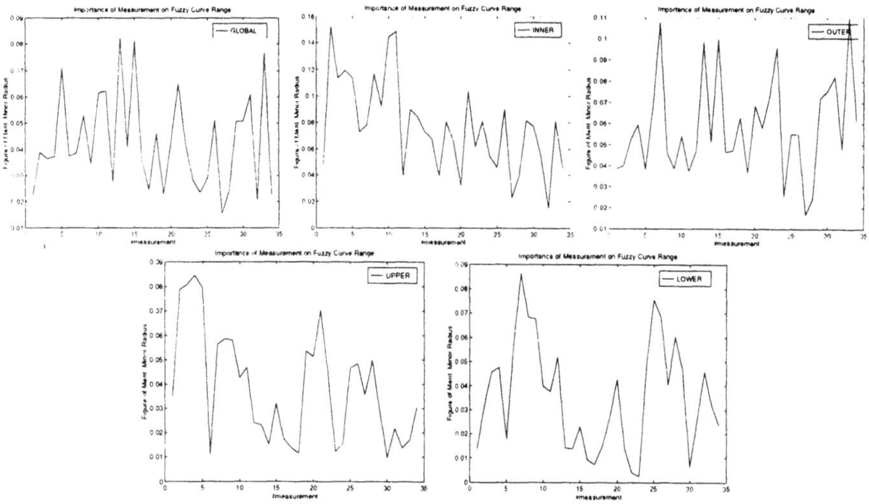

Fig.3.2 - Fuzzy figure of merit for *a*, for global regression and for the different plasma configurations.

on the corresponding variable axis, including the minimum and maximum values. The standard deviations of the different Gaussian functions are heuristically determined based on the mean derivative of the FC computed over the range of interest. Accordingly, a large standard deviation is associated to a flat region of the FC.

By analysing each FC, we are able to derive simple Fuzzy Rules qualitatively describing the input-output relationship. The rules extracted from different input measurements are combined to give a Fuzzy Associative Matrix. Figure 3.1 reports an example of the procedure. In the case of Fig.3.1, we heuristically decide of selecting either 3 or 4 fuzzy rules. As an example, the following rule holds

IF the input measurement *X11* is *SMALL AND X4* is *MEDIUM*
THEN the plasma parameter *a is VERY LARGE.*

As an example, Table 3.1 represents a two-input fuzzy rule matrix. Actually, we build our FS by using the three best ranked inputs and a subset of the possible rules. Each input variable is fuzzified by considering their membership in five Gaussian domains covering the whole range of the variable, with σ computed as mentioned above.

X_{11} \ X_4	VS	S	M	L	VL
VL	VS				VS
L		S		S	
M			L		
S			VL		
VS		M		L	

Tab. 3.1. Example of Fuzzy Associative Matrix for a two-input problem

These domains are VS (Very Small), S (Small), M (Medium), L (Large), VL (Very Large).On the basis of our experience, it seems unnecessary to take into account all of the possible preconditions obtained by assuming AND connectives of the input variables. This would give rise to already 25 preconditions in the case of two variables. Also for the output variable we use 5 Gaussian domains according to the above mentioned fuzzy values. The use of a reduced set of rules is surely useful to simplify the inference which in turn means a more rapid estimation. No fine tuning of the parameters has been carried out, because the NN part of the processor will yield the necessary fine correction to the model. Of course, the introduction of an adaptive correction of the FS parameters could be useful, but the expected improvement would not be so relevant, because we are using just three inputs, what leaves the problem yet ill-conditioned. In principle, the use of NN can instead take advantage of the simultaneous processing of the 34-dimensional input pattern. It is to be stressed that the NN is here trained to learn the difference between the true output value and its FS approximation.

	Models		
Parameters	NN	FS	NN+FS
ahor	18.7	29.3	16.2

Table 4.1 - Comparison of the performance of different network models trained to solve the proposed plasma identification problem. Each number represents the physical RMS error and is expressed in mm.

4. RESULTS AND CONCLUSIONS

The accuracy of the three-input approximated FS, of a *34-14-1* NN and of the proposed hybrid Fuzzy-Neural model which uses respectively 3 inputs for the fuzzy and just 5 inputs for the neural part are reported in Table 4.1. The number of nonlinear nodes of the hidden layer is heuristically determined but it is greatly reduced with respect to the basic NN models [2, 4]. The combined model strongly reduces the complexity of the optimization problem as well as the throughput time, without significantly degrading its performance in terms of accuracy. The final model yields a reduction of the number of sensors to be placed in the vacuum chamber of the reactor, allowing the determination of suitable locations for the sensors. From a control viewpoint, the recovery is very fast, and it is yet possible to improve the fuzzy part of the model by introducing subjective knowledge in terms of rules collected from experts. Moreover, after synthesizing the fuzzy part of the processor, it is possible to express it as a linear combination of fuzzy basis functions [5].

REFERENCES

[1] E.Coccorese, R.Martone, and F.C.Morabito, Identification of Non-Circular Plasma Equilibria Using a Neural Network Approach, Nuclear Fusion, 1994;34:10:1349.

[2] F.C.Morabito, Equilibrium parameters recovery for experimental data in Asdex-Upgrade elongated plasmas, Proceedings of the 1995 IEEE ICNN, Int. Conf. on Neural Networks, Perth, West. Australia, New York, NY, USA, IEEE Press, Nov 1995;2937.

[3] Y.Lin, and G.A.Cunningham III, A New Approach to Fuzzy-Neural System Modeling, IEEE Trans. on Fuzzy Systems, May 1995;3:2:190.

[4] F.C.Morabito et al, Identification of Plasma Equilibria in ITER from Magnetic Measurements via Functional Parameterization and Neural Networks, Fusion Technology, Nov 1996; 30:2:219.

[5] F.C.Morabito and M.Versaci, The use of fuzzy curves for the reconstruction of the plasma shape and the selection of the magnetic sensors, presented at the Symposium on Fusion Technologies, SOFT'96, Sept 1996, Lisboa Portugal.

MAIA NEURAL NETWORK: AN APPLICATION TO THE RAILWAY ANTI-SKATING SYSTEM[1]

G. Pappalardo, M.N. Postorino, D. Rosaci, G.M.L. Sarnè

Università di Reggio Calabria - Reggio Calabria, Italia
tel. 39 965 875204 - fax 39 965 875220 - E-mail: sarne@ns.ing.unirc.it

1.Introduction

The Neural Network (NN) model proposed in this paper has got a very strong biological analogy; in fact, the basic mechanisms of the signal transmission, particularly the frequency, among biological neurones are considered to model this kind of NN. The information on the NN synapses are transformed in a sinusoidal time-varying signal while in the traditional NN they are constant; furthermore, as in the biological case each neurone can have a proper working frequency. The complete theory of the *Modulated Asynchronous Information Arrangement* NN will not be presented here [14], but only the basic concepts as well as the techniques used to resolve both linear and non linear NN though the MAIA algorithms in supervised learning modality are presented.
The MAIA NN can be largely used and it has been tested to resolve different kinds of problems [6], [9], [10], [11]. In this paper it has been applied to the railway field, particularly in the refining of the performances of a railway anti-skating system, by comparing the results obtained with those of a supervised back-propagation NN.

2. The mono-neural linear MAIA NN

The following general problem can be defined: "*given two sets I and Y of atomic elements (respectively of cardinality equal to N and M), the unknown relationship F between the elements of I and the elements of Y has to be reached*". The aim of the MAIA NN is to search of the unknown relationship *F* [9], [10].
In order to obtain the general MAIA NN, it is convenient to define the mono-neurone NN, in order to characterize the basic elements of a NN: neurone and synapsis. Then, the following linear stationary system (LSS) described by the following equations and represented in fig.1 has been considered:

$$\dot{x} = Ax + Bi; \quad y = Cx + Di \tag{1}$$

where $\mathbf{i} \in R^N$ is the vector of inputs, $\mathbf{y} \in R^M$ is the vector of outputs, and $\mathbf{x} \in R^S$ is the vector of the system states. All these vectors can be considered as functions of the time t; **A, B,**

---

[1] M.N. Postorino dealt with the transport aspects , while G. Pappalardo, D. Rosaci, G.M.L. Sarnè dealt with the neural network aspects.

C and **D** are respectively the dynamic, the input, the output and the improper matrices (if **D**=0 the system is called proper) [2], [16].

Fig. 1- Schema of a LSS

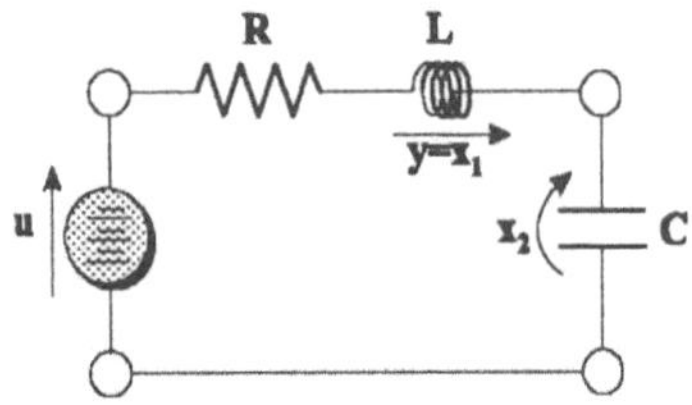

Fig. 2 - The electrical circuit represented by the system (1)

If the neurone is identified with a tension generator and the synapses with an elementary electrical circuit (fig.2), equations (1) can well describe this LSS in which u=u(t) is the tension generator, y=y(t) is the current in the circuit and $\mathbf{x}=[x_1(t), x_2(t)]^T$ is the vector of the state variables, identified in the tension at the capacitor and the current y. The Kirchoff equations [13] appied to this system provides the following relationships:

$$\begin{bmatrix} \dot{x}_1 \\ \dot{x}_2 \end{bmatrix} = \begin{bmatrix} -R/L & -1/L \\ 1/C & 0 \end{bmatrix} \begin{bmatrix} x_1 \\ x_2 \end{bmatrix} + \begin{bmatrix} 1/L \\ 0 \end{bmatrix} u \; ; \quad y = \begin{bmatrix} 1 & 0 \end{bmatrix} \begin{bmatrix} x_1 \\ x_2 \end{bmatrix} \tag{2}$$

The formal neurone can then be defined as an object to which a real function T of real variables is associated. T, called *transfer function*, converts an input i(t) time-variable in an output u(t)=T(i(t)) still time-variable [8][14]. The hypothesis of a transfer function not explicitly time-dependent (*without memory*) corresponds to an ideal tension generator; in the following a transfer function T without memory will be considered. In order to identify the elementary NN of fig.3 with the electrical circuit of fig.2, the transfer function has to be the identity function: u(t)=T(i(t))=i(t), and the synapses *m* coming out from the neurone has got as weight Z the electrical circuit of fig.2. The neurone-synapses system of fig.3 defines a very simple mono-neurone linear NN described by equations (2).

The behaviour of the mono-neurone NN depends on the nature of the input i(t). Generally, each LSS whose dynamic matrix has got eigenvalues with real part negative (as the system of fig.1), if subjected to an input time-limited and periodic with period T, will have a steady state output still time-limited and periodic with period T [2] [16]. If the input is a sinusoidal function of amplitude equal to i_n, initial frequency equal to ω_0 and initial characteristic impedance angle equal to α_n:

$$i_n(t)=i_n \mathrm{sen}(\omega_0 t+\alpha_n) \tag{3}$$

the steady state solution of equations (2) is:

$$y_m(t)=y_m \mathrm{sen}(\omega_0 t+\alpha_n+\phi_m) \tag{4}$$

where:

$$y_m = Z_m i_n \; ; \quad Z_r = 1\bigg/\sqrt{R^2+\left(\omega_0 L-\frac{1}{\omega_0 C}\right)^2} \; ; \quad \phi_m = -\mathrm{tg}^{-1}\frac{\omega_0 L-\dfrac{1}{\omega_0 C}}{R} \tag{5}$$

y_m being the amplitude of the sinusoidal output, Z_m the circuit impedance and ϕ_m the characteristic impedance angle produced by the circuit.

This kind of system can be used to perform a simple learning. The concept of learning of a mono-neurone linear NN is equal to the concept of one-variable linear regression and then is a very simple but also less interesting system. Nevertheless, it is the base of more powerful and more complex systems, as it will be shown in the following.

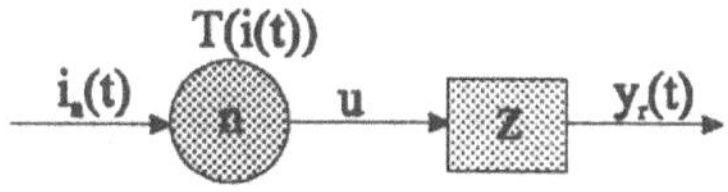

Fig. 3 - Mono-neurone neural network.

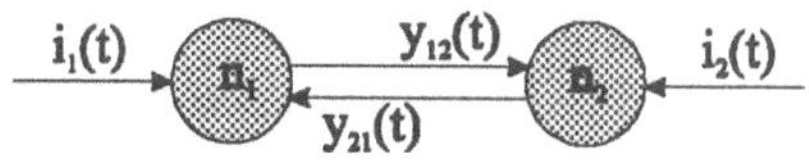

Fig.4.-Linear NN. Representation through an oriented graph.

3 Supervised MAIA learning for linear and non linear NN

The generalization of a mono-neurone NN is represented by a linear NN obtained by considering more mono-neurone linear systems. A simple linear NN is shown in fig.4; it consists of an oriented completely connected and recurrent graph. As fig.4 shows, the input to neurones is equal to the sum of the external inputs i(t) and the information coming from the synapses ending in it, that is y(t) [1].

The Kirchoff rule applied to the system of fig.4 provides a system of equation of the kind (1). Generally, the resolution of this kind of NN, formed by n neurones and with inputs of a sinusoidal nature, i.e.:

$$\mathrm{i}(t) = \left[i_1 sin(\omega_0 t + \alpha_1), i_2 sin(\omega_0 t + \alpha_2), \ \ldots\ldots, \ \mathrm{i}_n sin(\omega_0 t + \alpha_n)\right]^T,$$

i_n being the generic value of the data belonging to the set I, can be obtained by resolving a system as (1). This solution can be obtained though a matrix $\mathbf{W}(\omega_0)$, called *matrix of the harmonic response*, that under some hypotheses [2] [12] [13] exists and depends only on ω_0: $\mathbf{W}(\omega_0) = \mathbf{C}(j\omega_0\mathbf{I} - \mathbf{A})^{-1}\mathbf{B} + \mathbf{D}$ (the characteristics RLC being fixed); the following relationship, also called *symbolic equation of the system*, can then be written

$$\overline{\mathbf{Y}} = \mathbf{W}(\omega_0)\overline{\mathbf{I}} \tag{6}$$

where the vectors of estimated data $\overline{\mathbf{Y}}$ and $\overline{\mathbf{I}}$ are linked to the sinusoidal transformation y(t) and i(t) by the following relationships:

$$y_i(t) = \mathrm{Im}\left(\overline{y_i}e^{j\omega_0 t}\right), \quad i_i(t) = \mathrm{Im}\left(\overline{i_i}e^{j\alpha_0}\right) \tag{7}$$

Through $\mathbf{W}(\omega_0)$ and on the base of a training set (I,Y), a NN of this kind can learn linear relationships Y=F(I). In the case of a supervised NN [14], given a set of initial values and following an *a priori* fixed rule (*learning rule*) [7], the learning strategy consists in the modification of the values of the matrix $\mathbf{W}(\omega_0)$ till the convergence is achieved.

The modification of $\mathbf{W}(\omega_0)$ in the learning stage is obtained through the definition of a *state* S(t) of the neurone; it needs in order to obtain an updating of the unknown elements of $\mathbf{W}(\omega_0)$ to be estimated and it is defined as:

$$S = \frac{1}{1 + e^{\frac{-(inp+\Theta)}{\Psi}}} \tag{8}$$

where *inp* is the sum of the inputs ending to the neurone at the iteration k, Θ and Ψ are suitable parameters, introduced in order to give an initial different state to each neurone.

At the first step, the system characteristics RLC of the synapses are suitably initialized and the first input pair (i, y) is processed by choosing an initial values ω_0^1 and then evaluating $\mathbf{W}(\omega_0^1)$ through the (1). The system evolves through eq. (1) and at the presentation of the pattern p, on a synapsis m, at a time t_m^P the estimated value y_M^r is obtained, and it is compared with the expected value (y^p_m), belonging to the training set. The difference between the two values gives the *m*-synapsis error relative to the pattern *p*:

$$\varepsilon^p_m = y^p_m - \overline{y^P_M} \qquad (9)$$

that is used to modify the elements of $W^m(\omega\ _0^P)$ of the synapsis m={i, j}. Two methods can be chosen in order to obtain this modification in function of the states of the initial neurone *n* and the final neurone *k* of the synapses *m*: the *Hebb* [5] rule or the *Grossberg* [8] rule. Usually the first one is used with a learning rate Π belonging to the range [0, 0.1] so that:

$$\Delta w_n^m(\omega\ _0^P) = \Pi\ S_n S_k \qquad (10)$$

The updating of the elements of **W** for each synapsis can be obtained at a different time t_m^P, so this learning modality is called *asynchronous*, for this reason this class of neural networks is called *Modulated Asynchronous Information Arrangement*.

The procedure above described can be used only to resolve linear problem; a non linear working modality has then been introduced. In this case, the NN structure is similar to the linear one, but a non linear behaviour is introduced through the use of a suitable transfer function:

$$T(i) = tgh(ai+b) \qquad (11)$$

where a and b have to be calibrated together with the synapsis characteristics.

The MAIA NN so modified can be resolved only in a heuristic way. In fact, in this case the learning strategy is realized through the updating of the parameters a and b of the hyperbolic tangent (11) and the synapsis characteristics RLC. Therefore ΔR_m^P, ΔL_m^P, ΔC_m^P, Δa_m^P and Δb_m^P are computed as in (10) through the Hebb rule with a fixed the learning rate for R, L,C, a and b.

The updating of the synapses frequency is obtained through the search of the maximum values of the elements y, $dy_m(t)/dt$ that is where the elements are equal to zero. The interval between the first two maximum points is the semi-period of the new frequency on the examined synapsis.

The computing complexity of the MAIA algorithm, in the worst case for the non-linear case, and in the mean case, is respectively given by:

$$\frac{MP}{2\varepsilon}\left(\frac{1+e^{-\Theta/\Psi}}{tgh(b)}\right)^2 \qquad (12) \qquad\qquad \frac{MP}{\varepsilon}\left(1+e^{-\Theta/\Psi}\right)^2 \qquad (13)$$

where M and P are the number of synapses and learning patterns; ε is the percentage error between the expected value and that one computed by the NN; Θ and Ψ are parameters of the sigmoid function; b the parameter of the hyperbolic tangent transformation function. Therefore, the algorithm has got a linear complexity as regard the synapses and patterns, and it is inversely related to the desired error. Then, it belongs to the pseudo-polynomial in 1/ε set of algorithms.

4.Tests and results

The MAIA strategy above described has been applied to the railway system following a collaboration project with the Italian Railway Society (FS, Experimental unit of Florence), and the Parizzi Elettromeccanica company (FIAT group), which has made available the results of a set of tests performed on a commercial product [3]. The aim of the experiment was addressed to verify the opportunity to refine the evaluation of the reference speed of a train computed by the anti-skating system as regard the true one, the reference speed is very important for assuring an efficient functioning of a railway anti-skating system and furthermore for improving the overall safety level, decreasing the tear-and-wear of materials and improving the travel comfort [4], [15].

A railway anti-skating system [11] acts only in the event of an adherence loss of wagon axles, by constantly adapting the amount of braking to the current adherence. This technique aims at allowing the skating wheel to regain the most convenient zone of the adherence-skating curve. Generally, a railway anti-skating system is based on the detection of the speed of several vehicle axles; from the speed values detected a so-called *reference* speed is determined, which is assumed to be that of the entire train and in practice only slightly differs from the actual value. The reference speed is then used in order to control the activation of the anti-skating devices on each axle. This process is not particularly critical unless all wheels are simultaneously skating, in which case it is impossible to determine the train reference speed within an acceptable error limit. Various techniques exist to obviate this problem.

This work proposes an approach based on the use of NNs and therefore the patterns provided by the Italian Railway Society have been used. Data refer to the speeds of all axles sampled at 0.036 second intervals, the real train speed and the reference speed evaluated by the anti-skating system and the opening and closing time instants of each of the valves of the braking system.

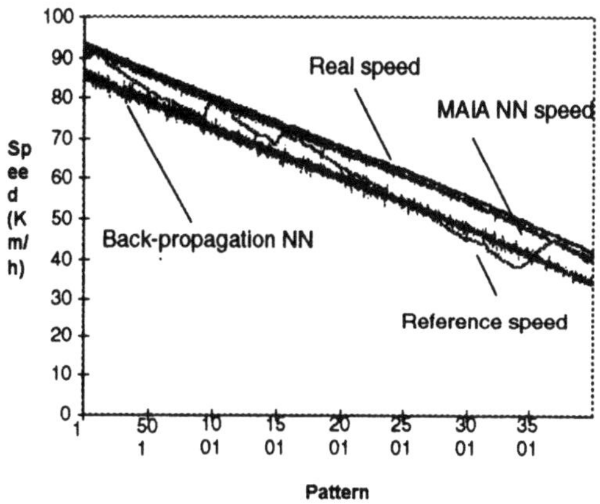

Fig. 5 - Results of the performed experiments.

One of the main problems encountered in this phase has been the lack of knowledge concerning the test conditions, in particular the slope of the railway line employed for the tests, which clearly affects both acceleration and deceleration

For the experiment proposed (i.e., the evaluation of the real speed) both NNs working with the MAIA paradigm and with the more known back-propagation (BP) algorithm have been tested

The MAIA NN topology used in this experiment is the same as the BP, the number of neurones in the input layer are equal to the speeds measured by the phonic speed detection wheels at t and $t+\Delta t$, the hidden layer are 50 neurones and the output layer is only one neurone for the reference speed. The results of the performed experiment are depicted in fig.5, where the reference speed computed by the algorithm of the anti-skating system and both by the MAIA NN and the BP NN are showed. As it can be seen, a combined use of both the algorithm of the anti-skating system and the MAIA NN represent the better solution; in fact, while the first one can faithfully reproduce the real speed when at least one wheel is in adherence, the MAIA NN is more efficient in the critical condition, that is in the event of simultaneous skating of all the wheels.

Numerically, the greatest measured error for the MAIA NN and the BP NN are respectively <2%, and <5.5%; the mean error is not relevant for this type of experiment.
The comparison between the MAIA NN and the more known BP NN shows that the MAIA NN is better as regard the capability to work with incomplete and wrong data. In fact, as already said, because of the exact test conditions are not known the data used are hardly incomplete and affected by error, but the MAIA NN is able to characterize the relationship existing among the data better than a BP NN.
At this time further development are in progress with the unsupervised MAIA NN. In this case, as well known, [8], only the input values are used in the learning stage, and the error term in this case is evaluated for each neurone as the Kirchoff sum of all the input ending in the neurone. If this sum is near to zero (i.e. less than a fixed small value) the learning ends.

Acknowledgements: The authors gratefully acknowledge the kind co-operation of Mr. Scarfone, Mr. Cocci, Mr Colombi and Mr. Solera and their organizations, the Italian Railway Society (FS) and the Eletromeccanica Parizzi company.

References

1.Arbib M.A. The metaphorical brain: an introduction to cybernetic as artificial intelligence and brain theory. Wiley-Interscience, New York, 1972.
2.Ballestrino A, Celentano G. Teoria dei sistemi, vol III. Liguori Ed., Napoli, 1982
3.Elettromeccanica Parizzi. WUPAR ETR460. Internal report, Milano, 1996.
4.Hay, W. W. Railroad engineering. John Wiley & Sons, London, 1982.
5.Hebb D.O. The organization of behaviour, New York, 1949.
6.Laganà D., Pappalardo G, Postorino M.N., Rosaci D. Sarnè M.G.L. A Hopfield like neural network in the simulation of traffic flow in a transportation network, In Proceedings of ICANN '95, Section Transportation, EC2&Cie, 1995
7.Mc Culloch W., Pitts W. A logical calculus of the ideas immanent in nervous activity, Neurocomputing :foundation of research, MIT Press 1988.
8.Nilsson N.J. Learning machines: foundation of trainable pattern classifying system. Mc Graw-Hill, London, 1965
9.Pappalardo G, Postorino MN, Rosaci D, Sarnè GML. Simulation of traffic flows in transportation nets with unsupervisioned MAIA NN, In Proceedings. of WIRN 96, 1996.
10.Pappalardo G, Postorino MN, Rosaci D, Sarnè GML. Unsupervisioned neural network in the compression and decompression of images, In Proceedings of WIRN 96, 1996.
11.Pappalardo G, Postorino MN, Rosaci D, Sarnè GML. (1997) Neural control of railway anti-skating system. Workshop on industrial application, Vietri
12.Pappalardo G, Rosaci D, Sarnè GML. Algoritmi e reti neurali MAIA. Internal report, Reggio Calabria, 1997
13.Ruberti A., Isidori A. Teoria dei sistemi. Boringhieri, Torino, 1979.
14.Rumelhart, D. E. and McClealland, J. L. and the PDP Research Group. Parallel distributed processing, vol. 1. Cambridge, MA: The MIT Press, 1986.
15.Vicuna, G. Organizzazione e tecnica terroviaria. Roma, CIFI, 1986
16.Zadeh L.A., Desoer C.A. Linear system theory. Mc Graw-Hill, New York, 1953.

On the Cognitive Behaviour of a Multi-Layer Perceptron in Forecasting Meteorological Visibility

Antonello Pasini, Vinicio Pelino and Sergio Potestà
Servizio Meteorologico dell'Aeronautica, 2° CMR, Aeroporto "De Bernardi"
Via di Pratica di Mare, I-00040 Pratica di Mare (Roma), Italy

Abstract

An investigation on the cognitive behaviour of a neural-network model worked out for fog forecasting in meteorology is presented. This analysis is performed in terms of the evolutionary dynamics of synaptic weights and forecast performances in learning and generalisation processes. We find that the visibility forecasting performed by the network is not a simple pattern recognition activity, but consists of a real feature extraction from the initial patterns, as in the XOR and parity determination problems. The results obtained allow to re-discover the chaotic behaviour of the atmospheric system in a new manner and show that neural-network models represent a successful forecasting method, alternative (in certain space-time ranges) to thermal-fluid-dynamical models.

1 Introduction

In recent years, neural networks, and in particular Multi-Layer Perceptrons (MLPs), have proved to be suitable for successfully tackling difficult tasks in a large variety of different domains [1]. In particular, our research group has shown [2,3] that models based on MLPs are able to forecast the values of a local meteorological variable like visibility with a great degree of accuracy.

Referring to the classification by Serra and Zanarini [4], we can distinguish two kinds of cognitive behaviours (related to the problems to solve) that a neural network can exhibit: pattern recognition and feature extraction. In the pattern recognition activity the output of the network is induced on the basis of the overlapping or similarity of input patterns, so that similar input patterns are related to similar outputs (in the coarse-grained classification case, to the same "prototype" output). This cognitive behaviour is typical in solving problems like the recognition of printed letters. Instead, in other cases, like the parity determination of a string of bits, where the most similar input patterns (those differing for a unique bit) have opposite parity, the network must classify these input patterns on the basis of some of their features. In order to produce the correct output, the network must realise some kind of internal representation that allows to discern distinct features in similar patterns. It has been proved that MLPs can solve even these more difficult problems and show a cognitive behaviour of feature extraction.

Thus, conversely, by adopting a MLP in order to solve a problem and analysing its cognitive behaviour one can obtain information on the nature of the problem itself.

The aim of this note is to present the physical results coming from an investigation intended to analyse the cognitive behaviour of a MLP model in forecasting meteorological visibility. In the next section, typical cases of pattern recognition and feature extraction are analysed in terms of the evolutionary dynamics of synaptic weights in the learning process and of generalisation performances. In section 3 the same analysis is performed for our model in cases of fog forecasting. Section 4 is devoted to the discussion of the physical relevance of the cognitive behaviour exhibited by our MLP model for better understanding and simulating the dynamical behaviour of the atmosphere. Finally, brief conclusions are drawn.

2 Pattern recognition vs. feature extraction in didactical cases

In this section we present the results obtained through the application of our original model, a MLP with one hidden layer and back-propagation least-squares training [2], to some didactical cases, and we search to identify some characteristic behaviours in learning and generalisation processes.

We consider three kinds of problems: a top-down recognition, the XOR problem and the parity determination problem for strings composed by 4 bits. The features of the first case-study are presented in table 1. The other two cases are well-known problems.

Table 1: top-down recognition

top	down		Input-hidden-output topology:
1 1 1	0 0 0		9-9-1
0 0 0	0 0 0	+ patterns with noise	
0 0 0	1 1 1		
target 1	target 0		

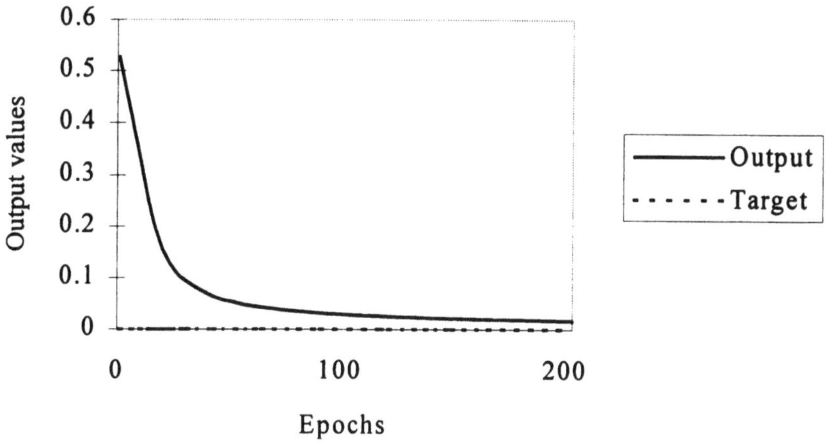

Fig.1. Top-down recognition: generalisation performances

Obviously, the top-down recognition is a problem in which the output of the network is determined by the falling down of similar input patterns into the same attraction basin leading to a unique prototype target. This is a clear example of a pattern recognition problem. It is interesting, therefore, to observe the evolution of the values of synaptic weights and outputs as the training cycles (epochs) increase. As a matter of fact, the evolutionary dynamics of synaptic weights and output values shows a monotonic course. In fig.1 the generalisation performances of our MLP in recognising a down pattern is shown.

In other case-studies of pattern recognition problems, here not presented for lack of space, we have found out the same behaviour in these evolutionary dynamics, so that we are induced to think of this behaviour as typical of this kind of problems.

The situation is very different for problems where a more difficult cognitive task is assigned to a neural network and the space of attraction basins is fragmented, as in the parity determination problem. Here the evolutionary course of synaptic and output values is no more monotonic, but shows several changes in the sign of its derivatives. Fig.2 shows weight variations in a case of parity determination, while in fig.3 the performances of our MLP in the XOR problem (1-1 inputs) are presented. In particular, this last figure shows as the network passes through several internal representations which lead to several distinct "hypotheses" for the output values (from the initial value 0.2 to the value 0.52, to the 0.4 *plateau* and, finally, to the asymptotic correct value 0).

While in pattern recognition problems the network produces outputs as induced by the similarity of input patterns, in feature extraction problems its internal representations allow to discern distinct features in similar patterns and permit that even similar patterns fall down into distinct attrction basins leading to different outputs.

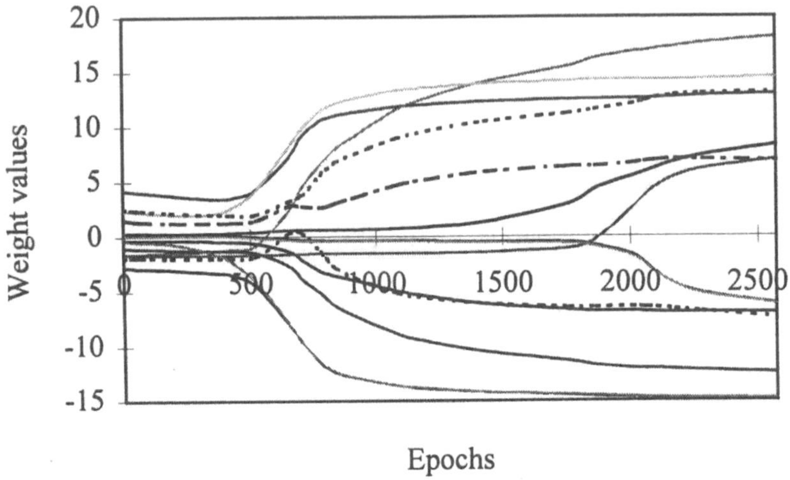

Fig.2. Parity determination problem: weight variations

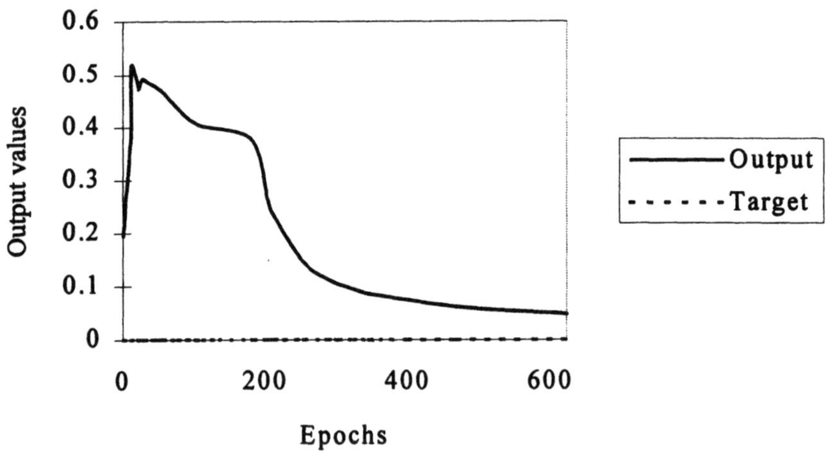

Fig.3. XOR problem: generalisation performances

This analysis leads to recognise distinct typical cognitive behaviours which represent the fingerprint of the class of problems under study.

3 MLP cognitive behaviour in fog forecasting

In previous papers [2,3] we have shown that our MLP models are able to forecast meteorological visibility and allow to increase the accuracy of our operational forecasting activity. We have recently worked out a model [3] which represents an improvement of the MLP model adopted in the case-studies of the previous section, a model in which the usual least-squares training is substituted by a weighted least-squares one, in order to properly take the errors associated to the observation of visibility into account. We wish to understand, now, if the cognitive behaviour exhibited by our MLP model in forecasting visibility is typical of a pattern recognition problem or of a feature extraction one. As we will see, the result can help to understand better the dynamics of the atmosphere and the attempts at simulating its behaviour.

Once established that the model works well in almost all the cases considered in our studies, we must stress that, as result of a subjective control, we recognise that similar input patterns sometimes produce similar (correct) outputs and sometimes put out well distinct (correct) results of forecasting, falling down into distinct attraction basins. This fact induces to think that an activity of pattern recognition is not sufficient for grasping and simulating the complex behaviour of visibility dynamics.

A more objective control is performed with the help of the evolutionary dynamics of synaptic weights and forecast performances of our model. As a matter of fact, in almost all the cases of forecasting, the course of synaptic and output values well resembles that encountered in the previous section for didactical problems of feature extraction. An example of these courses is shown in fig.4. Even now, in the majority

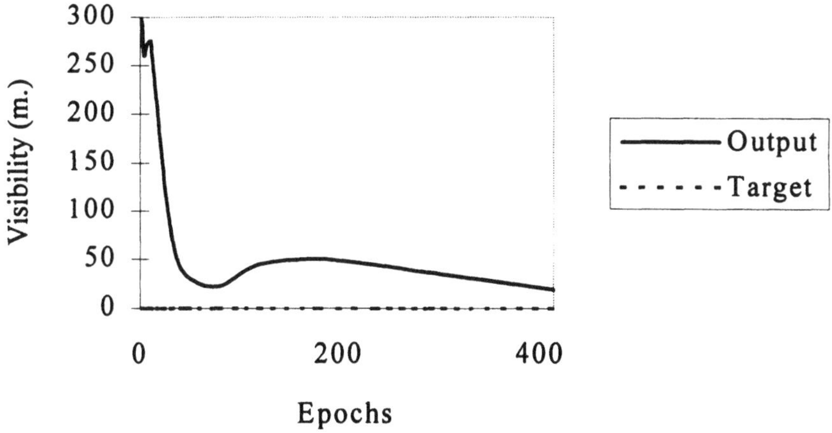

Fig.4. An example of visibility forecasting: generalisation performances

of cases, we are able to recognise several internal representations which lead to several distinct "hypotheses" for the output values, as the number of training steps increases.

4 Some physical considerations

As we have just seen, the cognitive behaviour of our MLP model in fog forecasting resembles more an activity of feature extraction than a pattern recognition conduct. As a consequence, which are the considerations that one can make on the nature of the physical system under examination?

The physical relevance of the evidence just obtained is twofold. First of all we establish the fragmented structure of the space of the attraction basins, thus re-discovering the chaotic behaviour of the atmospheric system in a new manner, i.e. by means of the dynamics of synaptic weights and output values. Furthermore, the fundamental results that even for similar input patterns we obtain correct forecasts leads to seriously consider neural-network models as valid alternatives (in certain space-time ranges) to thermal-fluid-dynamical models, which have inherent limitations in their deterministic non-linear structure that leads to an exponential growth of errors in time.

From the meteorological point of view, it is very interesting to find that a non-dynamical approach, such as the neural-network approach, is able to distinguish different meteorological evolutions from neighbouring initial states. Other approaches, such as the weather forecasting via analogues by Lorenz [5], have failed. Our results can explain this failure in terms of the fragmented structure of the attraction basins in the input multidimensional space.

If it will be confirmed in future studies that neural networks can grasp and simulate the complex behaviour of atmospheric dynamics, they will become good candidates for non-dynamical forecasting models, especially at long range, but even for local short-range forecasting.

5 Conclusions

We have shown that the cognitive behaviour of a MLP in forecasting meteorological visibility is typical of a feature extraction activity. This result allows to re-discover the chaotic behaviour of the atmospheric system in a new manner and lead to take neural-network models into account for an activity of forecasting, especially in those space-time ranges where dynamical models show their intrinsic limitations.

References

1. Swingler K. Applying Neural Networks. Academic Press, New York, 1996
2. Pasini A, Potestà S. Short-Range Visibility Forecast by Means of Neural-Network Modelling: a Case-Study. Il Nuovo Cimento 1995; 18C: 505-516
3. Pasini A, Potestà S. Towards Fog Forecasting in Meteorology by Means of Back-Propagation Neural Networks with Weighted Least-Squares Training. In: Marinaro M and Tagliaferri R (eds) Neural Nets: WIRN Vietri-96. Springer-Verlag, London, 1997, pp 263-269
4. Serra R, Zanarini G. Complex Systems and Cognitive Processes. Springer-Verlag, Berlin, 1990
5. Lorenz EN. Atmospheric Predictability as Revealed by Naturally Occurring Analogues. Journal of Atmospheric Sciences 1969; 26: 636-646

Classifying Magnetic Resonance Spectra of Brain Neoplasms Using Fuzzy and Robust Gold Standard Adjustments

Nicolino Pizzi
Institute for Biodiagnostics
National Research Council Canada
435 Ellice Avenue
Winnipeg MB R2N 2N4
CANADA
Tel: 204-983-8842
Fax: 204-984-5472
Email: pizzi@ibd.nrc.ca

Abstract

Magnetic resonance spectra are often difficult to analyze due to their complex nature and the presence of noise. Many preprocessing methods exist that transform the original input data in order to eliminate or diminish the effects of noise and/or reduce the dimensionality of the input space. Unfortunately, culling diagnostic information is further exasperated by the fact that the reference test or "gold" standard, against which a new and possibly imperfect magnetic resonance diagnostic test is measured, may itself be imprecise or even unreliable. However, little work has been done to investigate a methodology whereby the possible imprecision of a well-established but tarnished gold standard may be addressed while at the same time maintaining its vital discriminatory power.

Two strategies are presented to burnish such tarnished gold standards.

The first uses a fuzzy set theoretic preprocessing method to enhance the gold standard by incorporating non-subjective within-group centroid information.

The second uses a robust estimation of deviations from group medians for the reclassification of spectra in a training set.

These strategies were applied to a multi-layer perceptron classifier using magnetic resonance spectra of human brain neoplasms. The strategies garnered improvements to the classification accuracy of the neural network of 13% and 10%, respectively, as measured using test spectra. Furthermore, the remaining misclassifications were more conservative.

Introduction

It is often difficult to glean diagnostic information from magnetic resonance (MR) spectra due to their complex nature and the presence of noise. Many preprocessing methods exist that transform the original input data in order to eliminate or diminish the effects of noise and/or reduce the dimensionality of the input space. For instance, encoding using fuzzy set theory (1) has been successfully used in MR spectral classification problems as an input preprocessing technique (2). Culling diagnostic information is further exasperated by the fact that the reference test or "gold" standard (GS), against which a new and possibly imperfect MR diagnostic test is measured, may itself be imprecise or even unreliable. However, little work has been done to investigate a methodology whereby the possible imprecision of a well established but tarnished GS may be addressed while at the same time maintaining its vital discriminatory power.

As an extension to some previous work (3), two strategies are presented to burnish tarnished gold standards. The first uses a fuzzy set theoretic preprocessing method to enhance the GS by incorporating non-subjective within-group centroid information. The second uses a robust estimation of deviations from group medians for the reclassification of spectra in a training set. These strategies were applied to a multi-layer perceptron (MLP) classifier using ^{1}H MR spectra of human brain neoplasms.

Materials and methods

The data set comprises 206 1H MR spectra (360 MHz, 37°) consisting of 95 meningiomas (M), 74 astrocytomas (A), and 37 control samples of non-tumourous brain tissue from patients with epilepsy (E). The 550 data points in the region of 0.3–4.0 ppm were used in the analyses. The phased spectra were normalized (each datum was divided by the area of the spectrum) and randomly assigned to either a training set (n=80) or a test set (n=126). The training set contained 29 M's, 31 A's, and 20 E's. The GS was provided by a pathologist and was encoded using the vector $\{g_1, g_2, g_3\}$ where g_k=1, if the corresponding spectrum was assigned to group k, and g_j=0 for $j \neq k$.

The weighted distance, $d_{ik}=[\Sigma_j((x_{ij}-\mu_{kj})/\sigma_{kj})^2]^{1/2}$, of the spectrum, x_i from the group k centroid was computed (where μ_k and σ_k are the respective mean and standard deviation of the spectra assigned to group k). This distance measure was incorporated into the gold standard using fuzzy membership functions — functions in the interval [0,1] indicating the degree to which an element belongs to a set. Group k's membership function is defined as $f_k(x_i)=[1+(d_{ik}/q)^p]^{-1}$ where q and p describe the shape and amount of fuzziness for the distance measure; in general, the further a spectrum is from a group's centroid, the lower its membership value for that group.

The enhanced gold standard (EGS) was encoded by the vector $\{h_1, h_2, h_3\}$ where $h_j = f_j$ for $j \neq k$, if the spectrum was assigned to group k by the original GS, and $h_k = f_k^{1/c}$, where c is a concentrator that ensures the original GS assignment predominates. That is, a spectrum will never be reassigned to a class different from the class to which it was originally assigned, but if a spectrum is near another group's centroid then the corresponding output element for that spectrum will not be zero.

The median of the absolute deviations, MAD (median($|x-\text{median}(x)|$)/0.6745), is a robust estimator of the standard deviation. Only 40% efficient for normal data, it nevertheless is robust to outliers and long-tailed distributions (4). Although a univariate estimator, it may be extended to the multivariate case by computing a vector, MAD_k, whose elements are MADs for each spectral coordinate of group k. Specifically, for group k and its spectra, x_j ($j=1,\ldots,n_k$), the ith coordinate of MAD_k is $MAD_{ki} = \text{median}(|x_{ji} - \text{median}(x_{ji})|)/0.6745$ ($i=1,\ldots,550$). A coordinate value of a spectrum, x_j, is considered to be a group k coordinate i outlier if $|x_{ji} - \text{median}_{ki}| > 2.5 * MAD_{ki}$ where median_{ki} is the ith element of the group k median. Finally, for each spectrum, x_j, the distance metric $D_k^{(j)} = \Sigma_i d_{ji}^{(k)}$ is computed where $d_{ji}^{(k)} = 0$ if x_j has a group k coordinate i outlier, otherwise $d_{ji}^{(k)} = |x_{ji} - \text{median}_{ki}|$. A spectrum, x_j, from group k will be reassigned to group l, if $D_k^{(j)} \neq 0$ and $D_l^{(j)} = 0$. In other words, for a spectrum to be reclassified it must be sufficiently distant from its group's median and sufficiently near another group's median. Note that reclassification may only occur for spectra in the training set.

The MLP is a supervised feed-forward artificial neural network (5), a massively parallel self-adaptive system composed of fully-interconnected layers of processing elements, that iteratively minimizes an error function that compares the GS with the generated group assignment. The output of the jth processing element at the lth layer is $x_j^{[l]} = tr[\Sigma_i(w_{ji}^{[l]} x_i^{[l-1]})]$ where the w's are weights for the input values from the previous layer, and tr is typically the logistic function, $(1+e^{-x})^{-1}$, however, any sigmoid function is permissible (in our case the hyperbolic tangent function is used). The transfer function is applied to the summation of the outputs of the i PE's from layer $l-1$ multiplied by the respective i weights.

A typical global error function is $E = \frac{1}{2}\Sigma(d_k - o_k)^2$ where the d_k's and o_k's are the respective components of the desired and actual outputs and the weight changes are calculated using the gradient descent strategy $\Delta w_{ji}^{[l]} = -\alpha(\partial E/\partial w_{ji}^{[l]}) + \beta \Delta w_{ji}^{[l]}$ where α is a learning coefficient in the range [0,1] and β is the momentum coefficient. In general terms, an MLP may be considered a non-linear regression system that performs a gradient descent search through the weight space, seeking minima.

The MLP architecture used here consists of two hidden layers with three processing elements in the output layer (one for each group). Large learning and momentum values are used for the initial layers and the initial sets of iterations and smaller values for subsequent layers and sets of iterations. The end effect of this modulated learning strategy is to search for gross data features at the initial layers and during the initial sets of iterations and successively refining these detected features by subsequent layers and sets of iterations. The networks were trained on spectra from the training set using the GS and its adjustments.

Given an nxn contingency table of desired versus actual results, a typical measure of performance is $P_o = \Sigma_i n_{ii}/N$ ($i=1,\ldots,k$), where N is the total number of cases. Unfortunately, this measure does not take into account the agreement that might be due to chance, $P_c=[\Sigma_i(\Sigma_j n_{ij}\ \Sigma_j n_{ji})/N]/N\ (i=1,\ldots,k)$. Hence, we use the kappa coefficient, $\kappa=(P_o-P_c)/(1-P_c)$, as a chance-corrected measure of agreement between the desired and actual group assignments (6). If the agreement is due strictly to chance then $\kappa=0$. If the agreement is greater than chance $\kappa>0$ with $\kappa=1$ when there is complete agreement (if the agreement is less than chance $\kappa<0$).

Results and Discussion

Adjustments to the GS improved the overall diagnostic performance of the MLP compared to the original GS. Table 1 lists the performance results using the test MR spectra.

A 13% improvement in the κ score was achieved using EGS. EGS does not alter the original GS classification of the training spectra but it does modify the traversal of the MLP's weight space during the training process; those spectra that are near group centroids other than their own contribute less to the incremental changes to the MLP compared to those training spectra that are near their own centroids.

In the MAD-adjusted GS case, when the outliers were reclassified in the training set, a 10% improvement in the κ score was achieved. Interestingly, if these outlying spectra were removed from the training set, κ degraded to 0.62 for the test set (a 13% decrease from the original GS κ score). Although none of the spectra in the test set was reclassified, using the MAD criterion two test spectra were flagged as outliers (two M spectra were flagged as A spectra). In all three cases, GS, EGS, and MAD, these spectra were indeed misclassified as A spectra.

Finally, the classification errors were also more conservative for both EGS and the MAD-adjusted GS as compared to the original GS. That is, while the original GS classified 5 E's (non-tumourous) as either M's or A's (tumours) and 4 tumours as E's, EGS and the MAD-adjusted GS classified only 1 E as tumourous and 3 tumours as E's.

	Gold Standard (GS)			Outliers Adjusted (EGS)			Outliers Reclassified (MAD)			Outliers Removed (MAD)		
	M	E	A	M	E	A	M	E	A	M	E	A
M	61	2	3	58	2	6	57	1	8	56	4	6
E	1	12	4	0	16	1	0	16	1	0	16	1
A	9	2	32	5	1	37	5	2	36	13	5	25
κ	0.71			0.80			0.78			0.62		

Table 1: Performance results using test spectra

It is informative to examine the κ scores for the training spectra using the different methods (Table 2). Although the GS and EGS contingency tables are identical, the weights of the underlying MLP's are sufficiently different to exact a significant performance gain in the classification of the test spectra.

With the MAD-adjusted GS, three spectra were reclassified in the training set: a M spectrum to A; a E spectrum to A; and, an A spectrum to E. When reclassification took place, κ improved from 0.97 to 1.00. However, if those spectra were removed from the training set, as is often the case in classification problems, κ actually degrades to 0.93, suggesting that these spectra, although identified as outliers, have sufficient import to affect the learning cycle of the MLP. Further, the M and E spectra that were identified as outliers were classified as M and E spectra, respectively, using the GS. However, the A spectrum that was identified as an outlier (and reclassified as an E spectrum using the MAD criterion) was misclassified as an E spectrum using the GS.

	Gold Standard (GS)			Outliers Adjusted (EGS)			Outliers Reclassified (MAD)			Outliers Removed (MAD)		
	M	E	A	M	E	A	M	E	A	M	E	A
M	29	0	0	29	0	0	28	0	0	28	0	0
E	0	20	0	0	20	0	0	20	0	0	19	0
A	0	2	29	0	2	29	0	0	32	2	2	26
κ	0.97			0.97			1.00			0.93		

Table 2: Performance results using training spectra

Conclusion

The results demonstrate that the adjustment of a GS using a fuzzy or robust measure of deviation of MR spectra from their respective group centroids leads to a reduction in classification errors. Moreover, misclassifications tend to be more conservative. The MAD-adjusted GS is a more radical preprocessing strategy since a reclassified spectrum will necessarily deviate from the group assignment dictated by the well-established GS. However, if reclassification occurs, it only occurs for spectra within the training set; outliers within the test set are simply flagged but not altered using this method. Therefore, the accepted GS is left in a pristine state sullied only by its original tarnish.

References

Klir G. Developments in uncertainty-based information. Adv Computs 1993; 36:255–332

Pizzi N, Somorjai, R. Fuzzy encoding as a preprocessing method for artificial neural networks. In: Proceedings of the World Congress on Neural Networks, San Diego, USA, pp 643–648, 1994.

Pizzi N, Somorjai, R. To burnish tarnished gold standards: a classification strategy for MR spectra as applied to human brain neoplasm diagnosis. In: Proceedings of Society of Magnetic Resonance, Nice, France, p 1937, 1995.

Seber G. Multivariate observations. Wiley & Sons, Toronto, 1984.

Ripley B. Neural networks and related methods for classification. J Royal Stat Soc B 1994; 56:409–456

Everitt B. Analysis of contingency tables, Chapman & Hall, London, 1992.

Self-organization with a large medical database: Using GTM for prediction and clustering

B. Rosario, D. R. Lovell, M. Niranjan, R. W. Prager, K. J. Dalton† and R. Derom‡

Cambridge University, Engineering Department,
Trumpington St., Cambridge CB2 1PZ, UK
Tel: +44 1223 332754, Fax: +44 1223 332 662,
Email: {br,drl,niranjan,rwp}@eng.cam.ac.uk

†Cambridge University Department of Obstetrics and Gynaecology,
Rosie Maternity Hospital, Robinson Way, Cambridge, CB2 2SW, UK

‡Katholieke Universiteit Leuven, Center for Human Genetics,Herestraat 49,
B-3000 Leuven, Belgium.

Abstract

We present an application of the Bishop's GTM algorithm for the analysis of a large database of medical information and we explore a possible method to use the GTM for predictions.

The GTM algorithm finds the posterior distribution for each data point over a latent space; in this way it implements a topographic mapping from high dimensional data space into a lower dimensional latent space. Our idea is that, if the GTM preserves the intrinsic dimensionality of the data space, points "near" in the latent space should correspond to "similar" data in the data space, for instance data with similar risk. We apply the GTM algorithm to a learning set and we find for each learning point a corrisponding point in the latent space. We then consider a testing set and assign to each testing point the same risk as the "closest" training point in the latent space. While we only have access to retrospective data, we already know the risk for both the learning and the testing set, so we can calculate the error obtained in this way. We show that this error is comparable with the errors found by others methods for the same data.

Keywords: Unsupervised neural network, GTM algorithm, nearest neighbourhood, risk prediction.

1 Introduction

The goal of an unsupervised neural network is to find a good representation of the probability density function from which the data were generated; this kind of statistical model allows us to make good predictions about the new data presented.

In this paper we use an unsupervised neural network to explore low dimensional representation of information in a 700.000 record obstetrical database.

The model we use is the *generative topographic mapping* GTM [1], an alternative to the Self-Organizing Map [2]. The interest is both in the effective analysis of the obstetric data and in the study of the model. Previous empirical work with GTM has been restricted to a toy problem and a simulated dataset. Therefore, it seems interesting to analyse the performance of this method on a large, real-life dataset.

Moreover, we are interesting in finding new methods for predicting the risk of a bad outcome in pregnancy and this is the first unsupervised learning method used to analyse the obstetrics data.

In the next section we introduce briefly the principles of the GTM algorithm, in Section 3 we descreibe the data to be analysed and in Section 4 we present the results obtained with GTM to predict an adverse pregnancy outcome.

2 The GTM algorithm

The GTM algorithm [1] is an unsupervised neural network and can be considered an alternative to the Self-Organizing Map (SOM) algorithm of Kohonen [2]. Like the SOM, the GTM addresses the problem of mapping a high dimensional space into a low dimensional space; the mapping is a topographic one in the sense that it preserves the neighbourhood relations of the data points. Deriving from a statistical framework, the GTM overcomes some limitations of the SOM.

The GTM aims to find a representation for the distribution $p(\mathbf{t})$ of data in a D-dimensional space $\mathbf{t} = (t_1, ..., t_D)$ in terms of a number L of "latent" variables $\mathbf{x} = (x_1, ..., x_L)$.

Typically, the dimensionality L of the latent-variable space is less than D, since we would like to capture the fact that the data itself has an intrinsic dimensionality which is less than D and can be represented only by L variables.

We define a likelihood function $L(\mathbf{W})$, where $\mathbf{W}$ is a weight matrix and we use a form of the expectation-maximization algorithm to maximize $L(\mathbf{W})$ [6]. Let $\mathbf{W}^*$ be the weight matrix which maximizes the likelihood function. With the GTM algorithm we can calculate the probability distribution of $\mathbf{t}^n$, given $\mathbf{x}$ and $\mathbf{W}^*$, $p(\mathbf{t}^n|\mathbf{x}, \mathbf{W}^*)$ and the marginal probability $p(\mathbf{t}^n|\mathbf{W}^*)$.

Now, using Bayes' theorem, we can calculate the posterior probability of the latent point $\mathbf{x}$ given the data point $\mathbf{t}^n$ and the weight matrix $\mathbf{W}^*$

$$p(\mathbf{x}|\mathbf{t}^n, \mathbf{W}^*) = \frac{p(\mathbf{t}^n|\mathbf{x}, \mathbf{W}^*)p(\mathbf{x})}{p(\mathbf{t}^n|\mathbf{W}^*)} \tag{1}$$

where $p(\mathbf{x})$ is the prior probability distribution over the latent space.

We can then visualize the posterior responsibility map for individual data points in latent space. It is often convenient to summarize the posterior by its mean, given for each data point $\mathbf{t}^n$ by

$$< \mathbf{x}|\mathbf{t}^n, \mathbf{W}^* >= \frac{\sum_{i=1}^{K} \mathbf{x}^i p(\mathbf{t}^n|\mathbf{x}^i, \mathbf{W}^*)}{\sum_{i=1}^{K} p(\mathbf{t}^n|\mathbf{x}^i, \mathbf{W}^*)}. \tag{2}$$

This calculation gives, for each point $\mathbf{t}^n$, a corresponding point $\mathbf{x}$ in the latent space.

In their paper [1] the authors demonstrate the performance of the algorithm on a toy problem and on simulated data from flow diagnostics for a multi-phase oil pipeline. In the current paper, we see how GTM performs when applied to a large real-life dataset.

3 The obstetrics data

We used data from the Scottish Morbidity Register on 771,571 singleton births that occurred between 1980–91. The records were partitioned into a learning set consisting of births occurring between 1980–88, and a testing set consisting of births occurring between 1989-91.

The dataset comprises several dependent variables; in our analysis, we consider one such variable, failure to progress in labour. Put simply, failure to progress means that the natural course of labour has stalled before delivery, placing the wellbeing of both mother and child at risk.

Our ultimate aim is to determine how accurately a prediction of failure to progress could be made on the basis of the information available. We would like to develop a risk prediction system that could give an early indication of danger (*i.e.*, high risk) in order to allow prompt medical intervention.

We had to select the information relevant to the prediction of risk of this outcome. To select a relatively small set of features, we retained those features that afforded the greatest degree of discrimination between instances of failure to progress and normal labour. The criterion described in [3] resulted in the selection of 21 features shown in Table 1. We consider a 29-dimensional representation of these discrete features.

4 Using the GTM in predicting failure to progress

The GTM operates in the principle that the high-dimensional data we measure is the result of a generative process in a much lower dimension. If the GTM can find an information preserving mapping from data space to a latent space of lower dimension, can we use the latent space representation to make good prediction about the class of new data points?

We apply the GTM algorithm to the data described in the previous section. We divid our data into a *learning set* and a *testing set*; we apply the GTM algorithm to the learning set and we find the posterior responsibility (1) and the means (2) in the latent space for each learning point. We then consider the testing set and, given the $\mathbf{W}^*$ matrix found with GTM for the learning set, we can find *directly* the posterior responsibility (1) and the means (2) for the testing set.

The main idea is that, if GTM preserves the intrinsic dimensionality of the 29-dimensional data space, adiacent points in the latent space should correspond to "similar" data in the 29-D data space, *i.e.*, data with similar risk. We find, for each testing point, the training point which has the closest mean (2) and we assign to the testing point the risk of this training point. While we only

Selected predictors of failure to progress	
Predictor	**Incidence**
CSections	4.031%
MumAge	
NeoDxs	2.194%
Parity	
FEM STRESS INCONTINENCE	0.052%
PREM SEPARATION PLACENTA*	0.463%
ANTEPARTUM HEMORR NEC*	0.172%
THREATENED LABOR NEC*	3.087%
ANEMIA IN PREGNANCY*	6.218%
OTH CURRENT COND OF PREG*	1.841%
CEPHALIC VERSION NOS*	0.129%
TRANSVERSE/OBLIQUE LIE*	0.246%
HIGH HEAD AT TERM*	0.328%
MALPOSITION NEC*	0.482%
FETAL DISPROPORTION NOS*	0.027%
INTRAUTERINE DEATH*	0.244%
POOR FETAL GROWTH*	3.451%
EXCESSIVE FETAL GROWTH*	0.324%
OTH PLACENTAL CONDITIONS*	0.318%
GRAND MULTIPARITY*	0.079%
SUPRV HIGH-RISK PREG NEC	1.703%

Table 1: A list of the 21 predictors selected. The incidence of maternal conditions in the learning set of 540905 cases is shown in the right column. The maternal age variable `MumAge` is discretised into 7 groups: < 20, 20-24, 25-29, 30-34, 35-39, > 40, and "not known". The variable `Parity` can take on values 0, 1, 2, 3, ≥ 4. This discretization results in a 29 dimensional binary representation of the data.

have access to *retrospective* data, we already know the risk for both the learning and the testing set, so we can calculate the error obtained in assigning to the testing point the risk of the "nearest" (in the latent space) learning point.

We use the maximum-likelihood risk estimate

$$\frac{a_i}{a_i + b_i} \tag{3}$$

where a_i and b_i are the numbers of adverse and benign outcomes associated with the ith pattern. In this situation, the cross-entropy error function ([4], [5]) is appropriate since we wish to measure the quality of our probability predictions. Assuming that y_i is the output of the network for the testing point i (*i.e.*, the risk of the nearest learning point) and that t_i is the target, *i.e.*, the effective risk of the testing point, the error function can then be written in the form

$$E = -\sum_{i=1}^{N}(t_i \ln y_i + (1 - t_i)\ln(1 - y_i)) \tag{4}$$

If the ith pattern has a_i adverse and b_i benign outcomes, from (4) we get

$$E = -\sum_{i=1}^{N}(a_i \ln y_i - b_i \ln(1 - y_i)) \quad (5)$$

We then divide the error (5) by the total number of cases in the testing set in order to obtain the Average Negative Log-Likelihood. This number can be compared to the same Avg.Neg.LL found by other methods for the same data. The results are shown in the following table.

System	Avg.Neg.LL
Limit attainable on test set	0.2691
Ensemble of networks	0.2748
Nearest neighbour in the data space	0.2753
GTM 2D (Nearest neighbour in 2-D latent space)	**0.2756**
Hierarchical Dirichlet model	0.2756
GTM 1D (Nearest neighbour in 1-D latent space)	**0.2757**
Ensemble of direct weight networks	0.2757
Ensemble of logistic regressors	0.2759
Logistic regression	0.2759

The method to obtain the limit attainable on the test set is described in [3].

We can see the GTM performs a good mapping from a high dimensional input space to a low dimensional latent space; we lose little information considering a 2 (or even 1) dimensional latent space. This experiment is one of the first experiments to propose a sensible way to use the GTM for predictions.

5 Summary

We wanted to explore the idea that a low dimensional projection of the data could be useful in making prediction of bad outcome in pregnancy. We used the GTM algorithm to make such projection and found that the mapping performed by GTM preserves the information very well. Having data in a 29 dimensional space, and projecting them into a 2 or 1 dimensional latent space, we lose very little information.

6 Acknowledgements

We are pleased to acknowledge the assistance of Dr Susan Cole of the Information and Statistics Division of the National Health Service in Scotland, for collecting and providing us with access to data from the maternity scheme of the Scottish Morbidity Record system. This work was funded by the EuroPUNCH project and by the Quality Assurance in Maternity Care project, EC Biomed

Grant Ref. BIOMED 1 CT93 1113. The second author gratefully acknowledges the support of The British Council.

References

[1] C. M. Bishop, M. Svensen, and C. K. I. Williams, "GTM: A principled alternative to the self-organizing map," In M. Mozer, M. Jordan, & T. Petsche, *Neural Information Processing Systems*, 1997.

[2] T. Kohonen, "Self-organized formation of topologically correct feature maps," *Biological Cybernetics*, vol. 43, pp. 59–69, 1982.

[3] D. R. Lovell, B. Rosario, M. Niranjan, R. W. Prager, K. J. Dalton, and R. Derom, "Design, construction and evaluation of systems to predict risk in obstetrics," vol. Submitted to International Journal of Biomedical Computing, 1997.

[4] C. M. Bishop, *Neural Networks for Pattern Recognition.* Oxford University Press, 1995.

[5] J. J. Hopfield, "Learning algorithms and probability distributions in feed-forward and feed-back networks," *Proceedings of the National Academy of Sciences*, vol. 84, pp. 8429–8433, 1987.

[6] A.P. Dempster, N.M. Laird, & D.B. Rubin, "Maximum-likelihood from incomplete data via the EM algorithm," *J. of Royal Statistical Society, B39*, pp. 1-38, 1977.

Icarus Platform
Software Integration of Several Intelligent Systems

Giuseppe Russo
Institute for Research on Parallel Information Systems
Italian National Research Council (CNR)
Via P. Castellino 111, Naples, Italy

Abstract

The Icarus Software Platform contributes to the implementation of several intelligent systems based on innovative or traditional techniques for problem solving and decision support (DSS), and allows us to compare the obtained results in order to choice the best. It is a powerful tool capable to integrate many different technologies making very easy both the implementation of new kind of techniques and user interface. It is presented to the user by Visual Like Object Oriented modality with a differentiately graduated approach according to the user requirements; the user is provided with real and not (only) simulated realization of a set of tests.

The platform has yielded preliminary results with prototype approach on real world problems. Applications of interest are: Knowledge Discovering on very large databases, Personal Selection and Repay, Supplier Validation and EDP Balancing Load Prevision. The problems are presented, in turn or in parallel depending on the implementation environment, to the Icarus system, and are tested. The result of the test is a decision on the best technologies to utilize for the particular application. After choosing the method to be used, it is automatically set-up a user-friendly environment in order to make the real world application operative within a telecommunication company "Telecom Italia S.p.A.".

1 Introduction

In that area of applied research whose objects as its object the analysis and projection of DSS to hybrid motors (including artificial neural networks and fuzzy logic types) the realization of the ICARUS software platform - of generalized open type - is intended as a means to consent the integration and comparison of single motors with regards to applications in numerous centralized and/or distributed and/or incompatible environments. The present state of analysis and design of the ICARUS project has reached the realization of the software programme including many types of techniques: Neural Network paradigms as Back-Propagation, ANN/FIR NNs Temporal Back-Propagation, SOM, etc., Fuzzy Logic, Fuzzy C Means and symbolic Clustering Algorithms as ID3, CHAID, CART, UNIMEM, etc. The software is capable to implement further techniques of different technological backgrounds, the whole usable in environments such as HW parallel, X/Open, Unix, Dos, Windows, etc.

The platform is developed by mixed languages and it is presented to the user by Visual Like Object Oriented modality with a differentiately graduated approach according to the users requirements; the user is provided with real and not (only) simulated realization of a set of tests. The realization of the tests are assisted by interactive guidelines, that is motors of interest and specific inputs inherent to different motors but are located out according to the particular problem under examination but for the same problem [1] [2] [4], the test can be implemented rapidly and with flexibility by end/user graphic modality. Test results obtained on a motor problem-shooter prove usable, more measurable and comparable to simular results obtained by other motors in the same domain [5] [7] [9]. Furthermore reinforcing and evolutive algorithms can be inserted with the aid of the platform for predisposed motors. The platform has yielded preliminary results with prototype approach on real world problems (Knowledge Discovering, Personal Selection and Repay, Supplier Validation and EDP Load Balancing Prevision).

2 Intelligent techniques implemented

The software platform has the following capability, that make it a development tool very interesting. It contributes to the implementation of several intelligent systems based on innovative or traditional techniques for problem solving and decision support (classification, ranking, prediction, clustering, etc), and allows us to compare the obtained results in order to choice the best. It is a software tool capable to integrate many different technologies making very easy: the implementation of new kind of techniques, the customization or reinforcement of an algorithm, and user interface. It was created to make easy the portability and the compatibility on several operative environment.

The applications generated by the Icarus Platform are constituted by two software components: Expert element and End/User element. In the Expert phase, an expert user set up the whole project and is done the automatic implementation of the visual-like code that will be utilized by the user. In the End/User phase, it is possible, without any sort of background knowledge on the technologies applied, to load data from external sources and process them according to the rules estabilished during the expert phase [3] [6] [8] [10].

2.1 Neural networks

Among the numerous artificial neural networks which have been proposed recently, Backpropagation networks have been extremely popular for their performance. Backpropagation networks [2] are multiple-layered, feed-forward networks. Activations flow from the input layer through the hidden layer, then to the output layer. A Backpropagation network typically starts out with a random set of weights. The network adjusts its weights each time it sees an input-output pair. The Backpropagation network updates its weights incrementally until the network stabilizes.

FIR neural networks are classical multiple-layer networks whose connections are Finite-duration Impulse Response (FIR) filters. Let $w^l_{ji}(k)$ denote the weight that connects the neuron i in layer l-1 to neuron j in layer l. The signal $s_{ji}^{l}(n)$ appearing at the output of the i-th incoming synapse of neuron j is given by the linear combination of delayed values of the input signal $x_i^{l-1}(n)$ (convolution sum):

$$s_{ji}^{l}(n) = \sum_{k=0}^{M^l} w_{ji}^{l}(k) * x_i^{l-1}(n-k)$$

where n denotes the discrete time step. Hence summing the contributions of the complete set of p synapse, we may describe the output x_j^i of neuron j by using the following equation:

$$x_j^l(n) = \phi(\sum_{i=1}^{p} s_{ji}^{l}(n) - \theta_j)$$

where θ_j denotes the externally applied threshold, and $\phi(.)$ denotes the non-linear activation function of the neuron. Wan proposed a generalised version of the standard back-propagation learning algorithm (Temporal Back Propagation) and suggested the concept of reverse FIR filter, where delay units are replaced with advances units (real application on EDP Balancing Load Prevision)[14]. Neural network paradigms implemented in the Icarus platform can be reinforced, it is possible the integration with other techniques (hybrid algorithms).

On the basis of the data provided to the platform the neural network back-propagation was choosen together with the ID3 algorithm by the Icarus system in the case of the Personal Selection and Repay problems [9].

2.2 Fuzzy logic

Among the methods employing fuzzy reasoning, the so called rule-based fuzzy systems are commonly applied (Mamdami method) [11]. In these systems, every input and output variable have to go through the so called "fuzzification" stage, i. e. they have to be translated into linguistic variables and their membership functions have to be properly defined. The processing core of such a FL system is based on a collection of IF-THEN rules. The output of an entire collection of rules is of course a fuzzy set but in general it is advantageous to obtain from such a system a deterministic number. Thus, the resulting set is defuzzified or resolved to a single number.

It is possible, and in many cases much more efficient, to use a single spike as the output membership function rather than a distributed fuzzy set. This is known as singleton output membership function, and it can be thought of as a pre-defuzzified fuzzy set. It enhances the efficiency of the defuzzification process. The Takagi-Sugeno-Kang method of fuzzy inference was first introduced in 1985 [12] and support this kind of behaviour. Icarus platform supports also fuzzy pattern recognition techniques as fuzzy c means [11]. The software platform allow us to reinforce the fuzzy algorithms, by using a user-friendly interface. Further, it is possible the integration with other techniques (hybrid technologies).

On the basis of the data provided to the platform fuzzy logic and fuzzy c means techniques were choosen by the Icarus system as the best solution technologies in the case of the Supplier Validation problems.

2.3 Clustering algorithms

2.3.1 Symbolic Learning (ID3)

Quinlan's ID3 decision-tree building algorithm and its descendants are simple and yet powerful algorithms for inductive learning [13]. ID3 takes objects of a known class, described in terms of a fixed collection of properties or attributes, and produces a decision tree incorporating these attributes that correctly classifies all the given objects. It uses an information-theoretic approach aimed at minimizing the expected number of tests to classify an object. Its output can be summarized in terms of production rules. Its goal is to classify mixed objects into their associated classes, based on the objects' attribute values. The entropy value of an attribute describes how well that attribute can be used to classify (as a positive or a negative) - the lower the entropy value, the less uncertainty, the more useful the attribute.

Entropy is calculated by using the following function [13]:

$$entropy = -\sum_{j=positive}^{negative} p_j * log p_j .$$

where p_j is the probability of classification as positive or negative. ID3 by design is able to deal with both categorical attributes and continuous values. For categorical attributes, attribute values can be easily enumerated. For continuous values, ID3 performs a sweeping analysis of entropy reduction for all possible partition points (between any two consecutive values) and selects the partition point which provides the most entropy reduction [13]. In essence, the algorithm performs a binary partition. The Icarus platform allow us to reinforce the procedure Id3, it is possible the integration with other techniques (hybrid algorithms) and evaluation of a number of partitions greater than two.

On the basis of the data provided to the platform the ID3 algorithm was choosen together with the neural network back-propagation by the Icarus system in the case of the Personal Selection and Repay problems.

2.3.2 Cluster and exhaustive methods

A clustering procedures is a data analysis algorithm that enables users to quickly analyze and understand the relationships between variables in a data set. It performs a thorough, interactive analysis of linear and non-linear relationships and presents the results in the form of a statistical decision tree. In minutes, it performs the type of analysis that would take a skilled statistician days to complete. It is menu-driven. The results of an analysis are displayed graphically as a statistical decision tree using percentages or averages to communicate meaningful information. Only important results are produced while insignificant detail is left in the background. It is possible to direct your analysis by interactively previewing alternative results and generate rules. These rules can be stored as a knowledge base which lets you construct an expert system to conduct prediction, planning, diagnosis or consultation tasks.

The Icarus Platform support several classical clustering algorithms based on CLUSTER and EXHAUSTIVE methods. The Cluster method finds groups that maximize similarity within the groups and dissimilarity between the groups; it tends to find more natural patterns than Exhaustive. The Exhaustive method finds groups that maximize statistical significance; splits derived from the Exhaustive method display the most significant relationships. The Cluster method, when applied to a categorical variable, is often referred to as the CHAID technique [15]. When the Cluster method is applied to continuous variables, it is similar to the CART technique [16]. The Exhaustive method [17] was developed to address shortcomings in the Cluster method.

Among the different algorithms available and on the basis of the data provided to the platform the UNIMEM procedure was choosen by the Icarus system as the best techniques in our Knowledge Discovering problems.

3 Conclusions

The Icarus Software Platform has yielded good results with prototype approach on real world problems. The development of parallel systems is one successful factor for developing DSS systems. In the Icarus platform design are included the scientific and technical experiences developed on parallel systems. In particular, complex problems of knowledge discovering can be faced making available:

- multiple-techniques (mixed-languages) integrated in open platform,
- high computation capability,
- high dynamism, adaptability and performances.

Further step (already in progress):

a) including adaptive and evolutive systems from byological research,
b) improving automatic capabilities of the Icarus system to support R&S.

References

[1] McClelland, J.L., Rumelhart, D.E., Explorations in Parallel Distribuited Processing. A Handbook of Models, Programs and Exercises, pp 49-81, The MIT Press, Cambridge, MA, 1988.

[2] Rumelhart, D.E., McClelland, and PDP GROUP (eds), Parallel Distribuited Processing, Exploration in the Microstructure of Cognition, Vol.2 : pp. 7-57, the MIT Press, Cambridge, MA, 1986(edizione italiana : P.D.P. Microstruttura dei Processi Cognitivi, pp. 255-313, Il Mulino, Bologna, 1991.

[3] Fuminori, S., Fukuda, T., Two-Link-Robot Brachiation with Connectionist Q-Learning, in From Animals to Animats III : Proceedings of the Third International Conference on Simulation of Adaptive Behavior, a cura di D. Cliff, P. Hausbands, J.-A. Meyer e S. W. Wilson, Cambridge, MA, MIT Press-Bradford Books, 1994.

[4] From Evolution of Instincts to Evolution of Learning Structures in Robotic Agents, rapporto tecnico, Laboratorio di Microinformatica, Politecnico Federale di Losanna, 1995.

[5] Wallace, C., and Parick, J., Coding Decision Trees. Machine Learning, 11:7-22, 1993.

[6] Michaud, P., Simulated Computation in Automatic Classification in Applied Stochastic Models and Data Analysis Special Issue of Fifth International Symposium on A.S.M.D.A Granada 23-26 April 1991, Vol. 7, No.2, pp. 167-182.

[7] Vaccaro, R., Vanneschi, M., Design Methodologies to General-purpose Highly-Parallel computers: Phisical Machine and Architectural Supports, in IEEE Microarch, No.1, Vol. 6, pp.21-26, November 1991.

[8] SriKant, R.,and Agrawal, R. 1996, Mining Quantitative Association Rules in Large Relational Tables. In Proc. Of the ACM SIGMOND Conference on Managment of Data. Nearhos, J., Rothman, M., and Viveros, M. 1996.

[9] Applying Data Mining Techniques to a Health insurance information system. In Proc. Of the 22nd Intl Conference on very Large Databases.

[10] Sun Wu and Udi Manber, Text Searching Allowing errors, Comm. Of ACM(CACM), 35(10):83-91, October 1992.

[11] Gulley, N. and Jang, J.S.R. (1995). Fuzzy Logic TOOLBOX for use with Matlab, The Math Works Inc., Natick, MA, USA.

[12] Sugeno, M., (1985). Industrial Applications of Fuzzy Control, Elsevier Science Pub. Co.

[13] J. R. Quinlan. C4.5: Programs for Machine Learning. Morgan Kauffmann, Los Altos, CA, 1993.

[14] E. A. Wan, Finite Impulse Response Neural Networks with Applications in Time Series Prediction. PhD Thesis, Department of Electrical Engineering, Stanford University, 1993.

[15] G. V. Kass, An exploratory technique for investigating large quantities of categorical data, Applied Statistics, 24, 2, 1975, pp. 178-189.

[16] L. Breiman et al, Classification and Regression Trees, Wadsworth, 1984.

[17] Biggs et al, A Method of Choosing Multiway Partitions for Classification and Decision Trees, Applied Statistics, 18, 1, 1991, pp. 49-62.

SECTION 7

ARCHITECTURES AND ALGORITHMS

Plastic Tabu Search for Training Multilayer Perceptrons

Massimo Battisti, Pietro Burrascano**

Abstract

Tabu search is a global optimisation scheme allowing to escape from local minima in the cost function: it merges an iterative local search algorithm with heuristics aimed to avoid both limit cycles and confinements in a limited portion of the search space. The implementations proposed so far for its use in the training phase of a neural network imply the transformation of the learning task into a combinatorial optimisation problem by means of a preliminary quantisation of the real valued weights into n bits binary words: this early quantisation can significantly influence the final result and can be thus a limitation. The present paper proposes an original implementation of tabu search which, while retaining its basic characteristics, overcomes this limitation: it dynamically defines the set of feasible solution points at run time as the subset of cost function's minima encountered during procedure's run. The effectiveness of the proposed procedure is verified by means of experimental tests.

Introduction and Background

Different strategies are possible to overcome the problem of local minima, which consist in adopting optimisation techniques capable of being effective in continuing the search after the procedure reaches a first minimum. Simulated annealing [1] and genetic algorithms [2] have the above characteristics. A different approach to the problem of global optimisation consists in the use of tabu search (TS) strategies: they are usually implemented as combinatorial optimisation schemes that merge an iterative local search algorithm with heuristics aimed to avoid both limit cycles and confinements in a limited portion of the search space.

Different implementations of the tabu search based algorithm have been considered to train feedforward neural networks [3-4-5]: all them imply the transformation of the task in a combinatorial optimisation problem by adopting a scalar quantisation of the real valued weights into n bits binary words: this can be a limitation, because at the beginning of the optimisation procedure we have no prior information about the specific structure of the multimodal cost function. It follows that substantially different results can be obtained if the dynamic range and/or the number of bits associated to each weight is modified.

The present paper proposes an original global optimisation technique based on tabu search which, while retaining its basic structure, is particularised to the continuous (metric) case of training a MLP: the main characteristic of the proposed procedure, as it will be detailed in the following, is that the set of feasible points in the parameters space is not defined at the beginning of the procedure on the basis of a quantisation of the weight values, but is adaptively defined at run time as the subset of cost function's minima encountered during procedure's run; moreover, a portion of the parameters space is associated to each one of the feasible points (minima) identified at run time, in order to define a sort of adaptive vector quantisation of the parameters space. These regions are estimates of the basins of attraction associated to the

* Ist. Elettronica, Università di Perugia - Perugia - Italy; Email: burrascano@istel.ing.unipg.it

minima. The local search technique between the feasible points is performed by using a local metric which relies on the estimated shape of the region associated to the current point; the strategies to avoid limit cycles and confinements are a simplified version of those proposed in [5].

The Plastic Tabu Search Strategy

The search procedure is described in the following, divided into macro steps.

Step 0: initialisation. The procedure starts from a random point in the weight space.

Step 1: local minimisation. A gradient descent procedure is performed by means of the standard backpropagation algorithm and the minimum Mk is defined and the corresponding parameters vector is stored.

Step 2: the region. In order to define the region associated to the current minimum Mk, several sub steps are performed:

Step 2.1: shape of the region. Following [6-7], a distribution is associated to the current minimum Mk, evaluated as:

$$P_w^{(k)} = \frac{1}{\Xi} \exp\left\{ -\frac{1}{2} (\omega - \omega_n)^t [C_k]^{-1} (\omega - \omega_n) \right\} \tag{1}$$

where $(.)^t$ and $[\ ]^{-1}$ denote matrix transposition and inversion, respectively, the covariance matrix $\mathbf{C}_k$ can be evaluated by:

$$C_k = \frac{1}{n} \left[\nabla\nabla D (v_n, p(\omega_n))\right]^{-1} V_{v_n}\left[\nabla k (\mathbf{x},\mathbf{y},\omega_n)\right] \left[\nabla\nabla D(v_n, p(\omega_n))\right]^{-1} \tag{2}$$

where n is the number of training samples of the data set; $V_{v_n}[.]$ denotes the variance of the quantity in brackets with respect to the distribution $v_n(\mathbf{x},\mathbf{y})$; the normalising constant Ξ takes on the form:

$$\Xi = \sqrt{(2\pi)^m \operatorname{Det}[C_k]} \tag{3}$$

where m is the dimension of the parameters space $\omega \in \mathbf{W} \subset \Re^m$ and Det[ ] denotes the determinant.

The estimated covariance matrix C_k is stored. The gaussian distribution defined in this way gives a local description of cost function's shape in the region of the weight space surrounding M_k: our objective is to consider M_k as the centroid associated to a region whose shape is defined by C_k, but whose dimensions are still to be defined.

Step 2.2: size of the region. In our procedure an estimate of the basin of attraction associated to Mk is defined as the region to be associated to Mk. To estimate the basin of attraction, we defined a search procedure along random directions departing from Mk. The cost function is evaluated at regular steps along each direction kj: the step size in each direction kj departing from Mk is a fraction of the value of skj which can be derived from the matrix Ck in correspondence to the direction considered; the point where the derivative of the cost function, evaluated along the direction kj, becomes negative is stored as Pkj. This procedure is repeated for a number of directions, and the point Pkj leading to the minimum of the quantity Distance(Mk; Pkj)/skj is chosen as the point P*k defining the dimension of the basin of attraction associated to Mk and thus of the region Bk. Namely, the region Bk associated to the local minimum Mk is the ellipsoid centred in Mk whose shape is defined by Ck and passing in P*k. It is worth noting that a sufficient description of the space surrounding Mk implies a number of directions involved which exponentially increases with the number of network parameters (dimensions of the weight space).

Step 3: neighbourhood. After the current point Mk is defined together with its associated region Bk, the set of the feasible points in its neighbourhood has to be defined. To this end the points Pkj stored during the operations described in step 2.2 are used: they define the divide, along the direction kj, between the minimum Mk and other minima.

Step 3.1: local descents. A gradient descent procedure is performed starting from each point Pkj; the standard backpropagation algorithm is used.

Step 3.1.1: stored minimum During each gradient descent procedure, it is verified if the current point falls within the region Bh associated to a previously stored minimum Mh. If the check is positive, the gradient descent procedure is stopped and Mh is defined as a member of Mk's neighbourhood.

Step 3.1.2: new minima. If the condition of Step 3.1.1 is not verified, we are in a region of the weight space never explored before: the gradient descent procedure is run and the new minimum Mh is found and stored; it is a new member of Mk's neighbourhood. The characteristics of the new minimum Mh found in the neighbourhood of Mk are evaluated and stored by using the same procedure followed in Step 2.1: namely, the associated covariance matrix Ck is estimated and stored.

Step 4: the move. After Mk's neighbourhood is defined, the move to a different feasible point (minimum) in this neighbourhood is defined: at each step of the search, tabu search examines the neighbourhood of the current solution Mk and "moves" towards the neighbour which has a lower cost associated to it. This would essentially be a steepest descent algorithm; tabu search superimposes to it a meta-heuristics which avoids local minima entrapment.

Step 4.1: short term memory. Cycling around local minima is coped with the use of the tabu criteria: the set of feasible points in the neighbourhood of Mk is partitioned into the disjoint sets of the tabu moves and of admissible moves. A list of the most recently explored solutions, denoted with short term memory, is maintained and queried at each iteration of the search. The tabu criteria forbids the choice of recently explored solutions.

Step 5: end loop. After the move has been performed, if the stop criterion is NOT satisfied go to Step 3.

Experimental Results

Several experiments have been performed in order to validate the proposed technique and all them gave very satisfactory results; in the following the results of one of the experiments are reported, namely the *noisy rhomboid* classification task; moreover, we report the results of a comparison between the proposed learning procedure, denoted as plastic tabu search, with Reactive Tabu Search (RTS) and Simulated Annealing (SA). In the *noisy rhomboid* classification task the input samples are drawn from an uniform distribution in a bidimensional feature space; one of the two classes is associated to each sample according to its location in the input space; samples drawn from a zero mean σ=0.1 normal distribution are added to the nominal target values 0.1 and 0.9; the training set is reported in figure 1. Table 1 reports the main parameters adopted for running the training algorithm; Table 2 reports the minima detected, with evidenced the one leading to the lowest training m.s.e. . Figure 2 shows the partition in the input space defined by the best minimum; figure 3 shows the behaviour of m.s.e. along the different directions surrounding one of the minima encountered during learning: it is worth noting that the different curves, relative to different directions, share the same value of the ratio step/σ, while the steps span about one order of magnitude: nevertheless, the curves behave consistently up to several tens of σ. Figures 4 and 5 allow a comparison between the proposed algorithm and our implementations of RTS and SA in terms of both the best m.s.e. obtained and the computational effort associated to the overall procedure.

Conclusions

An original implementation of tabu search has been proposed in the paper which, while retaining the basic characteristics of tabu search techniques, overcomes the limitation associated to the transformation of the learning task into a combinatorial optimisation problem by means of a preliminary quantisation of the real valued weights into n bits binary words. The proposed procedure dynamically defines the set of feasible solution points at run time as the subset of cost function's minima encountered during procedure's run. The results of the experimental tests verified the effectiveness of the proposed procedure.

Acknowledgements

This research was financially supported by the Italian "Ministero dell'Università e della Ricerca Scientifica e Tecnologica" (MURST) and by the italian "Consiglio Nazionale delle Ricerche" (CNR).

References

[1] Engel J. Teaching feedforward neural networks by simulated annealing. Complex Syst. 1988, vol. 2, pp.641-648

[2] Whitley D., Starkweather T., Bogart C. Genetic algorithms and neural networks: Optimising connections and connectivity, Parallel Compu. 1990, vol. 14, pp.347-361

[3] Beyer D.A. and Ogier R.G. Tabu Learning: a neural network search method for solving nonconvex optimisation problems, Proc. Int. Join. Conf. Neural Networks, Singapore, Nov 1991

[4] de Werra D. and Hertz H. Tabu Search techniques: A tutorial and an application to neural networks, OR Spectrum,1989, vol. 11, pp.131-141

[5] Battiti R. and Tecchiolli G. Training Neural Nets with the Reactive Tabu Search, IEEE Trans on Neural Networks, September 1995, vol. 6, n.5 , pp.1185-1200

[6] Burrascano P. and Pirollo D. Training Feedforward Neural Networks in the Presence of Prior Information, Neural Nets WIRN Vietri-95, M. Marinaro and R. Tagliaferri Editors, World Scientific-1995; pp. 171-176;

[7] Burrascano P. and Pirollo D. Finite Sample Size and Neural Model Indetermination, 1997, in press

Table 1: Parameters adopted for running the training algorithm

Network structure	2 2 4 1
Training set cardinality	900
Max # of iterations	20
Tabu time	10
Max # of epochs for each local descent	40 000
Learning step during local descent	0.08
Max # of directions from each min	40
Step along directions (*σ)	1
Max # of points in the neighbourhood	7
Max exploration distance (*σ)	500

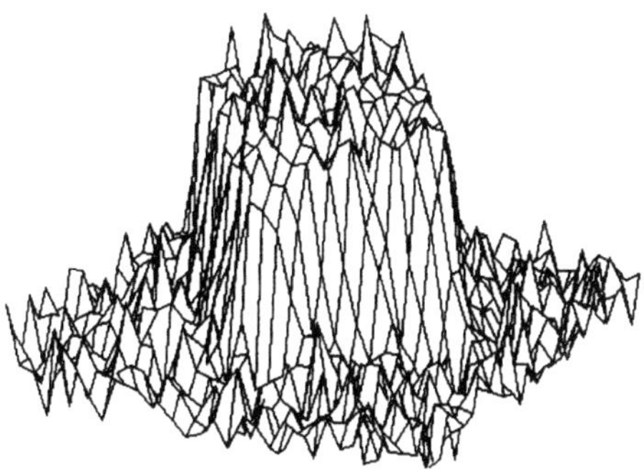

Figure 1 - The training set considered for the noisy rhomboid classification task.

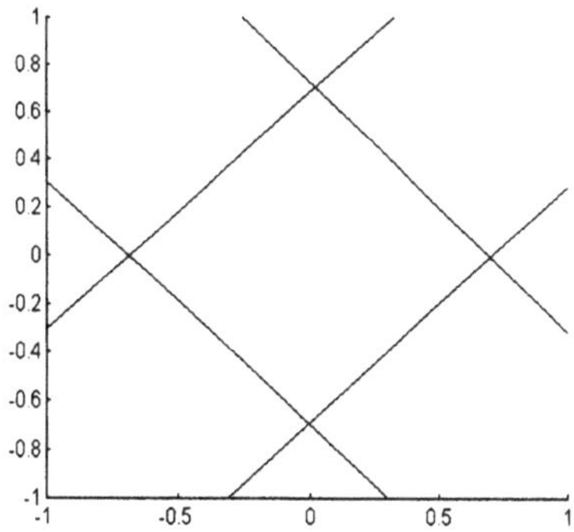

Figure 2 - Partition in the input space defined by the best minimum.

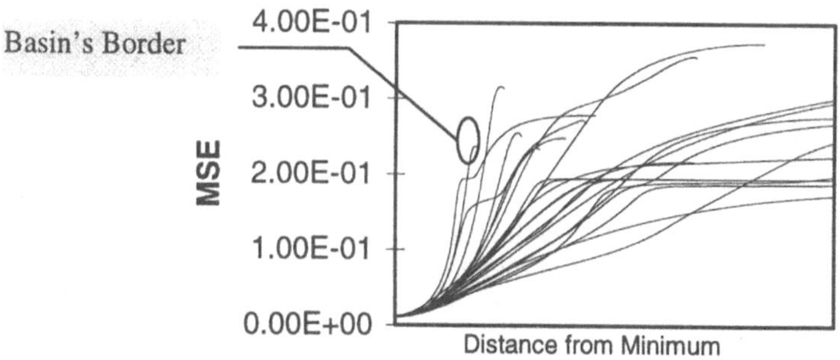

Figure 3 - Behaviour of m.s.e. along the different directions surrounding one of the minima encountered during learning.

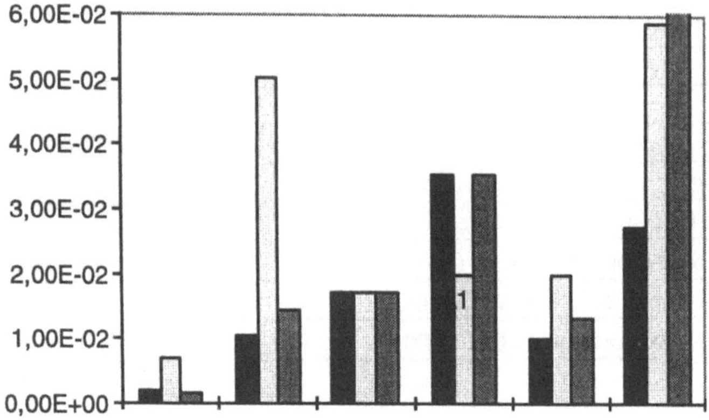

Triangle 4 squares Gauss1 Gauss2 Rhomboid Iris

Figure 4 - Comparison between the proposed algorithm and our implementations of RTS and SA in terms of the best m.s.e. obtained

LEGEND: Plastic Tabu: dark grey ; SA: medium grey; RTS: light grey

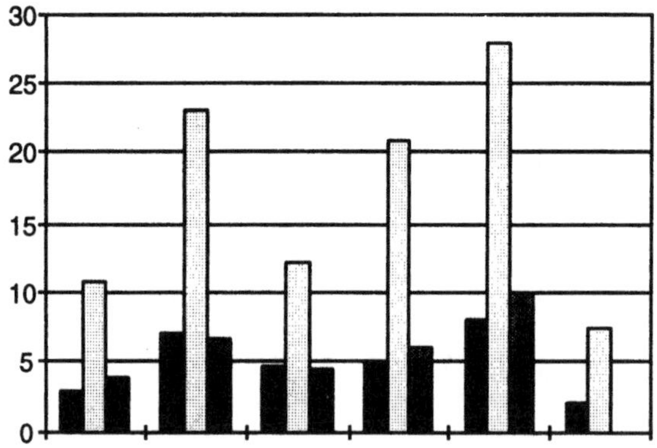

Triangle 4 squares Gauss1 Gauss2 Rhomboid Iris

Figure 5 - Comparison between the proposed algorithm and our implementations of RTS and SA in terms of computational effort associated to the overall procedure.

LEGEND: Plastic Tabu: dark grey ; SA: medium grey; RTS: light grey

Training Analog VLSI Multi Layer Perceptron Networks with Continuous Time Back Propagation

G.M. Bo, D.D. Caviglia, H. Chiblé, and M. Valle
Department of Biophysical and Electronic Engineering
University of Genoa, Via all'Opera Pia 11/A, 16145 Genova, Italy
ph:+39 10 3532287, fax: +39 10 3532795, e_mail: gian_bo@dibe.unige.it

Abstract

In this paper we discuss and investigate the main properties of the Continuous Time Back Propagation (CTBP) algorithm according to its usage for training Multi Layer Perceptron (MLP) networks. It will be shown that the CTBP algorithm allows a more effective analog VLSI implementation of MLP networks with on-chip learning, with respect to those presented in the literature. We will evidence the drawbacks of current analog on-chip learning implementations, the advantages of the CTBP formulation and its application to classification tasks.

1 Introduction

In the analog VLSI implementation of MLP networks with on-chip learning presented in the literature [1-4], weights control variables are usually stored as voltages across capacitors, and the weights update operation is performed by charging or discharging a capacitor (one weight capacitor per synapse) with a charge proportional to the weight update signal. This operation is usually controlled by a switch (one switch per synapse): by using a standard CMOS technology, the charge injection occurring at each iteration [7] generates an offset which affects the weight update values and introduces errors in the neural computations [11].

To overcome such drawback, we consider a different approach to the implementation of MLP networks with on-chip learning: the Continuous Time Back Propagation (CTBP) [10]. According to it, all the neural signals are coded by continuous time electrical variables and the weights are continuously adapted: following this approach, no switches are needed during the training process.

The paper is organised as follows. In Section 2 the by step learning approach used in most of the current analog VLSI implementation of on-chip learning neural network is briefly discussed. In Section 3 is introduced the CTBP learning algorithm while in Section 4 and 5 some consideration about the training behaviour are discussed. In Section 6 circuit simulation results are presented, while the conclusion are drawn in Section 7.

2 The by step learning approach

Let us consider a generic neuron with N synapses: the neuron output Sj is computed as:

$$S_j = f\left(\sum_{i=1}^{N} W_{j,i} S_i\right) \tag{1}$$

where $f()$ is the neuron activation function, S_i is the ith synaptic input and $W_{j,i}$ is the synaptic weight value between the ith synaptic input and the jth neuron. In the following, if not otherwise evidenced, we will consider as the neuron activation function $f()$ the hyperbolic tangent, thus S_i, and $S_j \epsilon [-1.0, +1.0]$.

As mentioned in Section 1, the weights updates $\Delta W_{j,i}$ are operated as the injection on the synaptic weight capacitors of a charge proportional to the weight update signal value [1-4, 11] for a learning time τ_1. Usually this operation is controlled by a switch (one per synapse). The weight update rule for a by pattern example presentation approach [5] can be expressed for the generic i^{th} synapses of the jth neuron as:

$$\Delta W_{j,i} = \eta \delta_j S_i \tag{2}$$

where $\Delta W_{j,i}$ is the weight update values , η is the learning rate, δ_j is the back propagated error term and S_i is the synaptic input. The parameter η summarises a set of circuit parameters (transconductance, time duration, capacitance, etc.) in a sort of backward gain [8].

According to the classical formulation of the BP algorithm [5], the signal δ_j does not change during the weight update operation; so the weight capacitors control switches have to be opened before a new example presentation could cause any change in δ_j. The duration τ_l has to be large enough to perform the update of the weight control voltage, but sufficiently small to avoid that the new weights updates generate a change in signals δ_j. This formulation implies that τ_l should be smaller than the feed forward plus back ward propagation delay.

In this perspective, the analog implementation is a direct mapping of the neural architecture onto a network of analog circuits: the trajectory in the weight space is followed through steps of finite value. We define this learning approach as a by step learning.

3 Continuous Time Back Propagation (CTBP) learning

In this Section we briefly explain the CTBP learning algorithm [10]; the rationale behind of CTBP is to consider Eq. (2) in a continuous formulation. In the following we suppose all the dynamics of the network concentrated in the synaptic weight storage units (i.e. weight capacitors). Considering an example presentation approach like the by pattern one and all the neural computation continuous in time; we can define the instantaneous square error cost function as:

$$C(t) = \sum_{k=1}^{N_o} [T_k(t) - S_k(t)]^2 \tag{3}$$

where N_o is the network outputs number, $T_k(t)$ and $S_k(t)$ are the target and the output signals of the kth neuron of the output layer at time t. The mean total squared error can be defined as [10]:

$$\varepsilon = E\left\{\int_0^{\infty} C(t)dt\right\} \tag{4}$$

where $E\{\}$ is the expectation operator. To minimise ε, the weights must be adapt in the direction of the negative gradients, thus the update rule is:

$$\frac{dW_{j,i}}{dt} = -\eta_c \frac{d\varepsilon}{dW_{j,i}} \tag{5}$$

where η_c can be defined as the continuous time learning rate. It has been demonstrated [10] that the update rule can be written as:

$$\frac{dW_{j,i}}{dt} = \eta_c \delta_j(t) S_i(t) \tag{6}$$

where $\delta_j(t)$ is the instantaneous back propagated errors term [5]. For the output layer we can write:

$$\delta_k(t) = 2\left[T_k(t) - S_k(t)\right]\left[1 - S_k^2(t)\right] \tag{7}$$

while for the hidden layers we can write:

$$\delta_j(t) = \left[\sum_{k=1}^{N_o} \delta_k W_{k,j}(t)\right]\left[1 - S_j^2(t)\right] \tag{8}$$

Given a MLP network with M synapses (and consequently M weights) and one pattern-target example, a set of M equations in the form of Eq. (6) can be written (one per synapse). The obtained equations described the trajectory of the network state in the weight space for the considered example. After the learning transient has expired , the weights signals reach a steady condition, which means that learning has been achieved for that example [6]. We can define with T_t the learning time constant: its value depend on the time constants related to the synaptic weight storage units.

We can refer to the learning occurring when a single pattern-target example is give to the network for a time duration τ as a learning phase. Iterating the examples presentation through the training set (e.g. in random order) implies to move through successive learning phases: this leads to the stochastic minimisation of the error ε, thus achieving the learning for the whole training set.

4 Analysis of the network learning: stability of the NOT network

To evaluate the stability of the network (and consequently of the learning process) through successive learning phases, let us consider first a simple network made of one synapse connected to one neuron, trained to learn the NOT logic function: $S_0(t)$ is the input signal, $S_1(t)$ is the output signal, $T_1(t)$ is the target signal, and $W(t)$ is the weight control signal.

To exemplify, let us assume that $S_0(t)$ and $T_1(t)$ are periodic with period 2τ with a 50% of duty cycle. Combining the feed-forward and the learning rule, we obtain a differential equation that describes the behaviour of the network (the time dependencies are omitted for the sake of simplicity):

$$\dot{W} + 2\eta_c S_0 \tanh(W \cdot S_0) - 2\eta_c S_0 \tanh(W \cdot S_0)^3 + \\ +2\eta_c S_0 T_1 \tanh(W \cdot S_0)^2 = 2\eta_c S_0 T_1 \tag{9}$$

The network has only one weight signal $W(t)$ thus Eq. (9) is a first order differential equation. In general, for a continuous time MLP network with N weight signals, the behaviour of the network is described by a system of N first order differential equations.

It is worth noting that, despite the network is small and the problem is simple, Eq. (9) is stiff. Anyway, some stability considerations can be made.

To analyse the stability of the network behaviour (the solution of Eq. (9)) we study the linearised homogeneous equation [9]:

$$\dot{W} + 2\eta_c S_0^2 W = 0 \tag{10}$$

Eq. (10) is a first order linear differential equation with variable coefficients (S_0 is a time function), whose solution is:

$$W(t) = W(0)e^{\left\{-2\eta_c \int_0^t S_0^2(\nu)d\nu\right\}} \tag{11}$$

where $W(0)$ is the value of the weight signal at time $t = 0$.

Since $| S_0(t) | \leq 1 \; \forall t$, the solution of Eq. (11) is asymptotically stable, as well as the solution of Eq. (9) [9].

5 Some consideration for larger networks

Let us consider now a MLP network with more that one synapse: the learning equations become very stiff and the stability analysis is consequently very complex; anyway, some heuristic considerations can be made.

Let us suppose to give to the network a pattern-target example for a generic time τ

- If $\tau \ll T_t$ (the learning time constant, see Section 3) we can suppose that the input/output signals corresponding to the presentation of a pattern-target example, are changed before the weights updates signals generate meaningful changes on the back propagated error signals. In such case the learning phase looks like a step, and the training process becomes similar to the by step learning described in Section 2.
- If $\tau \gg T_t$ the learning phase occurs for a time longer with respect to the learning time constant, thus the process becomes similar to a by pattern iterate learning. In this case the performance obtained during the learning process could be not so satisfactory, because this kind of learning often leads to instabilities.

In order to prevent instability of the learning process described so far (intended as the sequence of learning phases), the time duration τ can be modulated during the process itself, from a long interval (corresponding to a by pattern iterate example presentation) to a very short one (corresponding to a by pattern example presentation), optimising in this way the network training for a given applicative problem. For example, the training process can begin with $\tau = 5T_t$, and then have the presentation time reduced (e.g. linearly) during learning until $\tau = T_t/10$.

6 Circuit simulation results

In this Section, we present the results of the circuit simulation obtained by high level modelling the neural primitives by using HSPICE. We train an MLP network to learn the following function:

$$\begin{aligned} &if\ (x^2 + y^2 < 0.64) \\ &\qquad output = +1.0 \\ &\quad else \\ &\qquad output = -1.0 \end{aligned} \tag{12}$$

where x and y represents the coordinates of the bidimentional input space: their ranges is $[-1.0, +1.0]$. We refer to this train problem as the circle problem. The MLP network considered has 2 input (x and x), 8 hidden neurons, and one output neuron. The input space has been sampled with a step equal to 0.1: the overall number of pattern-target examples are 441. These examples has been given to the network for a time τ: this duration has been decreased during the training operations from $500ns$ to $50ns$. The continuous time learning rate has been set to $10^6 s^{-1}$, and we let the learning operations for $5ms$. In Fig. 1 the behaviour of some weight control voltages are shown. With the weight configuration obtained after 5ms of training, we verify the approximation performed by the neural network of the target function described by Eq. (12). Such approximation is shown in Fig. 2: the obtained results can be considered good, compared to those reported in [5].

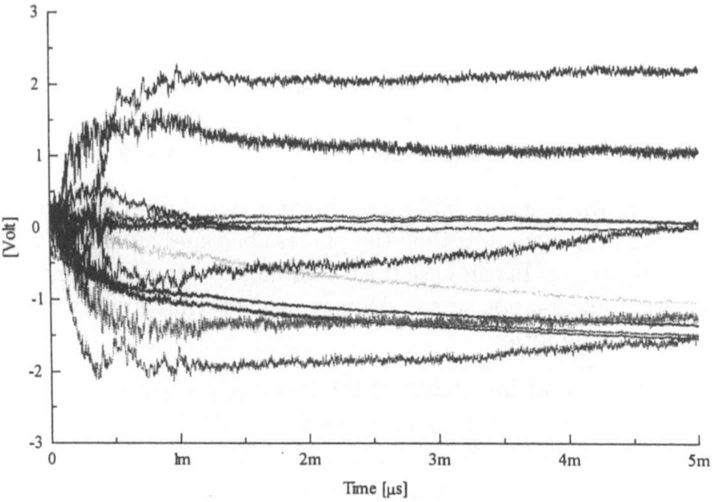

Figure 1: Behaviour of some weight control voltages for the circle problem.

7 Conclusion

In this paper we have discussed a Back Propagation learning algorithm called Continuous Time Back Propagation (CTBP), for the training of MLP networks. The CTBP algorithm is well suited for analog VLSI implementations of neural networks with on-chip BP learning: all the feed forward operations as well as the weights updates operations are performed in continuous time. With respect to the analog implementations of neural networks with on-chip learning presented in the literature [1-4], the switches necessary to perform weights updates operations (whose charge injections effects deteriorate the learning behaviour [11]) are not used during the training process.

Stability considerations, related to the continuous time training, has been done and a technique to prevent instability in the by pattern iterate learning behaviour has been discussed. To validate the algorithm, the result of a circuit simulation, obtained by high level modelling the neural primitives, has been reported and discussed: such result confirm the goodness of the continuous learning algorithm.

Future work consist of the study of the effects of the real dynamics of the neural primitives on the continuous time learning behaviour, and the design and fabrication of a test chip for its experimental validation.

References

[1] M. Valle, D. D. Caviglia, and G. M. Bisio. An Analog VLSI Neural Network with On-Chip Back Propagation Learning. Analog Integrated Circuits and Signal Processing, Kluwer Academic Publishers, Vol. 9, pp. 25- 40, 1996.

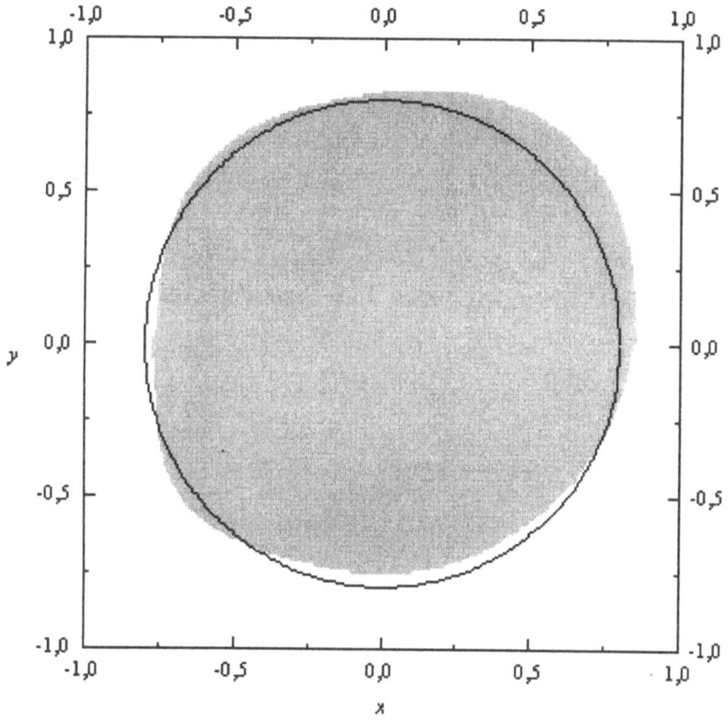

Figure 2: Graphical representation of the output of the neural network trained to learn the circle problem.

[2] T. Lehmann, and E. Brunn. Analog VLSI Implementation of Back- Propagation Learning in Artificial Neural Networks. Proc. of ECCTD93, Vol. 1, pp. 491-496, 1993.

[3] B. Furman, J. White, and A. A. Abidi. CMOS Analog IC Implementing the Back Propagation Algorithm. Neural Networks, Vol. 1, supl. 1, pp. 381, 1988.

[4] J. Cho, Y. K. Choi, and S. Y. Lee. Modular Analog Neuro Chip-Set with On-Chip Learning by Error-Back-Propagation and/or Hebbian Rules. Proc. of ICANN94, Vol. 3, pp. 1343-1346, 1994.

[5] R. P. Lippmann. An introduction to Computing with Neural Nets. IEEE ASSP Magazine, pp. 4-22, 1987.

[6] A. J. Owens, and D. L. Filkin. Efficient Training of the Back Propagation Network by Solving Systems of Stiff Ordinary Differential Equations. IJCNN, Vol. 2, pp. 381-386, 1989.

[7] G. Weigmann, E. A Vittoz, and F. Rahali. Charge Injection in Analog MOS Switches. IEEE Journal of Solid State Circuits, Vol. 22, No. 6, pp. 1091- 1097, 1987.

[8] H. Chiblé, M. Valle, G. M. Bo, and D. D. Caviglia. Evaluation of the Back- Propagation Analog Hardware Implementation. DIBE, Internal Report No. 19/96.

[9] D. A. Sanchez. Ordinary Differential Equations and Stability Theory: an Introduction. Dover Publications, Inc., New York, 1979.

[10] S. P. Day, and M. Davenport. Continuous-Time Temporal Back- Propagation with Adaptable Time Delays. IEEE Transactions on Neural Networks, Vol. 4, No. 2, 1993.

[11] A. J. Annema. Feed-Forward Neural Networks. Kluwer Academic Publishers, 1995.

EM Algorithm: A Neural Network View

Alessandra Budillon
Dipartimento di Ingegneria Elettronica, Università di Napoli Federico II
Via Claudio 21 I-80125 Napoli, Italy
budillon@diesun.die.unina.it

Massimo Corrente
Dipartimento di Ingegneria Elettronica, Università di Napoli Federico II
Via Claudio 21 I-80125 Napoli, Italy

Francesco Palmieri
Dipartimento di Ingegneria Elettronica, Università di Napoli Federico II
Via Claudio 21 I-80125 Napoli, Italy
Fax : 39-81-7683149 palmieri@nadis.dis.unina.it

Abstract

We show how to build accurately a continuous-time recurrent neural network architecture that implements the discriminating functions for a gaussian mixture. The network structure is obtained in batch after the distribution parameters have been estimated using the EM algorithm. Simulations show that the neural network at steady state is capable of being an accurate estimator for the posterior probabilities.

1 Introduction

A clustering problem consists in finding natural groupings in a set of data. It can be used for data encoding and compression. It has also applications to function approximation, image processing, statistical analysis and combinatorial optimization. We focus on an unsupervised learning approach where the classes must be found by the network itself from unlabelled input data. We search for a neural network with units and connections that display some degree of self-organization. Most of the work on self-organizing systems, especially within the neural network literature, has focused on competitive learning and feature mapping (Kohonen, 1990). In the networks based on competitive learning, the output neurons compete among themselves to be activated or fired, with the result that only one output neuron, or one neuron per group, is active at any time. Competition among the output neurons is based on the use of lateral inhibitory connections. Feature mapping is distinguished by the development through learning of significant spacial organization in the output layer. In the "Kohonen map" (1990), for example, the neurons are placed in a line or a plane and become selectively tuned to various input patterns. The locations of the winning output units convey information about nearby input patterns. In this case the effect of lateral feedback is emulated by a neighborhood function, a "Mexican hat" function, that produces excitatory or inhibitory effects, depending on the distance from the neuron. If we model the observed data as a gaussian mixture model, finding the clusters could be treated as a maximum likelihood problem. In the neural network literature and in the statistical pattern recognition literature, an iterative approach to maximum likelihood parameter estimation, the Expectation-Maximization (EM) algorithm, has become increasingly popular. The EM method has been found in most instances (Dempster et al., 1977; Redner and Walker, 1984; Jordan and Jacobs, 1994) to have reliable global convergence, low cost per iteration, economy of storage and ease of programming.

In this paper we try to answer this question : can we use a model similar to Kohonen network to derive a self-organizing architecture that implements the discriminating functions corresponding to a gaussian mixture ? In other words is it possible to learn with a self-organizing network the same statistical model learnt by the EM algorithm ? We answer to the question affirmatively showing how to derive a continuous-time neural network, composed by a set of standard sigmoidal units with lateral connections, capable of emulating the soft classifier emerging from modelling the data as a gaussian mixture. The main interest in this structure is to clarify the actual potential of a neural network to solve a given statistical model and to provide a solution directly realizable in analog hardware. Note that even though a CMOS implementation of the softmax function has been proposed (Waugh and Westervelt, 1993) the architecture described here is based on classical neurons with linear synapses and sigmoids.

2 The gaussian mixture and the EM algorithm

Assume a mixture model with N multivariate Gaussian components :

$$p(\mathbf{x}/\mathbf{\Phi}) = \sum_{j=1}^{N} \pi_j p_j(\mathbf{x}/\mathbf{\Phi}_j), \tag{1}$$

where $\mathbf{x} \in R^n$ is the observation space, $\mathbf{\Phi} = (\pi_1, \ldots, \pi_N, \mathbf{\Phi}_1, \ldots, \mathbf{\Phi}_N)$ a set of parameters, and

$$p_j(\mathbf{x}/\mathbf{\Phi}_j) = \frac{1}{(2\pi)^{n/2} \mid \mathbf{\Sigma}_j \mid^{1/2}} exp[-\frac{1}{2}(\mathbf{x} - \boldsymbol{\mu}_j)^T \mathbf{\Sigma}_j^{-1} (\mathbf{x} - \boldsymbol{\mu}_j)]. \tag{2}$$

According to this model from a set of observed data $\{\mathbf{x}_k\}_{k=1,\ldots,M}$ the EM algorithm (Dempster et al., 1977) can be used to find the set of parameters $\mathbf{\Phi}$, in this case $\mathbf{\Phi}_j = (\mu_j, \mathbf{\Sigma}_j)$. The EM algorithm is an iterative approach to maximum likelihood estimation and it is based on the idea of augmenting the original observed variables with a set of additional "hidden" variables, in such a way that the resulting "complete-data log likelihood" is easy to maximize. The algorithm is composed of two steps : an Expectation (E) step, that finds the expcted value of the complete-data log likelihood, given the observed data and the current model and a Maximization (M) step, that maximizes this function

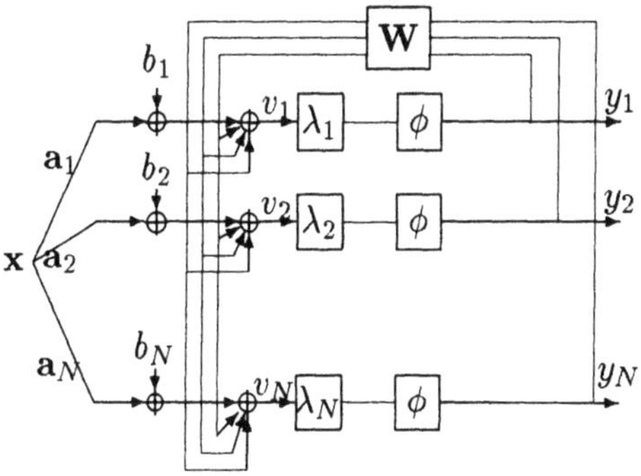

Figure 1: The Neural Network

to find a new parameter estimate. The mixture density estimation problem can be interpreted as an incomplete data problem, where the "hidden" variables are the labels indicating the class of the data.

For a given $(\pi_j^{(p)}, \boldsymbol{\mu}_j^{(p)}, \boldsymbol{\Sigma}_j^{(p)})$, the update $(\pi_j^{(p+1)}, \boldsymbol{\mu}_j^{(p+1)}, \boldsymbol{\Sigma}_j^{(p+1)})$ is given by

$$\pi_j{}^{(p+1)} = \frac{1}{M} \sum_{k=1}^{M} p(j/\mathbf{x}_k, \boldsymbol{\mu}^{(p)}, \boldsymbol{\Sigma}^{(p)}), \tag{3}$$

$$\boldsymbol{\mu}_j{}^{(p+1)} = \frac{\sum_{k=1}^{M} p(j/\mathbf{x}_k, \boldsymbol{\mu}^{(p)}, \boldsymbol{\Sigma}^{(p)})\mathbf{x}_k}{\sum_{k=1}^{M} p(j/\mathbf{x}_k, \boldsymbol{\mu}^{(p)}, \boldsymbol{\Sigma}^{(p)})}, \tag{4}$$

$$\boldsymbol{\Sigma}_j{}^{(p+1)} = \frac{\sum_{k=1}^{M} p(j/\mathbf{x}_k, \boldsymbol{\mu}^{(p)}, \boldsymbol{\Sigma}^{(p)})(\mathbf{x}_k - \boldsymbol{\mu}_j{}^{(p)})(\mathbf{x}_k - \boldsymbol{\mu}_j{}^{(p)})^T}{\sum_{k=1}^{M} p(j/\mathbf{x}_k, \boldsymbol{\mu}^{(p)}, \boldsymbol{\Sigma}^{(p)})}, \tag{5}$$

where $\boldsymbol{\mu} = (\boldsymbol{\mu}_1, \ldots, \boldsymbol{\mu}_N)$ and $\boldsymbol{\Sigma} = (\boldsymbol{\Sigma}_1, \ldots, \boldsymbol{\Sigma}_N)$. The posterior probability that $\mathbf{x}_k$ originated from the jth class for $j = 1, \ldots, N$ can be written as

$$p(j/\mathbf{x}_k, \boldsymbol{\mu}, \boldsymbol{\Sigma}) = \frac{\pi_j p_j(\mathbf{x}_k/\boldsymbol{\mu}_j, \boldsymbol{\Sigma}_j)}{p(\mathbf{x}_k/\boldsymbol{\mu}, \boldsymbol{\Sigma})} = \frac{exp(\xi_j)}{\sum_{i=1}^{N} exp(\xi_i)}, \tag{6}$$

where $\xi_j = -\frac{1}{2}(\mathbf{x}_k - \boldsymbol{\mu}_j)^T \boldsymbol{\Sigma}_j^{-1}(\mathbf{x}_k - \boldsymbol{\mu}_j) - \frac{1}{2}ln \mid \boldsymbol{\Sigma}_j \mid + ln\pi_j$, we note that $p(j/\mathbf{x}_k, \boldsymbol{\mu}, \boldsymbol{\Sigma}) = softmax(\xi_j)$.

3 A neural network architecture for the gaussian mixture

Consider now a continuous-time neural network with a single layer of output units. We associate one output cell to every class. Each unit is connected with the others and has a self connection, as shown in Fig. 1, with a standard logistic sigmoidal function $\phi(v) = \frac{1}{1+exp(-v)}$. The feedforward part is characterized by the weight vectors $\mathbf{a_i} \in R^n$ and the biases $b_i \in R$, the feedback part by the

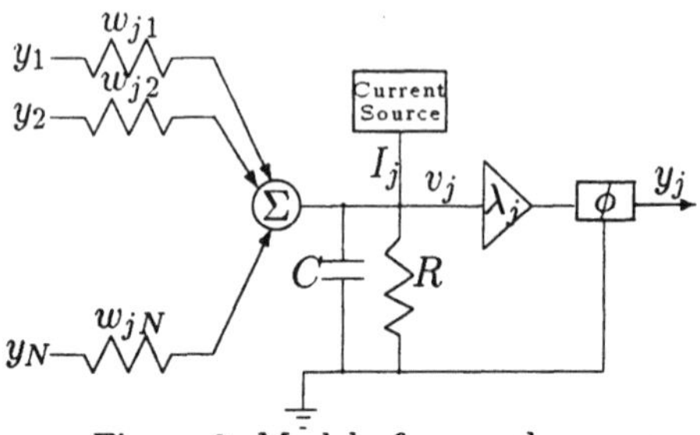

Figure 2: Model of an analog neuron

$N \times N$ matrix $\mathbf{W} = [w_{ij}]$. Each input to the sigmoidal function is scaled by a parameter $\{\lambda_i\}_{i=1,\dots,M}$ that controls the steepness of the sigmoid. We indicate with $\mathbf{\Lambda}$ the diagonal matrix containing the slope parameters λ_i, with $\mathbf{A}$ the $N \times n$ matrix of the weigths $\mathbf{a}_i^T$ and with $\mathbf{b}$ the vector of the constant biases b_i. We assume the model (1) for the data $\mathbf{x} \in R^n$, with $\mathbf{\Sigma}_i = \sigma^2\mathbf{I}$. This is a requirement of this architecture since the first network layer gives $\mathbf{Ax}+\mathbf{b}$ which is an affine trasformation that would not constitute a sufficient statistic for a more general case. The dynamics of the network is defined by the following system of coupled first-order differential equations :

$$\frac{dv_j}{dt} = -v_j(t) + \sum_{i=1}^{N} w_{ji}\phi(\lambda_i v_i(t)) + I_j \qquad j = 1,\dots,N. \tag{7}$$

This comes from the classical model of an analog neuron shown in Fig.2, after a normalization with respect to R and C, with $I_j = \mathbf{a}_j^T\mathbf{x} + b_j$ and $y_j = \phi(\lambda_j v_j(t))$. We desire to obtain a dynamic system that implements at steady state the discriminating functions $p(j/\mathbf{x})_{j=1,\dots,N}$, i.e. for $j = 1,\dots,N$

$$\lim_{t\to\infty} y_j(t) = y_{sj} = p(j/\mathbf{x}) = \frac{exp(\xi_j)}{\sum_{i=1}^{N} exp(\xi_i)}, \tag{8}$$

where $\xi_j = \frac{\boldsymbol{\mu}_j^T\mathbf{x}}{\sigma^2} - \frac{\boldsymbol{\mu}_j^T\boldsymbol{\mu}_j}{2\sigma^2} + ln\pi_j$.

Indicating with $\mathbf{y}_s(\mathbf{x})$ the steady state output vector we have $\forall\mathbf{x}$

$$\mathbf{y}_s(\mathbf{x}) = \phi(\mathbf{\Lambda}(\mathbf{Ax} + \mathbf{b} + \mathbf{W}\mathbf{y}_s(\mathbf{x}))). \tag{9}$$

The question is now how to associate to these values the mixture parameters, ideally we would like, for $j = 1,\dots,N$

$$\frac{exp(\xi_j)}{\sum_{i=1}^{N} exp(\xi_i)} = \phi\left(\lambda_j\left(a_j^T\mathbf{x} + b_j + \frac{\sum_{i=1}^{N} w_{ji}exp(\xi_i)}{\sum_{i=1}^{N} exp(\xi_i)}\right)\right).$$

We have found an approximate solution to this equality by trial and error on various simplifications. Let us assume first that the matrix $\mathbf{W}$ is an extremely simple one and has all its elements equal to -1. This induces competition and it is symmetric (we know that in these conditions the network is stable (Marcus and Westervelt, 1989)). We have

$$\mathbf{W} = -\mathbf{e}_N \mathbf{e}_N^T, \tag{10}$$

with $\mathbf{e}_N = [1, \ldots, 1]^T$. Inverting the logistic function ϕ we have :

$$\xi_j - ln \left(\sum_{i=1}^{N} exp(\xi_i) - exp(\xi_j) \right) = \lambda_j (\mathbf{a}_j^T \mathbf{x} + b_j - 1).$$

Suppose now that we ignore totally the ln term, we should have

$$\xi_j \simeq \lambda_j \mathbf{a}_j^T \mathbf{x} + \lambda_j b_j - \lambda_j.$$

To satisfy this relation we choose for the weigths the following values :

$$\mathbf{a}_j = \boldsymbol{\mu}_j \; ; \; b_j = 1 - \boldsymbol{\mu}_j^T \boldsymbol{\mu}_j / 2 + \sigma^2 ln\pi_j \; ; \; \lambda_j = 1/\sigma^2 \quad \forall j \in (1, \ldots, N). \tag{11}$$

It is somewhat remarkable that by using approximation (10) for the matrix $\mathbf{W}$ and values (11) for the feedforward weights we get already a reasonable approximations. Fig. 3a shows, with the solid line, the steady state outputs of the neural network as functions of the inputs, obtained on a synthetic mixture of five one-dimensional normal distribuitions and the posterior probabilities of the assumed model, with the dotted line. The parameters of the mixture have been estimated in batch using the EM algorithm. In the simulations $\mathbf{x} \in [0, 1]$, $\boldsymbol{\mu} = (0.01, 0.25, 0.4, 0.7, 0.9)$ and $\sigma^2 = 0.01$. To improve the results and to try to understand more about the matrix of the lateral weights, we have used the pseudo-inverse method for getting a better matrix $\mathbf{W}$. By indicating with $\mathbf{Y}_s$ the $N \times M$ matrix containing M desired outputs, i.e. $\mathbf{Y}_s = [\mathbf{y}_s(1), \ldots, \mathbf{y}_s(M)]$, and $\mathbf{X}$ the $n \times M$ matrix containing the corresponding samples, i.e. $\mathbf{X} = [\mathbf{x}(1), \ldots, \mathbf{x}(M)]$, we want to have

$$\mathbf{Y}_s = \phi(\boldsymbol{\Lambda}(\mathbf{AX} + \mathbf{b}\mathbf{e}_M^T + \mathbf{W}\mathbf{Y}_s), \tag{12}$$

with $\mathbf{e}_M = (1, \ldots, 1)^T$.

Using the pseudo-inverse method, we find the $\mathbf{W}$ matrix :

$$\mathbf{W} = (\boldsymbol{\Lambda}^{-1} \phi^{-1}(\mathbf{Y}_s) - \mathbf{AX} - \mathbf{b}\mathbf{e}_M^T)\mathbf{Y}_s^T(\mathbf{Y}_s\mathbf{Y}_s^T)^{-1}. \tag{13}$$

Note in Fig. 3b the almost perfect agreement between the neural network output, with the lateral weigths evaluated using (13) and the desired discriminating function of the statistical model. We have repeated similar experiments in two and more dimensions obtaining excellent results.

Table 1 shows the lateral weights evaluated with the pseudo-inverse method and corresponding to the parameters involved in the simulations. Note how the lateral weights tend to be negative and around the value -1. It is interesting as this result confirms the inhibitory nature of the lateral connections and our intuition that has caused choises (11). The particular characteristic of the matrix $\mathbf{W}$, that appears to show equal rows, has encouraged us to derive

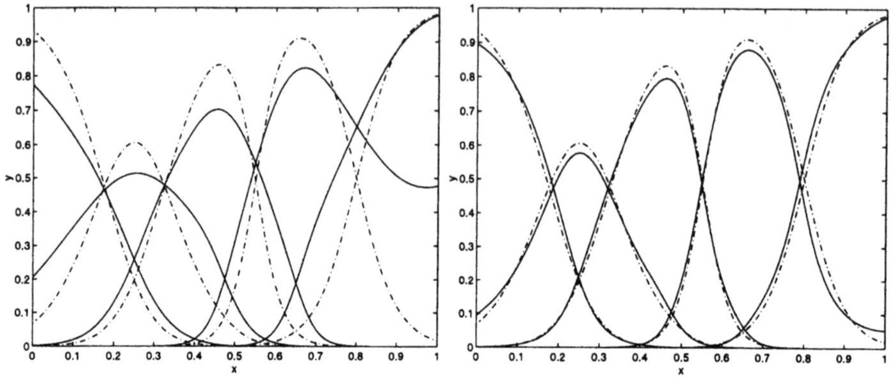

Figure 3: Discriminating functions and network outputs, using for $\mathbf{W}$ respectively approximations a) (10) and b) (13)

$W =$	−0.9754	−1.0321	−1.1015	−1.2040	−1.4539
	−0.9996	−1.0112	−1.1038	−1.2037	−1.4540
	−0.9980	−1.0293	−1.0839	−1.2047	−1.4537
	−0.9992	−1.0247	−1.1050	−1.1820	−1.4560
	−0.9986	−1.0269	−1.1020	−1.2074	−1.4258

Table 1: Matrix $\mathbf{W}$ evaluated using approximation (13)

an approximate expression for it depending in a single way from the mixture parameters. Let's assume the same values (11) for the feedforward weights and the following structure for the matrix of the lateral weights : $\mathbf{W} = \mathbf{e}_N \boldsymbol{\gamma}^T$ with $\boldsymbol{\gamma} = [\gamma_1, \ldots, \gamma_N]^T$, i.e. the ith column has all the elements equal to γ_i. Substituting in (9), results for $j = 1, \ldots, N$

$$\frac{exp(\xi_j)}{\sum_{i=1}^{N} exp(\xi_i)} = \phi\left(\frac{\boldsymbol{\mu}_j^T \mathbf{x}}{\sigma^2} + \frac{1}{\sigma^2} - \frac{\boldsymbol{\mu}_j^T \boldsymbol{\mu}_j}{2\sigma^2} + ln\pi_j + \frac{1}{\sigma^2}\frac{\sum_{i=1}^{N} \gamma_i exp(\xi_i)}{\sum_{i=1}^{N} exp(\xi_i)}\right).$$

Inverting the logistic function ϕ and reducing the same terms we obtain

$$-ln\left(\sum_{i=1}^{N} exp(\xi_i) - exp(\xi_j)\right) = \frac{1}{\sigma^2} + \frac{1}{\sigma^2}\frac{\sum_{i=1}^{N} \gamma_i exp(\xi_i)}{\sum_{i=1}^{N} exp(\xi_i)}.$$

By the following approximations :

$$ln\left(\sum_{i=1}^{N} exp(\xi_i) - exp(\xi_j)\right) \simeq ln\left(\sum_{i=1}^{N} exp(\xi_i)\right) \simeq ln(exp(\overline{\xi}_l)),$$

where $\overline{\xi}_l = (\xi_l)_{\mathbf{x}=\boldsymbol{\mu}_l}$, we find :

$$\gamma_l \simeq -1 - \frac{\boldsymbol{\mu}_l^T \boldsymbol{\mu}_l}{2} - \sigma^2 ln\pi_l. \tag{14}$$

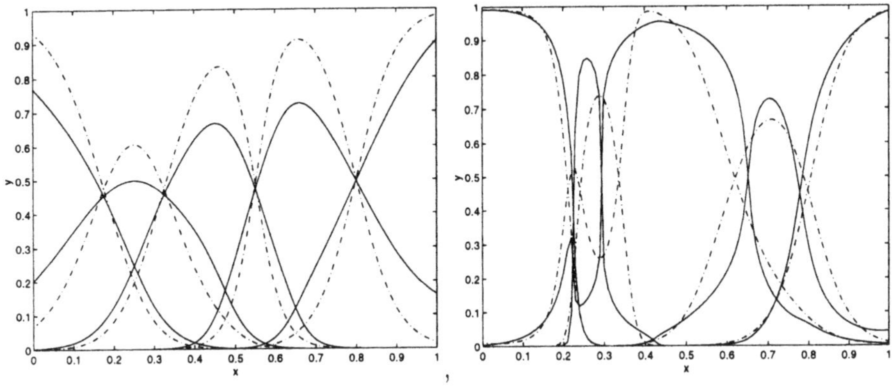

Figure 4: Discriminating functions and network outputs, using for **W** respectively approximations a) (14) and b) (13) but in this case $\mathbf{\Sigma}_i = \sigma_i^2 \mathbf{I}$

$$W = \begin{bmatrix} -1.0050 & -1.0312 & -1.0800 & -1.2450 & -1.4050 \\ -1.0050 & -1.0312 & -1.0800 & -1.2450 & -1.4050 \\ -1.0050 & -1.0312 & -1.0800 & -1.2450 & -1.4050 \\ -1.0050 & -1.0312 & -1.0800 & -1.2450 & -1.4050 \\ -1.0050 & -1.0312 & -1.0800 & -1.2450 & -1.4050 \end{bmatrix}$$

Table 2: Matrix **W** evaluated using approximation (14)

We have substituted the sum on $i \neq j$ with the sum on i and then it with the most significative term , which corresponds to the lth if the mean $\boldsymbol{\mu}_l$ is the closest to $\mathbf{x}$, then we have approximated $\mathbf{x}$ with the mean $\boldsymbol{\mu}_l$.

Comparing Fig.3a and Fig.4a reveals the improvement we obtained in the case of approximation (14) about **W** with respect to assumption (10). Comparing Table 1 and Table 2 shows how close are the values of **W** that we found using approximations, respectively, (13) and (14). Even if the statistics $\mathbf{a}_i^T \mathbf{x} + b_i$ are not sufficient for a gaussian mixture with $\mathbf{\Sigma}_i = \sigma_i^2 \mathbf{I}$, we got acceptable approximations using values (11) but with $\lambda_i = 1/\sigma_i^2$ and approximation (13) for **W**. Fig.4b shows the network outputs, as usually with the solid line, and the desired outputs, with the dotted line. Fig.5 shows the dynamics of the network, i.e. for a fixed input the behaviour of four outputs that after some possible oscillations converge to the desired steady state. We would like to emphasize that the key feature of the neural network is the continuous nature of its dynamics. Using the discrete version we found that it was very difficult to control the steady state behaviour. In fact in the simulations when we used a discrete-time version of the continuous equation (7) we had to use a very small stepsize for approximating the derivative with a finite difference. The order or magnitude of the stepsize has to be comparable to the inverse of the steepness parameter for the sigmoidal functions. We are currently working on extending the result to more general statistical models and on deriving a stochastic version of the

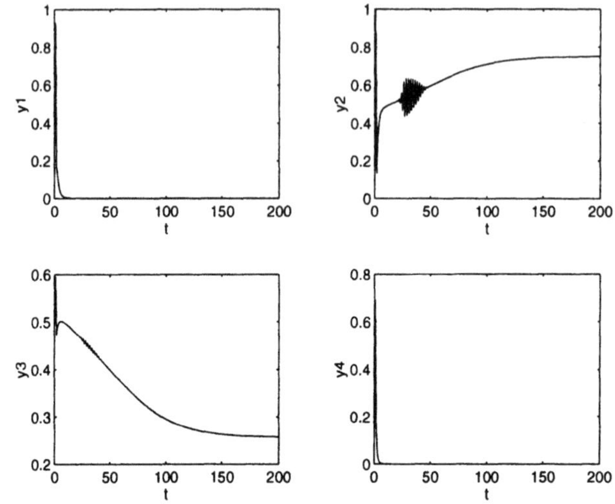

Figure 5: Network outputs during the dynamics

learning algorithm that can be directly implemented in continuous time hardware. Also the stability of the system has to be more rigorously estabilished because theoretical results are mainly referred to symmetric **W** (Marcus and Westervelt, 1989).

REFERENCES

Dempster, A. P., Laird, N. M., and Rubin, D. B. (1977). "Maximum likelihood from incomplete data via the EM algorithm". *Jornal of the Royal Statistical Society*, B39, pp. 1-38.

Jordan, M. I., Jacobs, R.A. (1994). "Hierarchical mixtures of experts and the EM algorithm". *Neural Computation*, 6, pp. 181-214.

Kohonen, T. (1990). "The self organizing map". *Proceedings of the IEEE*, 78, pp. 1464-1480.

Marcus, M. C., Westervelt, R. M. (1989) "Dynamics of iterated map neural networks". *Physical Review A*, 40, pp. 501-504.

Redner, R. A., and Walker, H. F. (1984). "Mixture densities, maximum likelihood and the EM algorithm". *SIAM Review*, 26, pp. 195-239.

Waugh, F. R., and Westervelt, R. M. (1993). "Analog neural networks with local competition. I. Dynamics and stability". *Physical Review E*, 47, pp. 4524-4536.

HW/SW Co-Design of a Complete Pre-Processing/Recognition System Based on Sgs-Thomson *OCR* Analog Chip

M. Costa, D. Palmisano, E. Pasero, R. Tosco
Department of Electronics – Politecnico di Torino
Corso Duca degli Abruzzi n. 24 – 10129 Torino (I)
E-Mail: costa@polito.it, palmisano@neuronica.polito.it, pasero@polito.it

Abstract

We embodied the fast ST EEPROM-based database filtering circuit currently known as *OCR* chip into a mixed HW/SW OCR system which incorporates data pre-processing without limiting the overall throughput. Those pre-processing operations handling the greatest amount of data are performed in HW by a dedicated digital device that has been first described in VHDL, then simulated and synthesized on a generic technology library using Synopsys tools. The original processing flow has been efficiently re-arranged so that the insertion of this new component allows to: substantially relax the speed requirements of the pre-processing operations not covered by the device; improve the recognition rate; reduce the total number of patterns stored into EEPROM to the extent that a net saving in silicon area results.

1 Introduction

With the support of "Programma Nazionale di Ricerca sulle Tecnologie per la Bioelettronica", joint research efforts have been recently carried out by some Italian industries and universities to set up an accurate and fast handwritten OCR system. After a preliminary selection, the k-NN based classifier proposed by the research group of DEIS – Università di Bologna [1] was chosen as the most promising algorithm because of its accuracy and flexibility. On the other hand, it requires the comparison of every unknown sample with all the ones stored into a labeled database. The computational expense of such comparisons makes unfeasible an entirely SW implementation of the algorithm. The Neural Network research group of ST Central R&D therefore devised a massively parallel EEPROM-based analog circuit [2], currently known as *OCR* chip, that filters the labeled database (i.e. extracts the indexes of the nearest neighbors) at a rate of several thousands unknown samples per second.

2 Present System Implementation

Fig. 1 outlines the structure of the existent OCR system, where the classification of NIST handwritten uppercase letters has been taken as a reference [3]. Starting from a B&W image located somewhere inside a 128*128 window, the SW pre-processing routine produces a 8*8 matrix of 5-bit integers that is passed on to several *OCR* chips. Here about 45000 labeled samples are stored using the same format. Since each chip can accommodate up to 2K such matrices, 22 exemplars are needed. The filtering process selects the indexes of 80 nearest neighbor candidates, which are then further decimated by the SW classifier routine according to a slightly different metrics. Finally an hypothesis about the most likely class is produced together with a confidence measure.

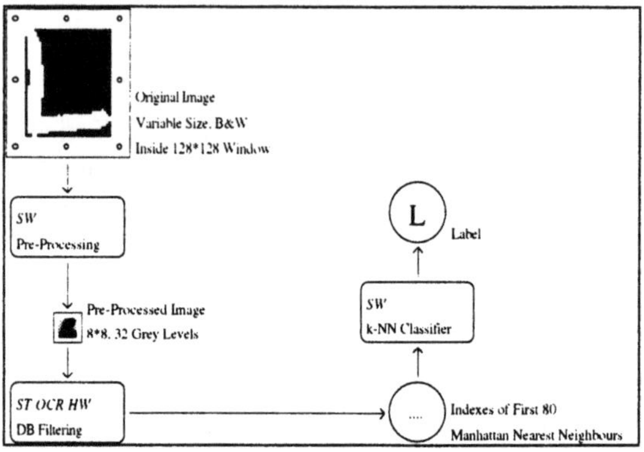

Fig. 1 – Overview of Present OCR System

3 Analysis of Computational Loads

In the following some considerations are summarized about the relative computational loads associated with the main functional blocks to serve as a guideline for possible improvements.

- Pre-Processing: high
  - Requires a limited number of **complex** operations
  - Handles a moderate amount of data
  - On the whole, suited for software implementation
  - Throughput provided by *OCR* chipset is hard to be matched
- Database Filtering: very high
  - Requires a huge number of **very simple** operations
  - Handles a huge amount of data
  - Well suited for dedicated, massively parallel hardware devices ⇒ *OCR* chipset
- Classification: small
  - Requires a moderate number of **very simple** operations
  - Needs the same data processed by the Database Filtering block (so that it must be equipped with a large memory), but handles only a small portion at a time
  - Suited for software implementation on a fast μP, mainly for flexibility issues
  - Throughput provided by *OCR* chipset can be matched without substantial design efforts

From this simple examination it turns out that the pre-processing block constitutes a real challenge for HW designers because of its complexity, but also a bottleneck inside the system if performed via SW. On the other hand, it is the main responsible for the high accuracy attained by the classifier. We therefore explored the feasibility of a mixed HW/SW approach.

4 Pre-Processing Block Partitioning

The pre-processing algorithm developed by the research group of DEIS – Università di Bologna essentially tends to eliminate as much as possible infra-class (i.e. non-informative) variability from the raw samples. Since the main sources of variability are: translation, scale, aspect ratio, slant and stroke width, the original image undergoes a sequence of corresponding normalizations, that is:

- ♦ Bounding Box Detection
- ♦ Size (32*32) & Aspect Ratio (1:1) Normalization
- ♦ De-Slanting
- ♦ Skeletonization

In addition, the skeletonized 32*32 B&W image gets ideally divided into 4*4 adjacent squares. Then for every such square the distance of the upper left corner from the nearest portion of the skeleton is encoded on a 5-bit gray level. Finally these gray levels are stored into the already mentioned 8*8 matrix.

Among the items above, it is certainly worth considering a digital HW implementation of at least the first two ones because of the following reasons:

1) they are preliminary to almost all the pre-processing algorithms conceived for template-based recognition systems (including artificial neural networks) of binary images;

2) they can be parallelized to a desired extent in a straightforward way;

3) they lead to a substantial reduction in the number of pixels to be processed: from 128*128 to only 32*32. Whatever subsequent operations handling such a smaller amount of data are likely to be performed via SW with a far lower efficiency loss.

Following these guidelines, the pre-processing block partitioning scheme we propose is outlined in fig. 2: bounding box detection plus size & aspect ratio normalization set up stage I and are covered by the dedicated digital HW design described later, while the remaining operations have been left in SW and put together into stage II.

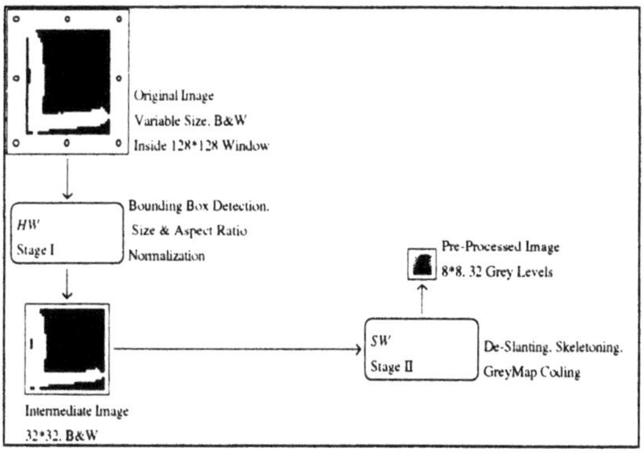

Fig. 2 – Pre-Processing Block Partitioning Scheme

5 HW Implementation of Stage I: the *Y-X-Zoom* Chip

The central idea underlying the operation of our circuit is very simple: the computational complexity of a bi-dimensional transformation performed on a N*N object may be decreased from order N^2 to order N if such transformation can be expressed (at least with a good approximation) as the product of two successive mono-dimensional ones. This property holds for stage I taken as a whole: therefore, *Y-X-Zoom* first performs both borders detection and size normalization in the vertical (*Y*) dimension, and then repeats the very same operations on the horizontal (*X*) one. As a result, aspect ratio gets normalized as well. Moreover, being the *Y* and *X* blocks so similar, they can be easily arranged into an efficient pipelined architecture.

In fig. 3 a practical example is shown that clarifies the main processing steps. Of course, border detection does not really give rise to a new image: only the indexes of the bounding rows/columns are stored.

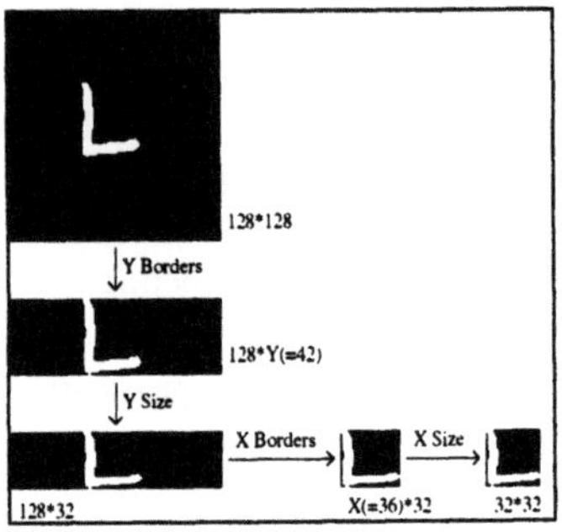

Fig. 3 – Normalization of a 36*42 Uppercase "L" through the *Y-X-Zoom* Procedure

The circuit has been fully described in standard VHDL and then functionally tested using Synopsys VHDLSim. Since we lacked precise interface specifications, it currently communicates with a generic host processor through basic data request/data ready signals controlling the access to the input and output external RAMs. However, the high degree of flexibility peculiar to the VHDL approach will make future customizations easier.

Excluding internal RAMs/ROMs and few library components requiring special licenses (owned by ST), we also synthesized *Y-X-Zoom* using Synopsys default technology library. The following list summarizes the results we obtained without exploiting any advanced optimization directives:

- Area: < 20000 gates
- Internal RAMs/ROMs: ~ 2.5 KB
- Maximum Clock Frequency: > 50 MHz
- Average Processing Speed at 50 MHz: ~ 5000 patterns/s

As it can be seen, the circuit is both small and fast. Moreover, performances can be substantially improved by eliminating some of additional functionalities we initially inserted for research purposes.

6 *Y-X-Zoom* in Action: a New Proposal at the System Level

Although the main computational load associated with pre-processing has been moved to HW, the speed requirements for stage II still remain quite severe. In order to drain the least amount of resources from the host μP, it would be desirable recognizing some unknown samples without invoking stage II at all. Now, if we ideally divide the intermediate 32*32 B&W image produced by stage I into adjacent 4*4 squares and encode the number of "bright" pixels inside every square on 17 gray levels, then the resulting matrix is compatible with the format accepted by the *OCR* chip. Well, such functionality belongs to the additional ones already built into *Y-X-Zoom*.

Of course, it is well known that the original pre-processing algorithm guarantees higher accuracy, or else the problem could be trivially solved. Anyway, we remind that the classifier outputs not only a label, but also a confidence. Therefore, one might set up a hierarchical OCR system that first tries to classify an unknown pattern using only the intermediate (fast) pre-processing. If it is confident about its own hypothesis then stage II is not invoked, otherwise a failed attempt event is said to be occurred (in analogy with the missing datum event of cache memories) and the slow but accurate route is selected to provide the final label.

Fig. 4 outlines the structure of the modified system: the two *OCR* chipsets accommodate differently pre-processed versions of the same labeled database. Problems arising from duplication will be addressed later.

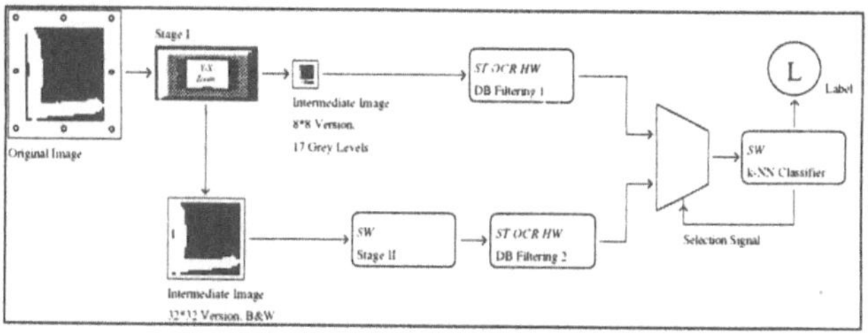

Fig. 4 – Overview of Proposed Hierarchical OCR System

The performances of the modified system in the recognition of handwritten uppercase letters have been compared with those of the original one by measuring the error rate on the standard NIST test database. Since we did not know some details about the specific k-NN classifier actually used (among these the value of k itself), we resorted to a program written by the research group of DEIS – Università di Bologna implementing a simple 1-NN classifier. Therefore only relative performances are relevant in this context. For what concerns the hierarchical OCR, we decided to declare failed an attempt whenever the first two nearest neighbors belong to different classes. The results are briefly summarized in the following list:

- Original OCR System:
  - Error Rate at 0 Rejection: 7.32%
- OCR System with Intermediate Pre-Processing Alone:
  - Error Rate at 0 Rejection: 8.38%
- Hierarchical OCR System:
  - Error Rate at 0 Rejection: 6.32%
  - Percentage of Failed Attempt Events: 9.92%

As it can be seen, even though as expected the intermediate pre-processing alone is less effective than the original one, the hierarchical combination of the two noticeably outperforms both instead of ranking in between. Event more striking is the very low rate of failed attempt events: this implies that, as a first approximation, the system is able to sustain a throughput of – say – 5000 unknown samples per second while including a SW pre-processing routine that might be slower by an order of magnitude.

7 Database Reduction

The unique but severe drawback of the methodology we just illustrated is the need of duplicating the labeled database, so that about 90000 instead of 45000 samples are to be stored. This might not be a huge problem for what concerns the classifier, since the advantages we shown are worth the cost of providing it with about 5.6 MB of RAM instead of the original 2.8 MB. However, also the number of OCR chips has to be doubled, and this of course is unfeasible.
We therefore looked at the chance of reducing the database by means of a refined version of a procedure known in literature as *condensed k-NN* [4]. Without entering into details we only say that, given a classifier (not necessarily a k-NN one), we devised an algorithm that utilizes the classifier itself to select only the least redundant samples. Unlike the original *condensed k-NN*, selectivity can be tuned to a desired degree.
In this way only 12437 + 15007 out of 2*44951 samples have been stored according respectively to the original and intermediate pre-processing. Performances attained by the hierarchical OCR system equipped with the reduced labeled database are summarized as follows:

- Error Rate at 0 Rejection: 6.78%
- Percentage of Failed Attempt Events: 15.9%
- Required Number of *OCR* chips: 15 (7 + 8)

The advantages arising from the proposed architecture are thus evident in every respect. In fact at the same time:

1) accuracy rate gets increased by nearly 0.5%;
2) the time-expensive SW stage II routine becomes a far less limiting factor on the overall throughput;
3) 7 *OCR* chips are saved at the prize of inserting a unique presumably 1 order of magnitude smaller device: the *Y-X-Zoom* chip.

8 Acknowledgments

This work was partly supported by EC Brite-EuRam project n. BE96-3433.

9 References

1. Kovacs ZM, Guerrieri R. *Massively Parallel Hand-Written Character Recognition Based on the Distance Transform.* Pattern Recognition 1995; 28: 293-301
2. Kramer AH, Canegallo R, Chinosi M et al. *55GCPS CAM Using 5b Analog Flash.* In: Proceedings of the IEEE International Solid-State Circuits Conference. San Francisco (CA), 1997, vol 40, pp 44-45
3. Garris MD, Wilkinson RA. *Handwritten Segmented Characters Database.* Tech Rep Special Database 3. National Institute of Standards and Technology, 1992
4. F ukunaga K. *Introduction to Statistical Pattern Recognition.* Academic Press, New York (NY), 1972

Interval Arithmetic Perceptron with pruning capability

Gian Paolo Drago
Istituto per i Circuiti Elettronici - CNR
via De Marini, 6 - 16149 Genova, Italy

Sandro Ridella
DIBE - Universita' di Genova
via Opera Pia, 11A - 16145 Genova, Italy

abstract- An Interval Arithmetic Perceptron (IAP) is a neural network where the usual perceptron topology uses the intervals as numerical representation of internal parameters and output: in this paper we present the learning of such a network and show its performance in weight pruning and in the consequent identification of the importance of input features. The applications to the Iris and the Breast Cancer database are presented and simple and efficient classification rules are obtained. IAP compares favourably with a well-established feature screening method.

keywords- Neural Network Computing, Learning, Interval Arithmetic, Fuzzy sets, Generalisation.

1 Introduction

In this work the use of Interval Arithmetic (IA) for identifying the importance of input features in a Perceptron Neural Network is presented.

An IA Perceptron (IAP) consists of a neural network with a single layer of weigths, each described by an interval rather than a real number, as well as output, which is also represented by an interval, while inputs are handled as real numbers. An interval represents the range of the possible values a variable may assume. The IA is able to identify a box in the weight space, where every point represents an acceptable solution for the problem under analysis [5]. The search for the extremes of the box may be very difficult from the computational point of view, but knowing them is extremely advantageous, since it lets one choose, inside the box, the most favourable solution with regard to additional constrains. Moreover, if the range of one weight comprises the zero value, this weight can be pruned. So, if the constraint consists in the need to prune as much as possible, one must look for a box with the greatest number of weight ranges including the zero value.

Obviously the pruned weights allow the identification of the less important input features. This pruning offers dual advantages: it improves the generalisation capability by lowering the number of learning parameters and consequently the Vapnik-Cervonenkis dimension [7]; and aids the understanding of the classification rule.

2 Interval Arithmetic Perceptron (IAP)

An interval is defined as a couple of real numbers representing the range between an upper and a lower value, which are identified by superscripts U and L [5] [1] In the following intervals and real numbers are represented by uppercase and lowercase variables respectively, so that an interval A is representable as $A = [a^L, a^U]$.

Mathematical operations and definitions we need (addition, product of an interval and a real number, product of two intervals, strictly increasing interval functions) are well known [5] [1].

Coming to the learning algorithm, the feedforward phase (as well as the backward one) is described in details in [5] [4], and it gives the interval perceptron output $Y = [y_p^L, y_p^U] = th(\mathbf{W}\mathbf{x}_p)$, where $\mathbf{W}$ is the interval vector weight and $\mathbf{x}$ is the real input vector. The interval cost function defined as

$$e_p^L = (t_p^L - y_p^L)^2; \quad e_p^U = (t_p^U - y_p^U)^2; \quad e = \sum_{p=1}^{n_p} e_p = \sum_{p=1}^{n_p} (e_p^L + e_p^U) \tag{1}$$

where $[t_p^L, t_p^U]$ is the interval target of the $p-th$ pattern and n_p is the number of training examples.

The weight update procedure follows the usual antigradient with an additional momentum term [4] [5]. The interval gradient, for the p-th pattern, is computed following [5]:

If $w_i^U x_{pi} \geq w_i^L x_{pi}$ then

$$\frac{\partial e_p^L}{\partial w_i^L} = -2(t_p^L - y_p^L)(1 - {y_p^L}^2)x_{pi}; \quad \frac{\partial e_p^U}{\partial w_i^U} = -2(t_p^U - y_p^U)(1 - {y_p^U}^2)x_{pi} \tag{2}$$

If $w_i^U x_{pi} < w_i^L x_{pi}$ then

$$\frac{\partial e_p^U}{\partial w_i^L} = -2(t_p^U - y_p^U)(1 - {y_p^U}^2)x_{pi}; \quad \frac{\partial e_p^L}{\partial w_i^U} = -2(t_p^L - y_p^L)(1 - {y_p^L}^2)x_{pi} \tag{3}$$

where k indexes the number of presentations of the training set; η and α are the learning rate and the momentum respectively.

3 Pruning

The algorithm described in the previous section is able to perform the weight pruning, provided that the interval target of each input pattern is suitably set (eqs. 1). Since we deal with a perceptron topology, the expression "input pruning" is equivalent to the pruning of the weight connected to the considered input. For the patterns belonging to one class we set $t_p^L = -tm_2$, $t_p^U = -tm_1$, while, for the other class, $t_p^L = +tm_1$, $t_p^U = +tm_2$, with $tm_2 \geq tm_1 > 0$. It is plain to see that, if $tm_1 = tm_2$, the algorithm described in section 2 reduces itself to the well-known Backpropagation; however, the interval weights, found through the weight update expressions, naturally lead to real weights instead of interval ones. When $tm_2 > tm_1$, the minimum of the cost function (1) corresponds to interval weights, and it is easy to predict that such weights will be confined within a box whose hypervolume is as larger as the extent to which tm_2 exceeds tm_1. However our specific interest does not lie in maximising the box size: we want to get the maximum number of weight intervals which include the zero value, leading to an equal number of prunable weights. Experience derived from computer simulations described in the following sections, showed us that having excessively large values of the difference $(tm_2 - tm_1)$ is of no use, and that these values depend on the complexity of the problems under analysis. More specifically, we found that for:

a) Iris: class 1 versus class 2 and 3: $tm_1 = .8$, $tm_2 = .9$
b) Iris: class 1 and 2 versus class 3: $tm_1 = .89$, $tm_2 = .9$
c) Breast Cancer: $tm_1 = .85$, $tm_2 = .9$.

As regards the algorithm start, the initial weight intervals have always been chosen with coincident extremes, whose values were produced through the SCAWI initialization technique [2]. The learning algorithm takes advantage of the multistart AMBP [3] tecnique. So the algorithm procedes with the search for the minimum of eq. 1, and, as soon as it finds a weight interval including zero, definitively prunes that weight and procedes to the minimum search. It is possible to perform a statistical analysis related to the priority of pruning for each weight: it is enough to store the position of every weight within the pruning sequence for all the trials done in the cost function minimisation. This analysis makes it possible to estimate the classification of inputs according to their importance: less important inputs are pruned more frequently with higher priority in the pruning sequence. In the following section this information will be used to facilitate the extraction of a rule for the file Breast Cancer. Indeed, it is well known [6] that the pruning of less important inputs is advantageous for a better understanding of the phenomenon under analysis, as well as for the extraction of simple rules describing it and for improving the generalisation capability, with regard to cases extraneous to the training set. On this point, it is important to recall that a reduction in the number of learning parameters leads to a decrease in the Vapnik-Chervonenkis dimension [7]

4 Numerical Examples

Two real-world applications will be considered, whose datasets have been obtained from the UCI repository of machine learning databases (Murphy & Aha databases). Since our interest here is in testing the pruning ability of our algorithm, we do not divide data files into training and test files: in fact, pruning with a larger pattern number is more difficult and it obviously maintains its validity if one reduces this number.

The first real problem is related to the Iris database, which contains three classes of 50 samples each. Here each class refers to a type of Iris plant: Iris setosa (class 1), Iris Versicolor (class 2) and Iris Virginica (class3). The inputs consist of four attributes plus the bias. Precisely: input 0: bias, input 1: sepal length, input 2: sepal width, input 3: petal length, input 4: petal width. All the input data have been normalised within the range $[-1, 1]$. Since our interest in this phase lies in the use of linear separators, we decided to divide the available data into two kinds of tests: the first refers to the separation of the first class (Iris Setosa) from the other two; while the second refers to the separation of class three (Iris Virginica) from the remaining two. Note that the first test deals with linearly separable data, while in the second linear separability is impossible.

In the first test, the IAP algorithm is able to show that two non-zero weights are enough to separate the data linearly. For a perceptron with 4 inputs there are five possible weights (considering the addition of the bias, whose weight is denoted by index 0) and 10 possibilities of pruning 3 weights among 5: 4 of these 10 possibilities satisfy the condition of linear separability of the data with only two non-zero weights. Table 1 shows these combinations (weights are numbered as the related inputs).

pruned weights	*not pruned weights*
0,1,3	2,4
0,1,4	2,3
1,2,3	0,4
1,3,4	0,3

Table 1: Results on the linearly separable Iris data

Coming to the second test, linear separability can now be obtained only if one classification error is accepted. The IAP algorithm is not able to do any pruning if maintenance of this performance is desired. When two classification errors were accepted, IAP shows that input 1 can be pruned, while when three errors were accepted, the input couple (1,2) or alternately input 4 can be pruned.

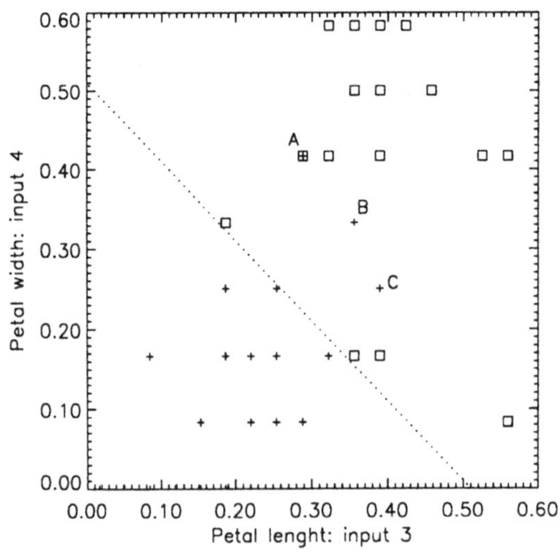

Figure 1

Figure 1, where class 2 and 3 are represented by cross and square respectively, shows a magnification of the portion of the plane of the inputs (3,4) of our interest: a possible separation of the data can be seen where the three patterns denoted by letters A, B and C are misclassified. Note that pattern A contemporarily represents a pattern belonging to class 2 and two patterns belonging to class 3, since input 3 and input 4 for these patterns coincide exactly.

The second real-world problem regards the data of the file Breast Cancer. This file includes 699 patterns, of which 458 (65.5 %) are Benign and 241 (34.5 %) Malignant; the nine input features are the following: 1. Clump Thickness, 2. Uniformity of Cell Size, 3. Uniformity of Cell Shape, 4. Marginal Adhesion , 5. Single Epithelial Cell Size, 6. Bare Nuclei , 7. Bland Chromatin , 8. Normal Nucleoli , 9. Mitoses .

Inputs have been normalised within the range $[-1, 1]$. Since 16 patterns feature comprise missing inputs, they have been removed: consequently 683 patterns were actually utilized, of which 444 are classified as Begnign and 239 as Malignant. A linear separator reveals an error percentage of 1.9%, corresponding to 13 missclassified patterns. In this situation all inputs are important. To be able to prune some of them, a higher error must be accepted: we found that if an error percentage of 3.95% is permitted, it is possible to prune 7 inputs. IAP only made use of the input couple (1,6): all others, except for bias, were pruned.

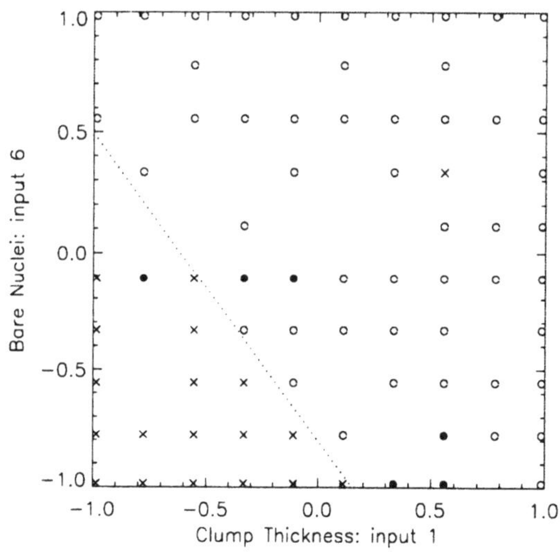

Figure 2

The graph in Figure 2 shows the plane corresponding to inputs (1,6). The 'Xs' represent points of the plane where the number of malignant cases overtakes that of begnin ones; circles refer to the opposite situation, while filled circles represent the case where the two classes have the same number of samples.

From the tests done using IAP, it has been found that the relative importance of the inputs, in decreasing order, is as follows: Bias, input 6, inputs 1 and 8, remaining inputs.

Finally, results with IAP have been compared with those obtained using the procedure described in [6]: this makes it possible to compute the variable t^* (eq.4 of [6]) for every input. The normalised saliency obtained in this way for the bias and the nine inputs is shown in Table 2.

Input	0	1	2	3	4	5	6	7	8	9	10
t^*	30.9	163.2	10.9	23.5	26.8	18.7	264.6	36.0	75.4	10.8	7.3

Table 2: Normalised saliency for Breast Cancer dataset

Input 10 consists only of noise and is used for setting a reference, as suggested in [6]. In comparison with the IAP results, satisfactory agreement is obtained in the estimation of the very important inputs 6 and 1 and for the relatively unimportant inputs 2,3,4,5,7,9, while in [6] much less importance is given to the bias. Moreover, in [6] even though input 8 appears quite important, it does not present the same level of importance as input 1, as revealed by our procedure.

5 Conclusions

This work presents a new technique for pruning the inputs of a perceptron using the Interval Arithmetic. Its application to real world data has given satisfying results.

In the future we intend to extend the method to Multilayer Perceptron Neural Networks. Improvement of the optimisation algorithm is also scheduled, since the search for minima in problems involving the use of IA is very difficult and represents a research field that has yet to be extensively explored.

aknowledgments This work was supported by the Italian Ministry for the University and Research (MURST 40 %) and by the National Research Council (CNR) of Italy.

References

[1] Anguita D. et al., Incorporating a priori knowledge into neural networks, *Electronic Letters*, Vol.31, no.22, october 1995.

[2] G.P.Drago, S.Ridella, Statistically Controlled Activation Weight Initialization, *IEEE Transactions on Neural Networks*, Vol.3, N0. 4, July 1992.

[3] Drago G.P. and Ridella S., An Adaptive Momentum Back Propagation (AMBP), *Neural Computing & Applications*, no.3, 1995, pp.213-221.

[4] Drago G.P. and Ridella S., Pruning with Interval Arithmetic Perceptron (IAP), *Internal Report ICE*, no.7, 1996.

[5] Ishibuchi H. and Tanaka H., An architecture of neural networks with interval weights and its application to fuzzy regression analysis, *Fuzzy sets andd Systems*, 57, 1993, pp.27-39.

[6] Steppe J.M. and Bauer K.W., Improved feature screening in feedforward neural networks, *Neurocomputing*, 13, 1996, pp.47-58.

[7] Vapnik V.N., The Nature of Statistical Learning Theory, *New York: Springer-Verlag*, 1995.

Hidden Recursive Models

Paolo Frasconi* Marco Gori† Alessandro Sperduti‡

*DSI. Università di Firenze. paolo@mcculloch.ing.unifi.it
†DII. Università di Siena. marco@mcculloch.ing.unifi.it
‡DI. Università di Pisa. perso@di.unipi.it

Abstract

Hidden Markov models (HMMs) and input/output HMMs are probabilistic graphical models for sequence learning. When thinking in terms of data structures, a sequence can be thought of as a linear chain. Depending on the task, however, the entities that need to be adaptively processed may be organized into data structures more complex that simple linear chains. In this paper we propose a theoretical framework to extend (input/output) HMMs for processing information structured according to any directed ordered acyclic graph. The resulting hidden recursive model (HRM) can be applied to problems of data structures classification or transduction. We report experimental results for tree automata induction tasks and in a simple logical terms classification problem.
Keywords: Learning data structures. Graphical models. Tree automata.

1 Introduction

Alternative approaches to pure symbolic systems for supervised and unsupervised learning in the case of temporal sequences have been extensively studied. For example, among probabilistic graphical models, hidden Markov models (HMMs) (Rabiner, 1989) are widely used for learning sequence distributions. In addition, recurrent neural networks (Williams & Zipser, 1989; Omlin & Giles, 1996) are a well known model for learning mappings from input sequences to output sequences. However, symbolic systems are still the more common choice when data is organized into more complex graphical structures (such as trees or grids). To the best of our knowledge, the only class of adaptive models that has been proposed is based on artificial neural networks with a recursive neuron model (Sperduti & Starita, to appear; Goller & Küchler, 1996).

This paper discusses a first attempt to build probabilistic models for supervised learning of structured information. The basic entity we are interested in adaptively processing is a data structure, mathematically described by a directed ordered acyclic graph (DOAG) with labeled nodes. Here for DOAG we mean a DAG $S = \{V, E\}$ with vertex set V and edge set E, where for each vertex $v \in V$ a total order on the edges leaving from v is defined. Each node v in the DOAG is labeled with a variable Y_v, which in general can be discrete or continuous, and possibly multivariate. Finally, we require the DOAG to possess a supersource, i.e., a vertex $s \in V$ such that every vertex in V can be reached by a path starting from s. A simple class which satisfies the above conditions is the class of linear chains, in which nodes v are associated to a serial order on the labels (i.e. v effectively corresponds to a discrete time index). In this paper, we restrict our attention to the case of discrete labels and we denote by $\mathcal{Y} = \{y^1, \ldots, y^{r_y}\}$ the state space (or alphabet) for the label variables. A DOAG having labels in $\mathcal{Y}$ will be denoted as $S_\mathcal{Y}$.

Generally speaking, the problem of learning data structures consists of making predictions based on the knowledge of a labeled graph $S_\mathcal{Y}$. The unsupervised learning problem corresponds to estimating the distribution $P(S_\mathcal{Y})$. For example, HMMs are a well known device for learning distributions of temporal sequences (i.e., linear chains, in our framework). The supervised learning problem, on the contrary, corresponds to estimating the *conditional* distribution $P(S_\mathcal{Y}|S_\mathcal{U})$, of an *output* DOAG $S_\mathcal{Y}$ given an *input* DOAG $S_\mathcal{U}$, where the alphabets $\mathcal{U}$ and $\mathcal{Y}$ are generally distinct. For example, input/output HMMs (Bengio & Frasconi, 1996) (IOHMMs) are an extension of HMMs for supervised learning in linear chains. The hidden recursive models (HRMs) we propose in this paper are probabilistic graphical models for dealing with structured information and generalize (input/output) HMMs from linear chains to arbitrary DOAGs. Like HMMs and IOHMMs, HRMs use hidden state variables to recursively capture contextual information. In this paper we discuss supervised and unsupervised learning in HRMs. As a special case, we derive a training algorithm for binary tree HRMs (BT-HRMs), that can be interpreted as a tree generalization of the Baum-Welch algorithm for HMMs. Finally, we report preliminary experiments showing that BT-HRMs can be employed to solve tree-grammars inference problems and simple learning problems in logic.

2 Hidden recursive models

2.1 Topology

Let us first consider a supervised learning problem. Assuming the input and the output structures share the same skeleton S, an HRM is constructed from S by introducing an input label node U_v, an output label node Y_v, and a hidden state node X_v for each node v in S. In a Moore model, edges are added so that U_v is a parent of X_v and X_v is a parent of Y_v. In a Mealy model an additional edge from U_v to Y_v is present. Hidden nodes are connected so that the subgraph induced by the set of X_v's is the transpose S. For example, when S is a linear chain, the resulting network is exactly an IOHMM. If the network is employed for classification of structures then S is the skeleton of $S_\mathcal{U}$ and only one output label node Y_s is present, where s is the supersource of S. Fig. 2.1 shows an HRM for classification of binary trees. If the network is employed for unsupervised learning, then S is the skeleton of $S_\mathcal{Y}$ and $S_\mathcal{U}$ is the empty graph. Evidence is normally entered through the visible nodes (input and output nodes during training, input nodes only when making predictions). The number of states of variables U_v and Y_v is constrained by the data at hand and does not depend on the particular node v in the original structure. The number of states of X_v is a design choice (like the choice of the number of states in HMMs). We denote by $\mathcal{X} = \{x^1, \ldots, x^{r_x}\}$ the hidden state space and we assume that $\mathcal{X}$ is also invariant with respect to v.

The *frontier* variables (the frontier generalizes the initial state in the case of temporal models) of the network may be supposed to be all instantiated with

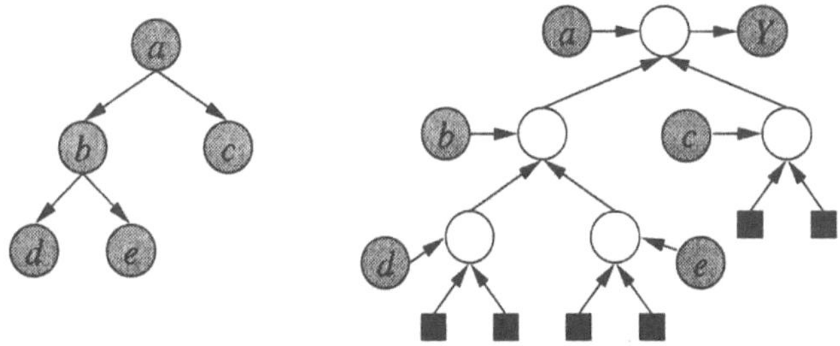

Figure 1: A binary tree and a corresponding HRM (dark square nodes denote the state frontier).

a known state.

The parameters in any Bayesian network specify, for the generic node A_v, the conditional probabilities [1] $P(A_v|\text{pa}_v)$. The simplest statistical model for these conditional probabilities is the unrestricted multinomial model. In this case the local densities are parameter tables that specifies the probabilities for each node given its parents. In particular, we shall denote by θ_{ij} the probability $P(X_v = x_v^i|\text{pa}_{X_v} = \text{pa}_{X_v}^j)$ and by ϑ_{ij} the probability $P(Y_v = y_v^i|\text{pa}_{Y_v} = \text{pa}_{Y_v}^j)$. We assume that all these tables do not depend on v, thus achieving an important reduction in terms of model complexity. In the case of HMMs and IOHMMs this assumption is commonly known as *stationarity* (in the case of recurrent neural networks, the very same idea leads to time-invariant weights).

2.2 Inference and learning in HRMs

The theory for inference and learning in HRMs is relatively simple once one recognizes that HRMs are just a special case of Bayesian networks in which the topology is known. Research concerning inference in Bayesian networks is now relatively mature, making available general and well understood algorithms. In the case of singly connected networks (or polytrees) inference can be performed directly on the Bayesian network using a local message passing algorithm often referred to as π–λ propagation (Pearl, 1988). In the general case, the DAG must be first "compiled" into a new structure, called junction tree, whose nodes contain clusters of variables; then inference relies on a local message propagation algorithm between the nodes of the junction trees (Jensen et al., 1990). An interesting solution to avoid compilation into separate junction trees for each training example consists of merging the whole training set into a supergraph (as done in (Sperduti & Starita, to appear)), so that only one junction tree has to be built. Alternatively, ad-hoc propagation algorithms for the class of DOAGs being considered may be derived. An example for the case of binary trees is presented in section 2.3.

Learning in HRMs correspond to the problem of learning the parameters in Bayesian networks with fixed structure. Since full Bayesian methods are intractable due to the presence of hidden variables, learning can be solved in

[1] We use the table notation for probabilities. For example $P(X)$ denotes the table $[P(X = x^1), \ldots, P(X = x^r)]$ and $P(X, y|Z)$ denotes the two-dimensional table with entries $P(X = x^i, Y = y|Z = z^k)$. $\sum_X P(X, Y, Z) = P(Y, Z)$ denotes the marginalization operator on tables.

the maximum likelihood framework, i.e. searching the parameters that maximize the likelihood function $P(\mathcal{D}|\boldsymbol{\theta})$. Common approaches for solving this optimization problem are gradient ascent and the expectation-maximization (EM) algorithm, which can be applied provided that the local conditional distributions belong to the exponential family. Both methods are iterative and, under certain regularity conditions, they converge to a local maximum of the likelihood. In the case of unrestricted multinomial distributions, the expected sufficient statistics computed during the E-step of EM are simply the expected vaules for the counts N_{ijk}: how many times the generic variable A_i was found in state a_i^k while its parents were found in the j-th configuration pa_i^j:

$$\tau_{ijk}^{(t)} = E[N_{ijk}|\mathcal{D}, \boldsymbol{\theta}^{(t-1)}] = \sum_{\boldsymbol{s}\in\mathcal{D}} P(A_i = a_i^k, \mathrm{pa}_i = \mathrm{pa}_i^j|\boldsymbol{s}, \boldsymbol{\theta}^{(t-1)}).$$

The above probabilities can be easily computed by solving a probabilistic inference problem with evidence $\boldsymbol{s}$ (i.e., instantiating the label nodes and the target nodes from the data structure $\boldsymbol{s}$ and propagating this evidence into the hidden nodes of the unfolded network with parameters $\boldsymbol{\theta}^{(t-1)}$). The maximization step consists of updating the parameters using the expected sufficient statistics:

$$\theta_{ijk}^{(t)} \leftarrow \frac{\tau_{ijk}^{(t)}}{\sum_{i,k}\tau_{ijk}^{(t)}}.$$

2.3 Inference in binary tree HRMs

The model we consider in this section is a generalization of IOHMMs for processing binary trees of categorical variables. We derive an evidence propagation algorithm specialized for this topology. The algorithm does not require to compile the unfolded network into a junction tree and can be seen as a specialization of Pearl's π–λ propagation.

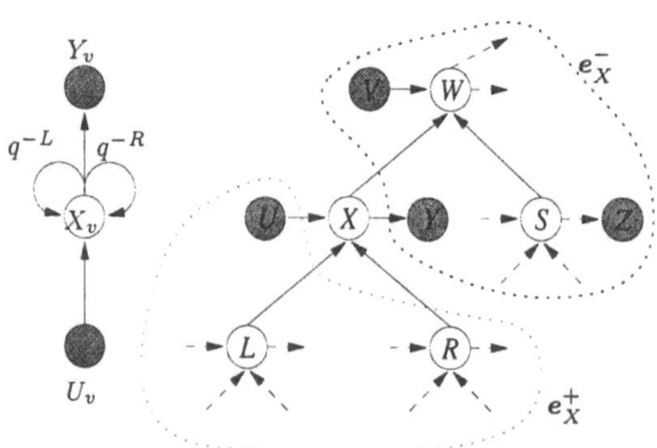

Figure 2: Left: Recursive diagram for a binary-tree HRM. Right: Slice of the unfolded network. Shaded variables receive evidence during learning.

With reference to Fig. 2.3, denote by v a generic node in the data structure $S_{\mathcal{U}}$ and let $X = X_v$, $U = U_v$, and $Y = Y_v$ denote the hidden variable, the input variable, and the output variable at node v, respectively (we drop the node subscripts to simplify notation). Let $L = q^{-L}X$ be the left child of X and $R = q^{-R}X$ the right child of X (the operators q^{-L} and q^{-R} are the binary-tree generalizations of the standard shift operator q^{-1} defined in the sequential domains as $X_{t-1} = q^{-1}X_t$). Assuming v is not the root node of $S_{\mathcal{U}}$, let W be a variable such that $q^{-L}W = X$ or $q^{-R}W = X$ (i.e., depending whether v is the left or the right child of his father in $S_{\mathcal{U}}$) and let V be the input variable connected to W. Moreover let $S = q^{-R}W$ if $q^{-L}W = X$, or $S = q^{-L}W$ if $q^{-R}W = X$ and let Z be the output variable connected to S. Let $\boldsymbol{e} = (\boldsymbol{u}, \boldsymbol{y})$ denote the evidence entered through the input and the output nodes. The aim of probabilistic inference is to assess the table $P(X|\boldsymbol{e})$ for a generic hidden node X. Denote by $\boldsymbol{e}_X^+ = (\boldsymbol{u}_X^+, \boldsymbol{y}_X^+)$ the evidence connected to X through X's ancestors and by $\boldsymbol{e}_X^- = (\boldsymbol{u}_X^-, \boldsymbol{y}_X^-)$ the evidence connected to X through X's descendants. Then we have $P(X|\boldsymbol{e}) \propto P(\boldsymbol{y}_X^-|X, \boldsymbol{u}_X^-)P(X|\boldsymbol{y}_X^+, \boldsymbol{u}_X^+)$. Introduce the "inward" table $\pi(X) = P(X|\boldsymbol{y}_X^+, \boldsymbol{u}_X^+)$ and the "outward" table $\lambda(X) = P(\boldsymbol{y}_X^-|X, \boldsymbol{u}_X^-)$. These tables can be recursively computed by the following inward/outward equations (that generalize the well known Baum-Welch's forward/backward propagation for HMMs):

$$\pi(X) = \sum_L \sum_R \theta_{X,L,R,u}\pi(L)\pi(R),$$
$$\lambda(X) = \vartheta_{y,X} \sum_W \lambda(W) \sum_S \vartheta_{z,S}\theta_{W,S,X,v}\pi(S).$$

Finally, the expected sufficient statistics for θ and ϑ are recursively computed (using Bayes' theorem) as:

$$E[X, L, R|\boldsymbol{u}, \boldsymbol{y}] \propto \lambda(X)\theta_{X,L,R,u}\pi(L)\pi(R),$$
$$E[X|\boldsymbol{u}, \boldsymbol{y}] = \lambda(X)\pi(X).$$

3 Experimental results

3.1 Induction of finite tree automata

In this section we consider the problem of inferring grammars defined on labeled binary trees, using BT-HRMs. Regular set of labeled trees can be accepted by binary *frontier-to-root* automata (FRAs) (Thacher, 1973). It can be observed that BT-HRMs are equivalent to FRAs in the limit case of 0–1 parameters (in that case $\delta(l, r, u)$ is simply obtained by taking the argument of the only nonzero parameter in the table $P(X|l, r, u)$).

We performed two experiments on induction of tree automata with boolean labels. In the first experiment the language to be recognized was defined as the parity on binary trees. It should be noted that the FRA that recognizes parity on trees has a symmetric transition function (i.e. $\delta(l, r, u) = \delta(r, l, u)$ for $u = 0, 1$). The language for the second experiment was generated by the two-states FRA shown in Fig. 3.1. Training sets of 100 samples were constructed by generating random trees (50 nodes and height 9, on average), with class labels produced by the accepting FRAs. We ran 10 trials with different initial parameters and using BT-HRMs with $|\mathcal{X}| = 2$. For the parity problem 5 out of 10 trials converged in 51.2 iterations, on average. In the other cases EM got

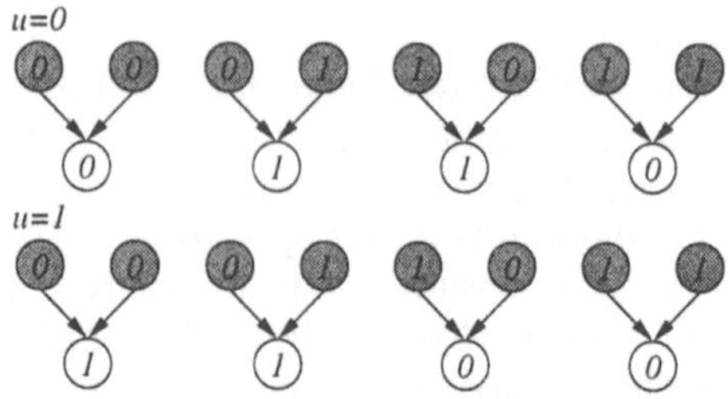

Figure 3: The FRA that generated the data for the tree-grammar inference task

stuck in some local maximum of the likelihood and training failed. By inspecting the parameters at the end of learning we noticed that the trained BT-HRMs were exactly equivalent to the FRA that recognizes the parity language. The equivalence was experimentally confirmed by testing on a separate set of 200 trees. In the experiment with the second FRA, 5 out of 10 trials converged in 29.4 iterations, on average. Again, the trained BT-HRMs were equivalent to the FRA that generated the data. To reduce the problem with local maxima we tried to increase the state space of the BT-HRM. Using $|\mathcal{X}| = 3$, all 10 trials converged for the grammar defined by the FRA of Fig. 3.1, yielding perfect generalization on the test set. For the parity problem no convergence improvements were obtained by increasing the number of states. We conjecture that the symmetry in the transition function may unavoidly lead to local maxima.

3.2 Classification of logical terms

In this section we consider the problem of learning heuristics to guide and control search processes in symbolic reasoning. All the different tasks that must be performed for learning control heuristics, like finding a rating for the applicable rules according to the current context, selecting the next subgoal, or realizing a generalizing lemma/failure-store, can be regarded as problems of learning a classification of symbolic structures of arbitrary size (Sperduti & Starita, to appear). In this context, we tested the feasibility of classification of simple ground logical terms by BT-HRMs. For this purpose, terms can conveniently be represented as trees, where function symbols are mapped to internal nodes, while constants are mapped to terminal nodes. The label of each node is used to store the symbol associated with the assigned entity. We trained a BT-HRM with 6 states on a training set of 280 logical terms randomly generated by an alphabet of 3 constants (a, b, c) and two functions ($f(\cdot,\cdot)$, $i(\cdot)$). The depth of the resulting trees was up to 6. Positive example in the training set contained the (sub)term $i(a)$ **or** the (sub)term $f(b, c)$. On 10 different trials the BT-HRM converged 7 times. The average number of epochs for these 7 runs was 46.42, while the average generalization error measured on an independent training set of 120 terms was 0.71%.

4 Conclusions

We have generalized discrete Markovian models to deal with structured information. The HRMs described in this paper are relatively simple and many extensions and improvements can be conceived. A first obvious generalization is to allow multivariate continuous variables as labels. Like in IOHMMs, continuous labels can be dealt with by using artificial neural networks for the conditional densities attached to the hidden nodes of the network. For example, in the case of binary trees $P(X|L = l, R = r, u)$ can be modeled using a set of neural networks N_{lr}, each having a softmax output function.

References

Bengio, Y., & Frasconi, P. (1996). Input-output HMM's for sequence processing. *IEEE Transactions on Neural Networks*, *7*(5), 1231–1249.

Goller, C., & Küchler, A. (1996). Learning task-dependent distributed structure-representations by backpropagation through structure. In *IEEE International Conference on Neural Networks*, pp. 347–352.

Jensen, F., Lauritzen, S., & Olesen, K. (1990). Bayesian updating in recursive graphical models by local computations. *Computational Statistical Quarterly*, *4*, 269–282.

Omlin, C., & Giles, C. (1996). Constructing deterministic finite-state automata in recurrent neural networks. *Journal of the ACM*, *43*(6), 937–972.

Pearl, J. (1988). *Probabilistic Reasoning in Intelligent Systems : Networks of Plausible Inference*. Morgan Kaufmann.

Rabiner, L. R. (1989). A tutorial on hidden Markov models and selected applications in speech recognition. *Proceedings of the IEEE*, *77*(2), 257–286.

Sperduti, A., & Starita, A. ((to appear)). Supervised neural networks for the classification of structures. *IEEE Transactions on Neural Networks*.

Thacher, J. (1973). Tree automata: An informal survey. In Aho, A. (Ed.), *Currents in the Theory of Computing*, pp. 143–172. Prentice-Hall Inc., Englewood Cliffs.

Williams, R. J., & Zipser, D. (1989). A learning algorithm for continually running fully recurrent neural networks. *Neural Computation*, *1*(2), 270–280.

Geometrical Constructive Algorithms of Binary Neural Networks

F.M. Frattale Mascioli, G. Martinelli, & V. Catini
INFO-COM Dpt., University of Rome "La Sapienza"
Via Eudossiana 18, 00184 Rome, Italy

Abstract

Binary neural networks are a very important and active research topic. In the present paper a geometrical constructive approach is discussed in comparison with similar methods, with the aim of obtaining nets with optimal structural complexity. Experiments show promising results.

1 Introduction

It is well known that any binary-to-binary mapping can be realized by a feedforward neural network with only one hidden layer and an output neuron. The determination of the net on the basis of the training set TS consists in deriving the number of hidden neurons with their synapses and those of the output neuron.

The usual learning algorithms are in general not efficient since they do not take into account the peculiar properties of the binary mapping. These properties stem from the geometrical characteristic of the problem to be solved. In fact, the TS can be conveniently represented in the input space by a labeled unitary hypercube. If N is the number of input bits of the problem, each vertex corresponds to one of the 2^N possible inputs. The label attached to it represents the binary output associated with the input. Each neuron of the hidden layer is represented by a hyperplane having coefficients coincident with the weights of its connections to input and bias. This hyperplane cuts the input space in two halves. The inputs corresponding to the vertices located in one of these halves yield a same output, 0 or 1. Each neuron consequently acts as a minterm of a Boolean function. The output neuron acts as an OR operator.

The learning algorithm can be defined as a tool for cutting the hypercube with hyperplanes for separating the vertices with label one from the others. Since the TS does not cover the entire binary mapping, it is important to optimize the generalization capacity of the net. The learning theory suggests to look for nets having the minimum number of neurons. Consequently, we must attain the said separation of the two types of vertices by means of the minimum possible number of hyperplanes. This requirement calls for constructive algorithms, corrected with a final pruning step.

It is important to point out that the information regarding the mapping to realize is not only contained in the TS, but also in the algorithm itself. This property was evidenced in [1, 2], where the said information was quantized in bits. The generalization of the net is complete when the sum of the cardinality of the TS and the previous information is just 2^N. However, it is difficult to apply the previous property by choosing the algorithm more suited to the problem at hand, since the said information is determinable only in very simple cases.

In conclusion, the learning algorithm should rely on the geometrical properties of the mapping and should be constructive. Algorithms of this type are available in the technical literature. We will consider the most recent of them [3, 4]. They fail to succeed when the mapping is poorly specified. For this reason, we develop a new method that overcomes these inconveniences. It is described in section 2. In section 3 several tests illustrate its performance.

2 Proposed algorithm

All the geometrical algorithms are characterized by the preliminary choice of a vertex V_I of the hypercube. In the following, we denote the vertices with label 1 as true vertices and false vertices the others. Since the mapping is not completely specified, there are also "do not care" vertices. Without loss of generality let us assume V_I as a true vertex.

The choice of V_I can vary from method to method. We will choose V_I as the true vertex more distant from the false vertices, the distance being measured in Hamming sense. The determination is undertaken by a simple approximate technique that is strictly related to the proposed algorithm.

After V_I is chosen, a hyperplane is found such that the halfspace Γ containing V_I does not contain false vertices but only true vertices. The optimal hyperplane corresponds to the maximum of true vertices in Γ. In the following we will denote the other halfspace as $C\Gamma$, the complement of Γ.

The difference among the geometrical algorithms available in the technical literature mainly regards the procedure followed for determining the hyperplane. This procedure is repeatedly applied until all the vertices of one type are separated from the others. For this reason, we will focus, in the following, our attention only on the said procedure without considering the details of the entire process. As said, we only discuss the two algorithms [3, 4].

The procedure followed in [3] for determining the hyperplane relies on the property that a set of vertices contained in a hypersphere is always separable from all the others by means of a hyperplane, having its coefficients directly determinable from the center of the sphere. This property is applied for adding to V_I true vertices, controlling at the same time that they are contained in a hypersphere. The inconvenience of the procedure is related to the determination of the center of the hypersphere, which is chosen equal to the center of gravity of the set of vertices added to V_I. Due to this approximation, the said control is not exact and the final effect is the determination of a number of hyperplanes larger than the minimum necessary to the separation. This inconvenience grows very rapidly with the dimension of the input space.

The procedure followed in [4] for determining the hyperplane is based on two topological properties regarding both the region Γ and the edges of the hypercube crossing the boundary between Γ and $C\Gamma$. The procedure requires to visit all the contiguous vertices starting from V_I. When the dimension of the input space is large, the procedure cannot be followed up to the farest vertices. Consequently, the procedure is prematurely arrested with the consequence of determining a superfluous hyperplane.

On the basis of the previous discussion a new geometrical procedure has been devised for determining the separating hyperplane. It relies on the determination of the N false vertices F_i, i=1,...,N closest to V_1. These vertices are inserted into a set denoted QVERT. Then, we consider the straight lines going from V_1 to the F_i and on each of them a point X_i at distance ε from V_1. Let us denote by V_1, F_i and X_i respectively the vectors having as components the coordinates of the vertices V_1, F_i and the point X_i. Then, it results

$$X_i = V_1 + (F_i - V_1) \cdot \varepsilon, \qquad i = 1,2,\dots,N\,. \qquad (1)$$

The distance ε from V_1 must be less than 1 in order X_i lies between V_1 and F_i.

The hyperplane HP defined by the N points X_i is characterized by a coefficient vector which does not depend on ε. In order to prove this property, let us consider the hyperplane defined by the N vertices F_i of QVERT. If C is its coefficient vector, it results:

$$C^t \cdot F_i = b, \qquad i = 1,2,\dots,N\,. \qquad (2)$$

We show that C is also the coefficient vector of HP. In fact, we have from (1) and (2)

$$C^t \cdot \left[V_1 + (F_i - V_1) \cdot \varepsilon\right] = C^t \cdot V_1 \cdot (1-\varepsilon) + b \cdot \varepsilon = q(\varepsilon)\,. \qquad (3)$$

Equation (3) shows that HP is parallel to the hyperplane defined by F_i; only q(ε) depends on ε.

REMARK: The value ε=1 cannot be chosen since the hyperplane HP in this case could contain several other vertices of the hypercube. In particular, it could be coincident with a face of the hypercube with the consequence of containing 2^{N-1} vertices, since the face is itself a hypercube of dimension N-1. In this case, it is probable that the entire TS is contained in HP, what could render impossible the separation of the two types of vertices.

Hyperplane HP is a valid choice if the remaining false vertices F_j, j=N+1,...,NF, where NF is the total number of false vertices, lie in CΓ. This condition may be easily ascertained, by considering the straight line from V_1 to F_j and determining its intersection with HP. By representing the line by

$$X_j = V_1 + (F_j - V_1) \cdot t_j\,, \qquad (4)$$

it is sufficient to determine the value t_j corresponding to the intersection. It holds

$$t_j = \frac{q(\varepsilon) - C^t \cdot V_1}{C^t \cdot F_j - C^t \cdot V_1}\,. \qquad (5)$$

Two cases are possible:

a) HP is valid. This happens if t_j is positive and less than 1 for all F_j, j=N+1,...,NF. In this case the procedure for determining the hyperplane is terminated. If the true vertices are also all located in Γ, then no further hyperplanes are necessary and the complete hidden layer is determined. When this last situation does not arise, it is necessary to restart the procedure for determining another hyperplane. The TS to be considered is reduced, since the true vertices located in the previous region Γ are omitted.

b) HP is not valid. There exists at least one false vertex F_j which lies in Γ. In this case, for all the F_j lying in Γ we determine the quantities

$$z_j = \max\left[-t_j, t_j - 1\right], \qquad (6)$$

which measure their "distances" from HP. We consider the F_j more distant from HP, i.e. that characterized by the largest z_j. Let denote it by F_k. We replace the last member of QVERT for F_k and repeat the procedure for determining the hyperplane with the new QVERT. If in the new region Γ there are still false vertices, we repeat again the procedure involving also the other vertices present in QVERT up to the first one, which is the one closest to V_1. The procedure continues. There are some controls in order to guarantee its convergence, by avoiding that a same false vertex enters and exits from QVERT more than one time. The computational cost of the procedure is drastically reduced by devising an optimized technique for determining the hyperplane defined by N vertices of the hypercube. This technique is described in the appendix.

3 Test and results

We have tested the proposed algorithm on known benchmarks. The resulting performance was very satisfactory. In the following we summarize some of them in order to illustrate its behavior.

3.1 AND function

The test regards a 30-bit mapping obtained by considering the AND operation of the first, 15-th and 30-th inputs. The TS and test set consist of 600 and 3000 random examples. In all the cases the complete generalization was achieved with one neuron.

3.2 Parity function

The TS used in this case contains only a part of the examples of the parity function (10 bits). After satisfying the TS, the neural net is checked on the remaining examples (validation set). In fig. 1 the generalization error versus the percentage of examples of TS is shown. Each result is the mean of 3 different trials.

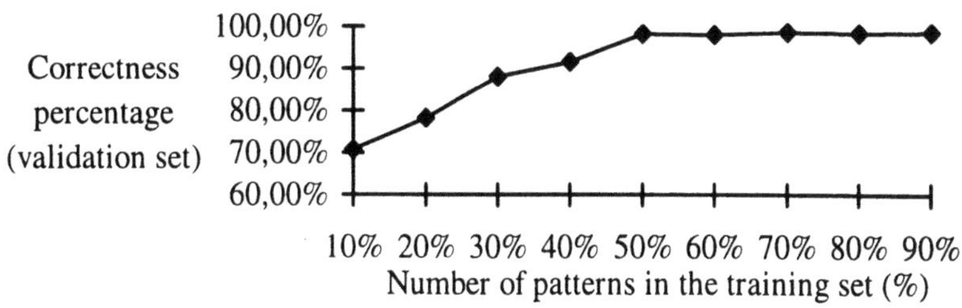

Fig. 1

3.3 Circle recognition

The test regards the recognition of a circular region in a square of 32x32 pixels. The problem is converted into a binary mapping by associating the pixels of the map with the vertices of a hypercube in a space of 32 dimensions.

The transformation is carried out under the constraint of preserving the neighborhood as close as possible. Namely, each of the two coordinates of the pixels of the square region surrounding the circle, spanning from 0 to 31, is converted into a string of 16 bits with the following rule:

$$\begin{array}{cccccccccc} 0 & 1 & 2 & \dots & 16 & 17 & 18 & \dots & 31 \\ \downarrow & \downarrow & \downarrow & \cdots & \downarrow & \downarrow & \downarrow & \cdots & \downarrow \\ 0 & 0 & 0 & \cdots & 1 & 1 & 1 & \cdots & 1 \\ 0 & 0 & 0 & \cdots & 1 & 1 & 1 & \cdots & 0 \\ \vdots & \vdots & \vdots & \cdots & \vdots & \vdots & \vdots & \cdots & \vdots \\ 0 & 0 & 0 & \cdots & 1 & 1 & 1 & \cdots & 0 \\ 0 & 0 & 1 & \cdots & 1 & 1 & 0 & \cdots & 0 \\ 0 & 1 & 1 & \cdots & 1 & 0 & 0 & \cdots & 0 \end{array}$$

Moreover, the pixel located at the left bottom has coordinates (0, 0). Consequently, its Hamming distance from the pixel (0, 31) and (31, 0) is 1. The overall number of input bits is 32.

If the TS is complete, i. e. all the pixels of fig. 2 are used, the algorithm yields a neural net with 10 hidden neurons which satisfies without errors the TS. If the TS is specified only with 50% of the pixels, as shown in fig. 3, the algorithm yields a neural net with 16 hidden neurons. Its performances are: 0% TS error, generalization error 7.6% (fig. 4). The behavior is improved, as shown in fig. 5, by allowing a 0.78% TS error. The resulting generalization error is 6.2% and the complexity is reduced to 13 hidden neurons.

These results compare favorably with similar experiments [5], since the present neural nets are simpler.

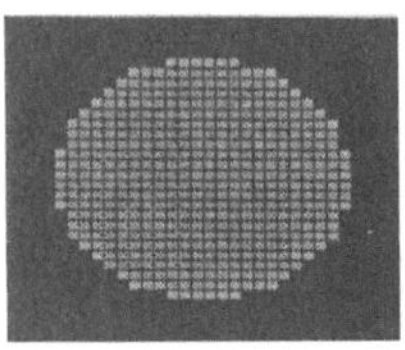

Fig. 2

Fig. 3

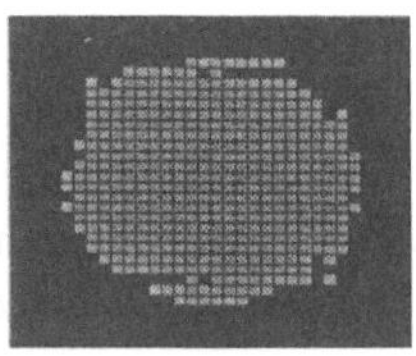

Fig. 4

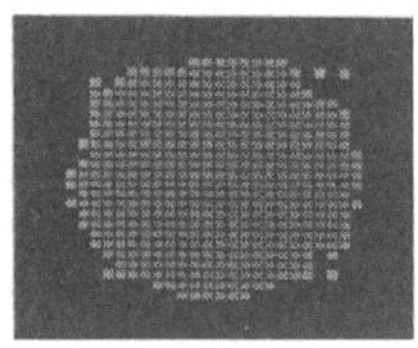

Fig. 5

4 Appendix: determination of the hyperplane defined by N vertices of the hypercube

Let us denote with Q_i, i=1,2,...,N the N vertices. Their components are equal to 0, 1. The equation of the hyperplane is

$$C^t \cdot X = b \,. \qquad (7)$$

Consequently, the vector of coefficients C meets the condition

$$C^t \cdot \left(Q_i - Q_j\right) = 0 \,. \qquad (8)$$

Depending on the Hamming distance DH between any couple of nodes, we derive very simple relations between the components of C. We illustrate them in the case DH=1 and DH=2.

Case DH=1. If the two vertices are Q_r , Q_s and the component they differ is the h-th one, then (8) yields

$$\left[Q_r(h) - Q_s(h)\right] \cdot C(h) = 0 . \qquad (9)$$

Consequently, the h-th component of C is zero.

In this case the h-th component of all the vertices does not affect (8) and can be omitted. Moreover, Q_r and Q_s without this component are equal. In conclusion, we can continue the process of determining C by considering a reduced set of vertices obtained by the previous one, as said.

Case DH=2. In this case Q_r, Q_s differ in correspondence to two components; let them be the h-th and k-th ones. (8) becomes

$$\left[Q_r(h) - Q_s(h)\right] \cdot C(h) + \left[Q_r(k) - Q_s(k)\right] \cdot C(k) = 0 , \qquad (10)$$

which yields

$$C(h) = \rho \cdot C(k) \qquad (11)$$

with ρ a suitable value obtainable from (10).

Since the two components of C are related each other, we can continue the process of determining C by relying only on one of them, for instance the k-th one. In fact, if Q_m, Q_n are two vertices, (8) becomes

$$\left[Q_m(h) - Q_n(h)\right] \cdot C(h) + \left[Q_m(k) - Q_n(k)\right] \cdot C(k) + ... = 0 , \qquad (12)$$

which can be rewritten as

$$\left\{\left[Q_m(h) - \rho \cdot Q_m(k)\right] + \left[Q_n(h) - \rho \cdot Q_n(k)\right]\right\} \cdot C(h) + ... = 0 . \qquad (13)$$

Therefore, we can continue the process of determining C by considering a reduced set of vertices obtained by the previous one by eliminating the k-th component and replacing the h-th one as suggested by (13), i.e.

$$Q(h) \longrightarrow Q(h) - \rho \cdot Q(k) . \qquad (14)$$

The two initial vertices Q_r and Q_s become equal.

It is clear from the previous discussion that the process of determining C is applied in successive steps to set of vertices of decreasing cardinality. The final equation yields a relation between two components. Taking account of the relations among components of C obtained in the preceding steps, we determine all the components of C in terms of one of them with a very reduced computational cost.

5 References

1. P. Carnevali, S. Patarnello. Learning networks of neurons with boolean logic. Europhysic Letters, Vol. 4, pp. 503-508, 1987;
2. ibidem. Exhaustive thermodynamical analysis of boolean learning networks. Europhysic Letters, Vol. 4, pp. 1199-1204, 1987;
3. I. H. Kim, S. K. Park. The geometrical learning of binary neural networks. IEEE Trans. on Neural Networks, Vol. 6, pp. 237-247, 1995;
4. F. M. Frattale-Mascioli, G. Martinelli. A constructive algorithm for binary neural networks. IEEE Trans. on Neural Networks, Vol. 6, pp. 794-797, 1995;
5. M. Muselli. On Sequential Construction of Binary Neural Networks. IEEE Trans. on Neural Networks, Vol. 6, pp. 678-690, 1995.

ON THE ADAPTABLE BOOLEAN NEURAL NET PARADIGM

F. E. Lauria, R. Prevete, M. Milo, S. Visco
Dipartimento di Scienze Fisiche dell' Università di Napoli
& Istituto Nazionale di Fisica della Materia
Mostra D' Oltremare, Pad. 19, I-80125 NAPLES (Italy)
lauria@na.infn.it

Abstract

We discuss the adaptable Boolean net neural paradigm together with its learning and generalization properties.

1 Introduction

Usually, neural networks are considered as classifiers, e.g. see [1], and very few attempts have been made to explore their different computational capabilities. Here, we discuss a different paradigm for the, adaptable, Boolean neural networks, see also [2].

In general, both the Boolean and the non-Boolean nets are characterized by state vectors containing the three subsets of components: the input, the hidden and the output component subsets, in some instance with common elements and often with a one component output vector. To simplify our presentation, we call input, hidden and output vector, respectively, the first, the second and the third of the state vector subsets. We present the time as a discrete variable, it unit is one τ. Moreover, we call "coupling coefficient" $C[h,k,d]$ the efficacy associated to the unidirectional connection between the node k and the node h, in the order, with a delay d, if the net nodes compute a linear combination of their inputs and confront the result with a given threshold, i.e., if they are linear threshold units. We call "weights" the same effects in the remaining nets. Eventually, we represent with $f[k,t-d]$, taking its value in the set $\{0, 1\}$, the state of the net node k at the time t-dτ before present and call T, a positive constant, the common threshold of the Boolean neural net nodes.

2 Classification versus transformation of knowledge

Usually, given a neural net we present to its input a vector and wait to know the net output, i.e., whether or not the input vector belongs to the set characterized by the predicate computed by the net. In other words, the net activity results in the computation of a function taking values in the binary set $\{0,1\}$. In some cases, the net output is a vector containing more than just one component, i.e., the net computes a predicate taking one out of finite many values. In other words, the net classifies its input vector as belonging to one of finite many subsets. However, the latter is no more than a finite sequence of yes-or-no decisions. An approach of this kind give rise to the generalized problem. Whereas a neural net has just one finite set I of input vectors, its weights can be chosen with some degree of freedom, because of the threshold T. That is, if it has been built to discriminate an I subset, then, we can ask whether or not it correctly discriminate the remaining input vectors. From a mathematical point of view there is no difference between a function taking values in $\{0,1\}$, or in a finite set of integers, and one taking values in the set of integers. However, from the point of view of the recursive function theory there is a difference between the two. To ask whether or not a vector has a given property, i.e. if it belongs to a given set, is conceptually different from computing the possible vector with a given property, belonging to a given set. E. g., to ask if a number is prime and to ask to compute the value, if it exists assumed by the given function in correspondence of the given independent variable value, are conceptually two different tasks and we cannot brush away their difference. By using neural net, there is an objectively different computational model to consider. Instead of asking the net to decide whether or not the input vector belongs to a given set, we can store in the net coupling coefficients the algorithm to compute a given correspondence, then its output vector sequence is the image, under the given correspondence, of the input vector sequence. Some illustrative example of the knowledge transformer paradigm for Boolean neural nets can be found in. Moreover, if we consider a neural net as a knowledge transformer, as opposed to a classifier, the generalization problem is automatically solved because, once implemented in the net coupling coefficients, the algorithm either computes the correct output vector sequence, for every input vector sequence, or it cannot be applied. There is a different aspect of a neural net as a classifier, namely the net storing capacity, we want to discuss it. To classify the input vectors the net weights must be suitably chosen. To this end, the net must contain a sufficient number of nodes and connections, i.e. of weights to store all the input vectors we want to classify. In other words, for a correct classification outcome the net dimensions must increase with the size of the input vector set. By contrast, in the knowledge transformer case, the number of different coupling coefficients depends on the way the algorithm is stored in the said coefficients, and does not depend on the input vector set dimensions.

Up to now we have considered nets with time independent efficacies: next we discuss nets with some coupling coefficients subject to a Hebbian rule, i.e., with some time dependent coupling coefficients. As is well known, there is no general way to implement a Hebbian rule in a Boolean neural net, e. g. see [3, pg.65]. However, applying the Caianiello formalism, see [4], we have proposed, see [2, 3] and the works there quoted, a quite general solution.

Let us call "Hebbian" any connection associated to a time dependent coupling coefficient $C[h,k,d,t] > 0$. For each h, let us represent with $C[h,k',d,t]$ the time dependent coupling coefficients associated to the Hebbian connections impinging upon the node h. The $C[h,k',d,t]$ value is computed every τ by applying the *Hebbian rule:*

If $\sum_{k'} C[h,k',d,t] < T$, *then:*
$C[h,k',d,t]$ *is increased if* $f[h,t] = f[k,t-d] = 1$,
$C[h,k',d,t]$ *is decreased of a small amount if* $f[h,t] = 0$,
$C[h,k',d,t]$ *is decreased of a greater amount if* $f[h,t] = 1 f[k,t-d] = 1$.
If $\sum_{k'} C[h,k',d,t] \geqslant T$, *then:*
$\forall h, dC[h,k',d,t]$ *becomes constant and is said to be frozen.*

As we are considering Boolean neural nets with absolute inhibition, but see also the discussion in [2, cap.4], it is meaningless to consider time dependent negative coupling coefficients and to extend the Hebbian rule to them. In the following we call "Hebbian-in", "Hebbian-out", a node receiving, sending, at least one Hebbian connection. In a net the presence of a Hebbian-in node implies the presence of a Hebbian-out node and of a Hebbian connection, and vice versa. However, because once frozen a coupling coefficient becomes constant, eventually the Hebbian attribute can be lost. We call "non-Hebbian" the nodes connected by time independent connections. We refer to the above mentioned increasing or decreasing coupling coefficient amounts as the "Hebbian parameters".

To start with, let us set some nomenclature questions about the neural nets with time dependent coupling coefficients. Usually, in the literature learning is qualified as supervised when the net output is measured against some known and desired goals, i.e., the net weights are adjusted at each training session until the desired output is obtained. By contrast, in the unsupervised learning the net weights are adjusted until some clustering of the input vectors is detected, i.e. until similarities in the latter are recorded in the output vector values. In both cases the learning process can be seen as a search for the weight values discriminating between the input vector sets, with the desired output vector sets known in the supervised case and unknown in the unsupervised case. Instead of, in the paradigm we are discussing, quite different from the unsupervised Hebbian learning studied in the classical paradigm, the Hebbian rule implementation causes the Boolean neural net to behave, in the learning sessions, like a filter in the time domain. Actually, it selects the input sequences to remember on the basis of their presentation behavior. That is, it selects and remembers the examples, no more than two or three consecutive input vectors are repeated a sufficient number of times. The sufficient number is determined by the values chosen for the parameters present in the Hebbian rule and on the examples very repetition cadence, i.e. how often the training sessions follow each other. Implicitly, the input vector sequences define a clock ticking on, inexorably, as the net ruminates its input. In turning, the clock presence implies the dependence the coupling coefficient variations on the repetition cadence of the training sessions. Accordingly, the teacher, in the net most general wiring blueprint, can be disposed of as its role is simply to shorten the learning process. At intervals as short as possible, the teacher lets in the wanted and eliminates the unwanted input vector sequences. In our simulations, see [8, 9], the number of training sessions increases with the increase of the noise to signal ratio, i.e. of the ratio between unwanted and wanted input vector sequences. However, for some particular wiring diagrams the teacher role is more pregnant, as the net so wired requires the learning examples to be broken down in sequences of elementary tasks. To avoid ambiguity with the classical learning paradigms, instead of supervised and unsupervised learning we propose to speak of assisted and unassisted learning.To understand the conditions needed to implement the Hebbian rule in a Boolean neural net, we must discuss how to assign the coupling coefficients so to guarantee a proper working net. Both in the Hebbian original formulation and in the subsequently proposed Hebbian rules, the coupling coefficient adjournment depends both on the activity of the transmitting node and on the delayed activity of the receiving node, as it ought to be. However, we are interested in nets containing more than one Hebbian-out and Hebbian-in node pair, besides the non-Hebbian nodes. That is, either we take the activities of the remaining nodes into account: an unrealistic as well as no practical solution we do not investigate further. Or we could satisfy the following condition (A): " To choose the net coupling coefficients such that no more than one Hebbian-in node can be active at any time". To satisfy (A), we have introduced the "assembly" net, see [2, 6, 7]. That is, instead of connecting N nodes to obtain a net learning to compute a given function f, we consider N smaller nets, the assemblies, connected so to obtain a larger net satisfying (A) and learning to compute f. Obviously, for a fault tolerant, i.e. redundant net, see [2, cap.1], in (A) the word "node" becomes "group of identically wired nodes".

The assembly wiring diagram has been presented in [2], here we discuss its more relevant aspects. Each assembly is characterized by an identifier, actually embodied in the coupling coefficients associated to its incoming sensory input connections. As the sensory inputs broadcast an assembly identifier just one "input control" module, the one belonging to assembly characterized by the said identifier, generates an output signal and, to guarantee the net proper working, inhibits the input channel. The input control contains the assembly two Hebbian-in nodes, independently trainable on the other assembly Hebbian-out node signals. As the "output control" module receives a signal from the input control, it sends an output signal on the first, i in the figure, Hebbian output connection. Concurrently, the latter signal, first, sets on the "store" module; second, is broadcasted to the other assemblies; third, tells to the "identifier" module to broadcast to all the other assemblies the very same assembly identifier. The signal coming from the output control, i.e. a signal on either the i or the ii connection, readies the store to hold an incoming identifier. Once the store module has accepted an incoming identifier, it enables the "compare" module to verify if among the incoming identifiers there is one equal to the stored one. As soon as the compare module detects an incoming identifier equal to the one the store is holding, then, it resets, i.e. clears the latter module and sends a signal to restart the output control. The first time the output control receives a signal from the compare, it sends an output signal on the same assembly second, ii in the figure, Hebbian output connection. Concurrently, the latter signal, first, sets on the store; second, is broadcasted to the other assemblies. By contrast the second time the output control receives a signal from the compare, it sends a signal on its third, iii in the figure, output connection concurrently to the input control and to the identifier module. As the latter receives a signal from the control, either on the i or on the iii connection, it broadcasts to all the other assemblies the very same assembly identifier. As the former receives a signal from the output control, namely a signal on the iii connection, it is reset, i.e., the assembly is readied for the next task by terminating its input channel inhibition. The output control module can have more than two Hebbian output connections. The upper bound on their number depends both on the Hebbian parameters and on the maximum delay allowed for the connections.

Besides the normal assemblies, there is a finite number of special purpose assemblies, the primitives, without Hebbian output connections. The net non-Hebbian output connections stem from the primitives to activate the system effectors so generating the elementary actions seen by the net environment. As confirmed by our simulations, see [2], a net composed by assemblies and primitives satisfies the condition (A) and learns, unassisted in a finite number of training sessions, to execute any finite sequence of elementary actions. Accordingly, if the latter is an universal set, the net can learn to compute any finite algorithm.

3 Conclusions

In [5] we have given a formal definition of learning in an adaptable Boolean neural net, i.e. in a net organized in assemblies which unassisted learns by examples to transform the sequence of its input vectors in accordance to the paradigm here discussed. Learning it turns out to be a property definitively acquired by the state vector sequence when the coupling coefficient matrix is subject to the given Hebbian rule. In the classical paradigm the knowledge is stored in the neural net by representing, in some way, the input bitmap in the net weights, some see this as an example of the subsymbolic knowledge representation. By contrast, an adaptable Boolean neural net learns, in finite steps, to execute an algorithm by storing the sequence of its elementary instructions, i.e. the sequence of the net primitive activities. Accordingly, in the adaptable Boolean net the knowledge is stored as the sequences of the primitive activities, as a kind of intentional knowledge representation, see [2, cap.5] for an illustrative example on this representation efficiency.

Acknowledgement: this research has been supported in part through the MPI/INFM 40% fund and the MPI 60% fund.

References

[1] Hassoun, Mohamad H. -"Fundamentals of artificial neural networks" MIT Press (1995) 511 + xxvi

[2] Lauria, F. E., M. Sette, S. Visco - "Adaptable Boolean neural networks" Fridericiana Scientia, Liguori (Napoli)(1996) 212.

[3] Rumelhart, D. E., J. L. McClelland and the PDP Research Group - "Parallel distributed processing. Vol I Foundations" MIT Press, Cambridge (Mass.) (1986).

[4] Caianiello, E. R. - "Outline of a theory of thought processes and thinking machines" J. Theor. Biol. 2 (1961) 204-235.

[5] Lauria, F. E. - "On some sufficient conditions for the Caianiello-Hebb transform convergence" Rend. Acc. Sc. Fis. e Mat., Napoli, Serie IV- Vol. LXII (1995) 7-42.

[6] Bini Verona, F., P. De Pinto & F. E. Lauria - "Toward a learning Boolean net: some cybernetic rules" R. Trappl ed. "Cyber. and Syst. '92" World Sc. (Singapore), (1992) 709- 716.

[7] Lauria F. E., M. Sette - "Teaching macros through program execution examples" E. R. Caianiello ed. "Neural nets WIRN Vietri-92" World Sc. (Singapore), (1992) 204-209.

[8] Lauria, F. E., M.Sette, S. Visco - "A Boolean neural network learning from a random environment" R. Trappl ed. "Cyber. and Syst. '96" Austrian Soc. for Cyber. Studies (Vienna) (1996) 491-496.

[9] Violi, T. - "Valutazione in presenza di rumore dei parametri di una regola hebbiana" (Valuation of the Hebbian rule parameters in presence of noise) Tesi di Laurea in fisica Dipartimento di Scienze Fisiche, University of Naples aA 1994-95.

Cluster Connections: A visualization technique to reveal cluster boundaries in self-organizing maps

Dieter Merkl, Andreas Rauber
Institut für Softwaretechnik, Technische Universität Wien
e-mail: {dieter, andi}@ifs.tuwien.ac.at

Abstract

The self-organizing map is one of the most prominent unsupervised learning architectures used to visualize the similarities of high-dimensional input structures. What remains by no means straight-forward, is an explicit representation of cluster boundaries in the final two-dimensional map display. The detection of these boundaries rather requires some amount of insight into the inherent structure of the input data which may not be expected in real-world application scenarios. In this paper we address this deficiency by suggesting an extension to the standard map representation that leads to an easy recognition of cluster boundaries. The general idea is the visualization of clusters within the input data items by connecting units representing similar data items while disconnecting units representing dissimilar data items. As a result we get a grid of connected nodes where the intensity of the connection mirrors the similarity of the underlying data items. Such a representation allows intuitive analysis of the similarities inherent in the input data without the necessity of substantial prior knowledge, and an intuitive recognition of cluster boundaries.

Keywords: Exploratory Data Analysis, Self-Organizing Map, Visual Representation, Cluster Detection

1 Introduction

Real-world data is often represented in high-dimensional spaces and hence the inherent similarities are hard to recognize and to illustrate. This fact makes it a challenging task to build tools that are able to visualize these similarities. By nature, visualization requires a mapping process from the high-dimensional input space to a low-dimensional output space. One well-known neural approach to dimension reduction is the *self-organizing map (SOM)* [3]. This model preserves the structure of input data as faithfully as possible and results can be visualized on a two-dimensional topographic map, thus indicating the similarities between input signals in terms of the distance between the respective units in the two-dimensional output space. In other words, the similarity inherent in the input data is visualized in terms of the distances between the units that represent the data. It still represents a non-trivial task, however, to determine the boundary between unrelated parts of the output space due to the usually high degree of dimension reduction in the mapping from the input onto the output space. In other words, the various clusters of similar input data often may only be detected when the person examining the map representation has some prior knowledge of the input structures. This clearly is one deficiency of the self-organizing map. Only recently, variations on the basic idea of self-organizing maps with a special focus on the facilitation of cluster boundary detection have been proposed. Some of these approaches rely on adaptive architectures as for instance *incremental grid growing* [1] and *growing cell structures* [2]. These architectures incrementally grow and split according to the specific requirements of the actual input data. As a result, these architectures produce isolated clusters of similar input data items. Other authors suggest the utilization of multiple independent self-organizing maps as for example *multiple 2-dimensional SOM* [8], or *hierarchical feature maps* [6]. The central feature of these architectures is that the independent self-organizing maps specialize on different clusters of the input data during the learning process. A general approach to visualization of vector quantization, the so-called *competitive Hebbian learning*, is suggested in [4] where a visual conntection is drawn between the winning and the second winning unit. This technique can be used with a number of vector quantization algorithms for using aging parameters to remove 'old' connections. All of these architectures share in common an intuitive visual representation of cluster boundaries. As the negative attribute of these architectures we should mention, however, that they require more "magic numbers", i.e. training parameters, to be specified before the training process starts. This makes these architectures much more susceptible to minor variations of the learning parameters as compared to the extremely robust model of self-organizing maps. Moreover, the recognition of inter-cluster relationship is not as easy as in SOMs, to say the least. These problems raise the necessity for a novel approach addressing the problem of cluster boundary detection while not interfering with the robustness offered by the standard SOM model. In this paper we present a visualization technique based on post-processing a trained SOM, which utilizes the distance between weight vectors of neighboring nodes to determine their degree of connectivity. Depending on their distance the nodes are connected by using connections of different intensity where the intensity corresponds to the nodes' mutual similarity.

The material contained in this paper is organized as follows. In Section 2 we present a brief review of the principles of the visualization technique which we refer to as *cluster connections*. Section 3 gives experimental results obtained from applying the cluster connection visualization to a trained SOM. A discussion of these results and the capabilities of the cluster connection representation is provided in Section 4. Finally, our conclusions are presented in Section 5.

2 SOM and the Cluster Connection Technique

Due to the limited space in this paper we assume the reader is familiar with the standard SOM learning rule. Instead of a review of its basic principles we rather refer to [3] for a thorough exposition of this neural network. The SOM implementation we used for the experiments described below is presented in [5].

Our *Cluster Connection (CC)* visualization technique is an approach relying on post-processing the information contained in the various weight vectors of a trained SOM. Pragmatically speaking, the distances between weight vectors of neighboring nodes are used to determine whether these nodes belong to the same cluster and should thus be shown as connected, or are located along a cluster boundary and should thus be not connected. In order to preserve the stability of the standard SOM, post-processing of the trained map is used to create CC representations finally showing the trained SOM as sets of nodes being connected according to the structures learned from the input data. In other words, the standard SOM representation is enhanced in the sense that nodes representing input items comprising the same cluster are shown as connected. In order to enhance the visual representation, a set of thresholds is used to visualize different degrees of similarity. As a result our visualization technique is capable of, first, revealing the inter-cluster relation of the input data items as well as, second, visualizing qualitative information on cluster membership.

Based on an analysis of the distances between pairs of neighboring units, a set of thresholds for a trained SOM may be derived in order to add connections of differing intensity to the standard SOM representation, showing both different degrees of similarity within clusters and mutual similarity of whole clusters. Different implementations of this core idea may serve the purpose of cluster visualization resulting in a variety of possible user interfaces, some of which are listed below.

1. A fixed set of two or more thresholds may be created – either automatically, based on the average, minimum and maximum distance between neighboring nodes' weight vectors, or (preferably) manually after analysis of the distances – to show connections with varying intensity.
2. A kind of 'slidebar' may be assigned to the distance-axis in a diagram showing the distances of the various pairs of nodes , allowing the user to decide, up to which distance the nodes should be shown as connected. Thus, the user can watch the set of connected nodes shrink and grow as she moves the threshold interactively, enabeling deeper insight in the structure of the input data.
3. All nodes can be shown as connected with the intensity of the connections being determined by their respective distances, i.e. the distances are directly converted to colors or greyscale values ranging from black for almost identical nodes to white for highly dissimilar ones.

3 Exploration of the Cluster Connection Technique

In the remainder of this paper we will use an artificial input data set as defined in [3]. We selected this specific data set because it is widely used and

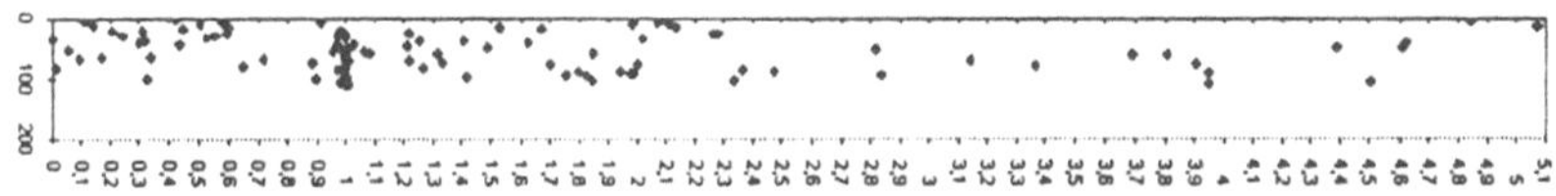

Figure 1: Distances between neighboring nodes of the map given in Figure 2

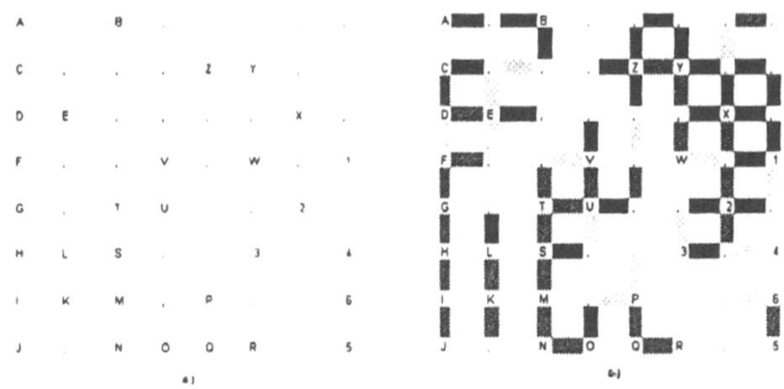

Figure 2: 8 × 8 SOM: (a) Standard representation, (b) CC representation

discussed as a benchmark data set in papers on related topics, thus allowing easy comparison of the results.

The result of the Cluster Connection visualization technique presented hereafter is based on three threshold values. We have chosen this strategy because its results may be mapped most conveniently on gray-scale levels needed for appropriate printed presentation. Neighboring nodes with a distance of their weight vectors below the first threshold value t_1 are connected by a black bar, followed by dark connections between nodes exhibiting a weight vector distance higher than t_1, but below a second threshold t_2. Analogously, weight vector distances between t_2 and t_3 are indicated by a somewhat lighter connection. Nodes showing a weight vector distance above the third threshold t_3 are not shown as connected.

We used the following exact figures for the three threshold values: $t_1 = 0.8$, $t_2 = 1.1$ and $t_3 = 1.6$. These thresholds were selected based on the analysis of the distance diagram as given in Figure 1. Please note that we do not claim to have selected the optimal set of threshold values for cluster detection in the results presented below. We should rather stress the fact that such 'optimal' parameters will not exist anyhow since cluster membership depends a lot on the desired granularity of cluster assignment.

Turning now to the result of the Cluster Connection visualization technique we first show in Figure 2 (a) the standard representation of an 8 × 8 SOM trained with the data set mentioned above. In this representation the winning units are labeled by the corresponding input signal. When we try to ignore our prior knowledge concerning this data set we might arrive at the honest conclusion that hardly any information on the branching structure present in the input data can be derived directly from the standard representation. This is especially true in areas, where almost all nodes are assigned an input signal as for instance in the lower left corner of the map.

For convenient comparison, the corresponding Cluster Connection representation is provided in Figure 2 (b). Here the branching structure inherent in the input data is clearly visible from the enhanced visualization technique. Starting with A - E in the upper left corner of the map, cluster F - J branches along the left side of the map (with this branch being less intensively connected due to the separation of F and C by the training process). K and L form a separate cluster, followed by the two connected branches M - R and S - V in the lower center. In the upper right corner W - Z form a cluster connected to the numbers *1* - *4*, from which *5* and *6* are separated.

As an argument in favor of an interactive selection of threshold values we want to stress that if we increase the threshold value t_3 the next connections to be added are *4* - *6*, I - K, L - S consecutively in this order, thus further visualizing the inherent structure of the input data.

Due to the limited space in this paper we cannot provide other results from the application of the Cluster Connections visualization technique. We rather refer to [7] for a number of other results as well as a more detailed description of the implementation.

4 Discussion of Cluster Connections

Cluster Connections allow the visualization and detection of clusters in a trained self-organizing map by post-processing of the information contained in the various weight vectors. Thus, the CC approach does not interfere with the training process in any way, leaving the extremely robust model of self-organizing maps untouched. Experience gathered with standard SOM training can be used further and already trained maps may be visualized using the CC approach without any modification.

By their very nature, Cluster Connections allow a very flexible approach to the cluster detection and visualization process. Visualization can be achieved fully automatically, be it by creating a set of thresholds based on an analysis of the distance diagram of the map (i.e. minimum, maximum and average distances between the nodes weight vectors) or by using the distances encountered directly to assign colors or gray-scales to represent the connections. Manual interaction with the thresholds and thus uncovering their influence on the growing and shrinking of connected regions, provides an indispensable tool for the exploratory analysis of the underlying input data set.

Both the basic cluster structure as well as the overall structure present in the input data can be visualized using Cluster Connections. Qualitative information about the relationship between linked nodes is given by the usage of different colors or gray-scales to indicate looser and closer connections.

Please note that Cluster Connections provide additional information about the nodes' similarity, which is present in any trained map yet unrevealed in the standard grid representation. Thus, in many cases this additional information is the only means to detect cluster boundaries within a trained SOM.

5 Conclusion

In this paper we have presented an enhanced visualization technique for self-organizing maps. The development of this visualization technique referred to as *Cluster Connections* is motivated by the fact that detection of cluster boundaries. Our extension enables both the visualization of similarity of input data comprising one cluster and the visualization of similarity between different clusters within the limits of the fixed grid topology of SOMs. CC are based on an analysis of the information contained in the weight vectors of trained SOMs, showing nodes of the final map either as connected or non-connected depending on the distance between the respective weight vectors. We have demonstrated the effect of this novel visualization technique on the basis of a prominent benchmark data set for SOMs. Since the representation is obtained by post-processing of a trained SOM, no additional parameters that influence the learning process are needed, thus retaining the stability of the basic SOM model. Given the wide variety of user interface solutions for Cluster Connections, exploratory data analysis may be enabled in a highly intuitive and interactive manner.

References

[1] Blackmore J. and Miikkulainen R. Incremental Grid Growing – Encoding high-dimensional structure into a two-dimensional feature map. *Proc of the IEEE Int'l Conf on Neural Networks.* San Francisco, CA. 1993.

[2] Fritzke B. Growing Cell Structures – A self-organizing network for unsupervised and supervised learning. *Neural Networks* 7(9). 1994.

[3] Kohonen T. *Self-Organization and Associative Memory.* Springer Verlag, Berlin, Germany. 1989.

[4] Martinetz T. Competitive Hebbian learning rule forms perfectly topology preserving map. *Proc of the Int'l Conf on Artificial Neural Networks (ICANN'93)* Amsterdam, The Netherlands, 1993.

[5] Merkl D. The Effect of Lateral Inhibition on Learning Speed and Precision of a Self-Organizing Feature Map. *Proc Australian Conf on Neural Networks.* Sydney. Australia. 1995.

[6] Miikkulainen R. Script Recognition with Hierarchical Feature Maps. *Connection Science* 2. 1990.

[7] Rauber A. *Cluster Visualization in Unsupervised Neural Networks.* Diplomarbeit, Technische Universität Wien, Austria. 1996.

[8] Wan W. and Fraser D. A Self-Organizing Neural Network for Contextual Analysis of Spatial Patterns of Multisource Data. *Proc Conf on Digital Image Computing, Techniques and Applications.* Sydney, Australia. 1993.

Discriminative Least Squares Learning for Fast Adaptive Neural Equalization

R.Parisi, E.D.Di Claudio, and G.Orlandi
INFOCOM Dpt., University of Rome "La Sapienza"
Rome, Italy

Abstract

In this paper a novel approach to learning in Recurrent Neural Networks (RNN) is introduced and applied to the problem of digital adaptive equalization. The proposed method extends to RNN a technique applied with success to feedforward NN and is based on the descent of the error functional in the space of the linear combinations of the neurons (the *neuron space*); it exploits the principle of *discriminative learning*, based on the minimization of an error functional which is a direct measure of the classification error considered in equalization problems. Main features of the new approach are higher speed of convergence and better numerical conditioning w.r.t. gradient-based approaches, while numerical stability is assured by the use of robust Least Squares solvers. Preliminary experiments regarding the equalization of PAM signals in different transmission channels are described, which demonstrate the effectiveness of the proposed approach.

1 Introduction

Fig.1 depicts the typical digital baseband transmission system; the channel model takes into account the effects of the transmitter, the transmission medium and the receiver, and is usually represented by a Finite Impulse Response (FIR) filter. The input to the channel is a sequence $\{s(k)\}$ of indipendent symbols

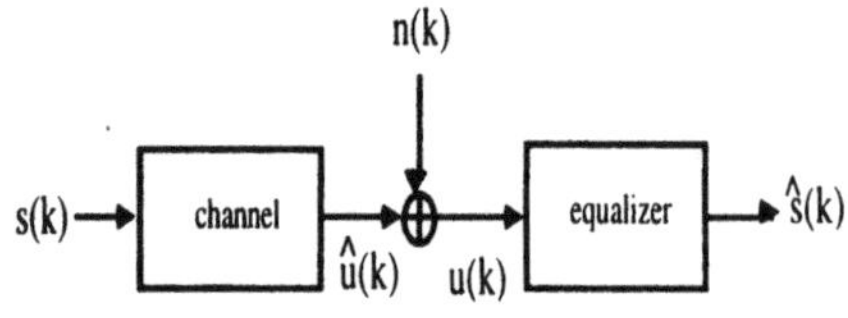

Figure 1: Schematic of data transmission system

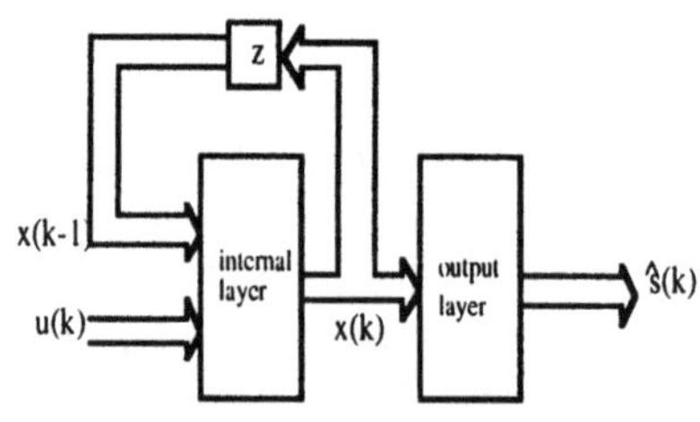

Figure 2: RNN equalizer

extracted from a specified alphabet; the channel output $\{\hat{u}(k)\}$ is corrupted by additive Gaussian white noise $\{n(k)\}$. Intersymbol interference (ISI) occurs as a consequence of the limited bandwidth of the channel and consists in spreading of the received symbol energy through several time intervals. The objective of equalization is to reconstruct the transmitted sequence and combat the effects of ISI and noise.

Linear equalizers have been preferred for long time, mainly due to their simplicity and theoretical tractability; anyway, for many typical situations the use of some form of nonlinearity is considered to be more appropriate [6]. In last years NN have been successfully applied to the equalization problem. In particular, Recurrent NN (RNN) [9] are attractive for the presence of feedback and their small size. *Kechriotis et al.* [10] applied fully recurrent NN trained with the Real-Time Recurrent-Learning algorithm (RTRL) [9] to the equalization of nonminimum phase, partial response and nonlinear channels; they compared their neural equalizer to linear FIR equalizers, trained with the Kalman algorithm.

Equalization can be viewed as a *classification* problem [6], in which the objective is the separation of the received symbols in the output signal space. Objective of the learning phase is thus the minimization of the classification error, defined as the ratio between the numbers of misclassified and received symbols. Anyway, most NN approaches use the Mean Square Error (MSE), that is not directly related to the classification error. In [7] a new error functional has been proposed which takes directly into account the classification error; the new method has been successfully applied to general classifier structures and in particular to NN. Authors called this approach *discriminative learning.*

Moreover, in the case of a "neural equalizer", due to its inherently nonlinear nature, the need of fast and stable training algorithms is particularly important. Many different approaches to NN learning exist; the most common involve the use of the gradient of the specified error functional (like the popular *backpropagation* algorithm [2] for feedforward NN). Anyway, gradient-based approaches, even if computationally simpler, are characterized by low rates of convergence and may not be suitable in applications where fast convergence is required. In analogy with the signal processing field, Least Squares (LS) methods could be employed to speed up convergence; anyway the application of LS concepts to highly nonlinear structures like NN requires an appropriate treatment.

In the present paper we introduce a novel LS-based learning method for fully recurrent networks which minimizes the classification error by application of the principle of discriminative learning. Preliminary description of the algorithm has been given in [11], where higher speed of convergence and numerical stability and robustness w.r.t. more common gradient-based solutions was demonstrated. In this work we extend that approach and apply the resulting *discriminative LS learning* to the problem of digital equalization.

2 Discriminative Least Squares learning (DLS)

In this section, we first briefly recall the fundamental concepts of discriminative learning, described in detail in [7]. Suppose that the aim is to associate an input pattern $\mathbf{z}$ to one of M possible classes. As a first step, M discriminant functions $g_i(\mathbf{z}, \mathbf{w})$, depending on some parameters $\mathbf{w}$, are introduced; they can be for example the outputs of a NN. Then an appropriate misclassification measure when the input belongs to the i-th class is chosen, which is continuous with respect to $\mathbf{w}$; a possible definition is:

$$d_i(\mathbf{z}) = -g_i(\mathbf{z},\mathbf{w}) + \left\{\frac{1}{M-1}\sum_{j,j\neq i} g_j^{\mu}(\mathbf{z},\mathbf{w})\right\}^{1/\mu} \tag{1}$$

where μ is a positive number. The third step is the definition of the following error functional:

$$l_i(\mathbf{z},\mathbf{w}) = l_i(d_i(\mathbf{z})) \tag{2}$$

where l_i is a differentiable zero-one function (like a sigmoid or an exponential). The objective of learning is the minimization of the error functional l_i w.r.t. the weights, performed by applying methods well-known in optimization theory. In [7] it is shown that NN, trained with the discriminative learning rule, are potentially able to converge to the true minimum Bayes risk.
Fig. 2 shows the NN herein considered; it consists of a fully RNN in cascade to a feedforward network. This structure is similar to the Elman net [5], with the addition of the feedforward part having the role of decisor.
Using a matrix formulation, forward propagation through the internal and the output blocks can be represented by the following equations respectively:

$$\left\{\begin{array}{rcl} [\mathbf{x}^T(k-1) \quad 1 \quad \mathbf{u}^T(k)]\mathbf{W}_i & = & \mathbf{y}_i^T(k) \\ \mathbf{x}^T(k) & = & f[\mathbf{y}_i^T(k)] \end{array}\right. \tag{3}$$

and:

$$\left\{\begin{array}{rcl} [\mathbf{x}^T(k) \quad 1]\mathbf{W}_o & = & \mathbf{y}_o^T(k) \\ \hat{\mathbf{s}}^T(k) & = & f[\mathbf{y}_o^T(k)] \end{array}\right. \tag{4}$$

In preceding formulas, $\mathbf{x}(k)$, $\mathbf{u}(k)$ and $\hat{\mathbf{s}}(k)$ are column vectors representing respectively the *state* of the net, the external input, and the output at time k (k=1,2,..), $\mathbf{W}_i$ and $\mathbf{W}_o$ are the weight matrices of the internal and the output sections, while $\mathbf{y}_i$ and $\mathbf{y}_o$ are correspondingly the outputs of the linear combinations (e.g. the inputs to the nonlinearities); f is the neuron activation sigmoidal-type function.
Objective of the learning phase is the minimization of an error functional E, coinciding in this case with the expression given in formula (2), where a sigmoidal function l_i is used.
The *neuron space* approach consists of two steps (see [12] for an extensive description):
1- in the first step the "optimal" $\mathbf{y}$ for each layer is estimated by performing a descent of the error in the space of the y's (the *neuron space*). This can be accomplished for example by a *gradient descent* in neuron space:

$$\hat{\mathbf{y}}(k) = \mathbf{y}(k) - \eta\nabla_{\mathbf{y}}E \tag{5}$$

where η is the *step-size* [3], also called *learning rate* in the neural field. At each iteration the gradient of the error is subtracted to the actual $\mathbf{y}$, giving the estimate $\hat{\mathbf{y}}$.

2- The second step consists in the computation of the weights by solution of a proper linear system. Namely, suppose that at the generic (k-1)-th step the QR decomposition of the solving system has been computed; then the new input can be appended to the triangular factor $\mathbf{R}$ and the following system formed for the generic layer:

$$\begin{bmatrix} \lambda^{1/2}\mathbf{R}(k-1) \\ (1-\lambda)^{1/2}\mathbf{z}^T(k) \end{bmatrix} \mathbf{W}(k+1) = \begin{bmatrix} \lambda^{1/2}\mathbf{C}(k) \\ (1-\lambda)^{1/2}\hat{\mathbf{y}}^T(k) \end{bmatrix} \tag{6}$$

In the preceding formula, vector $\mathbf{z}$ is defined as $\mathbf{z}(k) = \begin{bmatrix} \mathbf{x}(k-1) & 1 & \mathbf{u}(k) \end{bmatrix}^T$ or as $\mathbf{z}(k) = \begin{bmatrix} \mathbf{x}(k) & 1 \end{bmatrix}^T$ respectively in the case of the internal and of the output layer; λ is a proper *forgetting factor.* Initially $\mathbf{R}(0) = diag\{\epsilon\}$, where ϵ is a small number, and $\mathbf{C}(1) = \mathbf{0}$, while both weights and state inputs are initialized to small random values.

During learning, matrix $\mathbf{C}(k)$ is computed by the following matrix multiplication:

$$\begin{bmatrix} \mathbf{C}(k) \\ \cdots \end{bmatrix} = \mathbf{Q}^T(k-1) \cdot \begin{bmatrix} \lambda^{1/2}\mathbf{C}(k-1) \\ (1-\lambda)^{1/2}\hat{\mathbf{y}}^T(k-1) \end{bmatrix} \tag{7}$$

Proper treatment is required also by the state vector $\mathbf{x}$. Namely, after the weight update, $\mathbf{x}$ is perturbed according to the following equation:

$$\hat{\mathbf{x}}(k-1) = \mathbf{x}(k-1) - \eta \nabla_{\mathbf{x}} E(k-1) \tag{8}$$

The corrected state vector $\hat{\mathbf{x}}$ and the new external input are presented to the net and the algorithm proceeds. The state perturbation is consistent with the approach followed for $\mathbf{y}$ and is an example of *coordinate descent* approach [3]: the whole optimization process can be viewed as a sequence of steps in which the weights and the state are alternately corrected.

3 Computer experiments

In this preliminary study, we will consider the case of 2-PAM signals in which symbols are randomly extracted from the alphabet {-1,1}. In all the experiments a network with three recurrent units and two outputs and the values $\eta = 20$ and $\lambda = 0.999$ of the learning parameters were used.

In the first test we considered a channel with transfer function $H_1(z) = 1 + 0.7z^{-1}$; this is a simple minimum-phase channel which can be used as a preliminary test. The networks were trained with sequences of 20, 50 and 100 symbols, at different noise levels; the Bit Error Rate (BER) for each value of Signal to Noise Ratio (SNR) was evaluated on 10^5 more received symbols and averaged over 20 realizations. Fig. 3 shows the curves of the average BER versus the SNR, while varying the length of the training phase. These curves can be directly compared to those presented in [8], where 2000 symbols were used for learning; it can be seen that the new approach is able to provide the same performance with only 100 samples. No cases of ill-convergence were observed. The second example is a linear non minimum-phase channel with transfer function $H_2(z) = 0.3482 + 0.8704z^{-1} + 0.3482z^{-2}$; as pointed out in [8], this type of channel is closer to those encountered in real communication systems. Learning was performed on sequences of 100, 200, 300 and 500 samples; fig. 4 depicts curves of the mean BER versus the SNR. Also in this case, with respect to the gradient approach of [8], the proposed method is able to substantially reduce the number of training samples required to get the same BER. Also in this case, convergence was reached in all trials, demonstrating the robustness of the proposed method. An extensive description of the DLS approach, with more experimental results, will appear in [11].

4 Conclusion

This paper has introduced a new approach to adaptive digital channel equalization which makes use of Recurrent Neural Networks. Previous approaches were based on the minimization of the Mean Square Error (MSE) performed by a gradient descent procedure. Anyway the MSE is not necessarily related with the classification error (BER) that is considered in equalization problems; moreover, the use of gradient-based learning techniques is often hampered by slow speed of convergence and numerical ill-conditioning. Overcoming these difficulties, the proposed method minimizes an error functional that is a direct measure of the BER. Moreover, the determination of the optimal weights is performed by a procedure (*gradient descent in neuron space*) that is faster and numerically more stable and robust with respect to traditional gradient-based schemes. Experimental tests conducted on 2-PAM signals for different channels have confirmed the better performance of the novel algorithm.

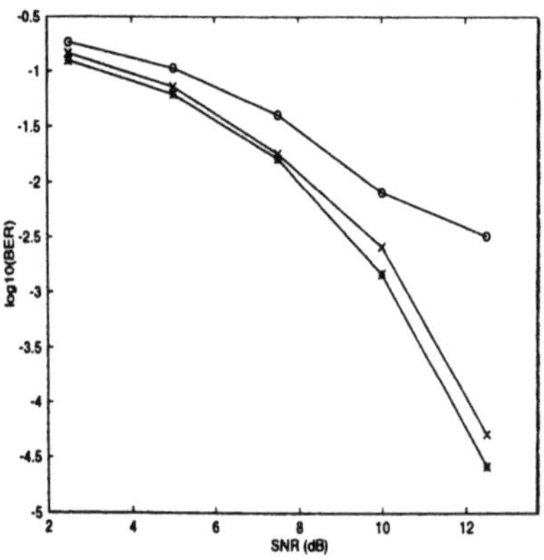

Figure 3: $H_1(z) = 1 + 0.7z^{-1}$, BER vs. SNR. o: after 20 samples in the learning phase, x: 50 samples, *: 100 samples

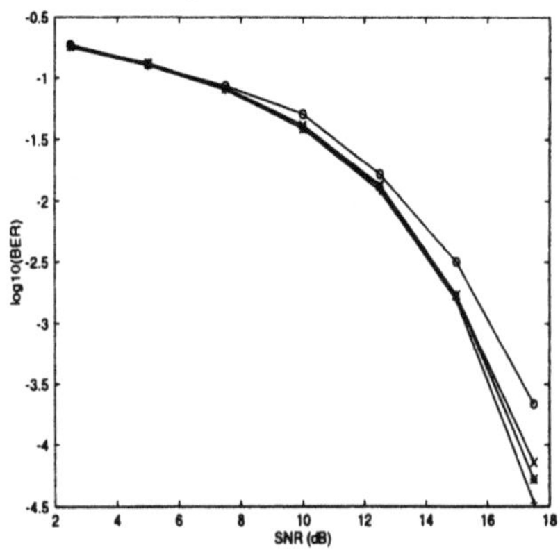

Figure 4: $H_2(z) = 0.3482 + 0.8704z^{-1} + 0.3482z^{-2}$, BER vs. SNR. o: after 100 samples, x: 200 samples, *: 300 samples, +: 500 samples

Acknowledgement

This work was supported in part by the Italian Ministery of University and Scientifical and Technological Research (MURST).

References

[1] D.E.Rumelhart, G.E.Hinton, and R.G.Williams, "Learning Internal Representations by Error Propagation," in *D.E.Rumelhart, J.L.McLelland (Eds.), Parallel Distributed Processing: Exploration in the Microstructure of Cognition*, vol.1, MIT Press/Bradford books, Cambridge, MA, 1986.

[2] D.G. Luenberger, *Linear and nonlinear programming*, Addison Wesley, 2nd ed.,1989.

[3] G.H.Golub, C.F.Van Loan, *Matrix computations*, The Johns Hopkins University Press, Baltimore, 1989.

[4] J.L.Elman, "Finding structure in time", *Cognitive Science*, 14, 179-211, 1990.

[5] G.J.Gibson, S.Siu, and C.F.N.Cowan, "The application of nonlinear structures to the reconstruction of binary signals," *IEEE Trans. on Sig. Proc.*, vol.39, no.8, Aug. 1991.

[6] B.H.Juang, and S.Katagiri, "Discriminative learning for minimum error classification," *IEEE Trans. on Signal Processing*, vol.40, no.12, Dec. 1992.

[7] S.Haykin,*Neural networks - A comprehensive foundation*, IEEE Press, 1994.

[8] G.Kechriotis, E.Zervas, and E.S.Manolakos, "Using recurrent neural networks for adaptive communication channel equalization," *IEEE Trans. on Neural Networks*, vol.5, no.2, March 1994.

[9] R.Parisi, E.D.Di Claudio, A. Rapagnetta, and G.Orlandi, "Fast training of recurrent neural networks by the recursive least squares method," *Proc. of the 8th Italian Workshop on Neural Nets, WIRN-Vietri'96*, Vietri (SA), 1996.

[10] R.Parisi, E.D.Di Claudio, G.Orlandi, and B.D.Rao, "A generalized learning paradigm exploiting the structure of neural networks," *IEEE Trans. on Neural Networks*, vol.7, no.6, Nov. 1996.

[11] R.Parisi, E.D.Di Claudio, G.Orlandi, and B.D.Rao, "Fast adaptive digital equalization by recurrent neural networks," to be published in *IEEE Trans. on Signal Processing*, special issue on Neural Network Applications to Signal Processing, Nov. 1997.

Author Index

MIX
Papier aus verantwortungsvollen Quellen
Paper from responsible sources
FSC® C105338

If you have any concerns about our products,
you can contact us on
ProductSafety@springernature.com

In case Publisher is established outside the EU,
the EU authorized representative is:
Springer Nature Customer Service Center GmbH
Europaplatz 3, 69115 Heidelberg, Germany

Printed by Libri Plureos GmbH
in Hamburg, Germany